LIVING HELL

LIVING HELL

The Dark Side of
the Civil War

Michael C. C. Adams

JOHNS HOPKINS

UNIVERSITY PRESS

—BALTIMORE—

© 2014 Johns Hopkins University Press
All rights reserved. Published 2014
Printed in the United States of America on acid-free paper
2 4 6 8 9 7 5 3 1

Johns Hopkins University Press
2715 North Charles Street
Baltimore, Maryland 21218-4363
www.press.jhu.edu

Library of Congress Cataloging-in-Publication Data
Adams, Michael C. C., 1945–
Living hell : the dark side of the Civil War / Michael C. C. Adams.
    pages cm
Includes bibliographical references and index.
ISBN 978-1-4214-1221-4 (hardcover : alk. paper)
ISBN 1-4214-1221-7 (hardcover : alk. paper)
ISBN 978-1-4214-1222-1 (electronic)
ISBN 1-4214-1222-5 (electronic)
1. United States—History—Civil War, 1861–1865—Social aspects.
2. United States—History—Civil War, 1861–1865—Psychological aspects.
3. United States—History—Civil War, 1861–1865—Casualties.
4. War and society—United States—History—19th century.
5. War casualties—United States—History—19th century. I. Title.
E468.9.A34 2014
973.7   1—dc23   2013021123

A catalog record for this book is available from the British Library.

Special discounts are available for bulk purchases of this book.
For more information, please contact Special Sales at 410-516-6936
or specialsales@press.jhu.edu.

Johns Hopkins University Press uses environmentally friendly book materials,
including recycled text paper that is composed

For the boys who fell
And the girls who mourned them

Mine eyes have seen the glory of the coming of the Lord:

He is trampling out the vintage where the grapes of wrath are stored;

He has loosed the fateful lightning of his terrible swift sword:

His truth is marching on.

JULIA WARD HOWE
"The Battle Hymn of the Republic" (1861)

CONTENTS

— *Preface* —

This book paints a graphic picture of the dark side of the Civil War, its pain, heartbreak, and tragedy. It describes the vicious nature of combat, the terrible infliction of physical and mental wounds, the misery of soldiers living amid corpses, filth, and flies. It also concerns the many civilians who endured loss, deprivation, and violations. To understand what the people of that time endured, I have relied heavily on bringing back their candid voices from the hushed past. That these eyewitnesses deserve to be heard again constitutes a core conviction of this book.

Because I want them to speak for themselves, I have neither corrected people's grammar nor interrupted their thoughts with that unpleasant expletive, *sic,* supposedly needed to flag linguistic errors. Instead, I rely on the reader's common sense to grasp the intended meaning of writings through which our forebears sought to reveal what they experienced.

Regarding terminology, I capitalize North and South as the major belligerent sections; by the same token, east and west, although major theaters of war, remain in lowercase. In the endnotes for each chapter, I cite sources used in the text. On first reference to a work, I give full information on author, title, and facts of publication. The author's last name and an abbreviated title only appear in subsequent notes for that chapter. The standard abbreviation for *The Official Records of the Union and Confederate Armies* is O.R., and I use this after each full reference in a chapter.

To achieve immediacy, I have at times attempted to create a sense of live action, as though we are experiencing an episode "on camera." This technique begins in the Opening, where we piggyback on Stephen Crane's arresting image of a road that moves with wounded soldiers shambling to the rear, in order to conjure for ourselves a gallery of Americans journeying together down the path of war. Just as Crane's road was not actually in motion, we will not really sprint down a neurasthenia ward with the animated Dr. Weir Mitchell. Nor would we in fact meet individual men from so many different units clustered together as we and they grope through the smoke on a firing line. We are staging a reconstruction, a reenactment, but one in which the players are the original participants. This modest stylistic device in no way distorts or detracts from the original documents, and I hope will prove valuable to the reader.

———•·•·•———

The intellectual debts contracted over a career are incalculable; mine would fill another book. Many of my creditors appear in the endnotes, but other sources of inspiration must remain unacknowledged. For example, I early learned from reading the late John Keegan to understand the real face of battle, but that particular piece of his work has no direct bearing here.

Marcus Cunliffe, a masterful thinker and writer, became the founding father of American studies in the United Kingdom, where I was raised. He was my mentor, and I remain grateful for his encouragement of my tendency to think a little sideways (or perhaps it is bass ackwards, as Lincoln put it). Although long gone, I imagine he still bends over my shoulder as I sit at my desk, taking his pipe from his mouth to make pointed comments.

I have benefited from discussions with numerous colleagues on the nature of war. For conversations specifically on the Civil War, I would like to thank John T. Hubbell, Civil War historian and past director of the Kent State University Press. Among several provocative comments, John once asked me if I had ever thought that much armed conflict might just be tribal in origin. Gabor Boritt twice asked me to speak in the Gettysburg College Civil War Institute. On our second visit, he hosted lunch for Bob Bruce, my wife, Sue, and me at his handsome farmhouse that had been a field hospital during the July 1863 fighting. On a beautifully clear, warm Pennsylvania day, Gabor showed us minnie balls with deep teeth marks: surgeons indeed told patients to "bite the bullet" so as not to injure their tongues.

Two of my fellow Regents Professors at Northern Kentucky University deserve a special mention: J. Robert Lilly and James A. Ramage. Bob has done incisive work on U.S. military justice; Jim is a national authority on partisans and raiders.

Nobody could hope for a better, more supportive editor than Robert J. Brugger. A combat veteran with the courage to talk about war while still in uniform, Bob enthusiastically advocates candid writing about war. He urged me to write the book, and his vigorous advice immeasurably enhanced it. Thanks also to Melissa Solarz, acquisitions assistant, for her enduring patience and ability to cut through Gordian knots. Helen Myers did a brilliant job of copyediting and proved to be a splendidly supportive reader. Juliana McCarthy, managing editor, smoothed the transition from typescript to book. Thanks also to all the other staff at Johns Hopkins University Press whose expertise and hard work have brought this project to fruition.

My wife, Susan Steves Adams (nee Kissel), and I have been constant companions and colleagues for thirty years. We read all of each other's writing. Sue not only encouraged and supported me fully in undertaking this work, she read, commented on, and improved the manuscript at each stage of its evolution. In a vital proofreading role, she restrained my urge to pepper the text with indiscriminate volleys of commas.

Thanks to all.

LIVING HELL

JIM CONKLIN AND GENERAL SHERMAN

×

MY TEENAGER YEARS IN THE UNITED KINGDOM COINCIDED with the centennial of the American Civil War. For me, the remembrance meant that I could acquire paperbacks normally unavailable to the general reader: Henry Kyd Douglas's *I Rode with Stonewall,* the memoirs of General Ulysses S. Grant, and the recollections of Confederate Admiral Raphael Semmes. I held a rather innocent view of the war at this time. I harbored romantic notions of dramatic exploits on the battlefield, of boys being forged into men through the ultimate test of combat. In part, Stephen Crane's 1895 novel *The Red Badge of Courage* inspired my vision. I read it in the Classics Illustrated graphic version around the impressionable age of twelve, then went on to devour the complete written text and to see John Huston's evocative 1951 black-and-white movie, in which Audie Murphy played the green youth transformed by the transcendent experience of battle. Henry Fleming's ascent into heroism seized my imagination.

In due course, I went to college and graduate school, where I wrote a dissertation on the war that became my 1978 book *Our Masters the Rebels.* In this work, I argued that Union generals, particularly in the east, had a tendency to talk and act as though awed by their Rebel opponents, whom they perceived as being from a more martial culture than their own. Their inferiority complex, as we might loosely label it, meant Federal army commanders lacked offensive spirit, displaying undue caution. Afflictions of "the slows" even affected their ability to follow up defensive successes, such as at Gettysburg.

I still think the thesis has merit. But I now see other reasons why generals were unable to capitalize when an enemy retreated: their own victorious forces often became too broken and wearied to mount effective pursuit. Today, my teenage images of battle-hardened veterans, endlessly enduring and consistently gallant, succored and sustained by stoic, long-suffering civilians, seem naive and misleading. I understand why Audie Murphy, a veteran who had seen more than enough combat in World War II, found Henry's flag-waving antics after returning to the regiment bitterly silly, and why, during shooting breaks, he wandered off the set, "as though lost in a distant dream." He had the two-thousand-yard stare of the emotionally spent combat soldier. He said as much, recalling: "Before the war, I'd get excited and enthused about a lot of things, but not any more."[1]

In a sense, this development in my understanding mirrors the journey from ignorance to enlightenment described by another combat veteran, General William Tecumseh Sherman. Speaking to a crowd of admirers at the Ohio State Fair on August 11, 1880, Sherman pointedly addressed young people in the crowd, asserting, "There is many a boy here to-day who looks on war as all glory, but, boys, it is all hell." The general carefully added that he did not espouse pacifism and would serve again if needed, but he urged people to look squarely at war's horrors.[2]

I want to stay with this point. I propose that we not go forward to watch Henry Fleming marching exuberantly off the field (he should not look quite so cheerful, anyway, as his next rendezvous with battle will be Gettysburg). Instead of moving on, let us dwell a while on the pains, the fears, and the blighted lives, indeed the tragedies of those who became the war's victims, like Jim Conklin, Crane's decent, tall soldier, shot through the body, milling along amid a crowd of other wounded, afraid of being run down by the artillery, wanting to be left alone to die. Jim experienced no transcendence, caught up in the mangle of war along with many thousands of other men, women, and children.

I am by no means the first author to argue for looking starkly at the grim features of the war. Walt Whitman, who worked in Washington, D.C., during the conflict and served as a volunteer hospital nurse, said the real war, the cruel war, would not get into the books.

But he tried in his prose and poetry to add some darker shadows. Much later, the distinguished historian Allan Nevins exhorted us to confront the war's hard reality:

> We should probe more deeply into roots, a process that will expose some of the weaknesses of our social fabric and governmental system. We should pay fuller attention to its darker aspects, and examine more honestly such misinterpretations as the statement it was distinguished by its generosity of spirit, the magnanimity with which the combatants treated each other; a statement absurd on its face, for no war which lasts four years and costs 600,000 lives leaves much magnanimity in its later phases. We should above all examine more closely the effects of the great and terrible war not on the nation's politics—we also know that; but on its character, the vital element of national life.[3]

My concerns are not coterminous with those of my distinguished predecessor, although I have become preoccupied, as he was, by the societal aspects of the war more than its politics. Also like him, I do not wish to deny the great issues involved and civic virtue shown, the fighting that produced prodigious courage, sacrifice, endurance, and magnanimity among soldiers and civilians. But I believe strongly that Professor Nevins correctly urged us to dwell more on the dark side. We should remind ourselves now and then about the grimmer realities of this struggle and, perhaps by extension, all armed conflicts. Many books consider in depth this or that important aspect of the bleak war. I hope to perform a service by pulling together all the strands into one large tapestry. The sesquicentennial presents the opportunity to do this, as once again we "celebrate" the conflict, a word I suspect could not be less appropriate.

To begin with, the Civil War's cardinal characteristic became its stunning bloodiness. It may be a commonplace, yet it still shocks us to remember that the fight cost as many lives as all of America's other major wars combined. Equally startling, the butcher's bill came for a contest neither sharply delineated nor fought by combatants bonded together in defense of clearly enunciated positions and universally held ideologies. The politics of division proved so complex, confusing, contradictory, and tangled that even today we hotly debate the reasons for the war.

Of course, it would be satisfying if we could find one single, straightforward explanation for the war. We try. Thus, one camp sees a clear-cut moral struggle between the forces of slavery and freedom. Agreed, slavery must have been a large factor, probably the biggest one, in the coming of the conflict. After all, the election as president of Abraham Lincoln, who opposed the further extension of slavery, led South Carolina fire-eaters to kick the lid off the cauldron and jump inside.

Yet, say skeptics, Northern opposition to slavery stayed so lukewarm that Lincoln did not even propose partial emancipation until fall 1862, and then not as a moral crusade but a military measure to put new life into the flagging war effort. Many white Northerners embraced racism as much as the next bigot: free blacks could not vote in much of the North, and several midwestern states excluded African Americans from living within their borders.

Some who downplay the debate over slavery counterclaim that the primary cause of the war may be found in Northern encroachment on Southern rights; Confederates fought a disinterested battle to uphold the principle of a states' right to resist centralized intrusion. Local rights included secession from the Union.

Again, the argument has some merit. Whether state or national authority should be paramount got a good airing during the war. But making this legal disagreement the focus of the contest still presents the problem that people do not normally precipitate a bloodbath to test an abstract constitutional principle. Appeals to state sovereignty usually masked other, more pragmatic, interests. Southerners embraced states' rights when convenient but insisted that national authorities return fugitive slaves, overriding the states' rights protest of Northern local officials.

Trying to broaden the debate, another school argued that we see an epic confrontation between an aristocratic agrarian South and a bourgeois business-industrial North doomed to collide. Charles and Mary Beard championed this argument between the world wars. It gained popularity both with Marxist historians and conservative apologists for the Old South. There must be some validity to the idea of rising industrial interests squaring off against older, entrenched agricultural concerns. But farmers and factory owners do not necessarily have to shoot each other over negotiable issues such as the height of protective tariffs. Midwestern farmers stayed loyal to the Union.

The only aspect of Southern agrarianism distinct enough to provoke a war remained plantation slavery. It lay at the base of the Southern way of life. Even though a majority of white people in Dixie might not own slaves, they subscribed to the caste system and could not conceive of a state of society in which blacks were free, let alone equal. So the argument turns full circle and the ravel of causes remains.

If we could say one thing with certainty, it would be that the war represented a profound failure of the political system; discord had broken government. The war does not qualify as a classic tragedy, fated to happen. The British Empire had abolished slavery peacefully between 1833 and 1838. Russian Tsar Alexander II ended serfdom without civil war in 1861. Only when the South closed its mind to rational debate of the Peculiar Institution late in the antebellum period did compromise become impossible in the United States, as Clement Eaton pointed out in *The Freedom-of-Thought Struggle in the Old South* (1940). John Brown's 1859 raid on the U.S. armory at Harpers Ferry, Virginia, although failing to spark a slave revolt, finished driving many Southerners into paranoia.

------◆------

When statesmanship failed, the calamity fell on a people with lives already steeped in hardship and loss. Victorian life, while not idyllic, still led many to see themselves at the apex of human development. They could evidence an intellectual flowering in New England, the polished manners of some Southern gentry, and the growing dynamism of the west that bred vigorous newcomers, like the Lincolns, Shermans, and Grants. The rise of the common man meant that more white males voted than ever before. Mass production enhanced daily life with cheap, plentiful goods, from ready-made furniture and clothing to newspapers and books. The middle class expanded, and the prosperous lived well.

Yet the mass of people did not. The scientific concept of a balanced nutritional diet, for example, scarcely existed. Many Southern yeomen, along with most poor whites and blacks, subsisted on a vitamin-deficient diet of cornmeal, molasses, and salt pork, leavened by occasional seasonal boilings of greens or beans. Urban workers had neither the time nor money to eat properly, their food often stale, badly cooked, monotonous. Fanny Fern, a pioneering female journalist, wrote in 1855 of cheap boardinghouses where clerks, apprentices, and seamstresses "bolt their meals with railroad velocity" amid "soiled table-cloths, sticky crockery, oily cookery." Ice for refrigeration remained scarce. Harriet Beecher Stowe, enduring humid June heat, complained, "I am sick of the smell of sour milk, and sour meat, and sour everything."[4]

Heavy, restrictive dress proved hard to keep clean and impeded overall health: vests and frock-coats encased men like stovepipes; women's stays constricted the lungs, while layers of pantaloons and petticoats dragged in the muck and caught fire in parlor fireplaces. Poor physical specimens abounded, as army surgeons examining recruits in 1861 could attest.

Medical practice stayed close to medieval. Young Sarah Morgan, partially paralyzed when her buggy overturned, endured frequent medical hot-cupping and bleeding. The doctor, she screamed, "has again been murdering me." Drugs to combat disease remained inadequate. A physician lost his daughter to convulsions, having only mustard plasters to fight the illness. Class proved no guarantee against sudden death: Mary and Abraham Lincoln, Varina and Jefferson Davis, Ellen and William T. Sherman, Mary and Robert E. Lee all lost children, as did other prominent couples. Known drugs, "heroic remedies," had drastic side effects. Calomel and "blue pills," commonly available mercury compounds used to treat bowel disorders, typhoid fever, and much else, produced gum disorders and kidney disease. Chloroform, prescribed for insomnia, and arsenic, found in widely advertised and readily available patent nostrums, killed.[5]

Because bacteriology remained in its infancy, public hygiene languished. Cities like Chicago, Baltimore, and Louisville had negligible sewer arrangements; scavenger pigs ate waste thrown in the streets and became emboldened to attack workers' children. For the poor and vulnerable, such as children under five, death rates stayed high. Typhus, cholera, and yellow fever struck hard. Almost eight thousand people died in the 1853 New Orleans yellow fever outbreak. The 1849 cholera epidemic killed five thousand New Yorkers alone. Only 2 percent of city homes had a water line that might have helped stop this water-borne disease. Rural areas also had no immunity: people built privies too close to kitchens, and animal waste fouled ground water. At Fort Riley, Kansas, in 1855, cholera killed the commandant's wife and fourteen others in one day.[6]

The accelerating pace of life added to physical and emotional stress. The telegraph enhanced communication but had unforeseen consequences, demanding radical human adjustments to technology. For example, the speed of the wire created havoc with military planning. A journalist could inform his newspaper of army movements virtually as they happened; an enemy agent might then relay the information to his side. Infuriated generals put reporters beyond the lines or threatened execution.

Steam power, applied to travel, propelled railroad locomotives, paddle boats, and screw-driven ships. But heightened speed jangled the nerves of people used to a horse's pace. Trains created air and noise pollution. Henry David Thoreau, seeking solitude at Walden Pond, heard wildlife agitated for hours after an engine roared through: the machine had invaded the garden. Disasters occurred frequently. Cows on the line derailed cars, foreshadowing interstate pileups. Fast steamers blew up. Charles Dickens, voyaging to America, depicted the ship's boiler as "a fire in hiding, ready to burst through any outlet, wild with its restless power of ruin and death." (In an 1865 shocker, the steamer *Sultana*, taking home Union prisoners of war, exploded, killing 1,700.)[7]

To alleviate stress and seize a modicum of comfort, Americans used tobacco with abandon, snuffing, chewing, and lighting up. New Yorkers smoked 75,000,000 cigars a year. People guzzled alcohol freely, along with readily available mood-enhancing drugs. Laudanum conveniently infused the two stimulants and proved handy for keeping children quiescent, daycare being virtually unknown outside of prosperous nurseries. Excessive imbibing caused debilitation, violence, and family abuse. One contemporary estimate had 60,000 homes ruined by drink per year. Drunken brawling infected Congress; in one 1857 scrimmage, a colleague knocked inebriated Representative Laurence Keitt of South Carolina across two tables, a shoe taking off in mid-flight.[8]

Americans regarded opium as a beneficial tonic and relaxant. They imported 24,000 pounds through northeastern ports in 1840, rising to 105,000 pounds by 1860. For women, with lives severely restricted by gender roles, opium served a similar function to Valium, prescribed in the 1950s for bored and depressed housewives. Alice James, sister of Henry and William, suffered attacks of neuralgia bordering on hysteria. Too bright for her stifling role, she fantasized knocking her father's head off while he sat stiffly reading. Instead, she resorted to self-medication, as did Mary Boykin Chesnut, one of the sharpest minds of the period. Denied the active public life of her senator husband, James, she struggled against overuse of opium and its derivative, morphine.[9]

We consider the nineteenth century a simpler, saner, more grounded time than our own, yet it looks similar in many ways. A grave equality gap existed between rich and poor. Hostility to immigrants manifested itself in a nativist movement. People found distraction in coarse entertainments such as freak shows, cockfights, gambling, and bare-knuckle boxing. They followed the latest fashions and fads. Prominent British personalities exercised their fascination, the public avidly following the indiscretions of the randy Prince of Wales or the handsome stage star, Frances Anne "Fanny" Kemble. Their faces adorned engravings, mugs, and handkerchiefs, to be superseded in 1861 by pinups of generals.[10]

Youth did not necessarily behave better. Bachelor young men rioted in their off hours, fighting pit bulls, getting stewed, and joining violent gangs. Elders protested against the fecklessness of their juniors. James Henry Hammond, a seaboard planter, called his boys "dead weights" that only hunted and fished. They "growl, grumble, sulk and do nothing," he complained.[11]

We easily exaggerate Victorian sexual probity. Limited contraception produced unwanted pregnancies. One physician estimated in 1860 that 20 percent of such cases terminated in abortion. Venereal disease thrived alongside prostitution. Many women without male support felt obliged to sell themselves for food. They faced an alternative of underpaid domestic service, with the threat of being forced by male household members, or doing work in factories with typical fourteen-hour days and minimal safety standards.[12]

"Accidents" in plants occurred frequently due to owner negligence. New York attorney George Templeton Strong recorded in his diary on January 11, 1860, that in Lawrence, Massachusetts, "a huge factory, long notoriously insecure and ill-built . . . suddenly collapsed into a heap of ruins. . . . Some five- or six-hundred operatives went down with it—young girls and women mostly." Strong wondered if Southern slaveholders could possibly treat their workers any worse than did the "misanthropes" of the North.[13]

The attorney had a point. Poor life expectancy and bad working conditions in the industrial North and in England often exceeded those on the plantation. But one factor separated slaves' status from any other and made it uniquely awful: they were property. (This allowed Lincoln to quip that although many held slavery to be a good, none wanted it for themselves.) State and national authorities deprived slaves of all civil and human rights. The U.S. Supreme Court held that they could not seek redress in court. They could not testify against a white. Slaves found themselves denied education, beaten, raped, and mutilated with impunity. The auction block separated slave families forever.

Uncle Tom in Harriet Beecher Stowe's 1852 novel endures the grim fate of being sold away from his loved ones downriver to Louisiana. There, Simon Legree, a New England Yankee (that complexity again), exploits land and people with equal callousness, thrashing Tom to death. Possibly while working a flatboat to New Orleans, Lincoln developed his repugnance to the Peculiar Institution. And, of course, South Carolina's hostility to Old Abe precipitated America's most destructive war.

———

Just how bloody became this conflict that engulfed the troubled land? Perhaps as many as 620,000 military died (360,000 from the North, 260,000 from the South). To give some context, soldiers had a 1 in 4 chance of dying versus 1 in 126 for Korea. Civil War military fatalities outnumbered U.S. losses in World War II by 50 percent. The statistics jar us even more if we consider losses as a percentage of population. A reliable estimate holds that at least 2 percent of Americans alive in 1860 died in uniform. This translates to more than 6,000,000 today. Union losses represented 1.6 percent of loyal state residents, the equivalent of 4.8 million now. Rebel dead, at 2.9 percent of white and black folk, equates to a stunning 8.7 million currently. And these figures fail to address the thousands that were physically or mentally maimed, or the civilians who suffered loss, malnutrition, displacement, death.[14]

I intend to place center stage the dark side of the war glimpsed in these figures. Author William Dean Howells said that Americans will only embrace tragedy if it ends happily. This implies that we must march on with Henry, wrapped in his red badge of courage. But I believe readers will wish to stay back with me a while, walking along that road where poor Jim Conklin staggers by amid a torrent of hurt humanity, brokenhearted Mary Lincoln weeps beside Varina Davis, and peppery General Sherman peers into hell.

In the eight chapters that follow, we will escort the reader down the dirty, dusty road of war, in a logical progression from military enlistment to camp, then on the march, to the battlefield, and from there to the hospital, the grave, and the haunted minds of psychologically damaged soldiers. As we draw the reader along, the landscape grows ever darker when we deal with massive civilian deprivation and social dislocation, invasion, and violations. The road then stretches away to the far horizon, charting some legacies of the war, even down to 2012.

Finally, in the Closing, we will take one more walk together. Conjure up the year 1898, and imagine we find ourselves on a dusty lane in Texas leading to the nearby railroad tracks. There a last great sadness awaits us.

CHAPTER ONE

GONE FOR A SOLDIER

✕

AS WE BEGIN OUR JOURNEY DOWN THE ROAD OF WAR, WE will sense around us an air of exuberant patriotism, because the bracing clarity of a call to arms has replaced the stress and uncertainty of the Secession Crisis. We will see boys invigorated by being asked to play a man's role. But dark shadows soon gather, for the exciting road leading into army life also delivers up disease, death, and disillusionment. Youths who have dreamed only of glory will be appalled by the reality, not only of battle, but of daily military routine, with its lowly toil, verbal and physical abuse, brutal and degrading punishments. Liquor and sexual excess lure some and disgust others. Recruits succumb to illness, not just venereal disease and alcoholism, but such camp sicknesses as measles, mumps, and nostalgia.

When volunteer enthusiasm fails, both sides resort to compulsion. But conscription laws tend to favor the rich and so ultimately produce a violent reaction, including armed resistance. To meet its manpower needs, the Union reluctantly authorized black recruitment. Many persons of color welcomed this opportunity, with its promise of racial advancement, yet they continued to face abuse and exploitation in a fundamentally racist society.

———◆•◆———

To begin, cheerfulness verging on euphoria greeted the cannon fire of April 1861. Many citizens felt relief that the wearing political bickering had ended. Southerners readied themselves to defend home and fireside from Yankee invasion, Northerners prepared to avenge the insult to Old Glory and preserve mankind's best hope—the Union.

Ella Thomas, a young woman from a prosperous Georgia slave-holding family, felt no man should stay "in the lap of inglorious ease" when threats to the homeland existed; her husband, brother, and brother-in-law all answered the call. She felt "proud to see them exhibit the noble, manly spirit which prompts them to go." After all, she felt, the fighting would be short, easily won by Southern cavaliers, each of whom could whip about a half dozen degenerate, money-grubbing Yankees. Some fire-eaters even promised to lap up any blood spilled in civil war.[1]

In the North, swelling enlistments promised regeneration for a section that seemingly had too often compromised to preserve a dishonorable peace, one designed to guarantee the continued flow of Southern cotton and capital to Northern factories and banks. "A nation hath been born again, Regenerate by a second birth!" boomed the poet W. W. Howe. No more sordid deals, declared Wisconsin's *Madison State Journal*. "A people long grown servile-necked," with "bowing under Mammon's yoke," had come to its senses and "to-day stand haughtily erect."[2]

Mothers might worry about the fate of their soldier sons, but girls inflamed by patriotic fervor insisted the beaux sign up. "If a fellow wants to go with a girl now he had better enlist," opined a volunteer. Older men could look with jaundiced eye at the coming fratricidal bloodshed and the infatuation of youth with the shallow trappings of patriotism. Virginian William Thomson told his fire-eating son, "The young and sanguine are rapidly carried away into dreamy fields and flawed visions." But a younger man, the New York 7th's Major Theodore Winthrop, better captured popular sentiment. Billeted in Washington at the Capitol, he determined the presence of troops in "our palace" necessary to amend the cowardice, bosh, and imbecility of the politicians "who had here cooperated to corrupt and blind the minds of the people."[3]

War allowed youth to assume a man's role while fleeing workaday grind and tedium. At the start of *Moby Dick* (1851), Herman Melville pictured office workers, stapled to their desks, who spent Sundays lining New York's wharves and piers, longingly scanning the ocean skyline for hints of adventure. He also created Bartleby the Scrivener (1853), a clerk who exemplifies the alienation of labor. Paralyzed by the soul-destroying work of sorting dead letters and copying documents, Bartleby becomes mentally and physically stultified, wasting away in a poor house.

Robert Gould Shaw, of the Boston elite, far more privileged than Bartleby, nevertheless cried out, "I am a slave now," after he graduated from Harvard and entered his uncle's mercantile business. He escaped into uniform early in the conflict. Boys, stigmatized as feckless by their elders, now turned the argument, posturing in the role of manly patriots. "We've been told of our degeneracy for years," wrote Henry Lee Higginson, son of a wealthy Boston merchant. But, he added proudly, the boys were proving to be "the same men who fought in '76, a thousand times better than any soldiers living."[4]

Service, deemed a rite of passage into manhood, brought boys eagerly flocking to the colors. Recruiters obliged them: "I didn't tell them that I was only fifteen. So I became a soldier," wrote Thomas Galwey, a youngster from Cleveland, Ohio, who joined the Union army in April 1861. Randolph Shotwell, from North Carolina, enlisted because it meant "the complete cutting loose from boyhood to assume the responsibilities and perils of manhood."[5]

Research suggests that both the innocence and enthusiasm of adolescence encourage volunteering. Boys in their late teens comprised the largest category of soldiers, at 40 to 50 percent of the whole. About 250,000 were just entering the teen years. These exuberant adolescents, packed with adrenaline, threw their kepis in the air and capered for civilians peering at their camps from passing trains. Joseph E. Crowell, a New Jersey volunteer, doubted that patriotism had motivated most boys to enlist. "To many it was a change from the ordinary humdrum of life. Others looked upon it as a picnic. And then in every boy's heart there is an inherent spirit of adventure."[6]

To poor or unemployed men, service offered a chance to gain self-respect and the promise of a steady wage (which subsequently created bitterness when pay became late). Enoch T. Baker, a Pennsylvania volunteer, wrote in late 1861 to his wife, who fretted about his leaving: "You know if i could have got work i wood not have left you or the children." Recent immigrants, often out of work or marginally employed in the worst jobs, could hope for financial stability in the military and a potential leg up into cultural acceptance by mainstream Americans. Half a million foreigners wore blue, including 150,000 Irish out of a total immigrant base of 1.5 million in 1860. Lesser numbers of Germans, Italians, Russians, Hungarians, and other Europeans fought for the Union. Fewer foreign nations were represented in gray, as many immigrants avoided the slave states because of distaste for human bondage or a reluctance to compete for jobs with a servile workforce.[7]

Inevitably, military fervor began to dissipate. We cannot say precisely when, but a fair estimate might be the spring of 1862. What caused the initial zeal to wane? First, exposure to battle proved sobering, even horrifying. We shall explore the subject of combat fully in chapters three and five, but we should mention the experience here just as a factor in declining enthusiasm. Romantic illusions failed to survive battle's grim truths. Recruits had been imbued with Currier & Ives' artful depictions of war, in which serried ranks of gaily uniformed soldiers, led by plumed officers on horseback, charged beyond the fallen, who assumed restful poses. Such fantasies bore no relation to the reality of metal projectiles disintegrating fragile bodies as men screamed and cried.

By August 1862, William Chunn of the 40th Georgia, serving in the western regiments, had decided that there existed "no beauties in the preparation for the whole sale slaughter of the human race. I see no glory in numbering those on the battlefield slain. It is nothing but horror from beginning to end." Elisha Stockwell believed himself to be the only survivor of Company I, 14th Wisconsin, at bloody Shiloh, April 6, 1862. Cowering under shellfire, his mind drifted "back to my home, and I thought what a foolish boy I was to run away to get into such a mess I was in."[8]

Fighting no longer seemed the answer for Theodorick Montfort, a lieutenant in the 25th Georgia, who watched as the surgeon lay out his grisly instruments in anticipation of Yankee warships beginning the bombardment of Fort Pulaski, Georgia, on March 31, 1862. "What a calamity is war," he moaned. "When will men cease to fight, & love their neighbors as themselves?" Captured when the fort fell, Montfort died in a Union prison that September.[9]

William B. Greene of the 2nd United States Sharpshooters had enlisted in a flush of patriotic fervor at seventeen. He quickly became disillusioned with the hard routine of army life, and discovered the actual experience of combat appalled him. At Cedar Mountain, on September 7, 1862, his unit was stationed in a copse. Rebel artillery shells smashed the treetops, bringing down vicious splinters of wood upon the sharpshooters. "Canister," containing "pieces of shell, railroad spikes, small bullets, etc.," made up some rounds. Terrified, Greene burrowed into the earth, later writing his mother that "the marks where I stuck my face into the ground" must still be visible. Although unwounded, he now started feigning illness to get a discharge and narrowly escaped trial as a deserter. A comrade unsuccessfully attempted suicide with his bayonet in a drastic bid to escape the service.[10]

Long casualty lists from unexpectedly bloody fields, amplified by soldiers' letters vividly describing combat and the death of friends, doused home front enthusiasm. Due to advances in photography, civilians could virtually experience the horror by peering at plates of the bloated dead displayed in store windows. You might examine corpses in 3-D by purchasing a stereoscopic viewer. The photographer, said the *New York Times*, October 20, 1862, "has done something to bring home to us the terrible reality and earnestness of war. If he has not brought bodies and laid them in our door-yards and along streets, he has done something very like it."

Soldiers widely interpreted civilian disillusion, even though it largely mirrored their own, as cynical avoidance of service to make money while soldiers risked their lives for less pay than a streetcar driver. By mid-1863, the Union Army of the Potomac's General Alpheus T. Williams thought that veteran resentment of civilian selfishness hurt re-enlistment. Georgia Private William Suttwell wrote from Fredericksburg, Virginia, in August 1863, that greed and godlessness undermined the cause: "We seek the creature and not the creator." As early as 1861, prominent Northern literary figure Henry Tuckerman had predicted glumly that idealism would wane in the face of fever-ridden camps, along with "a material prosperity that set new records for extravagance" and renewed political quarreling.[11]

The fading sacrificial spirit indicated that unity, initially fragile, had begun to fracture among civilians and soldiers. Confederate Colonel Williams C. Wickham, anticipating combat at Fredericksburg, December 1862, thought it a damned shame to die "for a cause of which I do not approve." Charles B. Haydon of the 2nd Michigan, serving in Virginia in late 1862, overheard rival pickets agreeing the fighting made no sense; why not "throw our guns into the river & end the d——d war!"[12]

The Richmond government's steady encroachment on states' rights antagonized Southerners, while the Emancipation Proclamation divided the North. Officers resigned commissions; some were cashiered, like Tennessean General James G. Spears, a brigade commander in the Union Army of the Ohio, broken for threatening to change sides, swearing "God damn the government, let her go to hell." Men who expected the military to rise above the petty squabbles of civil life became disaffected when promotion failed to recognize merit; passed-over officers, such as Ella Thomas's husband, Jefferson, who in 1861 thought it noble to serve in a Virginia regiment, resigned in high dudgeon the following year. Disgust with dissension in the high command furthered disaffection. Lack of success among Confederate generals in the west and Union commanders in the east bred recrimination and infighting. Captain William Lusk of the 2nd New York, furious at antagonisms among generals that helped cause Union defeat at Second Bull Run, a debacle in which he participated, complained that "there is no head on the field," only "lying reports," and "Old Abe makes a joke."[13]

———•◦•———

Discipline quickly made soldiers who had anticipated heroic escapades feel more like prisoners than some legendary Achilles. The boys "counted the days yet remaining before they would be discharged, the same as a convict does the remaining days of his imprisonment," confided Private Crowell. Soldiers had "little more freedom than the slave" swore New York Private Charles Gould. Similarly, from camp at Fort Bliss, Texas, June 1861, a Rebel cursed his captain as "a surly dictator" who "treats us more like slaves than anything else."[14]

Drilling elicited derision, as did wood cutting and digging latrines. "Spit and polish," scouring equipment with saliva and dust, seemed servile. Army life "comes hard sometimes for young men who have been raised to do no menial labor," admitted Georgia Private Theodore Fogle, slaving away in Richmond, Virginia, in July 1861. Nurses, too, became disenchanted, emptying slop pails instead of tending wounded gallants. John H. Brinton, a Union surgeon stationed at Cairo, Illinois, for much of 1861, said that many females flouted rules and expected dining service. He groused uncharitably, "Can you fancy half a dozen or a dozen old hags . . . surrounding a bewildered hospital surgeon, each one clamorous for her little wants?"[15]

Comparisons to slavery were not hyperbole; many military penalties echoed the degrading inflictions that marked the plantation and jail. Punishments included hanging by the thumbs, toes barely touching the ground; bucking and gagging, being trussed like a turkey with a bit cutting the mouth; spread-eagling on a spare wheel, mocking crucifixion; flogging; and branding. The horror of being ordered to brand a deserter during the 1864 Virginia Wilderness campaign permanently unhinged Union Surgeon William Chester Minor.[16]

Severity of punishment often appeared disproportionate. General Samuel Heintzelman spread-eagled an orderly on an artillery wheel simply for not removing his hat. This caused excruciating pain, according to Private Frank Wilkeson, 11th New York Artillery, Army of the Potomac. The victim's agony increased if tied horizontally, the body "pulling heavily and cuttingly on the cords that bound his upper arm and leg to the wheel." Soldiers felt officers habitually abused rank by bullying. A pilferer hit by General George Gordon Meade swore, "If it warn't for them shoulder straps of your'n, I'd give you the dam'dst thrashing."[17]

Harshness invited retaliation. Men of the 40th New York, en route to the front in Virginia, September 1861, endured frequent bucking and gagging at the hands of their colonel. Outraged, they "openly swear that they will shoot him the first time they have a battle with the enemy." When Lieutenant P. T. Keyes, 16th U.S. Infantry, Army of the Ohio, struck a straggler, the victim pledged, "I'll shoot you the first chance I get." The officer died in the next action.[18]

Officers often deemed severe discipline a necessity and in the soldiers' interest, for disobedience threatened life and health. In September 1861, Robert E. Lee wrote that many trainees had smallpox and measles. "They bring it on themselves by not doing what they are told. They are worse than children, for the latter can be forced." Other officers did not "spare the rod and spoil the child," forcefully confronting insubordination, especially in incidents involving alcohol and firearms. On April 12, 1863, Union General Michael Corcoran shot a drunken sentry who four times called him "a Goddamned Irish son of a bitch." Captain Nathaniel Southgate Shaler, commanding the 5th Kentucky Battery (U.S.) during the 1862 defense of Cincinnati, Ohio, knocked flat one of his men, "a bully of women and a drunkard," who had attacked him while resisting arrest. Shaler spreadeagled the gunner on a wheel until, when nearly dead, he "says he'll soger." [19]

For heinous crimes, soldiers faced execution. James Preble of the 12th New York, guilty of rape, caught drunk "with his Privates hanging out," was shot. Vice proved a bane of army life, even though officers, surgeons, families, ministers, and community leaders urged soldiers to adhere to a regimen of moral and physical cleanliness. Victorians preached the concept of death before defilement. Harriet Beecher Stowe felt happy that boys embraced war "as a bride, and are ready to die," but she fretted about her son Fred's exposure to soldier sins. [20]

Hard drinking headed the sinner's list. Many older men were habituated boozers. But imbibing also became a form of self-medication to ease miseries of mind and body. For many youngsters away from home constraints for the first time, acquiring the liquor habit made you a bold dog. Keeping the boys from liquor proved almost impossible. Corporal C. F. Boyd of the 15th Iowa, in camp at St. Louis, February 1862, watched his comrades "getting pretty old at the business of running the guard" to reach local saloons. "There seems to be no God here but more than the average amount of Devil," he said of duty in the city. Nurse Louisa May Alcott characterized D.C. as a city, "half of whose male population seemed to be taking the other half to the guard-house." [21]

The soldiers' nose for booze appeared uncanny. Despite all precautions, wrote Albert Fall, a gunner in Porter's Tennessee Battery (C.S.A.), from Bowling Green, Kentucky, December 1861, a sergeant got tight "and was engaged, with his corporal, who was also drunk, in loading and firing a horse-trough." Desperate officers dismissed sutlers (authorized merchants) and even flogged civilians who peddled liquor, but the flow continued. The concentration of troops in Richmond, the Confederate capital, overwhelmed the provost guard's resources. In a March 1862 diary entry, Edmund Ruffin, a passionate secessionist, reluctantly admitted that the city seemed reduced to "a sink hole of drunkenness, rowdyism, and crime."[22]

The rough company encountered in the army encouraged other vices, such as gambling and theft. Cornelia Hancock, a Union assistant surgeon with the Army of the Potomac, wrote after having her saddle stolen by soldiers, "The depravity of persons in the army is beyond belief." But the one abuse that joined alcohol as most damaging to soldiers' health and efficiency proved to be sexual promiscuity. No certain cures existed for the venereal diseases that, at times, threatened radical consequences, destroying the immune system and attacking the brain. They also proved highly infectious.[23]

Mercurial compounds served as the most common treatment, leading to the witticism, "A night with Venus, a lifetime with Mercury." Syphilis vaccination, created from active matter, proved risky and largely ineffective. Union Colonel John F. Williams reported his unit "so weakened by syphilis (from vaccination) that they cannot furnish many men for scouting purposes." Without good cures, the regulation of brothels probably proved the best prophylactic, ensuring uninfected women and clean establishments. In Nashville, for example, General R. S. Granger ordered the hospitalization of prostitutes likely to spread disease.[24]

The dimensions of the task ensured failure. D.C. alone boasted some 450 brothels with 7,000 women. These houses of ill repute continued to be unhygienic. A provost's guard raiding "The Hospital," a bordello near the Capitol, encountered sickening stench, filth, and a soldier in a louse-ridden bed. Prostitutes followed the armies. The Louisiana Tigers brought with them into service "disgusting looking creatures" passed off as ministering angels.[25]

The Christian Commission and other benevolent groups helped in the moral struggle, distributing Bibles and cautionary tracts, but the fight continued uphill. Older soldiers got "horny" and virgin youths wanted to experience sex before dying. Said Private Haydon of the 2nd Michigan, in May 1861, "If the men pursue the enemy as vigorously as they do the whores they will make very efficient soldiers." "Away from the restraints of society, and of home," observed Private Wilbur Fisk, 2nd Vermont, Army of the Potomac, in late 1863, "it is the easiest thing in the world to drop in with the current, call it the 'soldier's style,' 'live while you do live,' and let the end take care of itself." [26]

Probably one in twelve Civil War soldiers contracted a social disease. The Union army alone reported some 73,000 cases of syphilis and 109,400 of gonorrhea. Many hospitals dedicated a ward to VD. The epidemic hurt military functioning. Army of Northern Virginia General A. P. Hill, for example, suffered periodic incapacity due to the "clap," contracted as a cadet. Lower down the hierarchy, Colonel William Douglas of the 9th Ohio Cavalry, operating under Sherman, 1864, complained of men on sick call, "the result of their own licentiousness." [27]

Debilitation and death through dissipation thinned the ranks. "Whiskey and sexual vices carry more soldiers off than the bullet," charged Cyrus Boyd, 15th Iowa, an abstemious soldier. A case in point was the 71st New York's Private Patrick McCarty. Though only twenty, he became an alcoholic after signing up, destroying his immune system. Granted a furlough for re-enlisting, he "spent the whole time in debauch, came back bloated and shaking with incipient delirium tremens, fell sick with typhoid pneumonia and died as an old man dies whose constitution is enfeebled by age—." [28]

Unfortunately for moral cleanliness advocates, however, dissipation in fact caused only a minority of the many deaths from disease. In the British army during the Crimean War, 1854–56, disease produced four of five deaths, often from postoperative infection. Although the Civil War's two to one mortality rate of disease to wounds showed improvement, illness remained a personal tragedy and a problem for commanders. In 1861, 20 to 50 percent of men in any unit fell sick at one time, afflictions running the gamut. In August 1861, for instance, 645 of the 7th Louisiana's complement of 920 men reported sick.

Complaints ranged from acute diarrhea, the commonest problem, to VD, metal poisoning, epilepsy, and mental instability.[29]

The high sick rate resulted partly because physicians, keen to get bodies into the building armies, passed men as fit whose physical condition warranted rejection; inferior specimens, they would fail the challenges of camp life. Private Boyd, the Iowa volunteer cited above, alleged that "the surgeons are not all particular as the government wants men," and so passed all the boys. Another recruit, Alfred Bellard, 15th New Jersey, recalled that when inducted in 1861, he underwent no examination at all and only had to answer a few questions: "Were you ever sick in your life, have you got the rheumatism, have you got varicose veins . . . ?"[30]

Medical ignorance of the causes of disease and infection helped promote sickness. Volunteers' ungovernable behavior became another huge ingredient in fostering ill health. Short-term enlistees followed the sloppy example of citizen soldiers in the Mexican War of 1846–48, when disease boosted the U.S. death toll to 104,556. By 1861, the democratic people's army still often refused to be told where to defecate and when to wash. Even the well bred sloughed off, adopting the laxness of a hunting trip. Billets remained unclean. Private Rice C. Bull of the 123rd New York found the Soldiers' Rest in D.C. "the most filthy place I was ever in," and "crawling with vermin and rats which scampered in all directions."[31]

Exacerbating volunteer unruliness, the volume of recruits needing to be accommodated often overwhelmed quartermasters, leading to gross overcrowding. Marcus Woodcock of the 9th Kentucky (U.S.), Army of the Ohio, hospitalized for measles, November 1861, found two patients per bed. "The stench was horrible," resulting from the only sanitary arrangement provided, straw piled around the walls.[32]

Country boys found packed-in living particularly hard. Unused to cramped conditions, they fell prone to childhood diseases that men from congested urban areas had survived in youth. Mumps, measles, and chicken pox became virulent. Georgia General John B. Gordon recalled, "It was amazing to see the large number of country boys who never had the measles. They ran through the whole category of complaints that boyhood and babyhood are subjected to."[33]

Diarrhea and dysentery constituted the commonest diseases,

attacking soldiers of all ages and backgrounds; 700 of 1,000 men might have this at a time, physicians treating almost 500,000 cases per year. Causes included poor food, water, and sanitation, so that "vast acreages were essentially giant cesspools and garbage dumps." Officers did not always understand the sanitary aspect of their jobs. One report on the state of Union troops in camp at Cairo, Illinois, 1861, stated, "the company and regimental officers did not know how to care for the men, and the men themselves seemed to be perfectly helpless."[34]

Neglect caused needless deaths. New York Private Charles Gould's foot turned septic from an untended cut made while chopping wood; he died of blood poisoning complicated by typhoid fever. Sometimes, failure to seek medical aid came about because field officers distrusted surgeons who, taken on during initial army expansion, revealed their inexperience, even incompetence. The surgeon of the 31st Indiana, for example, treated cases of mumps with a futile application of a "caustic" solution to the back of the throat, using his swab repeatedly, guaranteeing transmission of the infection from man to man.[35]

Most physicians understood the inadequacy of their medical assets. Confederate assistant surgeon W. H. Taylor, on duty at a hospital in Charlottesville, Virginia, February 1862, recalled ruefully his only prescriptions for most complaints: "In one pocket of my trousers I had a ball of blue mass [a mercury compound], in another a ball of opium. All complaints were asked the same question, 'How are your bowels?' If they were open, I administered a plug of opium; if they were shut I gave a plug of blue mass." Drug supplies could run short but, in the North, medicines usually remained available, partly due to the efforts of the Women's Central Association of Relief and the U.S. Sanitary Commission. The South suffered a sustained drug shortage, partly due to the Union blockade targeting medical imports.[36]

In an environment of overused medical facilities and inadequate hygiene, physicians and nurses also became ill. Confederate hospital surgeon Dr. James McIntosh contracted erysipelas, a skin infection leading to painful inflammation of the tissue and organs, including the nose and mouth, making breathing difficult. Nurses had to cover his swollen face frequently with wet cloths and feed him a hominy paste for sustenance. On the Union side, volunteer nurse Louisa May Alcott predicted, "we have taken our lives in our hands, and may have to pay dearly for a brief experience." Within three months she endured "a sharp tussle with typhoid." Arabella Barlow, wife of Union General Francis C. Barlow, died of typhus in July 1864, the result of nursing sick soldiers at Fredericksburg, Virginia.[37]

Physical complaints, especially dysentery and diarrhea, could become part of a more complex disease broadly labeled nostalgia. In 1861–62, when the condition grew to its peak, it killed two to three soldiers per 1,000; it destroyed 5,000 Federals alone in the first year of the war. Nostalgia, a psychosomatic sickness, progresses in a circular fashion. If a patient had chronic diarrhea, the resultant weakening of constitutional hardiness could induce despondency, with chronic homesickness adding to the spiral of declining strength and energy. Or, the patient might begin by experiencing emotional pining; if there showed no improvement, this could deepen into depression and passivity, opening depleted constitutional resources to attack by disease. Private Ezra Bingham of the 61st Ohio became lonely and isolated, "much depressed in spirits and exceedingly homesick." One morning, he refused to get up. As his resolution faded, his pulse weakened, and he succumbed to a cough, fever, and "prostration." He effectively died of depression. Army routine had not provided him exemption from the Bartleby-style predicament of the modern worker.[38]

Physicians frequently diagnosed nostalgia in men of later middle age, those with insufficient resources to meet the challenges of camp life. But they saw the disease mostly in youths who often had been the most naively enthusiastic about enlisting for adventure, and who had neither the mental nor physical maturity to cope with adversity and disappointment. Cold reality began when the inductee received his uniform. Clothing often bore little relation to body size and did not fit glamorous images of plumed hussars and bearskin-capped guardsmen. A sixteen-year-old midwestern recruit described receiving his regimental costume in 1861: "My trousers were too long by three or four inches; the shirt was coarse and unpleasant, too large at the neck and too short elsewhere. The cap was an ungainly bag with pasteboard top and leather visor; while the overcoat made me feel a little like a nubbin of corn in a large husk."[39]

There followed months without the stimulation of action, under trying conditions of routine and drudgery, in unfamiliar and often unwholesome surroundings. The letdown produced indifference, depression, and craving for family. "I have been from home for months at a time," wrote Dick Simpson, 3rd South Carolina, from Fairfax Court House, Virginia, on July 4, 1861, "but I never wished to be back so bad in my life." Failure to receive pay or letters from home made volunteers feel neglected, forgotten, abandoned. On August 10, 1863, Union Private Joseph H. Diltz wrote plaintively to his wife after a seeming eternity without news: "I have Cum to the Conclusion that you have fergot me intierly. . . . I want to go home to see you all so bad i dont no what to do."[40]

Physicians recognized the symptoms of nostalgia as early as the seventeenth century, when the sickness was called the "Swiss disease" after being observed in mercenaries from that state serving years away from home. The complaint became documented frequently during the eighteenth to nineteenth century Napoleonic Wars. Many French soldiers, struggling to get back during the 1812 retreat from Moscow, succumbed to homesickness, compounded by exposure and malnutrition.

Some Civil War medical authorities acknowledged nostalgia as a legitimate and serious illness. Physicians in the field suggested the adoption of some quite enlightened remedies. A February 1863 article by U.S. assistant surgeon De Witt C. Peters seems particularly prescient. He began by deprecating "the policy of enlisting youths who have not attained their proper majority," arguing that they were "not sufficiently mature in mind and body to undertake successfully the arduous duties of a soldier."

After describing the physical and mental infirmities pitching youngsters into nostalgia, Peters offered excellent advice to surgeons and line officers: relieve the patient's mind of its "injurious burden" through kindness, exercise, bathing, and agreeable associations; accompany this treatment with a regimen to improve the tone of the stomach and bowels through generous diet and bracing tonics. Most patients, however, had a slim chance of receiving such benevolent medical handling. Many line officers saw their pasty-faced, lackluster men dragging about the tents as malingerers lacking in character, for whom the best medicine became hard discipline attended by punishment if necessary.[41]

Whatever the case, many sufferers died bleakly after illness wasted their bodies and exhausted their will to live. A Union army chaplain wrote to his sister from a hospital at Chapman's Point, Maryland, on November 3, 1861: "Away in gloomy hospital wards, with home a thousand miles away, and no really friendly voice but mine to soothe them or none to hold their hand in the dread hour and speak a word of comfort, the most of my boys died." In part to provide proxy mothers for boys dying alone and afraid, as well as to discourage impromptu sexual liaisons, the services chose plain matronly females, not young, attractive, and impressionable girls, as nurses.[42]

Nostalgia contributed to desertion. Private Boyd noted in late 1861 that, when tenting in bitter cold brought on husky voices and sore throats, "some of the boys began to think of their mothers and to talk of returning to their comfortable homes in the western counties." Joseph E. Crowell of the 13th New Jersey, a veteran, wrote in retrospect that "'T was not always cowardice that made soldiers desert. Something stronger than fear caused some to forget their oaths. . . . It was pure and unadulterated home-sickness." Senior officers proved largely unsympathetic. When a seventeen-year-old Iowan, caught deserting Sherman's command in November 1864, pleaded in extenuation, "I just wanted to see my mother," he was shot.[43]

———•◦•———

At least by the late summer of 1862, desertion by physically weakened and demoralized soldiers flowed from a stream into a flood. This, in turn, helped shrink the armies, depleted also by expiration of enlistments, and by deaths and disabilities from disease and wounds. Growing reluctance to enlist on the part of civilians meant authorities could not guarantee volunteers to make good these losses. Inevitably, the contestants resorted to compulsion for putting and keeping men in the army, even though both sides claimed to be fighting for individual liberties.

At first, local authorities and ad hoc bodies applied most of the force. Rebel and Federal officers, with little authority, pressed African Americans into laboring work, such as digging trenches, latrines, and graves. Some commanders punished veterans who refused to re-enlist by denying them furloughs. Other officers ignored the terms of service; men enlisted for one year in Braxton Bragg's command in the Army of Tennessee found their commitment arbitrarily extended. Those that resisted, Bragg quelled by force.[44]

Faced by chronic manpower shortages, military and civil leaders argued for formal national conscription, overriding state objections to heavy-handed use of central power. A universal draft turned out to be a particularly difficult position for Confederate authorities to defend, as they claimed to have gone to war partly to prevent central government from coercing sovereign states. Robert E. Lee found himself caught in this paradox, forced to argue that the Confederate Congress could veto state opposition to drafting to replenish the field armies.

The Confederacy acted first, through the Conscription Act of April 16, 1862. The law required troops in the army to remain for two more years. It made white males eighteen to thirty-five eligible for three years' service. However, exemptions existed for state and national officials, railroad engineers, telegraph operators, and, most controversially, large slave owners. You were permitted a substitute if a man not subject to the draft agreed to take your place. The amended law of 1863 raised the enlistment ceiling to age forty-five; by 1864 the range became seventeen to fifty, leading critics to jibe that the Confederacy "robbed the cradle and the grave."[45]

The elements of compulsion and exemption made the law unpopular, molding the conflict into "a rich man's war but a poor man's fight." Resentment continued after the abolition of substitution in 1863 because slave owners could still opt out through a $500 commutation fee. Unreasonably, wealthy men, who would lose most by Confederate defeat, could avoid service, even if staying behind served no vital public interest. The dispute over obligation to serve exposed cracks in the ephemeral unity inspired by the heady days of 1861.

Areas that had been lukewarm toward secession bitterly resented conscription. Their populations were largely of the middling sort, such as yeoman and subsistence farmers settled in the interior, including the mountains of Georgia, North Carolina, and Tennessee. "I could be at home if it warent for a fiew big rulers who I cannot help but blame for it," wrote a small farmer drafted into the 57th North Carolina. "These big fighting men cant be got out to fight as easy as to make speaches," he added. Fueling the fire, military commanders condoned such inequalities as giving officers leave to supervise cotton seeding, but denying furloughs to ordinary soldiers who needed to plant vegetables vital for family food.[46]

The North followed the South's example of compulsion, with the Militia Act of July 16, 1862, authorizing the President to draft state militias into Federal service. But of more import here was the Enrollment Act of March 3, 1863. This followed upon the initiation of state drafts by Maryland, Pennsylvania, and Wisconsin, precipitated by the crisis of 100,000 bluecoats being absent without official leave. This law, too, had flaws. It made men twenty to forty-five liable to conscription and disallowed exemptions. But, if called to serve, you could hire a substitute or pay a $300 commutation fee each time your name came up in the lottery, once again allowing the better heeled to get off the hook.[47]

The loopholes in both conscription acts suggested that Americans had not reached consensus on what should be the uniformly binding civic obligations of individuals in a time of crisis. In particular, it appeared that wealth could exempt a man from risking himself for the public good, despite being a recipient of society's greatest rewards. Buying one's way out seemed to carry little opprobrium in the best circles, and so prominent men exercised the option. In a typical defense of the substitution system, the *New York Times* declared complacently that this constituted the only sure method of preserving that class "who work with their brains—who do the planning and directing of the national industry."[48]

To many commentators, the practice of offering bounties to encourage volunteering seemed even more pernicious than substitution because they argued the bounty introduced a mercenary element into military service. Authorities and newspapers frequently blamed "bounty jumpers" (men who took the bonus, deserted, and reenlisted to get more money) for the majority of desertions. The evidence for so broad a claim seems questionable, although the problem did exist. And the pernicious practice of allowing bounty brokers to run a business in procuring recruits led to nefarious activities such as swindling and kidnap to get an illicit percentage of the victim's bounty. In any event, we have to suspect that the idea of a money transaction entering into a military arrangement probably bothered critics less than the fact that the bounty usually helped a poor man while substitution favored the rich.

Adding to perceived class discrimination, officers could resign their commissions to put their personal affairs in order; enlisted men usually had no such option to attend to family needs. Thus, Captain James Wren of the 48th Pennsylvania, after taxing service on the North Carolina coast and heavy fighting in Virginia, resigned his commission on May 18, 1863, even though he had signed on for three years on September 19, 1861. He gave as his reason for leaving that his partner no longer wanted to run his machine-tool business. He rationalized the decision by saying, "I think my services can be dispensed with, and be of no injury to the service."[49]

Similarly, officers more easily got temporary passes to enjoy amenities available in the vicinity of camp. Enlisted men did not get much recreational leave and many consoled themselves with booze. Robert Knox Sneden of the 40th New York, encamped at Leesburg, Virginia, noted in his diary, November 16, 1861, that officers received permission to visit the Washington sights. But, confined to camp, all that the boys could do was avoid the sentries and tie one on in neighboring Alexandria. Drunken fighting ensued and the guardhouse filled accordingly. "Sometime," he noted, "a whole company in camp have to be turned out armed and quell and arrest the rioters."[50]

In North and South, men resorted to subterfuge to beat the draft, including trying to fail the medical examination through bogus ailments certified by civilian physicians, either out of compassion for the draftee or payment of a bribe. Some men had their teeth pulled, as the army rejected those who could not masticate food or tear open a paper cartridge. Unfortunately, the faking of diseases such as epilepsy and poor sight led exasperated army doctors to pass men as fit who really did have these complaints.[51]

Conscription provoked violent resistance, a bleak underside to the mythic picture of patriotic devotion undergirding sectional unity in support of the glorious cause. In the South, although protests broke out in some major cities, core resistance tended to center in rural interior and upcountry areas that showed only lukewarm support for secession. Confederate provost marshals could not enforce the draft in large areas because of fierce push-back, sometimes by whole communities. It proved easy, too, in the many forested areas of the South, for draft evaders to fade into the woods where they might team up with Rebel and Yankee deserters, forming bands large enough to successfully resist army units sent against them.[52]

Northern opposition to the draft ranged from the marble quarries of Vermont and the Pennsylvania coalfields to the midwestern farming areas of Ohio, Indiana, Iowa, and Minnesota. But the fiercest riots occurred during 1863 in urban areas such as Detroit, where the 27th Michigan had to be called in to quell the mob. Moderate and Peace Democrats, afraid of Republican centralization of and potential abuse of power, orchestrated many of these incidents. As in the Confederacy, people on the lower socioeconomic rungs of society featured prominently in crowd makeup, as they had the weakest political voice, were most vulnerable to conscription, and had the least ability to provide for their families during enforced absence.[53]

The most notorious rioting occurred in New York City, starting on July 13, 1863, and lasting for five days. The first draft lottery drawing became pivotal in provoking the violence. Discrimination inherent in the substitution system figured largely in negative publicity. For example, on July 11, two days before the rioting began, the *New York Daily News* charged that the draft "virtually exempts the rich and fastens its iron hand upon the poor alone." Uncle Sam's hypocrisy seemed evident when, shortly before the riots, the socially elite 7th Regiment left for the front without 400 members who received permission to stay behind because of "business engagements."[54]

At first, protesting crowds showed a mixed composition, including native New Yorkers, Germans, and Irish. They began relatively peacefully, but, as demonstrations grew, young Irishmen increasingly took the lead. Although their compatriots had volunteered in large numbers early in the fighting, heavy death tolls and horror stories from the battlefield had chilled the war spirit. The boys had other grievances, feeling vulnerable to job competition from blacks while their brothers in blue suffered death for slave freedom. African Americans had recently replaced striking Irish stevedores.[55]

Also suggesting the caste and class roots of anger, the fiercest riot-ing boiled out of the wards with the worst tenements and living con-ditions. Dr. Stephen Smith, who ran the typhus ward on Blackwell's Island, observed the squalid environment of poor rioters. "In certain populous sections are fat-boiling, entrails-cleansing and tripe-curing establishments, which poison the air for squares around with their stifling emanations." A health inspector reported, in one two-block area, a stream of blood and slimy animal parts stretching from a slaughterhouse on 39th Street to the Hudson River. Completing the witch's brew, the riot's third day turned out to be the hottest of the year.[56]

Predictably, Radical Republicans, military officers, and African Americans proved prime targets of violence. The mob caught, tor-tured, and killed Colonel H. T. O'Brien of the city garrison, who had ordered his men to fire on a crowd. William Jones, a harmless black carter, suffered beating and hanging from a tree, his body set alight and burning while his killers danced around the corpse. Some in the city's political establishment gave their tacit approval.[57]

The rioting produced more than 300 deaths, with many more injured, and about 2.5 million dollars in property damage. Critics said the police would have had a better chance at containing the trouble if they'd had a mounted section like the London Metropoli-tan Police, with trained horses to scatter crowds. But British Bobbies rarely faced firearms that made riders into sitting ducks. The ineffec-tive and inconsistent response of civic and military authorities, which had done no contingency planning and felt unsure of the proper tacti-cal procedures, proved a more important reason for failure.[58]

The rioting burned out when elements of the Army of the Potomac were dispatched to the city. Also helping to assuage discontent, Tam-many Hall, like other local and state officials, put aside funds to help poor men with families buy substitutes or provide for their depen-dents during their absence, once again acknowledging the class discrimination inherent in conscription legislation. Associations throughout the warring sections made similar arrangements. Yet resentment continued, adding to a swelling desertion rate that finally reached over five thousand per month in both armies.[59]

Conscription provides us with some of the most compelling

vignettes of the modern state's machinery of compulsion in action. On an avenue in D.C. during a warmish afternoon, we may observe with Walt Whitman the chilling powerlessness of men caught in a moving prison box: "passing up, in the broad space between the curbs, a big squad of a couple of hundred conscripts, surrounded by a strong cordon of armed guards and others interspersed between the ranks." Or, in Atlanta, we can accompany men of Edward Walthall's Mississippi Brigade engaged in "conscripting a theater." Sealing all exits during the play, they create a huge mantrap that bags some three hundred souls caught without papers, sent then under guard straight to the Virginia front. Sergeant J. W. Simmons comments phlegmatically, "We knew the city was full of able-bodied men who ought to be in the army as well as us."[60]

Finally, on a street in Lexington, Kentucky, we might pause in September 1862 as a kindly local physician stops to talk with a young soldier, part of the invading Rebel army. The youth sits by the roadside, looking washed out. "My poor boy," says the older man, "you oughtnt to be here. You ought to be home with your mother." The youngster claps his hands in response to this gesture of sympathy: "Oh, I do wish I was home. I don't know who or what your are sir, but I am a union man & I was forced into the army else I wouldnt have been here." For this brief moment, an anonymous boy steps out of history's murk to deliver poignant lines; then he returns to obscurity, his fate unknown.[61]

Conscripted men never made up a majority in either section, because the draft laws aimed to stimulate volunteering in communities that wished to avoid being tagged with the unpleasant stigma of compulsion. Possibly just 20 percent of Rebel and 8 percent of Union forces resulted from conscription. Partly, the lower Federal number reflects a manpower resource available to assist volunteering and avoid drafting men, inconceivable in the Confederacy until too late in the war: African Americans.[62]

———◆◆◆———

Initially, most Federal commanders in the field hesitated to rattle the status quo, leaving the structure of slavery intact and returning fugitives to their masters. But by early 1862 the advantage of recruiting people of color appeared too clear to ignore. The Militia Act of July 16, 1862, authorized the President to use blacks "for any military or naval service for which they may be found competent." A month later, Secretary of War Edwin Stanton cleared General Rufus Saxton to enroll up to five thousand Africans, with equal pay for equal work (a promise later reneged on).[63]

Despite army prejudice against recruiting blacks, by fall 1862 their experimental deployment occurred in the Atlantic Sea Islands, Louisiana, Kansas, and Missouri. The Emancipation Proclamation of January 1, 1863, further encouraged the service of black soldiers. The final nudge came with March's Enrollment Act, which, with its threat to draft whites, made large-scale black recruitment attractive. In the blunt words of a popular verse: "In battle's wild commotion I shouldn't at all object If Sambo's body should stop a ball That was comin for me direct!"[64]

Many of the blacks recruited in areas of the South under Union occupation suffered forcible impressment, the authorities giving little thought to the impact on the conscripts' dependents (legislation had failed to provide for freeing slave families of soldiers). Abuses such as kidnap and false inducements occurred across the North, as agents for states like Massachusetts fanned out to find black "volunteers," saving trained white industrial mechanics from being conscripted.[65]

Yet a majority of African American recruitments resulted neither from force nor trickery. Corporal James Henry Gooding, 54th Massachusetts, who served in South Carolina and Florida before capture and death in Andersonville Prison, wrote on May 9, 1863: "Let every man of color consider that he has an interest in this war." Soldiers of color fought to free their people, and the more advanced thinkers hoped to use the cartridge box to win the ballot box. As the endless fighting sapped recruiting zeal, some sustained a higher level of enthusiasm than whites, even in the face of bad treatment and being sacrificed to save white lives. In bloody, suicidal, actions like the Petersburg Crater, July 30, 1864, they formed the "forlorn hope," thrown foremost into the assault and sustaining massive casualties.[66]

Inevitably, given the racist nature of American society, colored regiments fought a war on two fronts. Confederate authorities threatened to enslave or execute those captured, along with their white officers. The Rebels backed down when Lincoln guaranteed retaliation, but unauthorized murders still occurred frequently, at places such as Plymouth, North Carolina, with black prisoners lined up along the Roanoke River and shot. Following misguided medical theory that Africans did not suffer from diseases prevalent in summer heat, Union officers used them excessively as laborers, digging trenches, latrines, and graves.[67]

At Vicksburg, General Ulysses S. Grant rationalized his over-use of black troops on unhealthy fatigue duty by saying, "I do not want the White men to do any work that can possibly be avoided during the hot months." General John M. Schofield ordered such work for colored soldiers in North Carolina "so as to relieve the white troops from duty where they would be exposed to disease." Logic would suggest that, as black soldiers suffered a higher rate of pulmonary diseases, they would draw fewer fatigue details in cold, wet weather, but this did not happen. Unsurprisingly, while white deaths from disease versus wounds stood at a two to one ratio, for blacks it was ten to one.[68]

Black soldiers received more severe and frequent punishments than whites for disciplinary infractions, even though officers generally agreed men of color exhibited less drunkenness and individual defiance of orders. The only serious resistance to authority occurred in the matter of pay, for the army allotted black soldiers $10 per month, not $13, arguing they did not deserve the extra combat compensation for digging graves, etc. The discrimination led to organized protest, alleged to be mutiny by military authorities. Blacks accounted for 80 percent of soldiers shot for mutiny, including Sergeant William Walker of the 3rd South Carolina (U.S.), executed for stacking arms to protest pay discrimination.[69]

Soldiers of color faced charges and executions more frequently than whites for alleged rape. Esther Hill Hawk, a physician with Union forces in the Atlantic Sea Islands, recorded the execution of three black soldiers from the 55th Massachusetts accused of sexually assaulting a white woman. General Milton Littlefield hanged them immediately after a drumhead court-martial that allowed no time to muster a defense. He ordered three black regiments to attend and harangued them about the crime. Dr. Hawk observed bitterly that, if the general meted out the same punishment to white officers and men for raping black women, the firing squads would be very busy and the general "grown hoarse in repeating his remarks."[70]

Black soldiers met barriers to promotion, only a few rising to commissioned rank late in the conflict. Despite all the hurdles, men of color hoped their sacrifice would earn equitable treatment in postwar America. Clara Barton, tending a dying soldier of the 54th Massachusetts, felt moved by his belief that, through his struggle, his children would be free. Legally, they would be, at least by 1865. But General Littlefield's actions already hinted that the road they would travel in the postwar era would be hard and mostly unfair. Then, disillusionment and a keen sense of betrayal would, for many black veterans, tarnish pride in their war service.[71]

CHAPTER TWO

ON THE MARCH

×

AS THE REGIMENTS LEAVE THEIR ASSEMBLY CAMPS, WHERE the recruits have mustered and trained, we will accompany them on their march into the field and observe some of what happens on the road. Numbers of soldiers will find the open-air life healthful and invigorating, but all will be accompanied by the ubiquitous dirt, dust, and mud, along with millions of insects, ensuring that disease will remain a constant companion. Food rations will run short, and always the troops face a universal shortage of water, for drinking, cooking, washing clothes, bathing wounds, and cleaning surgical instruments.

Large concentrations of men move across the landscape, the biggest armies yet seen on the North American continent. They contain largely short-term citizen volunteers, unlike the small professional forces that characterized warfare before the American and French Revolutions of the late 1700s. Those turmoils changed the profile of warfare, making it more the people's struggles, in which plain folk had a stake and so might take up arms through dedication to a shared cause. The citizen soldier became a new model, radically enlarging the available manpower pool to include the whole masculine population.

In Europe, the early nineteenth century saw further attempts to extend political freedom through armed revolution at the barricades, while in the United States, building on concepts voiced in the Declaration of Independence, common (white) men surged to prominence during the 1830s presidency of Andrew Jackson. Jacksonian democracy confidently declared that the ordinary man could excel at any task to which he turned his attention. In a military context, this meant that he would exhibit innate soldierly abilities at least equal to those of a "book-learned" and hireling regular. Consequently, the young nation placed its security largely in the hands of a "well-regulated militia," amateur soldiers exercising their collective right to bear arms in organized state units.

As a result, the War between the States would be fought by massive levies of ordinary men in uniform—civilians in quieter times—albeit under the orders of commanders largely graduated from West Point and other military academies. The size of these armies became so great that they were compared frequently to moving cities. We have here a good image to bear in mind, because much follows from the analogy. The teeming multitudes of a city require shelter, food, clothing, warmth, water, and sanitary arrangements on a grand scale. The Victorian metropolis did not always succeed in meeting these essential needs. How much more difficult would it be, then, to cater to an urban concentration perpetually in motion, with no stable transportation terminals for supply, no guaranteed water resources, and so on? The city in motion found itself inevitably ill served.

———————

In theory, by 1860 the technological apparatus and organizational structures had reached a point where governments could put huge bodies of troops in the field and sustain them there. The railroad and steamboat could shift immense amounts of personnel and materials to any designated location, while an expanding network of roads provided links in this transportation grid. Mass production of uniforms, shoes, and equipment ought to have kept the levies clothed and shod. Industrial processing of preserved foodstuffs meant that troops could still eat when fresh meat and produce became unavailable locally.

The arrangements worked to the degree that the troops stayed in the field and on the march. But theory often failed when confronted by the harsh realities of practice. Railroads became degraded by heavy usage; the crumbling Confederacy could not maintain them. Raiders for both sides tore up track and burned bridges; natural disasters ruined the infrastructure. Ammunition and other vital supplies could be shipped on boats by whichever side controlled a particular waterway, but the final journey from the landing meant trundling over roads wrecked by war. In their construction, many highways had been neither graded nor drained to bear constant heavy traffic, being intended for local use only. F. Colburn Adams, a New York cavalry officer serving on the Virginia Peninsula, noted that, in violent storms, "trees were uprooted, tents blown down, the bridges over the Chickahominy nearly swept away, and the very earth flooded."[1]

Spring and fall rains reduced roadbeds to feet-deep mud churned up by marching boots, wagon wheels, and hooves. Mules drowned in deep potholes. "It is solemnly true," wrote General Alpheus S. Williams, "that we lost mules in the middle of the road, sinking out of sight in the mud-holes." In summer, haulage animals and beef cattle intended for the troops succumbed to heat, dust, and dehydration. Suffering the July heat in Mississippi during the 1863 Vicksburg campaign, Tom Taylor, 47th Ohio, asked, "Is it any wonder that men fell down in their tracks and that horses and mules reeled and fell under the saddle—sun struck was a familiar word." The mud interfered with military operations. Mud, along with diarrhea, stopped Grant's pursuit of the Rebels after Shiloh.[2]

Fodder for beasts ran short. Private William B. Greene, 2nd U.S. Sharpshooters, coming upon the carcasses of eighteen slaughtered horses at Bristoe Station, Virginia, on April 6, 1862, noted the Rebels must be short of feed to shoot their mounts this way. The Union alone lost 11,000 horses in the first fourteen months of war and more than a million perished in the overall conflict. Even when roads proved passable, hard-marching generals outran their supply wagons as the vehicles labored over rutted highways. Confederate General Dorsey Pender accused Stonewall Jackson of setting so grueling a pace that no supply train could keep up: "Jackson would kill up an army the way he marches," when added to "the bad management in the subsistence Dept."[3]

Bad management certainly constituted one factor. Particularly in the early months, thinly staffed quartermaster departments became routinely overwhelmed, but they also bogged down because of red tape and parsimonious accounting methods learned in the old army.

Thus, the department medical director at New Orleans denied a shipment of quinine badly needed by troops in the west because of "irregularity" in the submission of the requisition. Soldiers who had set off for war in fine new uniforms might go barefoot and nearly naked when replacement outfits failed to reach them. A New York woman who saw Gettysburg thought that many Union soldiers, "with their clothes ragged and dirty," resembled "inhabitants of the bottomless pit" of hell rather than respectable defenders of the Republic.[4]

Even newly issued uniforms might disintegrate because many consisted of "shoddy," run up quickly by suppliers for the government market out of a concoction of rag fibers bonded together. "Mud deep and growing deeper. Uniforms in bad plight—feet wet and cold and patriotism down to zero," declared Corporal C. F. Boyd, 15th Iowa, enduring extreme weather in the western theater, February 1862. The Union army, usually better shod than its opponents, still wore ill-made shoes, often cut to a standard shape, without proper sizing or arches and made for either foot, causing major discomfort. Cardboard soles fell apart on long marches. General Alpheus Williams wrote from the Virginia Peninsula in the Spring of 1862: "I have at least 4,000 men in my division who are shoeless completely, or so nearly that they cannot march."[5]

Confederate soldiers went shoeless in winter as well as summer, leaving bloody prints in the snow. "Many of our men are barefooted, and I have seen the blood in their tracks as they marched," attested Colonel John S. Williams, campaigning in Kentucky, in November 1861. A common expedient was fashioning crude moccasins from the untanned cowhide of cattle that had been slaughtered for meat, but these shoes shrank drastically as the hide dried, causing constriction and pain. The moccasins also proved so slick underfoot that men fell. Colonel Moxley G. Sorrel, on the staff of General James Longstreet, concluded: "The wearers, constantly up or down, finally kicked them aside and took the road as best they could." He added that the men had found a large supply of shoes sent from England to be shoddy, falling apart in one day of wet and mud.[6]

The gravest supply failure proved to be sustenance. Surgeon General William Hammond correctly asserted the designated Federal ration the most generous in the world, with ample allowances of meat, bread, legumes, rice, potatoes, onions, coffee, tea, sugar, salt, vinegar, and so on. But quantities in the field routinely fell short of the regulation allotment. Private John W. Haley, 17th Maine, admitted that hunger drove the boys to gobble entrails, called melts. "I have never before heard of eating such trumpery as melts, but necessity drives us to sample this disgustingly filthy mess."[7]

When fresh rations reached the lines, men might not be given time to eat them. Illinois Colonel William Camm, 14th Illinois, related the march being ordered before his broiling meat was warmed through, "and I ate my beef raw, without bread and the blood running over my hand." Gulping a mouthful of scalding coffee, he "swallowed it in agony, and a minute after drew all the skin from my palate with my forefinger." Private Lawrence Van Alstyne, 128th New York, described his company tearing raw flesh from freshly slaughtered beef. He dug at the warm liver, eating the sticky shreds that stuck to his fingers, and "kept it up until I had taken the edge off my appetite."[8]

Hunger drove men to actions that would have repulsed them in previous times. Nathaniel Cheairs Hughes of the Washington Artillery, Confederate Army of Tennessee, wrote in October 1863: "Daily starving soldiers crave of us permission to pick out of the dirt around the horses the soiled and trodden grains of corn that remained after feed time." Men in blue and gray ate rats and whole frogs. Private Silas Mallory, 64th Ohio, caught a frog, ripped it apart, ground it up with an ear of corn, and ate the mush for supper. Some also judged rat to be as tender as young squirrel. Desperate men rifled the dead. Private John Casler of the Stonewall Brigade admitted to taking crackers off a corpse, cutting away the bloody edges, and wolfing down the rest.[9]

When fresh rations failed, preserved substitutes had to suffice. Bacon found favor with the troops but, in hot weather, or if it had been in the cask too long, it could be rancid. Hungry men ate it anyway. Benjamin F. Jackson, 33rd Alabama, recounted to his wife in June of 1862 that the processed beef, permeated with saltpeter, required soaking overnight (when a water source existed); next, he said, "put it on and boil it half a day and then it will be so tough we can't chew it." Plain flour, mixed with water and cooked over the fire in bacon fat, if available, made a bread substitute. The results proved so resilient, wrote physician Esther Hill Hawk from a Union hospital in Florida, February 1864, that "If they could be worn as armor, it would make the men invulnerable." Prior-baked biscuit or hardtack formed a staple that kept body and soul together, but it took getting used to. Often, only a musket butt could break up this petrified cracker. When damp, it hatched weevils and black-headed worms an inch long. Texas chaplain W. J. Joyce pronounced the crackers "wormy moldy stuff" that irritated the thirsty tongue.[10]

Other preserved foods, more readily available to Northern than Southern troops, included condensed (dubbed "condemned") milk and desiccated ("desecrated") vegetables that came in brick-sized blocks. Both supplied vital nutritional elements. But the vegetables required long boiling in plenty of water; frequently, neither liquid nor cooking time was available. The boiling had to be done cautiously, for the fibers swelled alarmingly during the rehydration process, overflowing coffee pots and other impromptu cooking vessels. The reconstituted plants often became mushy or tough, tasting like "a lot of rags," recalled Private Joseph E. Crowell, 13th New Jersey. Canned and dried legumes contained important protein but, when not part of a balanced diet, caused intestinal problems. Private John D. Billings, 10th Massachusetts Artillery, described Sibley tents filled with the "nauseating exhalations from the bodies of twelve men." It is also likely that lead-soldered seams on canned goods helped to produce the metal poisoning found in some volunteers.[11]

Sutlers' wares, such as pies, pickles, and oysters, when available, enriched diets; but they were for individual purchase, and not all soldiers could afford them. Pay often showed up late or had to be sent home for essential family support. Lonely men eagerly anticipated packages from home, providing variety to the diet and comforting treats, but the parcels could arrive crushed or decayed. Captain Thomas N. Stevens, 28th Wisconsin, received "bread, cakes, pies, turkeys, cheese, &c. &c. moldy & rotten—whew!" Joseph H. Twichell, chaplain of the 72nd New York, in winter camp at Falmouth, Virginia, eagerly awaited his December 1862 Thanksgiving box from home, only to find it contained mince pie growing a crop of blue mold and a chicken pie "fast returning to dust."[12]

An inferior diet low in vitamins and minerals resulted in scurvy, an ugly, painful, and energy-sapping disease that increased as the war lengthened. In 1861, the Union reported five cases per one thousand; by 1864 more than twenty. Enlightened officers tried to obtain citrus fruits, onions, sauerkraut, fresh apples, and greens to combat the disease. They sometimes encountered push-back from citizen soldiers who wrongly associated fresh produce with cholera epidemics, and adequate supplies proved hard to find. Often, the only available course was to commandeer all produce grown near the line of march, stripping farm crops, and then sending out foraging parties to gather wild greens and onions.[13]

Even foraging could have deleterious results, as in Lee's 1862 Maryland campaign, where the general received criticism for marching north before the crops along his route fully ripened. The commander erred in "starting off with us before the corn was fit to eat," wrote North Carolina veteran Berry Greenwood. When the Army of Northern Virginia outran its supply lines, thousands of famished soldiers fell out or tried to march on green corn and sour apples. Mary B. Mitchell, a Maryland housewife, described Rebels gaunt from starvation begging food, always with the same explanation: "I've been a-marchin' and a-fightin' for six weeks stiddy, and I ain't had n-a-r-thin' to eat 'cept green apples and green corn."[14]

The consequent chronic dysentery thinned Lee's ranks. A Northern civilian who walked the Antietam field shortly after the battle said the Rebel lines could be traced "by the thickly strewn belt of green corn husks and cobs," with "a ribbon of dysenteric stools just behind." Malnutrition and diarrhea gravely impaired the efficiency of the armies, causing depression, lethargy, night blindness, muscular debility, neuralgia, and susceptibility to major diseases. Finally, emaciated men could not march or fight and died.[15]

Just as the armies stripped the countryside of food, with deprived civilians cursing them as a plague of locusts, the troops also ruthlessly drained the water supply. Men and beasts needed water to drink, a resource also essential for much cooking; for cleaning bodies, clothing, and utensils; and for washing medical equipment and operating tables. While surgeons might be criticized for lax sanitation, they often did not have water to clean instruments or their patients' blood-and-dirt-encrusted bodies. The needs of the martial city-on-the-march became so rapacious that desperate civilians disabled their water supply to avoid being left with none. "As we approached," recalled Confederate Colonel Marcus Stephens of campaigning in rural Mississippi, mid-1863, "the good people would remove the buckets, ropes, and Pumps from their wells or cisterns and no water could be had."[16]

Soldiers suffering dehydration, made worse by eating dry hard biscuits and salty bacon, resorted to desperate measures, routinely drinking foul water. Private Levi Ross, 86th Illinois, wrote of drought in Kentucky during the October 1862 Perryville campaign: "Much of the water we drink is mixed with the filth of the mules, hogs and goose." Confederate Private James Houghton confided to his diary, in the broiling heat of July, 1863, that his unit had taken stagnant water from a ditch: "we poaked the Skum one side with our cups then gave the water a spat to scare the bugs and wiglers to the bottom." No water could be rejected in extremity. Maine Private John Haley, camping on the 1863 Chancellorsville grounds a year after the battle, noted that water drawn from sources in proximity to hastily-dug graves had "a most horrible flavor," the water table being contaminated.[17]

Ignorance, slackness, and bad practice added to the inherent dangers of the situation. During the June 1862 heat in the western theater, Colonel William Camm of the 14th Illinois complacently watched his boys cracking jokes and singing as they filled their canteens from a brook. Turning in the saddle, he glanced upstream to where a dead mule lay in the water, covered with "millions of flies." The disconcerted officer had himself just enjoyed a careless drink from the same contaminated stream. Private C. W. Kepler, 4th Ohio, noted that a regiment in his brigade had been reduced to 185 men. They had camped downriver from other units, taking water from a stream "used as a latrine by the army, and . . . where lay in putrescent death horses, mules, and horned cattle."[18]

Thirsty soldiers greedily sucked up mud holes, bloody pools, and swamp water, inevitably encouraging disease. For example, bad water spread typhoid fever through both armies during the baking Atlanta campaign of summer 1864. Overall, the Union army formally recorded nearly 149,000 typhoid cases, of whom close to 35,000 died. The Confederates faced similarly severe losses. Bad food and water also helped keep dysentery and diarrhea as leading illnesses, causing close to 1,800,000 cases in the Federal army alone, with over 44,500 deaths. Intestinal pain could be so acute that victims like Texas State Trooper Jack Iago committed suicide (by slitting his wrists).[19]

◆━◆◆◆━

Water remained essential not only for drinking but washing. Soldiers became filthy from dust in summer and mud in winter; the dirt lay on them like a crust. Private Wilbur Fisk, 2nd Vermont, wrote from Gaine's Mill, Virginia, in June 1864, that the earth comprised piles of dust that got into clothes, coffee, blankets, haversacks. "It is universal, and there is no getting rid of it." That same month and place, Union nurse Cornelia Hancock wrote, "The weather is intensely hot, the suffering intensely great." Flies swarmed and "We have had scarcely one drop of rain for two weeks, the dust is shoe top deep." [20]

Mixed with water, dust became mud. Georgia Private Matthew Nunnally, enduring trench warfare at Yorktown, Virginia, during spring 1862 floods, noted, "We were on duty every other day and sometimes every day in the trenches up to our knees in mud, frequently without a morsel to eat for thirty-six hours, had but little sleep." Elisha Hunt Rhodes, 2nd Rhode Island, recorded in late November 1863: "It is raining, and we all live in mud, sleep in mud, and almost eat in mud." Another sufferer assured his brother he had now become expert on a rich assortment of mud, "from that kind of which you take up a ton every time you lift your boot, to that gayer and more sportive compound which spirts upon your knees, as you tiptoe through it. It is over-shoe everywhere." [21]

Captain Charles Minor Blackford, 2nd Virginia Cavalry, wrote from the field, October 1863, that it had been raining incessantly, "the air so dark and dank that it may be cut with a knife," the ground knee-deep in mud and slush. "I am stiff and cold and every joint is painful with aches and suffering." Tar from pine-tree fires added a piquant variety of filth, stickily coating hands, faces, and clothes. Only scrubbing with soap and water could remove the goo, and soldiers saw little of either solvent. The sweat of battle, powder smoke, and gunpowder residue from bitten cartridges provided a final touch of misery, dyeing faces and tongues indigo blue. Veterans in the field might resemble tramps. Tally Simpson, 3rd South Carolina, wrote from Fredericksburg, Virginia, in December 1862: "I am very ugly, my beard is shaggy, teeth black, clothes dirty and worn, finger nails long and black, nose little inclined to drip—I am a hard looking case." [22]

Lucky soldiers discovered a pool of dirty water to bathe in or took a plunge in a swamp. If in camp for a while, they would go far and wide for water. "The weather is exceedingly hot—and dusty. We send three miles for water," wrote South Carolina senator and short-term volunteer, James Chesnut, in the summer of 1861. Officers saw being stationary as a luxury because they might find a bend in the river to bathe away from the bivouac, protocol decreeing they should not wash in view of the men. Hence, they often had particular trouble keeping clean. Union Captain John W. DeForest depicted an officer's tunic "almost stiff enough to stand alone" with dirt and sweat. [23]

The pace of active campaigning often meant that soldiers could not clean up for weeks. During Lee's hard-marching 1862 Maryland campaign, a private in the 15th Georgia calculated that his regiment had not washed their clothes for forty-five days. Frances Peter, a physician's daughter in Lexington, Kentucky, watched invading gray ranks march by on September 18, 1862, and observed wryly that they looked "as if they hadn't been near water since Fort Sumter fell" in April 1861. The troops smelled, too, stinking of sweat, excrement, and urine. Dr. Lewis H. Steiner of the U.S. Sanitary Commission said that even pro-Secession citizens admitted to being glad when Lee's troops left, taking with them "the penetrating ammoniacal smell they brought with them." In the west, Sergeant Rice C. Bull, 123rd New York, fighting before Atlanta, figured he had neither bathed nor washed his clothing from May 20 to July 12, 1864. [24]

When opportunity finally allowed personal hygiene to be addressed, the results could be traumatic. As the hair of Union soldiers was cropped during their steamship passage to the Virginia Peninsula, April 1862, Colonel Charles S. Wainwright reported that "the pile of dirt disclosed beneath the earlocks of some must have been accumulating all winter," and the ship's pilot said the filth "would grow a hill of corn!" Clara Barton, a Union nurse tending a man whose socks had not been off during a month of campaigning on the Virginia Peninsula, 1862, felt horrified to witness that "his toes were matted and grown together and are now dropping off at the joint." [25]

———•◦•———

Dirty soldiers also became insect-infested soldiers. Ticks and fleas abounded in warm weather. "The trees are about in full leaf and vermin are becoming altogether too numerous," wrote Major Charles W. Wills, 8th Illinois, from Georgia, on May 2, 1864. "Every man is a vigilance committee on the wood-tick question." Chiggers created itchy misery. Union cavalry Captain Robert Burns wrote from before Atlanta that he and his company had become so filthy they might never get clean again. "To crown all, there is a little insect in the woods here called 'chickar' or 'jigger' which now almost torments us out of our senses. It is so small that it is almost imperceptible. It pierces the skin and makes a terrible itching. My body is covered with the marks of the remorseless little monster. . . . We are also troubled with the wood-ticks, scorpions, and all sorts of accursed bugs." [26]

The men voted lice the most ubiquitous "accursed bugs," because they colonized the human body by millions, creating a sensation of wretched humiliation so intense that the word "lousy" to describe feeling awful passed into the language. On first discovery of his being plagued by lice, Texas Private William A. Fletcher, 5th Texas, confided, "such a feeling of disgrace one rarely has." Being personally fastidious proved no deterrent since the close quarters of army living promoted the uninterrupted transmission from body to body. When Captain Nathaniel Southgate Shaler, 5th Kentucky Artillery (U.S.), pictured exhausted soldiers sleeping on a sidewalk, "crammed close as herring in a box," he was also describing the domain of insects. Lice colonies grew so thick, they could be seen like a blanket crawling over grass and tree trunks. Because they remained especially virulent in previously used campsites, soldiers came to dread old bivouacs. "Here I learned," said Fletcher, "that in moving and occupying the same grounds occupied by others, that cleanliness was no bar to lice." [27]

Lice proved hard to eradicate. When time permitted, soldiers boiled their clothing in soup kettles. But Texan William Lott Davidson, 5th Texas cavalry, decided this served merely to fatten the insects and "make the eggs deposited in the shirt hatch out." The artful employed another strategy, catching the lice as they wiggled out of clothing seams heated before a campfire, and then cracking them between nail and forefinger. "I have seen fellows so busily engaged in catching them that it reminded me of an old woman knitting," wrote Private Sam Watkins, 1st Tennessee (C.S.A.). At first, he recalled, the boys acted in a fastidious fashion and "would go off in the woods and hide to louse themselves, but that was unnecessary, the ground fairly crawled with lice."[28]

Veterans usually came to accept living with lice, just as they had to tolerate the millions of flies that accompanied the line of march. To understand why clouds of flies became omnipresent, we should reprise our moving city analogy. Cities must address sewage disposal by some method or other. But often the armies did not have time to dig latrines and, as we have seen, many volunteers ignored the sinks anyway, defecating where they wished, while animals could not use sanitary trenches. Charles Francis Adams Jr. wrote to his father that the army "is a city without sewage," waste and offal from slaughtered beasts scattered everywhere or hastily buried, "all festering under a mid-summer sun." Many soldiers with loose bowels from poor food and water defecated around their tents, while army horses indiscriminately dropped twenty to twenty-five pounds of manure a day. Hence the flies.[29]

S. Walkley, historian of the 7th Connecticut, remembered flies on food and maggot-infested beef. The men drank coffee with their eyes closed. South Carolinian Tally Simpson told his aunt that the flies "light on my face and stick so tight that I can scarcely knock them off with my fist." In moist conditions, multitudes of maggots squirmed from eggs. When Union General Kenner D. Garrard, campaigning in Georgia, in the summer of 1864, went to get a blanket from a pile that had been put away wet in his headquarters wagon, he disturbed a horde of freshly hatched maggots that groped blindly over his body.[30]

To be coated with dirt and insects degraded the soldiers' spirits, inducing low morale and despondency that, if unchecked, could disempower the victims and even end in death. Private Watkins, recalling the Army of Tennessee's 1864 occupation of Lookout Mountain, wrote, "Never in all my whole life do I remember of ever experiencing so much oppression and humiliation. The soldiers were starved and almost naked, and covered all over with lice and camp itch and filth and dirt. The men looked sick, hollow-eyed, and heart-broken, living principally upon parched corn, which had been picked out of the mud and dirt under the feet of officers' horses."[31]

The world of the army hosted a universe of threatening diseases. Lice and fleas transmitted typhus, also known as jail or ship fever, an epidemic disease that thrived in crowded, unsanitary conditions. The sudden onset of prostration, accompanied by severe headaches, rashes, high fever, and progressive neurological complications, characterized this illness. More frequently, physicians diagnosed diseases transmitted by flies. These flying insects widely spread *Salmonella* and *E coli* bacteria, found in contaminated feces, further encouraging typhoid fever and dysentery.[32]

The passage of the armies dislocated the natural environment. For example, mud can drown but, when disturbed, it also serves as a vector for such bacteria as tetanus and anthrax that live in the soil and enter hosts through cuts, sores, bites, and wounds. Army traffic also spawned mosquito-breeding sites by disrupting natural drainage channels, leaving standing water and waste matter. Species of mosquito carried two dreaded diseases, yellow fever and malaria. Yellow fever, although relatively rare in the Northern climate, attacked Yankees serving in Southern theaters. Fevers rose very high as the virus assaulted the organs, and victims vomited black blood; surgeons said that kidneys and intestines looked as though they had been dipped in boiling water. Physicians used calomel to empty bowels and quinine to attack the fever, but the treatments proved largely ineffective.[33]

Malaria, while less dramatic, proved more common. While physicians diagnosed roughly 1,350 yellow fever cases among Union forces, they found 1.3 million instances of malaria, resulting in over 10,000 deaths. All of the Unted States save a small area of the cooler northern and western states constituted malarious country. Doctors cited bad air as the cause, making a link to stagnant water without understanding that predatory flying insects, not poisonous bog gases, would ultimately prove responsible. Victims suffered incapacitating fevers, violent shivering, delirium, and, in extreme examples, destruction of red blood cells, causing death as the liver and spleen swelled, turning black. The disease punished the victim, recurring without warning.

A potent weapon to combat malaria, quinine, had been known since the seventeenth century, but limited supplies existed and not all physicians accepted this prescription, trying ineffective remedies such as whiskey or boiled dogwood bark.[34]

Troops attacked by clouds of insects tried their own prophylactic methods, such as pipe smoking or rubbing bacon fat on exposed skin, the salt supposedly repelling some pests. Very little helped. "There is a hopeless desperation chilling one when engaged in a contest with disease," wrote Major Charles Wills. "The unseen malaria has such an advantage in the fight." With no real protection, soldiers came to dread fighting in the swamps where "bad air" invited chills and fevers. A veteran of the 54th Pennsylvania avowed of the Chickahominy swamps, where the armies fought in summer 1862: "the mention of that name causes a shudder to run through the survivors of the Army of the Potomac." From the Louisiana bayous, Ben C. Johnson of the 64th Michigan, far from home, wrote bitterly that the slimy hand of fever dragged men down, there to be "laid away under the accursed soil of the swamp."[35]

Not all sickness derived from insects. Extremes of climate directly instigated illness. Let us acknowledge that certain men thrived on the challenges of living with raw nature in the rugged outdoors. Rutherford B. Hayes boasted that "These marches and campaigns . . . will always be among the pleasantest things I can remember." Captain DeForest maintained that the outdoors toughened up dyspeptic New England bookworms, rendering them "gaunt with bad food, fasting and severe marching; gaunt and wiry, but all the hardier and stronger for it, like a wolf." Those less feral fared more poorly.[36]

Exposure to harsh sunlight during summer campaigning felled men. The heat on the third day of Gettysburg grew so fierce that Lieutenant W. B. Taylor of the 11th North Carolina saw men faint all along the line. At other seasons, bleak cold and wet attacked the constitution, and failures in the supply system often meant a scarcity of tents. A South Carolina soldier moaned that he was "sad and dreary" from cold, having been rained on for four days, without a tent for protection. Union Major James Wren, 48th Pennsylvania, wrote from camp in Virginia, in November 1862, "Last night thear was a sharp frost & we, having no tents, we felt it. Very Coald. The men run short of rashons owing to the supply train not getting up with the Supplies."[37]

The troops also lacked blankets and waterproofs. In January 1862, eleven unequipped men of the 3rd Arkansas were found dead, frozen solid. John B. Jones, a Richmond bureaucrat, saw soldiers trudging along on a dark, sleety January 1865 day, "icicles hanging from their hats and caps, and their clothes covered with frost, and dripping." Colds, flus, and pneumonia resulted. Confederate Captain Charles Blackford, suffering chills and fever from incessant marching in rain and slush, complained that every joint ached, and he could not get up for three days. "It is a terrible feeling; one could court death when in my situation, for life seems robbed of all charm."[38]

Soldiers commonly complained of rheumatism and rheumatic fever. A Union corporal visiting his men in field hospital in February 1862, found "There are many cases of suffering there. Some with the Rheumatism seem to be the worst off—for they are completely helpless and suffer great pain." Without a cure, patients received opiates to relieve joint pain and quinine for general inflammation. Physicians blistered some on the pain spot, such as the knee, thereby only increasing their misery. "I've had very hard work today, dressing blisters is no easy task," confided Confederate Ada Bacot, a weary nurse in a Virginia hospital. One patient in particular, "a boy about eighteen was making considerable fuss about his blisters." Complaints of rheumatism became so widespread in the Union army during the first two years that surgeons were ordered to ignore them. Even so, the medical service officially recorded nearly 287,000 cases.[39]

———•◦•———

Older men with preexisting conditions could be very vulnerable to the rigors of campaigning. This category included many senior officers. Prior service had rendered them immune to childhood diseases such as mumps that struck down youths. But years of exposure wore down older regulars, who were at the same time experiencing the typical discomforts of aging. Edwin V. Sumner, a venerable Union general, had to remove his false teeth to bellow orders. Lower down the totem, a Lieutenant Dorrance, 123rd Illinois, swallowed his dentures in action November 1864, "and complains that they don't agree with him," according to his droll major.[40]

Marsena Rudolph Patrick, another older man and provost marshal general of the Army of the Potomac, endured agonies from hemorrhoids and rheumatism, driving him to ride in an ambulance, sedated with opium. Since the eighteenth century, scientists had experimented with electricity to curb rheumatism; Patrick had the telegraph operators hook him up to the wires and shoot a "dose of lightning" through him. He thought this helped him, as did a chloroform rub.[41]

Confederate General Daniel H. Hill's weakness began with probable childhood polio that left him perennially vulnerable. Writing in May 1862, during the retreat up the Peninsula, he confessed that "My bowels pained me so much that at times I was almost in despair." By January 1863, he felt so reduced that he tried to resign, pleading "a very feeble frame" since a boy. Urged to stay on in the crisis, he was transferred west to the command of waspish General Braxton Bragg, no great prescription for a sick man. Bragg spoke contemptuously of Hill's health issues, calling him a "croaker" who seemed defeatist and lethargic in action.[42]

Bragg himself came into the war with a history of accumulated ills, including migraines, stomach problems, and dysentery. He took a mercury compound for the liver and opium to ease digestive pain and soreness from boils. Illness and drastic medication in spring 1863 may account for his subsequent erratic behavior and frequent disorientation that eventuated in a breakdown, rendering him unfit until December.[43] The officer's privilege of riding might appear to offer benefits for weakened constitutions, but hours in the saddle could be torture for sick soldiers, especially cavalrymen. General George A. Custer may have suffered testicular pain from long periods spent bouncing in the saddle, possibly exacerbated by gonorrhea contracted in 1859. According to Captain Lewellyn G. Estes, aide to Judson Kilpatrick, that general "usually rode stooping and bent over the saddle" because "his kidneys troubled him and caused him a pain in the back."[44]

General George Stoneman's hemorrhoids delayed his movements during Sherman's 1864 campaigns and may have determined his choice of a quick but bloody frontal attack to get past Rebels at Sunshine Church on July 31, 1864, rather than trying a flanking movement that would have kept him in the saddle longer. Infantry generals feeling too sick to walk and forced to ride into action increased their odds of becoming targets. On the third day at Gettysburg, two of Pickett's brigadiers, James L. Kemper and Richard Brooke Garnett, reported too ill to attack Cemetery Ridge on foot and so rode forward; Kemper ended gravely wounded, Garnett dead.[45]

Pickett may not have recovered emotionally from the ruin of his division, and he affords a good example of how command stress, compounded by exposure, ground down senior officers. The general's health had been fragile since childhood; routine military service and the Mexican War added malaria and intestinal issues. By spring 1864 he had worn himself down to where, at successive intervals, he proved unable to exercise command, debilitated by hemorrhoids, dysentery, and strain. Observers described him as prematurely aged, his face bloated, eyes dull, hair lank and lifeless.[46]

Exhausted officers, however, enjoyed an option unavailable to the troops; they might resign. Colonel Thomas W. Higginson, 1st South Carolina (U.S.), retired North in October 1864, suffering prostration from wounds and overwork. Rebel Colonel Sterling A. M. Wood, 7th Alabama, went home, drained by loose bowels and injuries. But many officers felt constrained by the code of honorable conduct to remain at their posts. Confederate Brigadier John Echols stayed in the field despite "neuralgia of the heart" that sapped his strength. "Why doesn't Echols move forward?" complained his unsympathetic superior, John C. Breckinridge, during the 1864 Shenandoah campaign. "He is the slowest fellow." General Ormsby M. Mitchel, Union commander of the Department of the South, his system similarly depleted, died of yellow fever in October of 1862.[47]

To cope with pain, officers self-medicated with opium, alcohol, or laudanum, a mixture of both. Rebel General Henry H. Sibley drank heavily in the 1862 Southwest campaign to manage abdominal agony, affecting his command judgment. Whether near-invalids should have resigned for the good of the service remains debatable. Some received transfers to posts of lesser importance. General John B. Magruder helped slow McClellan's spring 1862 advance up the Peninsula, yet by the Seven Days Battles in late June he suffered stress, exhaustion, and chronic indigestion. Dosing himself with morphine, although probably allergic to the drug, he became erratic. Chief of Staff, Major Joseph L. Brent, described him as agitated, galloping up and down without purpose, reversing orders, obsessing on trivia. "I am feeling horribly," Magruder admitted, having lost "so much sleep that it affects me strongly." He suffered unfair accusations of intoxication, and Lee, whose own fuse grew shorter under stress, had him transferred to the Trans-Mississippi Department.[48]

Lee's famous lieutenant, Stonewall Jackson, also had performance problems during the Seven Days. Drained by constant campaigning in the Shenandoah Valley, he at times acted lethargic and dull. Returning from a night ride to confer with Lee, he collapsed, experiencing an adrenaline depletion. His slowness helped cost Lee a decisive advantage at Frayser's Farm, where Jackson clearly became befuddled, failing to support Pete Longstreet's heavily embattled troops. Exhausted, Jackson at one point fell asleep eating a biscuit. By July 8, he told his wife that he still "suffered from fever and debility" but felt he might be on the mend.[49]

Like many Victorians, Jackson suffered periods of ill health from youth, including attacks of intense gastrointestinal pain starting at fifteen. Hearing tell of a man driven to suicide by dyspepsia, Jackson said he understood. The general self-medicated and eschewed foods that he liked, convinced they must be bad for him. For recurrent eye pain, he used an eye bath, a chloroform liniment, and a glycerine/nitrate-of-silver compound taken through the nostrils. Exposure and the burden of command caused premature aging. John Jones, who witnessed Jackson and James E. B. "Jeb" Stuart at a Richmond gathering, thought that both men, though not yet forty, looked older and "war-worn."[50]

Robert E. Lee provides the most famous example of the destructive effect of command stress and long months in the field. Due in part to his long military career, Lee periodically suffered from diarrhea, malaria, lumbago, probably arthritis of the spine, and, most critically, progressive heart disease partly attributable to acute rheumatic fever. The war brutally wore Lee down. By the Fredericksburg campaign of late 1862, he became forced at times to travel in an ambulance and, by March 1863, felt seriously ill from rheumatism and heart trouble. After the strain of Gettysburg, he confided in a letter to President Davis, August 8, 1863, that "I sensibly feel the growing failure of my bodily strength." Lee's admission that "I have not yet recovered from the attack I experienced last spring" has led one biographer to speculate that sickness may have diminished the general's leadership capacity in the summer of 1863.[51]

Sickness confined Lee to an ambulance again for a chunk of September-October of that year, his debilitation interfering with his conduct of the Bristoe Station campaign. For example, he could not supervise the savage fighting on October 14. His physical condition continued to decline. In late May 1864, illness cost him an opportunity to hit Grant when the North Anna River divided the Union army into three sections. The war cost Lee his cause, but it also ruined his health and shortened his life expectancy.[52]

<hr />

Debilitation not only affected generals' individual performances. Factors of disease, climate, and environment also circumscribed what they could achieve with the men under them, also struggling against the same natural enemies. Generals faced challenges in three areas of command: the ability to plan campaigns and move troops forward to battle; the facility to direct their actions when engaged; and finally the opportunity to follow up encounters effectively.

First, disease that affected a high percentage of troops hamstrung offensive operations. For example, in extenuation of his torpidity in late June and July 1862, General George B. McClellan pleaded that 29 percent of his roughly 103,000 men had become unfit. Onslaughts of malaria, typhoid, and yellow fever hampered early Union attempts to establish solid bridgeheads along the Confederacy's Atlantic coast. In the west, similar outbreaks, especially of malaria, stymied Grant's initial operations against Vicksburg. The 1st Kentucky Brigade (U.S.) alone lost one-third of its strength to disease in a month.[53]

Cautious generals hesitated to risk their men in extreme conditions. Colonel James Garfield, operating in the Kentucky winter of 1861–62, wrote, "there are fathers and mothers in Ohio that I hardly know how I can endure to meet." Most of his 42nd Ohio came down sick. "This fighting with disease is infinitely more horrible than battle." When, in early 1864, Lee demanded to know why Jubal Early had not forded the icy Rapidan to get at the Yankees opposite, Early asked what would happen to the resultant "pneumonia patients."[54]

When armies did march, weakened men battled heat, dust, drought, rain, and mud that helped to thin the ranks. Able men felt challenged to march thirty miles a day carrying forty pounds of equipment, but a third or more of a unit's strength, if already in poor condition, and especially if also suffering battle fatigue, might drop out on long marches. Hiking toward Gettysburg, Private John Dooley saw comrades in the 1st Virginia fall "by tens, twenties, nay by hundreds along the dusty roadsides." Virginia Captain Charles Blackford said his men suffered greatly on this campaign: "Some died on the roadside from the effects of the heat." Union Private Wilbur Fisk, approaching the battle from the opposite direction, witnessed "many men fall out to fall in no more." Those still in rank might stumble onto the battlefield exhausted. A Union lieutenant in the 2nd Corps, marching into battle during Grant's 1864 summer campaign, slumped comatose on the firing line: He "had a ball enter his shoulder and it embedded itself under the shoulder blade and he never waked up at all."[55]

Some officers put straggling down to ill discipline and cowardice. While overexposure to combat did turn men into malingerers, a Union veteran also made a point in responding to criticism of the ranks: "When a man is physically unable to walk, all the discipline in the world will fail to keep him in the ranks when the regiment marches." He always prayed for a night's rest before battle; otherwise "along those ranks could be seen a great many thin faces, whose bodies were weakened by exposure and consequent disease, and who were poorly able to endure." Shortage of footwear, noted above, increased straggling and failure to reach the line of battle, particularly on the Rebel side. A. L. Long blamed lack of shoes, along with malnutrition, for much of the chronic straggling in Lee's army during the 1862 Maryland campaign, winnowing effectives down to 45,000. John H. Worsham, 21st Virginia, thought barefooted men falling out helped to cost Early his chance to get into D.C. in 1864.[56]

Dehydration, rather than strategy or tactics, could dictate where troops fought. The armies that mauled each other at Perryville, October 1862, marching in fierce heat, found their movements dictated by the search for water sources. A Union staff officer complained of "all this dreadful dust no water to be met with for miles, but stagnant pools and slimy ponds redolent of the odor of the cattle of the neighborhood." As the forces deployed into line, Union General Daniel McCook moved five miles out of position to find water, saying he had no choice. Reflecting on Gettysburg, Colonel William C. Oates of the 15th Alabama noted that parties of men had been out of line searching for water when he ordered the attack on Little Round Top. Their absence contributed to the pivotal failure to take the hill and turn the Union left flank. Officers' inability to prevent men, particularly famished Rebels, from stopping to eat food abandoned by retreating enemies, stalled advances. Plundering supply wagons cost Patrick Cleburne's command their momentum in the attack at Bald Hill, July 22, 1864. Rebels on day one of Shiloh lost the benefit of their surprise attack, delaying to eat Yankee breakfasts.[57]

Exhaustion and sickness curtailed postbattle movement. General Abner Doubleday described his condition after Chancellorsville as wretched:

> I am so cut, scratched, and bruised that I can hardly hold a pen in my hand. My limbs are covered with swellings from the bites of insects and torn from forcing my way through briers and thorny bushes; my eyes close involuntarily from lack of sleep and excessive fatigue. My legs are cramped from so much riding, and I have not yet succeeded in getting rid of the chill caused by sleeping on the wet ground in the cold rain. My clothes, up to last night, had not been taken off for a week. As I lay down every night with my boots and spurs on, my feet are very much swollen.[58]

Nothing romantic could be found in death and disabling by disease and exposure. Bacteria robbed many boys of gallant dreams as they wasted away in faraway places. They died for country but without a red badge of courage. "He who so longed for a heroes death on the battlefield, died of wasting fever," recorded South Carolinian Grace Brown Elmore on May 11, 1862, after hearing cousin Willy Taylor was gone. "None of his own people were there to smooth his pillow and receive his last sigh."[59]

Being among strangers made the losing struggle against ravaging sickness even worse. Civilian endings usually took place at home, with consoling rituals of deathbed visitations by friends and relatives, giving meaningful opportunity for reconciliation, resolution, and farewell. By contrast, soldiers' deaths frequently took place "lonely, solitary, and anguished, without the comfort of companionship, without the possibility of being 'good' deaths."[60]

The religious took consolation from faith. With family absent, a soldier could still receive God's loving comfort and grace at the end. A captain in Kershaw's brigade, marching in Virginia mud in February 1863, took pity on a twelve-year-old stumbling along. But the boy, too proud to leave the ranks, refused to ride the captain's horse. Shortly, he fell dead and received a hasty burial. The officer ruminated that the lad would have no headstone, but "God, who notes the fall of a sparrow will not forget the gallant boy." Georgia Private Shephard Proyer wrote his wife from the front: "If I should fall, my dear, grieve not for me. Be assured that I die in the faith and hope of a crown of glory that awaits me above where there will be no more wars or troubles of any kind. I want you to meet me there."[61]

For believers and skeptics alike, photography offered the comfort of sending home a likeness for about $1.50, ensuring that a tangible image of the soldier would survive. But some men found no consolations. A Confederate nurse divulged the death of a young soldier: "a melancholy case, he was very much frightened, & I'm told wept nearly all day yesterday." She had been off duty but felt sorry her presence could not have helped "to ease his last moments. I havent a doubt he was some mothers pride, & perhaps her only prop & stay in this world tis too sad."[62]

As we leave this section of the road we have marched down with the boys of 1861–65, let us recapture a few moments in the lives of ordinary individuals that illustrate the harsh experiences of campaigning. On a hot dirty road in Maryland in the summer of 1862, we pause to watch Alexander Haskell, a Rebel staff officer, leap from his horse to examine a straggler who has crawled into a fence corner. Perhaps he suspects malingering. But the boy cannot speak and barely breathes, choking because snotty dust clogs his mouth and nose. The officer tries frantically to clear the lad's nostrils.[63]

We next peer over the shoulder of a Union regimental commander who has lost his drummer. The dead man had cared for the colonel during an illness and they developed a bond. The officer grieves because he wanted the family to have the remains, but "I cannot send the body home on account of the disease." The drummer died of smallpox and requires immediate burial; not even shipment in a zinc-lined coffin, with a bed of charcoal to absorb putrefaction, becomes permissible when pox is on the loose.[64]

We drop in to eavesdrop on the boys of Company B, 33rd Alabama, Army of Tennessee, who wonder whether Private Alfred Bridges, who had severe bowel problems and just died of an opium overdose on August 12, 1862, committed self-murder. A comrade has heard that "He had some opium in his pocket and he took a large dose of it" (opium eased intestinal pain and helped firm soupy stool). Maybe death occurred accidentally, yet "they said he caused his own death."[65]

Finally, we listen in to the scuttlebutt circulating in Company G of the 47th Ohio on a hot day in August 1861. A private has shot himself rather than face another grueling march under the sweltering Virginia summer sun. According to rumor, he said at the end that "if he was going to be killed by marches, he might as well die first as last."[66]

That "last" he talked about, the end stage of the march, takes soldiers to the battlefield.

CHAPTER THREE

CLOSE-ORDER COMBAT

×

THE ROADS DOWN WHICH MOST OF THE SOLDIERS TRUDGE through dust and mud propel them toward "the elephant," the taste of battle. Many boys enlisted mainly to see this exotic beast. Only the greatest circuses featured an elephant so that, in the circumscribed world of plain folk, to have seen this fabulous creature gave extensive bragging rights. So, too, the volunteer might hope that participating in the circus of war would be uniquely exciting and confer some special status back home. In actuality, volunteers could find combat invigorating, but more frequently they found it horrifying, sometimes both. All were caught in terrible episodes where the elephant bellowed and trampled. Some veterans wrote of the experience, then or later. What they say may shock us, but we must not flinch away. For how can we hope to understand or profess to celebrate them if we do not confront what they endured?

When the mass armies, those mobile cities, collided, they wreaked havoc on one another. Developments that put great citizen armies in the field, such as the spread of democracy and innovations in manufacturing, also conspired to put many thousands on the firing lines and equip them with modern, efficient weapons that inflicted enormous casualties. Killing on an industrial scale had arrived. It is hard for us to conceive of the massive losses inflicted by modern arms. But we can do better than simply try to imagine the slaughter; we can relive it in the words of the combatants.

The standard 1860's shoulder weapons look deceptively antique, akin to the flintlocks carried by earlier generations, such as the British Brown Bess or Tower musket, used from the seventeenth into the nineteenth centuries. This gun fired when the flint struck a spark from the lid of a pan containing gunpowder, causing a combustion that travelled through a touchhole to the charge in the barrel. Because of wear of the mechanism, dull flints, damp or clogged powder, flintlocks often misfired twice in the dozen. The military favored a smoothbore musket without the grooved tube that spins a rifle bullet to impart velocity and accuracy. Admittedly, a smoothbore's effective killing range was only one hundred and fifty yards, and the ball could even fly wide over fifty yards. But the smoothbore was fast firing; the ball, inserted from the muzzle end, dropped easily down the firing tube as it had no rifling to fit, so a good musketeer could achieve two to three discharges per minute. These characteristics led officers to rely on rapid volume of unaimed fire delivered by packed ranks at "whites of eyes" range, backed up by the bayonet.

From the mid-eighteenth century on, armies issued rifles like the British Baker and American Pennsylvania, but to picked men only. Rifles remained true at a distance, they sustained accuracy for sniping, yet also had the deficit that they continued to be expensive to craft and slow to load. The ball had to be hand cast and painstakingly screwed or hammered down the rifling, which took about a minute-and-a-half, an unacceptably slow rate in close action.

By the mid-nineteenth century, three developments radically improved the standard issue weapon. First, precision machine tools made interchangeable parts that allowed economical mass-production of high-quality weapons. Second, by the Mexican War, a percussion mechanism began superseding the flintlock device. A metal cap containing an explosive charge fitted onto a nipple that replaced the powder pan. When hit by a hammer, the ignition in the cap fired a powder line from the nipple to the main load. Relatively immune to wet weather, the percussion musket, if kept clean, proved 99 percent efficient.

Third, fast-firing rifle bullets appeared, ones that dropped down the tube like a smoothbore load but, when propelled by the discharge, exited as a rifle round. This increased hitting power and accuracy to something like a thousand yards. Although attributed to a Frenchman, Claude E. Minié, who fitted the ball with a wooden base that swelled on discharge to embrace the rifling, James H. Burton, an American armorer, devised the version most used by Civil War soldiers. Burton's conical lead bullet featured three concentric rings around a hollow base. When the charge fired, gases forced into the cavity pushed the rings out, making a smooth fit with the rifling. The troops dubbed the bullet a "minnie." The leading percussion rifles, the U.S. .58-calibre Springfield and the British .577 Enfield, conveniently accepted the same round.

In 1861, many troops made do with percussion smoothbores, even flintlocks or shotguns, often loaded with buckshot and ball, deadly close in but erratic at longer range. Large quantities of dubious surplus weapons imported from abroad included used Belgian rifles reputed to be little better than bayonet stands. Steadily, Enfields and Springfields dominated. By 1862, repeating weapons like the Sharps and the Spencer carbine became available, especially in the North, but saw limited service as they expended ammunition at an unsustainable rate. Sharpshooters and cavalry mainly received repeating weapons to offset their disadvantage in numbers when opposing infantry. Troopers also carried revolving pistols, as did officers.

Artillery saw similar advances, both heavy guns in permanent installations and lighter pieces for fieldwork. Grouped in horse-drawn flying batteries, the latter included rifled iron guns, often firing a three-inch calibre shell, effective to a mile and a half. The 1862 Parrott rifle, throwing a 10 lb. projectile, proved particularly lethal. At closer range, the 12 lb. bronze or brass smoothbore Napoleon howitzer effectively smashed enemy formations.

The devastating firepower of the new weaponry might have been expected to change battlefield alignments. We would anticipate commanders spreading out the traditional blocks of men to provide less dense targets, and opening fire at longer ranges, breaking up attacks to avoid face-to-face butchery. French Colonel Ardant du Picq advocated this adaptation in *Battle Studies* (1870). But during the Civil War, old practices dominated. Officers still packed men together in close-order columns or firing lines and withheld defensive fire until the enemy came within murderously short range. One study, based on eyewitness reports, estimates that, on average, musket volleys in the Civil War began at 127 yards' range. In a 113-case sample, no units opened fire over 500 yards, 80 percent waited to 250 or less, 60 percent to 100 or fewer yards.[1]

Why so? It seems to be a general rule of human nature that our circumstances change faster than our ability to adapt to them. Many officers simply did not see an imperative need to alter. Further, they lacked full faith in citizen soldiers' discipline under fire: troops spread into a skirmish line with yards between them would lack comforting shoulder-to-shoulder contact; unless highly trained, they might break under the stress of isolation. As late as 1876, crumbling morale on the extended skirmish line helped destroy the 7th Cavalry at the Little Big Horn and British redcoats at Isandhlwana in 1879, panicking under Zulu attack.[2]

Regular officers often doubted the marksmanship of amateur levies, boxing them together as in the past to deliver a wall of fire in the enemy's faces, hoping to land a knockout punch, even with indifferent musketry. At Ivy Mountain, Kentucky, in November of 1861, Colonel John S. Williams held fire until the Union advance reached point-blank range, inflicting "terrific slaughter" as each shot "took effect." However, if you mauled without crushing the attacker, a savage and indecisive firefight usually ensued. In Gettysburg's Wheatfield, July 1, 1863, the enemy formations exchanged savage volleys at 100 yards; "men were falling like leaves in a storm" and, according to an officer of the 23rd North Carolina, "blood ran like a branch." Sometimes, as in the Virginia Wilderness fighting of 1864, discharges took place at muzzle point.[3]

Many officers also failed to register that defensive firepower had shifted the tactical advantage away from the offense. Military training, emphasizing study of the Napoleonic Wars, seemingly reinforced by the Mexican War experience, taught that vigorous battlefield attacks won decisive victories. But in a war where not just a professional army had to be beaten, but a whole people's will ground down, no single day's triumph, no matter how dramatic, could bring outright victory. The most famous example is Lee's gamble on July 3,

1863, that he could achieve a decisive breakthrough by cracking the Union center, opening the road to D.C. and ending the war. It would be a modern Waterloo. The resulting assault failed, with nearly seven thousand casualties. Told to reassemble his division in anticipation of a Union counterattack, General Pickett replied, "General Lee, I have no division now."[4]

Whether Confederates like Lee, commanding numerically inferior forces, should have stood entirely on the strategic and tactical defensive, forcing the enemy into costly offensives, remains debatable. Had the Confederate armies concentrated on holding the heartland, taking advantage of a largely sympathetic population, interior communications, familiar terrain, and the ability of smaller numbers to hold ground against an attacker, it might have been possible for the South to exhaust the North's will to conquer. Perhaps this constitutes second-guessing, and might demand too much innovation of Confederates steeped in the ingrained tradition of the offense. Whatever the case, Lee appears to have been temperamentally unsuited to a passive defensive role, his preference laid bare in a response to Longstreet's urging of a less costly flanking movement at Gettysburg: "The enemy is there and I am going to strike him."[5]

Faith in the offense remained hard to shake. Lee had earlier lost five thousand men in a sweeping attack at Malvern Hill on July 1, 1862. General Porter E. Alexander, studying the open ground with its clear field of fire for Union gunners, puzzled as to "how on God's earth it happened that our army was put to assault such a position." The Rebels did not have a monopoly on disastrous frontal assaults. At Fredericksburg, December 13, 1862, Ambrose E. Burnside lost nearly 13,000 men hurling waves of compact lines at Confederates well entrenched on elevated ground. He was shortly replaced but, for the most part, more cautious generals did not find favor with authority, perhaps because they seemed to lack results. McClellan was chary of squandering lives, but Lincoln was also almost certainly right in worrying that George had "the slows."[6]

George H. Thomas seems to have been criticized more unfairly. His preference for winning through superior deployment misled others into believing he lacked pugnacity. Thomas's careful preparations for delivering the coup de grace to Hood at Nashville frustrated his superiors, U. S. Grant and Henry Halleck. Sherman fared better, though he, too, valued maneuvering to find the enemy's weakness, remarking, "I don't want to lose men in a direct attack when it can be avoided." The 1864 jostling between Sherman and Joe Johnston in Northern Georgia has been likened to two canny prizefighters probing for an opening. Jefferson Davis tired and replaced Johnston with John Bell Hood, the epitome of impetuous offensive spirit.[7]

Early, if costly, tactical successes at Gaine's Mill and Second Manassas reinforced Hood's aggressive predilections. In defending Atlanta, he bled his army in wasteful, badly coordinated attacks. The disasters culminated at Franklin, Tennessee, where Rebel charges cost six thousand men in an afternoon, one brigade losing 419 of 600 effectives. At times, Hood's allegiance to the all-out assault seemed to waver, but he never repudiated it entirely. Indeed, writing after the war, he asserted in his memoirs that only encouragement of the "devil-me-care" spirit created a soldier that "when ordered to charge and drive the enemy, will—or endeavor to—run over any obstacles he may encounter to his front." He concluded, "I expect to die more proud of my defense of Atlanta & my Tenn. campaign than all my career as a Soldier."[8]

In preparing for frontal assaults, generals sought to minimize casualties by artillery bombardment to soften up the target; by coordinated supporting attacks, staggered to drive into the enemy en echelon (or at a slant) and so difficult to break up; and by having troops close fast, starting at the quick step and accelerating into double quick time. The results disappointed. At Fort Wagner, July 1863, the preliminary bombardment failed to dislodge the garrison from its bomb proofs; the supporting brigades, badly handled, had no room to maneuver; and double quick time failed to save the 54th Massachusetts, leading the attack, from suffering 40 percent losses. Colonel John Elwell, watching the attack, cried, "My God, our men are being slaughtered." The question might be why he was surprised.[9]

The volume of fire encountered in battle stunned combatants, leaving an indelible impression. General Joshua Lawrence Chamberlain said descriptions of projectiles "darkening the air" were not hyperbole but a "dead-level fact." Cartridge expenditure proved immense. Army of the Cumberland records show 3.5 million rounds expended in June 1864, 2.25 million in July, 3 million in August. (Authorities gave replenishing the ammunition train a haulage priority, explaining why troops often went without rations.) A Rebel brigade under Samuel French, sent to collect spent balls on the field, gleaned 2.5 tons. The general noted, "the ground was literally covered with them—oxidized white like hail-stones."[10]

The noise of musketry deafened soldiers, veterans likening it to brick buildings collapsing or a hard rain clattering on a tin roof, while artillery fire, like claps of thunder, made the ground shake and fence rails jump. Projectiles mowed down any vegetation standing in the way. General Raleigh Colston observed at Chancellorsville trees cut off a few feet above the ground as if scythed, and brush fractured in every branch. "The bullets seemed to fill the air and to be clipping every little weed and bush and blade of grass around us," wrote Corporal C. F. Boyd about Shiloh. "Acres and acres of timber such as small saplings and large underbrush were mowed down and trees one foot in diameter were cut down as if a mowing machine had gone through the field and limbs fell like autumn leaves in the leaden and iron storm."[11]

Human flesh fared no better. The musketry grew so intense at Spotsylvania, 1864, reported Major Thomas Hyde, 7th Maine, that many a corpse resembled "nothing but a lump of meat or clot of gore." One man could be identified only by beard color as his face could not be recognized, "but appeared more like a sponge." The features of Frank Arnold, one of William Quantrill's raiders, hit in the head five times at Baxter Springs, Kansas, in October 1863, "could not be recognized as belonging to a human being." The corpse of a sixteen-year-old private of the 55th Illinois, hit by seven balls at Shiloh, looked "as red as if he had been dipped in a barrel of blood." Colonel Charles Phillipps, 52nd Georgia, sustained wounds successively in the left arm, right leg, knee, and cheek at Champion Hill, Mississippi. Also in that engagement, Iowa private John Myers said heavy fire "cut us all to peases and scatred our Regiment." He got shot in the left ankle and "i hat my bick toe shot off and was struck with a spand grape shot [a spent iron solid shot, golf-ball sized, hurled in a cluster from a Napoleon] on the right nea and left elbow."[12]

The metal storm cut down troops en masse. William Fletcher, 5th Texas, in spring 1862 fighting at Gaine's Mill, Virginia, described Union corpses lying "so close that it put one in mind of a railroad grade with ties laid for ironing." In one small episode at Antietam, Union General Alpheus S. Williams watched two Napoleons fire canister into oncoming Confederates. "Each canister contains several hundred balls. They fell in the very front of the line and all along it apparently, stirring up dust like a thick cloud. When the dust blew away no regiment and not a living man was to be seen." Over two hundred had perished, "in two ranks, as straightly aligned as on a dress parade." Repeatedly, survivors testified that you could walk on bodies without touching earth. Union Colonel William Averell counted over five thousand Rebels sprawled on Malvern Hill. "A third of them were dead or dying, but enough were alive and moving to give the field a singular crawling effect." Dead Yankees lay so thick in front of the 11th North Carolina's position in the 1864 Wilderness that they built a breastwork of corpses.[13]

The maelstrom quickly decimated even large units. In five hours at Franklin, the Confederates lost more troops than U.S. forces did in nineteen hours on D-Day, 1944. At Cold Harbor, seven thousand Yankees fell in twenty minutes. One company of the 4th Alabama dropped 75 out of 105 men at First Manassas. Of the 1st Minnesota's 384 men at Gettysburg, 234 went down. One Rebel regiment lost 128 of 265 effectives at Kennesaw Mountain. Of 250 in the 6th Georgia at Antietam, only 24 remained unhurt. After Shiloh, General Patrick R. Cleburne reported his brigade reduced from 2,700 to 800. The 2nd Tennessee and 6th Mississippi had virtually ceased to exist. Nearly 30 percent of Ohio troops at Gettysburg fell. On July 1 alone, 70 percent of the 82nd Ohio's 258 were lost.[14]

Statistics for overall army losses tell the same tale of concentrated slaughter. At Antietam, combined casualties in close-order combat came to over 22,700. In the Seven Days Battles, McClellan lost nearly 10,000 or 10.7 percent of his army, Lee close to 20,000 or 20 percent. Each side suffered about 9,700 casualties at Shiloh, spread over two days. Chickamauga cost the North 16,550 and the South 17,800 in a day. Lee lost 28,000 at Gettysburg or nearly 40 percent of his force; the Federals 23,000 or 25 percent. At Stone's River, the Union sustained 31 percent casualties, the Confederates 33 percent. Most stunning, in the month from the Wilderness to Cold Harbor, May 5 to June 3, 1864, Lee lost 32,000 or 46 percent of effectives, Grant 50,000 or 41 percent.[15]

Rather than old-fashioned saber or bayonet thrusts, small arms and artillery inflicted most wounds. Musket balls did massive damage to the body. Unlike a modern high-velocity steelhead bullet in the .30-calibre range, a .57 or .58 lead ball frequently lacked the force to drive through and exit the target, instead staying in the victim, wrecking bone and organs. The 71st New York's chaplain, Joseph Twichell, "saw one man who received a ball in his cheek and, glancing over his jaw, it was taken out between his shoulders." Another "was hit in the side, yet some how or other the ball found its way up to behind his ear." The construction of the minnie ball magnified this roaming characteristic.[16]

When the rifle fired, the minnie spread out in the barrel, meaning the pliable lead could no longer hold up on impact but became unintentionally a dum-dum or soft-head bullet. Meeting the resistance of flesh and bone, it flattened out further, even assuming the diameter of a half dollar. As it slowed, it travelled the victim, wrecking everything in its way. This is why experienced officers cautioned against crouching during an advance; the ball would travel the body lengthwise. This is also why surgeons amputated so many shattered limbs; physicians lacked the time, tools, operating facilities, or medical knowledge to reconstruct splintered bones. They had to remove the limb before gangrene and peritonitis attacked. "The shattering, splintering, and splitting of a long bone by the impact of the minie were, in many instances, both remarkable and frightful," recalled a surgeon.[17]

Minnies inflicted truly horrific damage, their ravaging wounds being excruciatingly painful. During the fighting at Kennesaw Mountain, Rebel Lieutenant Charles Johnsen of the Washington Artillery sustained a fatal shot as he bent over. "A bullet took him, low down, about his waist and in his left side, and ranged up diagonally through the entire length of his body, tearing through his kidneys, bowels, stomach, lungs, and coming out at his shoulder." He screamed in agony "I am killed" and then managed "Mother," as blood gushed from his mouth. Hit men might wish to die. At Ball's Bluff in October 1861, Lieutenant Oliver Wendell Holmes Jr. 20th Massachusetts, shot by a ball that plowed left breast to right, feared lung damage as he spat up blood. Even though his sergeant had managed to squeeze out the bullet, he considered a laudanum overdose to end the awful pain.[18]

Minnies shattered the facial structure. At Cold Harbor, 1864, the man standing next to New York gunner Frank Wilkeson took a ball in the face. "A tiny fountain of blood and teeth and bone and bits of tongue burst out of his mouth. He had been shot through the jaws; the lower was broken and hung down." In Virginia fighting, Georgia private William White saw a Union infantryman similarly wounded, when "an Enfield rifle ball entered the back part of his right jaw, passing inside his mouth, tearing the tongue out by the roots and shivering the upper jaw into small fragments." Bullets disfigured and disabled. On day one at Gettysburg, Union Brigadier General Gabriel Paul had both eyes shot out; he lived on in darkness. Earlier, in June 1862, Colonel William Duffield, 4th Michigan, shot through the left testicle and thigh at Murfreesboro, Tennessee, suffered a wound "very painful and bleeding profusely." The genital damage left him in grave pain and mental anxiety. Men with tearing wounds might not survive long enough to get aid. Sixteen-year-old Abe Hanna bled to death after a ball broke his spine and severed a major vein in the pelvis. At Second Bull Run, Robert Sneden of the 40th New York noted a colonel trying to get to the rear who "had been shot through the head which now had swollen to three times its natural size!"[19]

There is more; let us step along the battle line a moment where the elephant rears and trumpets. Men still in one piece load and fire as fast as they can, ignoring the mule kick of the musket butt that bruises the shoulder black and blue. Union infantry colonel James A. Mulligan described the misery of soldiers fighting all day "without water, their parched lips cracking, their tongues swollen, and the blood running down their chins when they bit their cartridges and the saltpeter entered their blistered lips." Some have soiled themselves through fear and excitement, or simply because dysentery refuses to take a holiday during combat. Now and then a soldier pauses to urinate in his rifle barrel; without water this becomes the only way to cool the weapon and keep the rifling free of clogging. We see constant movement on the line, some men coming up, but more staggering to the rear with serious wounds.[20]

We watch Corporal James Quick stumble back as a bullet enters behind his left jaw and exits through the nose. He is just twenty-two. Next to him, Lieutenant William Taylor has been hit in the neck by a bullet that missed the arteries but severed his windpipe. He clasps his hands to his neck, trying to stanch the flow of blood and air hissing through the wound. Private Keils runs past, "breathing at his throat and the blood spattering" from a neck wound. "His wind-pipe was entirely severed," Colonel William Oates curtly informs us. We avoid Private George Walker because his right arm is off, severing the artery, and blood "on certain movements of the arm, gushed out higher than his head." Blood spurts, too, from a Federal officer shot behind the bridge of the nose; he wanders about, continuing to blink even though both eyes are gone, "opening and closing the sightless sockets, the blood leaping out in spouts."[21]

Over here, a young Rebel in great pain from a shattered arm runs "up and down, forwards and backwards, by the side of a huge fallen tree, always turning at the same point and retracing his steps to and fro," agony making him oblivious to the enemy fire attempting to kill him. He tries to avoid men on the ground, writhing and shrieking; some have been pierced through the abdomen, which makes an awful wound, usually fatal. One fellow's knee shatters. "I neaver heard a man hallow so in my life," his captain, James Wren, assures us. There are more head-injury cases. One is New Hampshire soldier Frank Hersey: "The bullet entered his eye and passed through, the blood spirting in jets." His comrade, Henry Stockwell, has also fallen, shot through the head and "his brains had partly run out." So, too, have those of a 12th Corps man who lies moaning underfoot while gray matter oozes out at every breath.[22]

This is the work of the muskets. What of the big guns? We may recall the rifled cannon-fired shells that, when detonated by a timing fuse or exploded on impact, hurled jagged metal fragments over a wide area. At Gettysburg, the extreme force of one shell bursting in the close-ordered ranks of the 6th Wisconsin took down thirteen; another landing among the 2nd Wisconsin flattened seven. Shells ripped men apart. The blast of a shell exploding right in the chest of Lieutenant Daniel Featherstone threw body parts ten feet in the air and twenty feet over the ground.[23]

At Second Manassas, Private William Fletcher, 5th Texas, stood gazing at a courier galloping his mount across the field, when "a shell struck them and exploded, and there was a scattering of parts of both man and horse, and I took it to be a percussion shot that exploded when hitting." Colonel Edward Cross, 5th New Hampshire, fell gravely wounded at Gettysburg after being hit by 12 lb. shell fragments that made a deep wound above the heart and almost caved in his breastbone. Shrapnel lacerated his face, destroying three teeth, and damaging his left leg below the knee. Private Nick Weekes described shells bursting through the ranks of the 3rd Alabama at Chancellorsville. He saw "an arm and shoulder fly from the man just in front, exposing his throbbing heart. The foot of another flew up and kicked him in the face as a shell struck his leg. Another, disemboweled, crawled along on all fours, his entrails trailing behind, and still another held up his tongue with his hand, a piece of shell having carried away his lower jaw."[24]

Such macabre shell wounds unnerved those still living. Private Randolph Shotwell recalled being "horrified at seeing a man running, struck by a shell and his head blown square off at the neck, and tumbling before the corpse as it staggers and falls!" At Fredericksburg, a shell hit portly Union Captain William Stewart in the chest, sending his corpse cartwheeling through the ranks. Also at Fredericksburg, Captain James Wren, 48th Pennsylvania, witnessed one of his company sliced apart: "Michael Divine was Cut right in 2 pieces with a shell & his insides Lay on the grass alongside him." At Gettysburg, a youngster's corpse startled 1st Virginia Private John Dooley: "the boy's head being torn off by a shell is lying around in bloody fragments on the ground."[25]

Joseph E. Crowell, a survivor of the 13th New Jersey, penned haunting recollections. Here he describes the mutilation at Antietam of a 107th New York private, hit by shell fragments that took off both legs at the knee. "None had ever heard such demoniacal shrieks." But Crowell accounted the sight worse than the screaming: "there protruded from the lacerated flesh the ends of the bones of the legs in a most horrible manner, making a sight that was simply sickening." At Chancellorsville, Crowell saw the chin and lower jaw of a staff officer snatched off: "In its place was a mass of blood, raw flesh and gore! A piece of shell had come along and torn away the entire lower portion of his face." Eerily, the missile traveled so fast the eye missed it: for no earthly reason, the officer suddenly lacked half a face. Understandably, "I involuntarily shrieked." Just before, a shell had landed in the ranks. "Two men had been literally torn to pieces. Their remains were strewn over the roadway from one side to the other. One man's heart was still throbbing. Pieces of skull and human brains lay here and there!"[26]

Serving the powerful engines of war conferred no immunity to damage. Gunners' ears bled from the concussion of the cannon, their eardrums often shattering and their hearing permanently impaired. Battery to battery counterfire caused some of the worst injuries. Crowell recounted what happened at Chancellorsville when a shell landed on the ammunition stored in a wheeled artillery caisson: debris from the wagon and the remains of men and horses filled the air. One gunner dropped from the sky to the ground right beside him. "'For the love of God,' it said, 'for the love of God, shoot me! Put me out of my misery!'" The sufferer had gone up amid the flames, and fire had roasted off all his clothes, burning the flesh to a crisp. His eyes had been seared away and the ears gone. The ends of his fingers had charred to the bone and a white kneecap protruded through charcoaled flesh. "Such a sickening sight was never seen. And yet the thing was alive, and not only alive, but conscious."[27]

Other eyewitnesses offered similar depictions of ghoulish scenes from hell. Corporal C. F. Boyd, 15th Iowa, remembered seeing after Shiloh twenty-six battery horses lying dead in one small area. The gunners "are torn all to pieces leaving nothing but their heads or their boots. Pieces of clothing and strings of flesh hang on the limbs of the trees around them." From the Rebel side, Philip Stephenson, 15th Arkansas, related seeing two artillerymen destroyed completely from the waist up. "We found long strips of flesh high up on the trees behind them." A mutilated battery horse, mad with pain, ran around frantically, finally ramming its head into a tree, the body falling at the base of the trunk in an odd squatting position.[28]

Compared to the rifled cannon, the smoothbores may seem to belong to an earlier age. But they had a vital role in close action, their discharges devastating at short range. Smoothbores tossed solid round shot, varying from 3 to 12 lbs., at an advancing enemy when still at a distance. The ball bounced along the ground, dismembering any bodies in its path. Lieutenant William Wheeler, 13th New York Independent Battery, testified that "I saw an infantry man's leg taken off by a shot, and whirled like a stone through the air, until it came against a caisson with a loud whack." At Shiloh, Corporal Boyd recalled seeing five attacking Rebels mangled by one 6 lb. ball: "One of them had his <u>head</u> taken off. One had been struck at the right shoulder and his chest lay open. One had been cut in two at the bowels and nothing held the carcass together but the spine. One had been hit at the thighs and the legs were torn from the body. The fifth and last one was piled into a mass of skull, arms, some toes and the remains of a butternut suit." [29]

At Second Manassas, John Worsham, 21st Virginia, saw a single solid shot kill four men. A captain's corpse remained upright after the head had been knocked off, "with a stream of blood spurting a foot or more from his neck." The shattering of heads produced harrowing experiences for those in close proximity to the victim. In action at Fort Harrison, Virginia, 1864, Union General Edward Ripley got "dashed in the face with a hot steaming mass of something horrible," like an unsavory warm pudding. He first thought that his own features had been blown off, as the foul detritus had temporarily blinded him to his situation. But the debris proved to be from the wrecked head of a soldier standing in front of him, blasted backward. Opening his own blouse, the general remembered, "I threw out a mass of brains, skull, hair and blood." In another incident, Union Major Thomas Hyde found his mouth similarly stuffed involuntarily with brain matter, bone, and blood, when the smashed pulp of a private's skull smacked him full in the face. [30]

When the enemy persisted in coming on despite round shot, smoothbores switched to grape (small iron balls in a rack or held together by slender stems that snapped on firing) or canister (containers filled with musket balls and miniature shrapnel). The effect proved so devastating to the senses that it left gunners themselves haunted by violent memories. Fighting in defense of Cincinnati, 1862, Union Captain Nathaniel Southgate Shaler, 5th Kentucky Artillery (U.S.), had the nightmare experience of being ordered to fire canister into a mixed melee of blue and gray, as they grappled with one another, threatening to overrun and submerge his battery. He carried away with him a horrifying image of the result: the heat from the roasting gun barrels had created a convection current above the battery, swirling body parts, eyeballs, teeth, shards of uniform and equipment through the air:

> And they are blown out, rent by hurricane
> To bits and shreds that spatter down to earth
> What once were men—good friends and foes alike.

At Antietam, General John Gibbon, watching the impact of double rounds of canister on Hood's advancing division, witnessed whole ranks go down in piles, men visibly torn into pieces. He remembered "an arm go 30 feet into the air and fall back again." Although gazing upon his sworn enemies, he felt no jubilation, only sickness at the slaughter, confessing, "It was just awful." [31]

———————

In the metal storm of combat, officers had an even higher percentage risk of injury and death than rankers. The figures give a stark picture. In both armies, the proportion of officers killed reached 15 percent more than enlisted men, and generals had a whopping 50 percent higher likelihood of dying. General Abner Doubleday, who fought in the east, compiled a list of generals killed and wounded at Gettysburg. He provided names, perhaps to humanize the numbers. On the Rebel side, six generals died: Armistead, Barksdale, Garnett, Pender, Pettigrew, and Semmes. Four sustained major wounds: Anderson, Wade Hampton, Kemper, and Scales. Union general officers fared no better. The fighting killed five: Farnsworth, Reynolds, Vincent, Weed, and Zook. Thirteen fell wounded: Barlow, Barnes, Brooke, Butterfield, Doubleday himself, Gibbon, Graham, Hancock, Paul, Sickles, Stannard, Warren, and Webb. [32]

The cost at the regimental level proved equally exorbitant. Not only were all three brigadiers in Pickett's division casualties, but thirteen colonels fell also. Even before the killing fields of Gettysburg, there had been a severe loss of field grade and mid-level commanders. Yet, if anything, the attrition worsened as the fighting became more desperate, and the concomitant slaughter intensified during the last campaigns of the war. For example, May 4–June 3, 1864, twenty-two of fifty-eight generals in the Army of Northern Virginia became casualties. In one afternoon at Franklin, the Army of Tennessee lost 50 percent of its regimental commanders, some fifty-four officers wounded or killed, along with six generals who died.[33]

Why did such a high proportion of casualties winnow the officer corps, particularly at senior levels, especially when compared to most later conflicts? The battlefield did eventually spread out in acknowledgment of the new, rapid-firing, high-velocity weaponry. To a good degree, by the turn-of-the-century conflicts, the Spanish-American, Russo-Japanese, and Boer Wars, and more so during World War I, units tended to go forward in loose skirmish lines or small groups, as exemplified by German storm trooper tactics, the generals meanwhile overseeing troop movements from the rear. (Old practices nevertheless died hard. As late as the Somme in 1916, British infantry in close-order formations received orders to walk in line abreast across no-man's-land toward German machine guns firing 500 rounds per minute; the generals had assumed their artillery bombardment would obliterate the enemy front lines, which it had failed to do.)

With soldiers scattered over a much wider field, commanders down to the regimental level could no longer control their whole force directly by immediate eye and voice contact. Communications technology came to their aid: through wireless, an officer in a command post could hope to know the positions of all units, whether in open view or not. Then, too, as smokeless powder came into use by 1900, commanders and their staff no longer needed to be like their predecessors, grouped in the very heart of action on the firing lines, anxiously peering through rolling dense white sulphur clouds, trying to ascertain what was happening. It made sense that officers who no longer needed to be in the advance to function should keep in the rear, where less chaos existed and they enjoyed a greater chance of survival, preserving their brains to direct events and leaving the brawn to others.

Those lower down the totem pole did not always appreciate the change in leadership style. British Tommies in the Great War joked grimly that they had never seen a dead staff officer, and they believed the generals were indifferent to the staggering suffering because they never had to witness it, safely ensconced in their chateaux. Even generals with a hell-for-leather reputation, such as George S. Patton in World War II, could be cordially resented. Troops noted cynically that on Patton's trips to the front he conspicuously drove in a jeep; on the way back he took a plane. The GIs also noted of Patton's nickname, "Old Guts and Glory," that it meant "your guts, his glory."

By contrast, in the earlier Civil War, officers still adhered to the maxim that necessity required leadership from the front, as their brethren had done for centuries. Generals believed they must, in person, direct the disposition of their troops in the "fog of battle" or chaos would ensue. And they had precious few staff officers to assist them in this. Stonewall Jackson fell fatally wounded by his own men while riding beyond his lines after dark, trying to ascertain the relative position of the combatants. A sniper picked off Major General John Reynolds, mounted and vulnerable, in plain view of both sides, as he led his command into their positions on July 1, 1863. At Pine Mountain, Georgia, on June 14, 1864, a deliberately aimed Union artillery round eviscerated General Leonidas Polk, while he and his staff exposed themselves on rising ground to observe enemy positions. The Yankee Parrott shell passed through his left arm, body, and right arm, before exploding against a tree.

The poor visibility and tremendous racket of battle required officers to appear in easily recognized dress and equipment, wearing a sash and waving a sword, as they bellowed commands to overcome the fearful noise. Charles E. Davis of the 13th Massachusetts explained how commands were issued: "In Battle the order to charge is not given in the placid tones of a Sunday-school teacher, but with vigorous English, well seasoned with oaths." During Pickett's charge, to direct his men into the target on Cemetery Ridge, the copse of trees, General Lewis A. Armistead put his black hat on his sword, making himself conspicuous to his brigade and the enemy. He just reached the Union guns beyond the stone-wall crowning the rise when balls in the chest and arm took him down. He died on July 5.[34]

We must remember that, had officers not gone first, many men might have balked at entering the maelstrom. For good reason, the officers' code demanded that an exemplary leader should never ask his men to do and endure what he would not. This ethic led officers to expose themselves to risk so as to give confidence to the ranks. General John C. Breckinridge, according to J. Stoddard Johnston, one of his colonels, did not seek shelter, but rather "he kept himself in view of his troops and inspired them by his presence." A price was often paid. Despite repeated urgings to take cover during the September 1862 Battle of South Mountain, Confederate General Samuel Garland Jr. insisted on staying in the open, receiving a mortal wound.[35]

The ethic of leadership by example also demanded that officers stay at their posts as long as they possibly could, even if seriously wounded. A famous example is General Albert Sidney Johnston, in command of Confederate forces at Shiloh, who bled to death on the field after refusing to seek aid for a leg wound. On the second day of Gettysburg, Mississippi General William Barksdale, wounded by a rifle ball above the left knee, nevertheless remained on the field. After a solid shot hit his foot, he could not stand and so continued mounted, although bleeding heavily and in great pain. A plain target now, he was knocked from his horse by a bullet entering the left breast, and he died the next day. Rebel General Francis Cockrell had better luck. Though wounded in both hands by shrapnel that broke the bones and stripped off three fingernails at Kennesaw Mountain, he lived to be shot four times at Franklin, yet survived the war.[36]

Georgia Brigadier General John B. Gordon, who held a crucial position in the sunken lane at Sharpsburg, remains a vivid instance of stubborn gallantry. A shot went through the right calf and then another hit higher in the same leg. He managed to stay on his feet after a further ball tore up flesh and tendons in his left arm, sending blood streaming down the limb. A fourth bullet ripped through his shoulder and yet, almost unbelievably, he still stood at his post when a fifth ball hit him full in the head. He fell face forward in his hat, unconscious, and would have drowned in his own blood had it not run out through bullet holes in the cloth. Although not fully recovered, he returned to duty to see out the war, even though wounded again over the right eye and in the leg. During the 1862 Kentucky campaign, a ball hit General Pat Cleburne in the cheek, removing two teeth. Because of this disfigurement, his voice developed a harsh hissing sound when raised to issue commands. Cleburne returned to duty in time to be wounded above the ankle at Perryville and later die at Franklin of a ball to the abdomen.[37]

Sacrificial adherence to duty was not simply a matter of mythic Southern gentlemen's honor; the concept also held sway in the Northern officer corps. Union General Francis C. Barlow suffered a serious wound at Antietam, leaving the left side of his face badly scarred. But he was back in time for Gettysburg, where on the first day a bullet tore through his side, lodging in the abdomen. Although he nearly died, he took the field again during Grant's 1864 Virginia campaign. So did Winfield Scott Hancock, wounded in the groin on Cemetery Ridge, and still carrying bone fragments in the abdomen that frequently caused incapacitating pain. Lesser known examples include Major Henry A. Barnum, 12th New York, shot at Malvern Hill, the ball entering the abdomen and exiting the posterior. A stubborn abscess formed in the wound, which remained inflamed and continued to generate pus. A linen thread had to be drawn through the wound regularly to drain it. Nevertheless, the colonel held his command to the end of the war.[38]

We may wonder whether heroic courage shaded into foolhardiness when command capacity diminished with injury. General Richard S. Ewell sustained a light injury before a leg was shattered in fighting on August 28, 1862, the damage necessitating amputation. Afterward, he used a poorly fitted wooden leg that caused abscesses and abrasions. A spent ball, hitting him in the chest in June 1863, added to his injuries, and he endured frequent falls because the artificial leg prevented him from fully controlling a horse. By May 1864, he had become physically wasted, visited by scurvy and dysentery, now forced to travel in an ambulance. Lee came to doubt Ewell's fitness for the field and sent him to command the defenses of Richmond. Indeed, it can be argued that his abilities had been eclipsed earlier, by mid-1863. Writing to the general on January 18, 1864, Lee admitted that, because of Ewell's injuries and general debility, "I was in constant fear during the last campaign that you would sink under your duties or destroy yourself." [39]

The most controversial case may be that of John Bell Hood. Already noted for his dash and personal bravery, on July 2, 1863, at Gettysburg, he was hit by shell fragments that ranged through the left hand, forearm, elbow, and biceps, rendering the arm largely useless. He returned to Longstreet's corps in time to be hit in the right leg by an exploding bullet at Chickamauga. A surgeon took off the shattered limb at the thigh. Hood suffered terrible pain that aged him, and frequent heavy medication may have made him erratic, as well as adding to his debility. He may not have been up to the burden of commanding the Army of Tennessee. For example, he failed to exercise proper oversight of the frontal fighting outside Atlanta, especially during a critical phase on July 19, 1864. He also missed a vital opportunity to catch General John M. Schofield's command in a trap because heavy doses of laudanum for incessant pain had put him to bed. We may reasonably conclude from Hood's and other case studies that grave impairments and critical losses of leadership adversely affected army operations on both sides. [40]

Although our task is dedicated to depicting warfare on land, because this by far dominated the majority experience of the American people, it might prove instructive at this point to briefly sketch in naval combat. Although sailors' lives paralleled those of soldiers in many ways, we may discern differences. Sailors enlisted as regulars and so came under a more stringent discipline than short-term volunteers. They had more opportunity to keep clean while on active service and regulations required them to do so. But in other ways the experiences paralleled. Though chowders and other fish dishes varied the seamen's diet, they also steadily ingested hardtack, called ship's biscuit, dried navy beans, and salt meat, often rancid bacon and beef turned green in the cask. Officers had been educated about the need for fresh fruits and vegetables (the term "limey" came from the Royal Navy's early pioneering use of citrus fruit and juice rations), but they often proved unavailable on prolonged blockade duty or ocean tours. Poor diet and bad drinking water resulted in scurvy, dysentery, and typhus. Sailors also contracted malaria on many stations. It was not unusual for over 4 percent of a crew to be on sick list.[41]

Like soldiers, naval ratings self-medicated with, and found consolation in, alcohol and drugs. Herman Melville, who served as a "white jacket" on an American man-of-war prior to the secession conflict, averred that grog constituted the sailor's enemy, men going to any length to smuggle it on board, "and if opium were to be had, many would steep themselves a thousand fathoms down in the densest fumes of that oblivious drug." Alvah Hunter, a ship's boy on the ironclad monitor *Nahant*, 1862–63, noted an episode at Charleston, Massachusetts, when "Some despicable creature had smuggled some liquor into the navy yard and sold a quart or two to a group of our men," so that "half a dozen of our best sailors were fighting-roaring drunk." The Master-at-Arms and petty officers overwhelmed the culprits, bucking and gagging them to cut off a stream of blasphemous oaths. "One of them was as handsome a man as would be seen in a day's journey, a model seaman, and as he looked up at me from his 'trussed up' position on the deck I felt greater sorrow for him than I would have thought it possible to feel for a stranger."[42]

Sailors routinely faced a horrible death relatively uncommon on land: drowning. High seas and gales sunk ships and drove them onto rocks, or vessels foundered when they struck submerged snags in rivers. Union monitors proved particularly vulnerable: they were never intended to be ocean-going vessels, so the sea washed over their decks even in calm waters, and sailors considered them floating coffins in a squall. Crews fought frequent leaks, meaning they had little air when rough weather required closing the ports, and the ship's lights flickered for lack of oxygen. Monitors sank quickly, allowing few crewmen time to escape. When the *Weehawken* went down off Charleston in December 1863, thirty-one hands drowned.[43]

As in the armies, veterans of past service carried bodily damage. A smoothbore ball from the War of 1812 still lay buried in the shoulder of the commodore under whom Melville served, and he would be seen often "doubled up from the effect of his wound." Naval encounters had always been savage affairs, but improved ordnance (firing larger calibre projectiles, up to 20 inches in diameter in seacoast batteries) made them worse. In addition to solid shot, naval armaments included rifle shells, grape shot, and chain shot (two balls linked by chain, intended to cut rigging and sweep decks at kneecap level). Gunners lobbed hot shot to incinerate enemy vessels, and seamen dreaded roasting in the inferno of a ship on fire, just as wounded soldiers on land feared burning up in blazing brush. This horrible fate happened to the crew of the wooden-walled *Congress*, burned in battle with the ironclad *Virginia* on March 8, 1862.[44]

As soldiers dreaded cannon shot into tree tops, because it brought down lethal wood shards, sailors feared vicious splinters from shattered decks and railings, along with a new threat, rivets and bolts on ironclad sheathing that, when dislodged by the concussion of incoming rounds, ricocheted around the hull. One rogue nut on a monitor in action against Fort Sumter, on April 9, 1863, struck the wheel officer, Edward Cobb, "upon the side of his forehead, tearing off a piece of his skull about five inches long by three wide, inflicting a mortal wound." It next struck Pilot Scofield near the spinal column at the base of the neck, "effecting a paralysis of the body because of the shock to the nerves." The nut then glanced off the pilot-house roof, wounding Captain Downes in the foot. On June 17, 1863, off Savannah, a 15-inch Dahlgren smoothbore round fired by a monitor smashed through the armored casemate of the C.S.S. *Atlanta*, metal and wood fragments flying along the gun deck, killing one and wounding fifteen. The concussion knocked out forty. A further hit sent iron balls from the *Atlanta's* broken shot racks careening across the deck.[45]

Although there were few open-sea encounters, such as the June 1864 battle between the *Alabama* and *Kearsage* off Cherbourg, France, vicious exchanges occurred between Union vessels supporting ground forces that operated along the seaboard and Confederate coastal fortifications. In the Union bombardment of Fort Sumter, April 7, 1863, the Yankee ironclad *Keokuk* received ninety hits, including steel-pointed rifle shells. The hull sustained nineteen punctures below the waterline. Hits to boilers proved particularly horrible as escaping steam killed and maimed. When a shot from a Brooke rifle on the Confederate ironclad *Albemarle* penetrated the starboard boiler of the wooden-walled *Sassacus*, a blast of hyper-heated steam scalded and blinded most of the stokers.[46]

The newly invented torpedoes held a special terror for crewmen engaged in river warfare. Detonated by contact with a percussion charge or from shore by electrical cable, these explosives lurked unseen beneath the surface, waiting to hole unsuspecting vessels. Boats opened below the waterline sank fast. The monitor *Tecumseh*, hit by a torpedo in Mobile Bay, sank in twenty-five seconds, taking down 93 of 114 crewmen. George R. Yost, on the *Cairo*, described the vessel being struck on December 12, 1862, by two torpedoes in the Yazoo River: "In 5 minutes the forward part of the Hold was full of water and the forward part of the gundeck was flooded." Although beached on a sand bank, the ship quickly submerged. Confederates manning gunboats on inland waters faced great odds, as most of the fleet consisted of vulnerable wooden paddle steamers, hastily reinforced with railroad irons. Sinking by holing, fire, or explosion quickly destroyed the majority. In the Battle of Memphis, June 6, 1862, Union gunfire annihilated seven of the Rebel flotilla's eight vessels in sight of the stunned citizenry.[47]

As soldiers faced dismemberment on the firing line, projectiles tore sailors to pieces on the gun deck. The wooden walls of the *Cumberland* proved no match for the ironclad *Virginia*. One Rebel shell killed all of a starboard gun crew save the powder monkey and gun captain, although a round ripped the latter's arms off at the shoulder. Crewmen dragged corpses to the port rails for later sea burial. A survivor told the correspondent for the *Baltimore American* that "The decks were slippery with blood, and arms and legs and chunks of flesh were strewed about." John C. Kinney, signals officer on the *Hartford*, engaged in Mobile Bay on August 5, 1864, said, "Shot after shot came through the side, mowing down the men, deluging the decks with blood, and scattering mangled fragments of humanity so thickly that it was difficult to stand on the deck, so slippery was it."[48]

For individuals, such death and destruction must have been as awful as that facing soldiers on land. But, if it is not completely obscene to suggest a distinction, not of kind but degree, then we might note that naval actions and their resulting casualties constituted a minor chord in the massive chorus of war. To help realize the point, let us bring

Melville back into the conversation (rarely a bad idea). The great teller of sea stories described the aftermath of battle as recounted to him by a black sailor named "Tawney" who had seen action on the U.S.S. *Macedonian*. He said that intact corpses were thrown overboard during fighting to clear the decks and mitigate the visible horror. But more detailed cleanup necessarily waited until after battle. The fighting had splattered blood and brains all around. "About the hatchways it looked like a butcher's stall; bits of human flesh sticking in the ring bolts." The ship required washing down and the galley cooks sprinkled the decks with hot vinegar "to take out the shambles smell from the planks."[49]

Finally, the crew threw overboard a pig that had run around, rooting amongst the chunks of flesh, so that its face and hide had become soaked in human blood. The men said it would be cannibalism to eat the animal now, a prospect sufficient to give anyone a lifetime of nightmares. But note that this occurred to a crew of just hundreds, with abundant water on hand to wash wounds and surgical apparatus, as well as to clean decks. The sea also functioned as a convenient cemetery for expeditious burial of the dead. And, finally, they needed to deal with only one domesticated scavenger.[50]

What when the dead and wounded numbered not hundreds but ten, twenty, or thirty thousand, the devil's work of just one day or two in a small area of the earth? What about scarcity of water to bathe and refresh the wounded, and numberless bodies requiring burial with shovels in hard ground, along with a multitude of dead horses needing to be burned? And what when not one pig, but herds of wild hogs snuffled and chewed among the entrails of the dead and not-yet-dead lying on the field? What then?

CHAPTER FOUR

CLEARING THE BATTLEFIELD

×

AFTER THEIR FIERCE ENCOUNTER, THE TROOPS MOVE ON, relieved to have survived intact at least one more bloodletting. The generals will engage in maneuvers to gain strategic advantage until, finally, they inevitably confront each other violently again. We will not march away with them but stay for now to witness desperate attempts to clear the field of both living and dead. Combat always produces an ugly detritus. The margins of the Bayeux Tapestry, a contemporary graphics account of the Battle of Hastings, 1066, show severed heads, arms, legs, chunks of horses hewn apart by broadsword and axe. European fighting from the Hundred Years War through the Napoleonic conflicts inflicted great carnage.

But the sheer efficiency of machine-age weapons produced a seemingly unparalleled butcher's bill. World War I soldiers compared combat to a giant sausage machine, whole men fed into the hopper, a mishmash of ground flesh dropping from the blades. The Civil War introduced America to wholesale killing. One student of the violence likens a Civil War battle to two huge beasts, one gray and one blue, clawing at each other, "spouts of waste issuing at the rear, an offal of bleeding parts of bodies, arms, legs, hands, dead men, wounded men screaming" and "a slag of dead horses."[1]

The medical and burial services must comb over the bloody floor of this abattoir, trying to retrieve those who still live and get them aid. Then they must dispose of the cadavers. We often tend to rush over this subject, cursorily referencing the flag-draped coffin and the official words of consolation. But this misleads us as to the real character of the grim landscape left by combat. The Duke of Wellington, British victor at Waterloo, 1815, famously said that, next to a battle lost, the saddest thing is a battle won. Let us begin to see what he meant, as the stretcher bearers start groping among battle's offal.

--------◆•◆•◆--------

The clearing of the field appears chaotic and clumsy, especially in the first phases of fighting. Nobody envisaged the scale of the coming slaughter. Southern politicians offered to drink all the blood spilled in fratricidal conflict. Northern leaders promised that just one advance on Richmond would burst rebellion's balloon. Why bother to build a large, expensive surgical corps or fleets of ambulances? So the authorities remained underequipped to cope with the immense slaughter that occurred at such battles as Malvern Hill, Virginia, in the late spring of 1862, where Major Henry K. Douglas of Stonewall Jackson's staff found himself trying to lead his trembling horse through reeking fetlock-deep blood pools. That day's work produced 6,000 wounded and 1,400 dead. Earlier, at Manassas, in July 1861, the first major eastern engagement, the armies simply abandoned many wounded for want of means to help them.[2]

At first, two-wheeled unsprung ambulances predominated, carrying only two casualties apiece. Desperate transportation officers also pressed into service farm wagons and commercial vehicles to act as impromptu conveyances. As late as Fair Oaks, June 29, 1862, Robert Knox Sneden, on Union General Samuel P. Heintzelman's staff, noted lines of wounded needing help "but few ambulances were to be seen— And they were all full of dying and desperately wounded men. Thin streams of blood ran out of the sides and bottoms of these vehicles, while the drivers were lashing the horses, and going over stumps in a reckless manner, jolting the remaining life out of the occupants."[3]

Early on, the only medical corpsmen available to collect the wounded might be bandsmen, temporarily relieved of other duties. It took four corpsmen to carry a body in a makeshift conveyance, a blanket that tortured victims. Serving on Virginia's Tidewater battlefields in 1861–62, Private Sidney Lanier, 2nd Georgia, heard pleas from the maimed to go steady: "Easy walking is desirable when each step of your four carriers spurts out the blood afresh, or grates the rough edges of a shot bone in your leg." Hoping to hang on for help, men tried to stanch their wounds. At Kelly's Ford, Virginia, on November 8, 1863, Sneden saw a dead Rebel whose "leg had been wrenched off at the knee, exposing all the arteries and tissues." Despite the agony lastingly engraved on his face, he had managed to improvise a tourniquet, but he still bled to death. "He was covered with dust and dirt, and his long yellow hair was matted with blood, presenting a terrible sight."[4]

Those who could still walk stumbled to the rear, nursing a shattered limb, body wound, or broken face. On this road of ruin, Stephen Crane's Jim Conklin takes his final bow. Some, without hope, crawled away to die. Sergeant Amos Hurriston, 154th New York, mortally wounded at Gettysburg, expired in seclusion, clutching a family photograph. "I got the likeness of the children and it pleased me more than eney thing that you could have sent me," he'd written home. In the first battles, finding a field hospital did not guarantee relief because many remained badly equipped. Charles J. Stillé, of the civilian U.S. Sanitary Commission, noted some wounded from summer 1862 Peninsula fighting laid on bare ground, "just as they had been left by the fortune of war (four days before); their wounds, as yet undressed, smeared with filth and blood, and all their wants unsupplied." Frederick Law Olmsted, also a Commission member, reported that ambulances, failing to locate field hospitals, dumped men by a swamp in inches of water. As late as December 1862, Walt Whitman wrote grimly of "the wounded lying on the ground" with "No cots; seldom even a mattress. It is pretty cold."[5]

Nevertheless, by late 1862, medical attention by both sides showed a perceptible improvement. Bigger, four-wheeled, sprung ambulances became available. Field hospitals increased in number and equipment. Rational procedures had been established. The wounded might hope for a temporary field dressing immediately behind the firing line: a tourniquet, rudimentary wound cleansing, and bandaging. Then, alone or supported, they looked for an ambulance pickup point, to be driven to a field hospital for diagnosis, treatment, and emergency surgery. Whenever possible the medical services located these facilities in sheltered houses, barns, under trees, and by a deep well or brook. Red flags identified them.[6]

Still, immediate retrieval of the wounded continued to be hamstrung by factors beyond the medical services' control. Many casualties remained lying in no-man's-land while the conflict ebbed and flowed over them, making retrieval hazardous. Sharpshooters targeted relief parties, even if under a white flag as they attempted to bring in enemy casualties. The piteous cries of the suffering, clearly audible after firing died for the night, haunted soldiers waiting for the next day's combat. Major Samuel Hurst, 73rd Ohio, recalled being unable to sleep nights at Gettysburg: "It was the most distressful wail ever listened to. Thousands of sufferers upon the field, and hundreds lying between the two skirmish lines, who could not be cared for, through the night were groaning and wailing or crying out in their depth of suffering and pain." As late as 1915, Major Wilbur Crummer, 45th Illinois, could still hear the night sounds of the wounded begging for water at Shiloh and Vicksburg.[7]

Even after the armies disengaged, sharpshooters continued to pick off relief workers because white flags went unrecognized until commanders signed a formal truce. Both sides hesitated to initiate this, because it looked like an admission of defeat. At Cold Harbor, June 3, 1864, thousands of wounded lay under a blazing sun while Grant and Lee waged a war of semantics. Although the Union assault had failed, Grant balked at straightforwardly requesting a truce until June 7.[8]

Torrential storms frequently fell after major battles, blackening the sky and turning the field to mud, impeding salvage work. Explanations for the rain varied. Perhaps reverberating cannonades disrupted cloud systems. Or hot air from gunfire condensed in the upper atmosphere to be precipitated as rain. The fanciful opined the storms represented angels weeping over the slaughter. Whatever the cause, rain lashed down after New Market, Malvern Hill, Shiloh, Second Manassas, Chancellorsville, Gettysburg, Murfreesboro, and more. Grant noted how downpours stopped him following up Shiloh. Again, in Virginia, May 1864, he recorded "five days of almost constant rain without any prospect of clearing up. The roads have now become so impassable that ambulances with wounded men can no longer run between here and Fredericksburg."[9]

Men experienced the nightmare of falling disabled while missiles still whistled overhead. At Antietam, Jonathan P. Stowe, 15th Massachusetts, managed to scribble, "I am wounded!" He added, "And am afraid shall be again as shells fly past me every few seconds. . . . Am in severe pain." Herds of riderless horses and escaped mules trampled the wounded in crazed stampedes. Flying batteries, coming into action, ran over the helpless. Captain Nathaniel Southgate Shaler, 5th Kentucky Artillery (U.S.), depicted gun teams that "dare not swerve for Christ or brother," whose "leaping wheels cut deep the field thick strewn With dead and wounded." The wounded wave hands, hoping the guns will avoid them, but then "The helpless bow their heads, the wheels roar on—" further crushing bodies, ending lives.[10]

Before crashing rains could quench the flames, brush and grass fires started by red-hot projectiles consumed many wounded. Soldiers universally feared this end, and it traumatized men unable to save the crippled from the advancing inferno. The screams of roasting men, bellies ripped open by exploding cartridge boxes that ignited with a cheerful firecracker popping, haunted veterans. In 1867, Sherman vividly recalled "on Shiloh's field, when our wounded men, mingled with rebels, charred and blackened by the burning tents and underbrush, were crawling about, begging for someone to end their misery." In extremity, some who could still use an arm, and had a gun, prepared to shoot themselves. Other desperate men seeking shelter thoughtlessly crawled into haystacks and burned there. Major John Edwards, adjutant to Rebel General Joseph O. Shelby, recalled of Prairie Grove, Arkansas, December 7, 1862, roasted corpses in a blackened hayrick, gorged on by swine. "Intestines, heads, arms, feet, and even hearts were dragged over the ground and devoured at leisure."[11]

Hogs also ate the living. At Cross Keys, Virginia, on June 8, 1862, Major R. L. Dabney, chaplain to the Stonewall brigade, recorded that corpses, "with some, perchance, of the mangled living, were partially devoured by swine before their burial." Being eaten haunted Confederate veteran Thomas J. Key: "It is dreadful to contemplate being killed on the field of battle without a kind hand to hide one's remains from the eye of the world or the gnawing of animals and buzzards." Human scavengers, stragglers and depraved civilians who robbed bodies, also degraded the fallen, and sometimes finished off their victims. At Missionary Ridge on November 25, 1863, Captain Tom Taylor, 47th Ohio, helped a near-naked sufferer who had been stripped even of his shirt. The thieves tried to rip the boots off his grapeshot-shattered legs, but "he made such a noise because of the agony and suffering from the pulling they desisted."[12]

Men lying exposed desperately needed water, but little was to be had unless they could drag themselves to bloody pools. A seventeen-year old in New York's Excelsior Brigade, disabled by a leg wound in fighting before Richmond in June 1862, told his brigade chaplain, Joseph Twichell, that he used his fingers to clear goo constricting his throat and then "was forced to moisten his lips and throat with his own urine." Dehydration produced madness. Corporal Cyrus Boyd, 15th Iowa, witnessed wounded men at Shiloh, "so near dead from exposure they were mostly insane." One Rebel who had "died in great agony" lay "on his back with his hands raised above his head" in supplication.[13]

Neglect advanced the rotting of damaged tissue and bone. General Alpheus S. Williams recalled that one of his men at Chancellorsville "had been wounded through the hips, and his feet had lain in the water until they gangrened and more than half the flesh had fallen off, leaving the bones of the feet protruding fleshless, nothing but skeletons of toes and outer bones." Often, a life might be saved only because maggots, hatched from eggs laid by flies in wounds, ate the rotten tissue.[14]

———•◦•———

Reaching a field hospital failed to guarantee prompt attention. Although overwhelmed surgeons worked nonstop, many wounded went untended. According to Sneden, during heavy fighting on the Peninsula in late June 1862, the work so overwhelmed doctors that, "in a short time the surgeon sinks under prostration which paralyzes every vital power." Federal nurse Cornelia Hancock estimated that at Gettysburg three hundred surgeons worked five days to perform the amputations. Lack of water often made conditions worse. Medical facilities came under fire: a Chancellorsville house and a Gettysburg barn used as hospitals both took fire and burned with the nonambulatory patients in them.[15]

John Stuckenberg, chaplain of the 145th Pennsylvania, sketched the daunting task facing the staff of a Gettysburg field hospital: "Here lies one with his leg shattered the flesh torn by a shell, nothing but shreds being left. There lies one shot through the abdomen, the intestines protruding—his life cannot be saved, perhaps even opium gives him but little temporary relief." And on: "Here lies one with his arm almost severed from his body—waiting for amputation. There lies one young and handsome shot through the face and head—his eyes swollen shut and covered with a yellow, putrid matter, his hair clotted with blood, his jaws torn, and a bullet hole through each cheek."[16]

The surgical staff steadily increased, rising to 11,000 in Federal service by 1865, a ratio of 1 per 133 men; the South had 1 per 324 yet somehow achieved about the same survival rate. In theory, personnel attending the wounded followed clearly prescribed procedures. Under optimum conditions, which rarely prevailed, a regimental surgeon rendered immediate attention to a casualty behind the lines to stop bleeding, superficially cleanse, and then dress wounds. Patients got a drink of water, if available, along with an opiate. U.S. surgeon W. W. Keen remembered the crudeness of administration—"doled out with a pocket knife [powder sprinkled directly into the wound] without worrying about superfluous exactitude in doling out the blessed relief that morphine brings to men in pain."[17]

Senior surgeons met the wounded at the next stage, a division or corps field hospital. As soon as possible, they carried out a thorough diagnostic examination to ascertain the degree of damage and the action required. They used fingers and metal probes to locate foreign bodies in wounds, simultaneously extracting accessible debris and securing bleeding vessels. Physicians now performed minor surgery, quickly and perhaps without anesthetic, especially if the soldier appeared exhausted or in shock. However, he might receive whiskey and a bullet or twig to chew on. Joseph E. Crowell, 13th New Jersey, wounded in the hand at Chancellorsville, bit on a stick while the surgeon snipped off the remains of a finger. This expeditious intervention saved him from gangrene. If the surgeon prescribed no further procedures at this time, an attendant re-bandaged the patient and administered a stimulant of alcohol and tobacco. Unfortunately, with little water and disinfectant, surgeons' hands and dressings became contaminated, leading to blood poisoning with complications such as lockjaw.[18]

Those requiring more radical intervention would be laid out for the head surgeon to inspect, attended by his assistants. Normally, the chief flagged complex abdominal or chest wounds for removal to major hospitals with superior facilities. He marked the remainder with a chalk line on the damaged limb, showing where amputation or resection cutting would occur. Often, a room in a house became the theater, the operating table a door laid across two barrels. Federal surgeon Patrick Binford recalled blood collecting in deep pools on the floor of a house used as a field hospital at Champion Hill, Mississippi, May 1863. Finally, he ordered drainage holes drilled through the floorboards under the table to drain off the fluid. Ether and chloroform administered via a cloth held over the face constituted the most common anesthetics available to Federal surgeons. Opinions differ on the consistency of Southern supplies, but Confederate medical staff reported local shortages by late spring 1862. Physicians commonly preferred chloroform. The flammable properties of ether made it dangerous when surgeons performed many procedures by naked lamp or candle flame.[19]

"Guillotining" predominated as a method of amputation in the field. With a knife, the surgeon sliced to the bone the soft tissue just above the damaged area, and then completed severance with a hacksaw. He then tied off the arteries with oiled silk, the streamers left long enough for the rotted arterial ends to be tugged free days later. Good surgeons completed complex procedures in under two minutes. Naturally, men resisted losing their limbs, especially in an era when most jobs required physical dexterity, and such impairments meant social rejection. Michigan private Thomas A. Perrine, whose lady friend shortly ditched him, complained bitterly the war left him with "an empty sleeve, an empty heart."[20]

To avoid amputation, surgeons might try excision and recision, procedures designed to save limbs by removing pieces of damaged bone from the shaft, leaving natural mending to bridge the gap. However, these long and complicated procedures incurred a greater chance of hemorrhage and infection. Unhealed ex-sections could abscess. Southern professor of medicine J. J. Chisolm observed of such cases: "the bones are carious [decayed]; the abscesses are interminable sinuses, from which are kept up a constant discharge." Restoration of motor ability could not be assured: "the wound has healed, but the limb remains weak, shrunken, stiff, painful and nearly useless." Artificial limbs often functioned better and, overall, surgeons favored amputation.[21]

Given the difficulties army surgeons faced, they achieved acceptable results, keeping the death rate from all causes, including disease, to 14 percent, versus 16 percent for the Crimea, and 15 percent in the Franco-Prussian War. Military surgeries posed greater challenges than civilian: poor, filthy facilities; wood, metal and leather driven into wounds; a greater number of patients in poorer physical condition. Yet doctors in uniform achieved better success, with a mortality rate of 26.5 percent versus 50 percent. Why then did the public hold army surgeons in contempt as drunken butchers? Admittedly, some drank or took drugs, usually to stand the strain of overwork and danger, including threats of hospital infections. They feared what happened to Dr. Robert W. Gibbes, South Carolina's Surgeon General, who became disabled, "poor creature, he is losing the joints of his hand from an operation he performed on a gangrenous wound." Stories of boozy sawbones, based on a minority in the medical corps, unfairly brought all surgeons into disrepute.[22]

Also, ignorance of the fact that amputations often offered the only way to save lives also fed ill-informed hostility. Surgeons looked the part of butchers, smocks and arms drenched with blood, limbs piled nearby. Johann Stuber, 58th Ohio, described a field hospital outside Vicksburg: "The house, the halls, the yard, even the attic was pressed full of wounded. I saw the doctors on the verandah with knives and saws working as diligently as butchers at the meat market." Outside, former slaves, who had sought refuge and work within the Union lines, buried limbs. Burial details struggled to keep up. "I notice," said Walt Whitman at Fredericksburg, "a heap of amputated feet, legs arms, hands, &c., a full load for a one-horse cart." In the same location, Union private William Hamilton described animals enjoying the windfall: "There was a Hospital within thirty yards of us . . . about the building you could see the Hogs belonging to the farm eating arms and other portions of the body." Joseph Crowell estimated his squad buried eight hundred limbs at Gettysburg.[23]

Misunderstanding of anesthetic procedure further colored images of medical callousness. In the field, physicians could only roughly gauge patient bodyweight, important to measuring the dose. Shock, blood loss, and weakness also complicated estimates, so that physicians dared not apply deep anesthesia for fear of killing patients. They ordered a shallow draft to be administered, leaving patients insensible to pain but semiconscious. Drugged and fearful, seeing the knife and saw, patients hallucinated ghost pain, screaming or moaning in imagined hell, leading uninformed observers to mistakenly conclude that surgeons were callous monsters who left men in agony. The real suffering came later when the patient fully awoke to disability with all its emotional distress and physical ramifications, including the torture of prolonged swelling, inflammation, infection, and fever.

———————

As soon as possible, postsurgical patients left for major hospitals, usually located in urban centers, to complete their recovery. But even with the wartime expansion in medical transportation, many delays occurred in moving casualties from field hospitals. The sheer volume of wounded from a major engagement temporarily overwhelmed resources. The ubiquitous rains stopped traffic, as did the depredations of raiders, taking out railroads and bridges. While on hold, postoperatives endured dirt, thirst, and hunger. Colonel James A. Mulligan, Union commander in the fight at Lexington, Missouri, September 1861, recalled: "Our supply of water had given out and the scenes in the hospital were fearful to witness, wounded men suffering agonies from thirst and in their frenzy wrestling for the water in which the wounded had been bathed."[24]

With inadequate numbers of cots, men awaiting evacuation lay on bare ground. This fate awaited a private in the 48th Pennsylvania, wounded in the thigh. He lay exposed to the elements, going without food for seven days. Cornelia Hancock, nursing in a Union hospital during the Wilderness fighting of May 1864, described men on church floors and pews, rain pouring through bullet-riddled roofs "until our wounded lay in pools of water made bloody by their seriously wounded condition." In July of that year, George Templeton Strong of the Sanitary Commission saw about six thousand men lying around Grant's headquarters under a blistering sun, covered in clouds of dust, while turkey buzzards hovered overhead.[25]

When the sufferer did get a ride to the main hospital, shortages of more advanced ambulances even late in the war meant that this last journey frequently occurred in an unsprung vehicle. Rebel Walter Lenoir, who lost a leg fighting against General John Pope on August 31, 1862, endured torture in a wagon that made only twenty miles in five hours, jolting patients at every rut, causing "a pang which felt as if my stump was thrust into liquid fire." General John Imboden, commanding the Confederate medical column taking wounded to Virginia after Gettysburg, could not forget the suffering. Many patients remained without food for thirty-six hours as rain pelted down. He watched unsprung wagons, without even straw cushioning, bounce brutally over rocky, washed-out roads:

> The jolting was enough to have killed strong men, if long exposed to it. From nearly every wagon as the teams trotted on, urged by whip and shout, came such cries and shrieks as these:
> "O god! why can't I die?"
> "My god! will no one have mercy and kill me?"
> "Stop! Oh! for God's sake stop just for one minute; take me out and leave me to die on the roadside."[26]

The condition of men arriving at permanent facilities shocked nurses. Rushing to unload ambulances coming from the Fredericksburg battlefield, D.C. nurse Louisa May Alcott met "a regiment of the vilest odors that ever assaulted the human nose," and shortly after there assembled around the stove "the dreariest group I ever saw— ragged, gaunt and pale, mud to the knees, with bloody bandages untouched since put on days before." Numbers temporarily overwhelmed facilities. Kate Cumming, a Confederate nurse in Corinth, after Shiloh, said the staff initially worked without cots or blankets for the men, and without plates to serve food. She said filth and vermin covered the incoming.[27]

Yet the effort to provide adequate facilities continued throughout the war, especially for white soldiers. Black troops experienced more neglect from both sides, some of it intentional. The wounded from

Fort Wagner lay out for thirty-six hours, producing cases of gangrene. Segregated hospital units for African Americans, generally inferior structures, and less well equipped than those for whites, gratuitously raised the mortality rate. Still, by 1865, the Northern and Southern medical services between them operated some four hundred hospitals of an unprecedented magnitude and sophistication, boasting nearly 400,000 beds. More than one million soldiers had received care in Northern facilities alone.[28]

Daunting challenges faced physicians and nurses in providing long-term care. As medical science had gained little understanding of bacterial infection and no antibiotics existed, many patients regressed despite successful surgery, succumbing to secondary complications. Stonewall Jackson, whose weakened system fell prey to pneumonia and general debilitation following amputation, might have been saved today by postoperative treatment. Wounds frequently refused to heal without modern hygienic procedures and pharmaceuticals. At the D.C. Armory Square Hospital in February of 1863, Walt Whitman met a young New York soldier shot through his bladder half a year earlier. Waste water still oozed from the boy's gaping wound, "so that he lay almost constantly in a sort of puddle—." Excisions became infected. George Fisk, an eighteen-year-old Union private, took a bullet at Fair Oaks on May 3, 1862. The wound festered when the surgeon performing an upper arm ex-section failed to locate all embedded bone chips. The arm and shoulder became a dead weight, immobile and swollen. Finally, the wound exploded in a bloody eruption, killing the boy.[29]

Problems required repeat surgeries. Infection and blood poisoning that led to gangrene necessitated recutting flesh and further amputation to remove cankered tissue and bone. Threads tying off arteries broke loose, needing to be sewn again. Georgia private Milton Clark endured this renewed procedure at Reed's Hospital, Lynchburg, Virginia, in August 1864. Minimally sedated, he allowed as how it "was very painful to me." Days later, a second artery broke, requiring the removal of further flesh and bone to expose fresh artery for retying. This time, Clark got chloroform.[30]

Extended surgery often failed. A bullet hit Union Corporal James Quick in the face at Fredericksburg. Despite wound cleansing, bacteria attacked, ulcerating numerous blood vessels within the skull. Hemorrhaging became frequent. Surgeons tried tying off the left common carotid artery (one of two vessels supplying most of the blood to the neck, head, and brain). The treatment failed to take. After a massive effusion of blood, Quick became comatose and died minutes later. Autopsy revealed the carotid artery rotted through at the site of the suture.[31]

Patients suffering massive facial damage, such as crushed jaws, had little hope of a full recovery and normal life. Mary Boykin Chesnut, nursing at a Virginia hospital, The Wayside, in November 1864, daily spoon-fed hominy rice, gravy, milk, and softened bread to four men unable to chew. "One was shot in the eye, but his whole jaw was paralyzed. Another—and the worst case—had his tongue cut away by a shot, and his teeth with it." Without the technology to intravenously feed patients with utterly ruined jaws and swollen, lacerated throats, nurses could not provide enough nourishment to sustain life. The victims died of malnutrition.[32]

Many wounds involved nerve damage, causing immense pain and discomfort, while proving hard to cure. The war brought to prominence a gifted practitioner in the developing field of neurological science, Weir Mitchell. Later, he gained notoriety for a controversial isolation cure that he prescribed particularly for female patients he labeled "hysterics." Today, the treatment appears insensitive, even cruel. Charlotte Perkins Gilman made it infamous in her story, "The Yellow Wallpaper" (1899), about a woman driven mad by medical incarceration. Mitchell could be extreme in his views; according to repute, he once set a patient's bed on fire to jolt him out of depression. Whatever his eccentricities and later misjudgments, he dedicated his wartime career to helping men with neurological damage, achieving results in many cases. Mitchell impressed Federal Surgeon General William Alexander Hammond enough to be placed in charge of the Turner's Lane Hospital in Philadelphia, a 400-bed facility for nervous diseases.

The doctor wrote up many of the cases he treated there in *Injuries of Nerves and Their Consequences*. This detailed study allows us to inspect the wards along with this eminent practitioner. A tall, gaunt, sharp-bearded man, the soldiers nickname him "Uncle Sam." His manner intense and animated, he stalks along at a frenetic pace; we must hurry to keep up. We first meet a New York soldier, shot through the biceps of the right arm at Gettysburg on July 2, 1863. His injury spawned neuralgia and joint disease. The arm exhibits swelling, feels hard, like marble, is glossy, and extremely sensitive to the touch. It must be kept wrapped in a wet cloth. Over time, the ordeal has caused chronic emotional stress. He cannot stand even the blowing of a nurse's breath on his arm, and complains that the sound of her dress rustling by his cot causes distress. He has declined enough mentally that some staff consider him insane.[33]

Moving on, we come next to an Irish soldier of the 69th Pennsylvania, shot in the left forearm six months ago. He has developed neuritis and joint disease. Dr. Mitchell tells us that a course of blistering failed to increase blood circulation and muscle mobility. The patient looks "thin, anaemic, nervous, and pain-worn." His record states that he "sleeps badly, and has ague and dyspepsia. The arm is generally wasted; he keeps the hand wet." Pain in damaged limbs becomes a problem for many men; they find relief only through soothing applications of cold water to combat inflammation. Even though the constant drip, drip has a wearing effect on the patient's nervous resolution, some must continuously keep the affected limb under a tap.[34]

Mitchell uses leeches to stimulate areas with injured nerve endings. He advocates liberally dispensing morphine and, in extreme cases, arsenic drops to relieve excruciating misery: "The pains of traumatic neuralgia are so terrible," explains the lanky head surgeon, "that we are usually driven at once to the use of narcotic hypodermic injections." Opium plasters present a further option: when placed over injured areas, they introduce soothing narcotic effects directly into the affected region. Sergeant A. D. Marks of the 3rd Maryland (U.S.), shot in the neck and chest at Chancellorsville, typifies such cases. The damage resulted in partial paralysis of his neck and left arm, accompanied by pleurisy and congestion of the lungs. Treatments include icing the arm, blistering the shoulder, and then dressing it with opium plaster. The sergeant needs frequent morphine injections and electrical treatments for increasing pain. Applications of leeches also ease the patient's suffering. (Marks's record shows sufficient improvement for him to be released in April 1864, but still without the use of his left hand.)[35]

We proceed to the bedside of Private Joseph H. Corliss, 14th New York, shot through the left biceps at Second Bull Run, August 1862. He lost the use of both hands, his left arm frozen across the chest, and his right arm hanging limp. After months in hospital, recovery remains elusive. The left hand withered to a hard, thin, claw, with deformed nails. Paralysis now reaches the left leg, so he must not only drip water on both hands but also into his boot to ease the pain. Many such severe cases require constant medical attention. At Cold Harbor, in the spring of 1864, a minnie ball hit Captain A. F. Swann, 16th Pennsylvania Cavalry, in the left arm and elbow. Needing frequent morphine shots, "Both arms are covered with the punctures of the syringe, discolored, and the cellular tissue indurated." Operations to remove the damaged nerve tissue have failed to effect a cure.[36]

The cases go on. Patients sit or lie with arms molded to chests, limbs shrunken and without movement in their fingers. Keeping injured areas wet occupies them constantly. Family and friends fail to recognize casualties emotionally debilitated by their ordeal. For example, Mitchell points to the case of Private David Schively, 114th Pennsylvania, seventeen years old. A minnie ball that ranged up through the right arm into the cheek hit him on July 2, 1863, at Gettysburg. The surgeon notes he "is nervous and hysterical to such a degree that his relatives suppose him to be partially insane." Private John C. Dyre, 71st Pennsylvania, occupies the last cot we pause by. A bullet entered behind his left ear at Gettysburg. By February 1864, the wound has distorted his features, pulling the face to the right and slurring his speech. Neurological damage paralyzes the left side, and Dyre cannot close one eyelid. Chewing food causes him great pain. No procedures, including electrical treatments, help; the physicians see no relief in sight.[37]

We take our leave of Dr. Mitchell here, but pause to consider that, in addressing both the physical needs of such stricken men and also attempting to help them keep up their spirits, the hospital nursing staff also played an essential role. Many patients developed a son-to-mother relationship with their caregivers, perhaps at times childlike in its intense need and dependency, but still of positive benefit in their predicament. The nurses not only provided this feminine comfort, they fed, cleaned, and administered soothing medications to the suffering. Inevitably, this burden of responsibility put a brutal stress on the nursing staff, at least 10 percent of women attendants breaking down under the load.

Many nurses helped patients bear their encroaching mortality. Kate Cumming of Mobile, serving at a Corinth hospital, wrote: "At home, when a member of a family is about to go to his last resting-place, loving friends are around the couch of the sufferer, and by kind words and acts rob King Death of half his terrors. . . . But here a man near dissolution is in a ward with perhaps twenty more," and only a single nurse keeps vigil. After Shiloh, she tended a wasted boy named Wasson. The youth suspected he was mortally wounded. "What was the matter," he asked, "was he going to die?" Kate softened her answer, but then a surgeon bluntly told the boy he was finished. Wasson accepted his end, but told Kate it seemed hard to go so young and without seeing his family. She sat with him, cushioning his last hours, until she went to sleep, exhausted.[38]

The women of the wards cried for the boys they came to know and love. Ella Thomas nursed at the 3rd Georgia hospital in Virginia. She talked sadly of a soldier dying in late July 1864. In a delirium, he mistakenly cried out gleefully, "I am going home, I have a furlough to go home." She wished she had an address for the family so she could write and tell them where and when their son died, adding "but I would not have them know how he died." Nurses every day wrote final letters for dying soldiers. On top of these painful duties, nursing staff also had to cope with the moral and physical decline of surgeons who broke under the strain of overwork and responsibility. New Englander Hannah Ropes, serving at the Union Hospital in Georgetown, near D.C., wrote that her ward physician stayed drunk all day and performed the rounds "like a somnambulist!" Sitting by dying boys, fearing hospital infections such as contracting gangrene, all the while themselves nervously and physically frayed, many nurses hung on day-by-day, wondering when breakdown would debilitate or kill them.[39]

No job proved worse than disposing of the dead littering the battle-fields. Ironically, this involved more slaughter, as military details had to shoot herds of rogue mules and horses roaming the battlefield, along with many writhing and screaming animals mutilated by missiles. Work details burned the corpses of animals, though often they lacked the time to do a thorough job, leaving half-burned remains smoldering in decaying, stinking piles, attracting flies and scavengers. Human remains also decayed quickly, especially in hot weather at the height of the campaigning season. Until orders moved the regiments on, living soldiers coexisted with the dead. Virginian David Hunter Strother, a Union staff officer, explored the field after Antietam. He noted with distaste that "our troops sat cooking, eating, jabbering, and smoking; sleeping among the corpses."[40]

Cadavers quickly swelled to twice their normal size. Gases distended stomachs that then burst, emitting foul and, to Victorians, deadly odors. The sickly sweet, heavily cloying smell of death hung over the killing fields. At Shiloh the stench reputedly overpowered the scent of spring blossoms. The dead took on a nightmarish appearance as their faces disintegrated. Strother, again, described the lack of distinguishing features among the dead at Cedar Mountain, where fierce August heat had obliterated any human form. "The eyes had bulged through their apertures in the flesh, distended to the size of eggs, and their hair lay long, tangled and matted with blood, over a forehead blue and yellow by exposure and hastening corruption."[41]

According to Sergeant Thomas Meyer, 148th Pennsylvania, on grave duty after Gettysburg, in the next stage of decomposition faces became "black as charcoal and bloated out of all human semblance; eyes, cheeks, forehead and nose all one general level of putrid swelling, twice the normal size, with here and there great blisters of putrid water, some the size of a man's fist on face, neck and wrists." The shining fetid mass crawled with maggots as corpses began to fall apart, the rotting pieces joining the body parts already scattered by missile fire. Disposal of this human detritus assumed monumental proportions. Sherman Norris, 7th Ohio, burying the dead after Gettysburg, said, "I shall remember that day and its ghastly dead. We took them from perfect lines of battle as they had fallen; we dragged them out from behind rocks; we found them behind logs or lying over them, with eyes and mouths distended, and faces blackened by mortification." In just one half acre before the Union lines at Vicksburg, thirty decomposing bodies of Rebel attackers were counted.[42]

The refusal of opposing commanders to cooperate in retrieval delayed the cleanup and made it more oppressive for the workers. When possible, Union commanders delegated the gruesome task of interment to black soldiers and contrabands employed for this kind of unsavory chore. Slaves fulfilled a similar function in the Confederate service. However, when necessary, generals pressed whites on both sides into the work. As an example, after New Market in the Shenandoah, May 17, 1864, Confederate commander John C. Breckinridge unsuccessfully petitioned his opposite number, General Franz Siegel, to help Rebel details bury Yankee dead.[43]

Usually, officers instructed soldiers to bury friendly dead first in individual graves, marking the name and unit of the occupant clearly on a piece of wood, rock, or other impromptu headpiece. This could not always be accomplished, as missiles disfigured bodies and the elements decayed features, making identification impossible. Fallen officers stood the best chance of being recovered, their bodies often retrieved while the fighting raged. They, along with the dead from prosperous families, might be sent home in charcoal-lined zinc coffins. Shipping services, such as Adams Express in the North, made the service available to those who could pay. In one unusual instance, some men in the 5th Corps, Army of the Potomac, clubbed together to send home comrades' body parts in cracker boxes so that the remains might lie in familiar soil.[44]

Whatever the efforts made, most common soldiers ended up in anonymous mass graves. Workers shoveled remains into handy rifle pits, hastily dug trenches or convenient folds in the ground. William Martin, a Union veteran, confessed that, after the fighting at Ezra Church outside Atlanta in 1864, Rebel dead received no respect—"laid three or four deep and we covered them like cabbage." Another old soldier recalled: "The common soldier that fell in battle was thrown into a trench with no winding sheet but his blood-stained garments, and no covering but the cold clods thrown over him by unsympathizing strangers."[45]

Because of the sheer numbers to be interred, the soil chucked over the common grave might be only eight to ten inches deep. What amounted to dumping bodies like garbage concerned many soldiers in a period when death was supposed to be a highly ritualized, dignified departure from life, normally attended by grieving family and cherished friends. Punning on the word shooting (a common term both for discharging weapons and for disposing of waste), cynical Union veteran Ambrose Bierce wrote in *The Devil's Dictionary* (1911) that a regimental standard might be taken as a sign advertising that rubbish might be shot here.

Soldiers tried to improvise techniques for shifting the dead to help make the labor more palatable. Pennsylvania army chaplain A. M. Stewart commented on what happened after Spotsylvania in May 1864. In the heat, "The hair and skin had fallen from the head, and the flesh from the bones—all alive with disgusting maggots." To cope, burial details stuffed their nostrils with young green leaves, blocking the stench. They fashioned hooks from bent socket bayonets and stuck these on poles to drag the corpses to prepared pits, keeping the operation at arm's length. Even then, said Samuel Compton, 12th Ohio, "The bodies had become so offensive that men could only endure it by being staggering drunk."[46]

In the end, despite misgivings and later feelings of guilt, burial details resorted to desperate and devious devices to finish their obnoxious assignment. They chucked bodies down wells, stacked them in icehouses and other outbuildings, stuffed remains under porches, and shoveled the decayed matter into compost piles. Dick Simpson, 3rd South Carolina, admitted that the corpses they were responsible for at Vienna, Virginia, in August 1861, stank so badly that "some were covered up with brush with their head and feet left out, and very often the latter were eaten off by the hogs." Inevitably, shallow layers of soil and brush covering common graves eroded, washing away under the pressure of rain or the busy efforts of scavenging creatures.[47]

This exposure of badly decayed flesh filled the air once again with foul smells. Sergeant Berry Benson, 1st South Carolina, wrote that, when his regiment marched back over the old Seven Days field, erosion of burial sites meant "we endured at times almost agony from the horrible stench that in one locality or another pervaded the air." A young Louisiana officer, R. A. Pierson, acknowledged that, months after Fredericksburg, the Confederate army had not yet fully buried the Union dead; half-exposed corpses were still evident: "our troops were so worn down with fatigue from the three days fight, that they took but little pains in burying them; they are still exposed to view in many places, some with their heads and arms sticking out, while others' heads are projecting and present the most hideous features; their teeth glistening as though grinning at the passers by."[48]

On the Union side, Rice Bull, 123rd New York, revisiting Spotsylvania in spring 1865, counted one hundred Rebel skeletons, given scant burial, now visible in a two-hundred-foot area. When orders made troops camp on sites proximate to the communal graves dug after previous encounters, they found that, in the words of Private Alfred Bellard, 5th New Jersey, "it was our morning's work to clean the ground of worms, that had been washed from the graves during the night by the rains. Our well, that was merely a barrell sunk in the ground had to undergo a general skimming before we could get water for coffee."[49]

———————————

Eventually, the troops left. But many civilians remained in the area devastated by battle, unless driven off by soldiers or frightened away from the district, fleeing as refugees. Some of them failed to evacuate before the fighting because they had nowhere to go; others felt uneasy about trusting themselves and their children to the open road, where they would be vulnerable to robbery and worse without the protection of menfolk away in uniform. Some simply refused to desert their homes as the fighting approached, somehow hoping to protect and preserve their property. Whatever the case, these civilians caught in a battle zone experienced all the devastation of battle and then the task of sorting out the wreckage left by the armies.

The fighting proved profoundly traumatic for noncombatants. Little in their previous experience or imaginative lives, neither pictures nor literature, including soldiers' letters from the front, could prepare them for the terrifying reality of combat. Soldiers frequently remarked on the number of civilians in combat zones who had gone mad, at least temporarily, through overwhelming fear. During the fighting at Fredericksburg, Union soldiers dragged a woman from her cellar bomb shelter, demanding that she show them where they might find a well for water. Robbed of cover, she seemed to lose her senses. Thomas Galwey, 8th Ohio, recognized her later, sitting among corpses, hair disheveled and staring vacantly into space. He supposed that, suddenly plunged into hell, she "must have gone mad with fear."[50]

During the 1862 Maryland campaign, Colonel Elisha Rhodes, 2nd Rhode Island, observed a woman in the town of Burkettsville wandering among the bodies of dead soldiers, apparently bereft of reason. Captain William Willis Blackford, 1st Virginia Cavalry, witnessed women and children in Sharpsburg, driven from the shelter of a stone house by shell fire, consumed by hysterics, "like a flock of birds . . . hair streaming in the wind and children of all ages stretched out behind."[51]

In small towns like Gettysburg, Sharpsburg, and Franklin, quartering officers commandeered intact buildings as medical stations, whole communities becoming one vast hospital zone, the wounded laid out in barns, houses, stores, and churches. Soldiers requisitioned blankets, bedsheets, petticoats, food, water, anything that could help the casualties. The ratio of the mutilated to the normal population must astound us. In one day at Franklin, a community of 2,500 inhabitants, 10,000 casualties piled up. At Gettysburg, with a population of 2,400, the number of wounded to be accommodated reached 20,000. Sometimes a town visited by fighting more than once virtually ceased to exist save as one huge medical center. Such happened to Fredericksburg, Virginia, which civilians did not reoccupy until the war ended.[52]

Colonel W. D. Gale, a Confederate staff officer at the Battle of Franklin, described the seizure of Mrs. Carrie McGavock's large two-story house for placement of the wounded. "This was taken as a hospital, and the wounded, in hundreds, were brought to it during the battle, and all the night after. Every room was filled, every bed had two poor, bleeding fellows, every spare space, niche, and corner under the stairs, in the hall, everywhere—but one room for her own family." At Shiloh, newspaper correspondent Charles Coffin peeked into the home of a middle-aged lady with three young children: "On Monday night one hundred wounded were brought to her house. Her two horses had been seized, her corn eaten, and no equivalent returned." Already, seven mounds in her garden indicated the burial places of patients who failed to survive surgery.[53]

The numbers and condition of the wounded shattered the composure of civilians who previously had no conceivable idea of the potential magnitude of carnage. Sally Putnam wrote vividly of Richmond becoming a universe of suffering during the 1862 Peninsula fighting: "We lived in one immense hospital, and breathed the vapors of the charnel house. . . . Every family received the bodies of the wounded or dead of their friends, and every house was a house of mourning or a private hospital. . . . Sickening odors filled the atmosphere and soldiers' funerals were passing at every moment. . . ." A veritable abattoir engulfed everyone caught in the aftermath of combat. Fannie Beers, setting off to tend soldiers wounded close by in the 1864 Georgia campaign, came first upon a vast number of mangled, living beasts. "The plaintive cries and awful struggles of the horses first impressed me. They were shot in every conceivable manner, showing shattered heads, broken and bleeding limbs, and protruding entrails." Many "struggled half-way to their feet, uttering cries of pain, while their distorted eyes seemed to reveal their suffering and implore relief."[54]

Residents spent months rebuilding their communities, cutting up shattered trees, clearing and plowing ruined fields, razing shattered buildings. Acres of debris exhibited broken weapons, torn knapsacks, ruined canteens, pieces of uniform and equipment, smashed wheels, gun limbers and carriages, ration cans, blankets, shrapnel, and, of course, bodies. As we have seen, military burial details inadequately disposed of corpses. In a Yorktown house on the Virginia Peninsula, a sniper killed during the 1862 Peninsula fighting had "tumbled down the flue in a doubled up position and stuck thus in the fireplace," making a dreadful spectacle, "shot between the eyes and the back of his skull was all blown out." Even when the building burned, the sharpshooter's charred corpse stayed as a grotesque monument, a Gothic horror rivaling Ambrose Bierce's tortured creations.[55]

Deserted buildings became bizarre mausoleums. After Bristoe Station, August 28, 1862, two Rebel corpses remained uncollected in an old stone house. On the first floor a soldier killed by a bullet through the forehead while in the act of loading still sat on a bed with his rifle across his knees; the second body lay sprawled in blood on the upper story. After being officially evacuated, structures used as field hospitals might still contain blood-soaked rags, amputated limbs, even dead patients. Contamination of the water supply added to the health hazards facing civilians. On examination, one well at Sharpsburg disgorged the bodies of fifty-eight Rebels unceremoniously dropped down the shaft.[56]

Although souvenir hunters desecrated the dead, civilians usually tried to inter remains properly. Elizabeth Hook and her family took a young Rebel's body into their home to preserve it for burial, fearing the hogs would eat it. She became haunted by memory of "the continual drip, drip of the blood from his wounds." Bodies discovered too close to homes, found in hastily made graves under porches and in gardens, had to be exhumed and reburied properly. A farmer at Cross Keys dug up and relocated one hundred soldiers planted too near his house. A soldier of the 34th New York, revisiting Fredericksburg after the armies had moved elsewhere, reported that "every doorstep was a tombstone," awaiting attention at the end of hostilities when civilians might reclaim their community.[57]

A woman returning to Manassas after the August 1862 fighting confronted acres of debris and bodies in a ditch hastily covered over: "their hands and feet were visible from many. And one poor fellow lay unburied, just as he had fallen with his horse across him, and both skeletons." The stench from unsealed pits lingered for whole seasons. One hired hand on a Sharpsburg farm remembered with horror the pall hanging over the countryside. "We couldn't eat a good meal and we had to shut the house up just as tight as we could of a night to keep out that odor."[58]

Sometimes, the traumatic events visited on civilians shaped the remainder of their lives. One of them, Carrie McGavock, whose house had been taken as a field hospital at Franklin, dedicated her life to re-interring, in a proper cemetery with individual headstones, the 1,500 Confederates buried on her land. She wandered her hallowed ground continually, rarely missing a day of stewardship in the cemetery, continually checking her book of the dead, still haunted by one fateful day in November 1864.[59]

For the soldiers, repeated exposure to the terrible sights, sounds, and smells of battle could overpower their emotional resolution. The road down which they marched to war progressively darkened, shadowed by awful memories of the unimaginable. Victorians lacked a clinical diagnostic language to describe what happened to the psyche of mentally wounded fighting men. They called it simply but vividly "shook over hell" because that is what it looked like.

— CHAPTER FIVE —

THE EDGE OF SANITY

×

OFTEN, WE SEEM TO THINK THAT COMBAT'S EMOTIONAL damage largely began with the shocking trauma of trench fighting in the Great War, World War I. We tend to conceive of Civil War soldiers as hard-bitten and unlikely to break down under adverse conditions. Actually, every description of psychiatric wound identified since 1914 had precedent in the 1860s. In this chapter, we shall look at the Civil War's emotional battle damage, which drove men to the edge of sanity and beyond. We may fail to appreciate the widespread extent of these psychological wounds because the field of psychiatry did not become fully fledged until the 1890s and only burgeoned in the first years of the new century. Consequently, no psychiatrists appeared at the fighting front before the 1905 Russo-Japanese War. Thereafter, they became an intrinsic element of military medical services, and the diagnosis of mental wounds took a giant leap forward.

One-seventh of British Great War casualties, often recorded as shell-shock cases, had psychiatric issues and constituted 20 percent of disability discharges. Although U.S. forces engaged in heavy fighting for less than a year, they officially sustained 106,000 emotional casualties. By World War II, the number of identified mentally disturbed U.S. patients rose to one million, usually labeled combat fatigued. During initial stages of the Korean War, psychiatric wounds reached 240 per 1,000. Many suffered posttraumatic stress disorder (PTSD), a complaint that grew in frequency through the Vietnam War to Iraq and Afghanistan. In one key manifestation of the condition, patients suffer the nightmare reliving of profoundly disturbing episodes. Psychological damage may produce extremes of character, including unreasonable anger, violence, alcohol addiction, and loss of concentration.[1]

The prepsychiatric era had no clinical terms to describe what physicians were seeing, so that doctors misdiagnosed mental wounds as cowardice, character loss, or lack of patriotism, whereas today we might discern a profile of damage inflicted by war. In the Napoleonic age, for instance, we can, from a modern perspective, detect cases of chronic combat exhaustion. British General Sir John Colborne, commanding a brigade on the Spanish Peninsular, 1809, retired from the field, feeling "fit for nothing." He confessed, "I was so nervous that I used to be obliged to say, 'Give me a glass of wine, I am going to cry.'" General Sir Thomas Picton begged the Duke of Wellington not to include him in the 1815 Waterloo campaign, pleading, "My Lord, I must give up. I am grown so nervous, that when any service is to be done it works upon my mind so that it is impossible for me to sleep at nights." The Iron Duke insisted he needed Picton, and his subordinate general died leading his division into action.[2]

In examining the Civil War, medical historians frequently cannot characterize behavior precisely because both observers and victims, with limited understanding and lack of a clinical vocabulary, leave us inadequate clues. In late 1864, Captain J. McEntire, a U.S. provost marshal, wrote of Private William Leeds, an Army of the Potomac deserter in his charge, that "he has been strolling about in the woods . . . mourning for the loss of his character." This seems a moral more than a medical judgment. Consider as a further instance the plight of General James Longstreet, wounded in the Wilderness in May 1864. At home recuperating, the general appeared "very feeble and nervous and suffers much from his wound." He "sheds tears on the slightest provocation," a humiliating experience. "He says he does not see why a bullet going through a man's shoulder should make a baby of him." Longstreet could not diagnose his symptoms as those of combat fatigue that reached a crisis when he was wounded.[3]

Soldiers gained little helpful insight from practitioners of the infant neurological sciences. Earlier, we witnessed Dr. Weir Mitchell addressing nerve complications resulting from physical injuries. But if no major bodily damage had occurred, Mitchell and his colleagues scathingly denounced seeming debility as deliberate "malingering." They had no understanding of the somatic symptoms of distress, condemning "feigned epilepsies, paralyses, and the like —." Line officers showed similar skepticism about wounds they could not see. General Horace Porter, aide-de-camp to General Grant in the 1864–65 campaigns, observed that, for some time after combat, men "would start at the slightest sound, and dodge at the flight of a bird or a pebble tossed at them." Yet, this evidence of mental distress failed to make him sympathetic to those who could not bear the strain. Writing after the war, he announced that only braggarts and weaklings broke; he characterized the more delicate members of his own class witheringly as milksops, "leading an unambitious, namby-pamby life, surrounded by all the safeguards of civilization." To his mind, they needed a dose of the Victorian medicine for stunted "manliness"—time roughing it in the wilderness to advance muscular development of body and brain.[4]

Soldiers' reluctance to be stigmatized by confessing to emotional upset makes it hard to quantify Civil War mental wounds. A lack of bureaucratic precision in describing individual cases compounds the problem. For example, in desertion cases the exact cause often went unexamined, so we cannot know if a subject suffered from mental wounds or had other motives for running. We do know that huge numbers deserted, especially as the destructive fighting ground on. At least 105,000 Rebels and 279,000 Yankees officially absconded, and probably many more did so who were never cataloged. Thirty-four thousand deserted from hospitals, suggesting they were fleeing mental traumas. But we lack certainty. Bounty jumpers or other criminals hiding behind the uniform frequently ran off; other deserters suffered from nostalgia perhaps unrelated to combat experience; still more responded to a call from home to protect a starving family. Further complicating matters, the services often failed to distinguish between men simply AWOL, perhaps wandering around stunned after a battle, and those who lit out for good. We cannot always discover the severity and longevity of mental anguish in given cases. But we can say that thousands suffered mental wounds, some clearing up quickly, others lingering and possibly healing over time, while some combat traumas never receded.[5]

Exact numbers do not matter because we want primarily to paint a human, rather than a statistical, portrait of the causes and consequences of mental injuries. To accomplish this in a complex and fluid diorama of combat, we should continue our model of accompanying the troops as they struggle down the road into battle, the emotional sky clouding for many of them. Even before we reach the field, we recognize signs of stress. Mary Livermore, a civilian who observed Northern soldiers en route to the front, said rookies displayed "boisterous enthusiasm," perhaps to allay nervousness, but men who had been under fire moved along "in a grim silence that was most oppressive." We might extrapolate that, as they approached the front, they recalled past encounters. For example, Louisiana soldier Will Pinkney, who went to war "devil-may-care, hearty, laughing, mischief loving," after fighting in the defense of New Orleans, where the garrison came to feel inadequately reinforced, became "woe begone, subdued, care worn, and sad!"[6]

As the sounds of distant battle swell, we notice the columns of marching men thinning down. Their ranks shrink partly through straggling due to the physical stress we examined in chapter two, with exhausted men dropping by the roadside. But some soldiers "skulk" away to dodge the coming fight. A consensus existed among veterans that the men who "played off" before an engagement could deplete a unit of half its strength. Edward Wightman, 9th New York, explained that the "beat," as a skulker was known, "is always missing in a fight. The beats of a regiment sometimes number one half." They hung around the rear of armies until fighting ended, often mingling with resigned, long-term stragglers too physically or mentally destitute ever to become proper soldiers again, yet afraid to disappear for good. Skulkers and stragglers (at some point the men and terms merge) often could not face battle because they had been there too often. The herds of displaced men milling in the rear area constituted an unfortunate consequence of placing quickly assembled and partly trained citizen armies in the field: "That was one of the features of the war due to the disordered, anomalous condition of things," recalled Confederate Philip D. Stephenson, 13th Arkansas, a veteran of the western theater.[7]

Soldiers labeled skulkers "coffee coolers," because men who stayed in rank got peremptory orders to move out and had to drink their coffee scalding, whereas coffee coolers lingered back, taking their time. Provost guards routinely forced men back into line at bayonet point, scaring many into the woods where pursuit became harder. Frank Wilkeson, 11th New York Battery, observed coffee coolers in Virginia during the latter stages of the war: "These men had dropped out of their commands as they approached the battle line, and had hidden in the woods. There were hundreds of them in the army at Cold Harbor. There were hundreds of them around Petersburg." Some men who had "lost their character" felt emboldened through desperation to act like banditti, preying on civilians in the wake of marching columns, stealing food and searching for liquor to drown their misery. Northern journalist Whitelaw Reid described Frederick, Maryland, plagued by malingerers on the eve of Gettysburg: "the town is full of stragglers, and the liquor shops are in full blast . . . drunken soldiers are making night hideous; all over the town they are trying to steal horses or sneak into unwatched private residences or are filling the air with the blasphemy of their drunken brawls."[8]

Generals railed against demoralized behavior. But enlisted men by no means accounted for all the booze swigged. Officers, who maintained their own liquor supplies, drank to stand the strain of responsibility and the constant personal exposure demanded by their combat role. According to regimental chaplain Joseph H. Twichell, Colonel George Hall of the 71st New York needed his drinks to start the morning: "Early in the day before he is braced up, he is as one deprived of a back-bone." Julius Gieseke, a lieutenant in the 4th Texas, complained that on the march his "Colonel stayed behind and tanked up considerably." Braxton Bragg arrested Generals George B. Crittenden and William Henry Carroll for drunkenness on the eve of Shiloh. Colonel William Dewey, 15th Iowa, approaching the same battle, would "wheel his horse around," away from observation, "and take some consolation through the neck of a pint bottle," reported Corporal C. F. Boyd. At Fredericksburg, Generals Orlando B. Wilcox and Samuel D. Sturgis became too inebriated to lead their troops. During the 1864 Virginia battles, General Thomas F. Meagher frequently became drunk as a "beast," sending his servant to find liquor, "& keeping his bed <u>wet & filthy</u>!" complained General Marsena Rudolph Patrick, the Army of the Potomac's top policeman.[9]

Tobacco, less immediately damaging to the constitution, served as another tonic for nervousness. Billy Yank happily traded food and coffee to Johnny Reb for good Southern chewing and smoking tobacco. The seemingly immovable General Ulysses S. Grant chain-smoked cigars (and would die of throat cancer). Major Sam Byers, 5th Iowa, observed the general in action outside Vicksburg, May 16, 1863, where he appeared "Calm as a Statue." Byers speculated that "possibly smoking so much tranquilized his nerves a little, and aided in producing calmness." Grant, he surmised drily, "was calm everywhere, but he also smoked everywhere."[10]

As the troops moved into combat positions, each stage of their deployment induced stress and nervous depletion. While the men waited, drawn up in firing lines, they faced a grueling physical and emotional test. Robbed of motion, they became subject to all manner of misgivings. Colonel Ardant Du Picq, a contemporary French soldier, noted that the physical strain and mental anguish that preceded "going in" drained away morale. Joseph E. Crowell, 13th New Jersey, felt the same. Every man got scared during a fight, he recalled, "But the worst part of it is just before you go in—when you're waiting to go in." At Antietam, the apprehension felt so palpable that "a peculiar atmosphere of impending disaster surrounded us that was indescribable."[11]

World War I troops experienced an equivalent situation waiting to go over the top in a big push. In both conflicts, being stationary under shellfire and unable to answer back intensified the anguish. The physical concussion and emotional terror of incoming rounds produced shell shock. Lieutenant William Nathaniel Wood, 19th Virginia, swore that, of "all mean things, the climax is reached when compelled to receive the fury of cannonading with no opportunity to inflict damage." Foreshadowing the Great War, prolonged trench warfare in 1864–65 provoked an acute sense of impotence. Soldiers before Petersburg in 1864 described trench work as promoting chronic tension through ceaseless vigilance, enforced immobility without rest, and a general apprehension that never went away. Cannonading could paralyze men, robbing them of volition. Private Wilbur Fisk, 2nd Vermont, described the effect of shelling on New Jersey men waiting in line at Fredericksburg: they "did not run, but their regiment became so completely broken up that but little could be expected of them." They hugged the ground, trembling, "too demoralized in the knees to be capable of effective service."[12]

For some volunteers, just one exposure to the experience of exploding shells proved too much. At the Battle of Cumberland Gap, 1862, a shell burst tossed Daniel Cupp, a Union rookie from Tazewell, Tennessee, into the air. He ran off and, afraid to go home, never went there again. Captain Jacob Roemer, 2nd New York Artillery, recorded that a lieutenant of the 34th New York Light Artillery lost his wits under artillery fire at Second Manassas. He crawled quivering under a bush and had to be removed gibbering from the field. A New Jersey boy, lightly wounded physically at Fredericksburg, nevertheless had waking nightmares according to his nurse, Louisa May Alcott: "often clutching my arm, to drag me from the vicinity of a bursting shell, or covering up his head to screen himself from a shower of [canister] shot." Billy Vaught, of the Washington Artillery (C.S.A.), got caught in a shrapnel blast at Marietta, Georgia, June 18, 1864. Suffering deafness and neuralgia, he went home to recover but never returned. Shell shock had morphed into PTSD.[13]

As an engagement developed and regiments became embroiled in musketry, stress from the uproar increased exponentially. Captain John William DeForest, 12th Connecticut, wrote vividly of the "incessant spattering and fiery spitting of musketry, with whistling and humming of bullets; and constant through all, the demoniacal yell advancing like the howl of an infernal tide. Bedlam, pandemonium, all the maniacs of earth and all the fiends of hell, seemed to have combined in riot amidst the crashings of storm and volcano." Men hyperventilated, and for many, the strain progressed to an irregular cardiac condition known as "soldier's heart." The thousands affected experienced "fits of fluttering cardiac action" and "cardiac irritability," with pulse rate fluctuations as high as 120–150, severe shortness of breath, even coughing up of blood. We can tell that many soldiers on the firing line succumbed to extreme emotion from the number of dropped muskets loaded multiple times without being discharged. Of

27,500 single-shot shoulder weapons gleaned from the field after Gettysburg, 12,000 had two unused loads in the barrel, 6,000 had three to ten rounds, one was stuffed with twenty-three. In other words, at least 18,000 men, in a highly distracted mental state, loaded and over-loaded their weapons, oblivious of never having fired them.[14]

As fierce fighting continued, men broke and ran. To prevent this, noncoms took station behind the ranks, backed by officers and sometimes cavalry, all authorized to bring down terrified bolters. In orders to his cavalry division during the Gettysburg campaign, General Jeb Stuart flatly stated: "let the artful dodger on the battlefield receive the retributive bullet of his gallant comrade." Captain Oliver Wendell Holmes Jr. 20th Massachusetts, stood behind his men at Fair Oaks in June 1862, swearing he would shoot any runners. He attributed his company's steadiness to his stand. Yet men still contrived to bolt, "skulking" behind trees, rocks, in barns, and other shelters. A *Richmond Weekly Dispatch* correspondent wrote from Sharpsburg, September 26, 1862: "Candor compels me to say that the straggling and desertion from our army far surpasses anything I had ever supposed possible."[15]

Fearful men tried to disguise their weakness. In the spring 1864 Wilderness fighting, Private Frank Wilkeson, 11th New York Battery, watched a colonel rubbing gunpowder on his face to appear combat blackened: "Instantly he was transformed from a trembling coward who lurked behind a tree into an exhausted brave taking a well-earned repose." Desperate men pretended to be injured. Private Joseph Dimmit Thompson, 38th Tennessee, told his wife that at Shiloh "some of our Company disgraced themselves by falling back, pretending to be very lame."[16]

Not just new recruits or "fresh fish" shied away when the elephant trampled. Only in myth do soldiers get used to combat and always stay steady under fire after surviving their first exposure. An exceedingly trying episode could break any man at any time. An American army report commissioned in World War II explains: "Each moment of combat imposes a strain so great that men will break down in direct relation to the intensity and duration of their exposure." Confederate John Dooley, 1st Virginia, concurred: "I must confess that the terrors of the battlefield grew not less as we advanced in the war."

He thought this held true for most soldiers, "For, in every battle they see so many new forms of death, see so many frightful and novel kinds of mutilation, see such varying fortunes in the tide of strife, and appreciate so highly their deliverance from destruction, that their dread of incurring like fearful peril unnerves them for each succeeding conflict." A private named Barrail, Washington Artillery (C.S.A.), fought through the Army of Tennessee's many campaigns until, in 1864, at Dalton, Georgia, he lost his nerve. Unable to carry on serving the guns, he crept under a caisson. A comrade wrote: "he seemed crushed."[17]

Sometimes, a whole company or more would head for the rear. At Perryville, Terrill's 33rd Union Brigade caved, officers without swords and men without guns stampeding for the rear. Troops coming up in support "just fell down on our faces, and let the cowardly herd pass over us," wrote Captain Wilberforce Nevin, 79th Pennsylvania. Such disasters usually occurred when an unexpected or overwhelming threat suddenly changed the course of action for the worse, creating mass panic and demolishing the discipline that normally held troops together. The catalyst might be a flanking movement or an unusually fierce frontal assault. Terror in such cases became infectious. Wilbur Fisk admitted he bolted along with others during the May 1864 Virginia fighting. He grew tired, hungry, and spooked when a dead friend fell on him. He felt "shamelessly demoralized," admitting, "My patriotism was well nigh used up, and so was I, till I had some refreshments." The last remark reminds us that many soldiers returned to their units after regaining their self-possession.[18]

Running could be a reaction to feeling asked to do too much: the demand appeared unreasonable. At Second Bull Run, N. K. Nichols and others in the 101st New York fought well until ordered to assault artillery: "they marched us up to Reb battery and we skidaddled then I fell out and kept out all day. Laid in the wood all night with 5 or 6 others." At times, we appear to witness a collective attack of PTSD. Colonel D. K. McRae's Confederate infantry broke at Antietam, burrowing into haystacks, traumatized by memories of being flanked at South Mountain. Collapsing morale could be a response to feeling betrayed, deliberately sacrificed by one's own generals. At Kennesaw Mountain, the 34th and 86th Illinois seemingly heard they would make only a feint and that the generals had scheduled the major attack elsewhere. Upon realizing they must in fact assault the heart of the Rebel position, the shock induced collective paralysis. They wandered the field aimlessly, clutching pots and pans. The enemy, recognizing a mass eclipse of the senses, held their fire. Union officer David Hunter Strother felt that, in such instances, an active imagination often caused loss of courage. "Men will coolly face a visible danger, who will stampede and disgrace themselves on some false report or fancied terror."[19]

One of the most notorious instances of troops degenerating into an hysterical mob took place at Shiloh where a spirited early morning Rebel attack caught Union troops still in camp and unawares. As Northern soldiers fled their tents, retreat became rout, terror infecting a large portion of the army. A demoralized crowd of thousands huddled on the riverbank, struggling to get on the steamers trying to land fresh troops. On one boat, Lieutenant Ambrose Bierce, 9th Indiana, noted that "this abominable mob had to be kept off her with bayonets." Northern war correspondent Henry Villard counted "an immense panic-stricken, uncontrollable mob" of some 7,000 to 10,000 men, including field officers, "all apparently bereft of soldierly spirit." Mass despair gripped them, stealing their will to fight. General Grant believed the refugees "would have been shot where they lay, without resistance, before they would have taken muskets and marched to the front to protect themselves."[20]

Charging into a hail of fire got harder each time feet had to be forced forward. At Fredericksburg, December 1862, Major Abner Small, 16th Maine, "saw one soldier falter repeatedly, bowing as if before a hurricane. He would gather himself together, gain his place in the ranks, and again drop behind. Once or twice he fell to his knees, and at last sank to the ground, still gripping his musket and bowing his head." Small refused to call the boy a coward, saying simply: "his legs would not obey him." At Kennesaw Mountain, June 1864, Lieutenant Albert Theodore Goodloe, 35th Alabama, observed the same inability to will a physical response: "There were some with whom the sense of danger was so oppressive that they had to be literally pushed along as we advanced upon the enemy, being overcome by a dread of death, which to them was very humiliating; patriots they were nevertheless and often fought like tigers when the battle was fully joined."[21]

—•◆•—

A soldier's resolution might fail in one episode but not in others. During an advance, Captain Crawford, 85th Illinois, saw a boy start for the rear. Asked if hit, he replied with tears in his eyes: "no, but I'm just scared to death, can't I go back." With unusual compassion, Crawford gave him a message to take back, and the next day the soldier looked right as rain. In the 1864 campaigns, when the butchery achieved unparalleled proportions, whole divisions could not step out. By June, said General Patrick, Union troops in Virginia failed to heed the charge and officers would not expose themselves to encourage the men.[22]

Fearful carnage left whole battalions emotionally drained. Contemporaries frequently used words like "dazed" and "despondent" to describe behavior after Shiloh, Antietam, Gettysburg, and Franklin. Numbed soldiers wandered around in a trance, temporarily deranged by horror. After Sharpsburg, Lee himself begged his stunned soldiers to get back in line. In a sampling of feelings expressed by soldiers of both sides in the aftermath of Shiloh, their first bloodbath, 75 percent felt "in despair."[23]

Many were undergoing what psychologist Pierre Janet calls "dissociation." That occurs when the mind shelters itself by temporarily blocking out the injurious source of trauma in the surrounding reality. According to Lieutenant Henry Livermore Abbott, 20th Massachusetts, his colonel, Raymond Lee, became "very much shaken in his intellects" by Antietam. The day after battle, he mounted his horse and, without leave of absence or explaining his purpose, apparently meandered off some ten miles. His men found the colonel "without a cent in his pocket, without having changed his clothes for 4 weeks, during all which time he had this horrible diarrhea."[24]

Disoriented soldiers might be suffering neurological damage from traumatic head injuries. Some healed over time, while others did not. Captain Frederick William Stowe, Harriet's son and an aide to General Adolph von Steinwehr, got hit in the head by shrapnel at Gettysburg. He never fully recovered his senses. Invalided out,

Fred endured depression and headaches. In 1867, he went through an alcohol recovery program. In 1871, he simply wandered off into oblivion. Private James Melton of the 7th Ohio, hit over the left ear, also became deranged. He disappeared from hospital. A shell burst overhead stunned Lieutenant Colonel John B. Estes, 44th Georgia, engaged at Ellison's Mill, Virginia, on June 26, 1862. The blast addled his brains, although he showed signs of recovery over time. Surgeons hospitalized the men discussed above, while others remained in the ranks despite being "lost in character." John Bumgardner, 26th Indiana Light Artillery, got knocked down by concussion from a shell blast. The medical officer diagnosed him as fit to carry on, yet he had lost his reason, crying out, "There they come men," when no enemy was in sight, and "run boys run they are after us."[25]

Astounding numbers left the ranks during heavy campaigning. After Fredericksburg, the woods filled with Union stragglers; a little later, during the infamous Mud March, a contemporary estimate put the AWOL at 3,000 officers and 82,000 other ranks. On the Rebel side, Lee blamed straggling for the curtailment of his 1862 Maryland campaign, telling Charles Squires, commanding the Washington Artillery: "The infantry, sir, are straggling, they are straggling," adding, "Captain, our men are acting badly." The government in Richmond calculated 40,000 men had left the line. Lee again charged that absenteeism thwarted his Pennsylvania offensive, asserting, "The number of desertions from the army is so great and still continues to such an extent that unless some cessation of them can be caused I fear success in the field will be severely endangered." In the Union camp, provost marshal General Patrick opined that, unless Meade "does something to keep better discipline in his command, there will be few troops to put into action." He complained that "the whole country is full of stragglers."[26]

Senior officers generally shared Patrick's severe attitude to dereliction of duty. After Malvern Hill, Colonel Francis Bartow berated soldiers as misfits and cowards who reported unfit, although physically unharmed. When a man asked permission to drop out, Bartow "cursed and swore at him," then "began to punch him with his fist," and finally ordered him out of sight as "not fit to be with my brave men." Confederate General William Dorsey Pender called men in

nervous collapse a "filthy unprincipled set of villains." Many temporarily stunned by combat returned to their units, but not all. A Confederate surgeon wrote after Gettysburg that ten North Carolinians,
previously of good report, had lit out for home. A pursuing police
patrol captured seven, subsequently sentenced to be court-martialed
and shot.[27]

Authorities failed to appreciate that most troops, if kept in a
combat zone for long enough, continuing on without rest, inevitably
reach the end of their mental and physical tethers. Military doctors
identified this condition in World War II as combat exhaustion. Field
studies of the 1940s showed that initially a soldier's experience and
competence rose over time to a peak of efficiency, but then dropped
off quickly to final breakdown unless positive intervention occurred,
such as a furlough. Physical deprivation and repeated exposure to
trauma downgrade bodily strength and mental resilience. New York
Private David L. Thompson recalled struggling with himself to stay
in line at Antietam. He explained, with admirable understatement,
that "Between the physical fear of going forward and the moral fear
of going back, there is a predicament of exceptional awkwardness."[28]

Endocrinologist Robert Sapolsky provides a scientific context:
under stress, all animals secrete hormones. This helps in weathering
a crisis, but ultimately leads to a kind of "emotional suicide" when
the immune system becomes degraded. The deterioration appears in
physical symptoms like blood thickening and clots, resulting in heart
attack and stroke, along with a steady loss of brain function, possibly
ending in dementia. In lay terms, British psychiatrist and combat
veteran Lord Moran notes in *Anatomy of Courage* (1987) that each
soldier owns moral capital in a personal bank deposit. Combat makes
withdrawals on that account until it is empty.[29]

The results may be seen in repeated descriptions of combat-
exhausted soldiers as listless, lethargic, vacant. Edward Wightman,
9th New York, described the multitude of army stragglers as "mis-
erably worn. Their countenances are sunken and melancholy and
indifferent almost to stolidity." During the vicious fighting around
Spotsylvania, Virginia, spring 1864, when many men bankrupted
psychologically, a lieutenant in the 15th New Jersey wrote that the
troops, "are listless and feel doomed," adding that "day after day we

stupidly and drearily wait the order that summons us to the dreadful work." A senior officer, Colonel Charles S. Wainwright, chief of artillery for the Army of the Potomac's 5th Corps, recorded he had never seen such lethargic, sleepy men.[30]

High rank gave no immunity to the degenerative effects of repeated combat exposure. Libbie Custer recalled meeting, in Fall 1864, "a tired General [Alfred A.] Torbet," who seemed without "life and animation." Basil Duke, Confederate General John Hunt Morgan's right-hand man, described his chief in 1864 as depleted by command responsibility, imprisonment, and longing for his wife Mattie. He appeared, said Duke, "greatly changed. His face wore a weary, careworn expression and his manner was destitute of its former ardor and enthusiasm." Part of Morgan's problem lay in the perennial soldier's dilemma of divided loyalties: a grinding tension between the obligation to die for the cause and responsibility to live for loved ones.[31]

We often most clearly see the progress of combat fatigue in generals' lives because their careers have been relatively well documented. When the war began, Confederate General Richard S. Ewell at times agonized over his share of responsibility for the killing. After Malvern Hill, staff officer Moxley Sorrel found him in a shed piled with bodies. The general sat doubled up on the floor, hands clasped to his head, sobbing, and beside himself at the result of Lee's frontal attack. He asked: "Can you tell me why we had five hundred men [from his command alone] killed dead on the field yesterday?" (Of the same engagement, D. H. Hill commented bitterly: "It was not war. It was murder.") Nevertheless, Ewell continued to serve effectively until badly wounded in the Second Manassas campaign, where he lost his left leg below the thigh. Thereafter, the general became increasingly unhappy about the war's human costs. This possibly affected his command performance. Although he had his defenders, detractors accused him of lacking the aggressiveness that might have crushed Meade on July 1 at Gettysburg.[32]

British military observer Colonel Arthur Fremantle met Ewell before the battle. He described the general as exhibiting "a haggard, sickly face: having so lately lost a leg above the knee, he is still a complete cripple, and falls off his horse occasionally." Fremantle noted Ewell employed the classic military method of coping with stress, being a "great swearer." The general performed unevenly in the Spring 1864 campaign, shock at the loss of Stuart and Longstreet's wounding adding to his nervous strain. Lee observed his subordinate beating runners at Spotsylvania with the flat of his sword, swearing fearfully, his composure blown. Appalled by any man's loss of character, Lee chided Ewell: "How can you expect to control these men when you have lost control of yourself? If you cannot repress your excitement, you had better retire." Seven days later, Ewell lost all presence of mind and lay prostrate on the ground. Lee removed him from command.[33]

George B. McClellan's chronic over-caution and habitual overestimation of the odds against him to excuse inaction have been well documented. Even though we cannot precisely gauge how far these traits constituted defense mechanisms against committing troops to the slaughter, command stress appears in the mix. "I am tired of the sickening sight of the battlefield, with its mangled corpses & poor suffering wounded!" McClellan wrote to his wife, Ellen, during heavy Peninsula fighting, June 1862. "Victory has no charms for me when purchased at such cost." In a later letter he declared: "Every poor fellow that is killed or wounded almost haunts me." The stress became so unbearable that he apparently retreated into dissociation. On June 30, as Lee launched an all-out attack at Glendale Crossroads to crack the Union army, McClellan and his staff boarded the gunboat Galena and sailed off up the James. They stayed away all day, inspecting river defenses, no job for the commanding general. In the Fall campaign, McClellan suffered painful neuralgia attacks from South Mountain through Antietam. He wrote Ellen that "the want of rest and anxiety" wore him down. On the key morning of battle, September 17, he kept to his tent until 7 a.m., leaving his generals to pace. Suffering severe neuralgia, he failed to renew hostilities on the 18th. Lincoln's removal of McClellan may have precluded a breakdown.[34]

Two heroes of Gettysburg proved less fortunate. George Pickett fell in love with a young belle, LaSalle Corbell, in September 1861. Their relationship deepened his wish for peace, adding to the pain felt by a West Pointer over a classmates' war. "Oh, my darling," he wrote, "war and its results did not seem so awful till the love for you came. Now—now I want to love and bless and help everything, and there are no foes—no enemies—just love and longing for you." After the attack on Cemetery Ridge shattered his division, several officers observed the general staring into the distance, weeping uncontrollably. In September, with Pickett's performance faltering, Lee replaced him in field command.

General Gouverneur Kemble Warren, a Northern hero of Gettysburg, who commanded the Army of the Potomac's artillery train, was the first to grasp the tactical importance of putting troops on Little Round Top, key to the Union left flank. Rushing units forward, he secured the position, preventing potential disaster. But mounting losses as the fighting ground on made Warren irascible and unpredictable, his condition made worse by heavy drinking, all symptoms of combat exhaustion. Colonel Wainwright described him thus at Cold Harbor, June 6, 1864: "He appears to have sunk into a sort of lethargic sulk, sleeps a great part of the time, and says nothing to anyone. I think at times that these fits of his must be the result of a sort of insanity." Meade felt obliged to replace Warren.[35]

Even vehement exponents of the spirited offense suffered guilt over their part in the killing. Joshua Lawrence Chamberlain became famous for his madcap bayonet charge down the slope of Little Round Top. Nevertheless, he agonized over the fate of men he had sent to die, and two months after Gettysburg went home to recover from nervous prostration. Returning to his command for the last Virginia campaigns, the general precipitately ordered the 18th Pennsylvania to assault a strong Rebel position at Five Forks in January 1865. As a stretcher party carried the 18th's dying leader to the rear, the colonel cried out accusingly: "General, I have carried out your wishes." This imputation of his personal accountability struck Chamberlain to the core with horror: "What dark misgivings searched me as I took the import of these words!"[36]

John Bell Hood, a vigorous proponent of offense as the decisive tactical weapon, still grieved at times over the human cost. By 1865, he appeared quite physically and mentally threadbare. Mary Boykin Chesnut described him at a social gathering in Richmond as "perfectly abstracted, was gazing in the fire—his face livid, spots of perspiration on his head. He was back evidently in some moment of his bitter trial. Willie Preston's death—the fields of dead at Franklin—the panic at Nashville. Who can tell—but the agony of his face was fearful." Officers she knew said they had seen Hood on previous occasions staring into the flames with the same tortured expression. The general probably had PTSD brought on by the weight of fatigue, death, and defeat. (After the war, when rested and partially restored, Hood would strongly reassert his faith in the offense at all costs.) Less well-known generals whose mental resources failed included Confederate William Ward, whose troops called him "Old Shaky" because of his tremors. General Philip St. George Cocke, C.S.A., made sickly and despondent by the burden of brigade command, killed himself during Christmas 1861. General Francis E. Patterson, Army of the Potomac, faced court-martial for cowardice after he begged off sick before battle; disgraced, he shot himself in November 1862. Confederate General G. W. Smith suffered a nervous breakdown after Seven Pines.[37]

Even seeming monuments to stoicism such as Grant and Meade could approach the edge of sanity. In the 1864 fighting, both showed vile temper and skewed judgment. Historian Fletcher Pratt concluded: "The ceaseless vigilance, the strain of daily battles, was beginning to tell at Union headquarters, everyone's nerves were frayed. Grant gruffed at the adjutants; Meade took a perverse pleasure in making his staff uncomfortable, colonels hardly dared to speak to him." As a result of one snarling exchange, Grant testily ordered Meade to assault on June 3, a blunder costing 7,000 casualties in ten minutes. By August 18, General Marsena Patrick concluded ruefully: "Grant is not at all well, & there are fears that he is breaking down." Grant and Meade held on. General James Ledlie could not. While his troops fought over the bloody Crater at Petersburg, July 30, 1864, Ledlie, his resolution shattered, stayed in his bombproof drinking medicinal alcohol.[38]

Extreme emotional stress resulted in sleep deprivation. Nightmares, particularly common after major actions, wrecked the restorative value of rest. "Even when I sleep," moaned Major Charles Harvey Brewster, 10th Massachusetts, "I hear the whistling of the shells and the shouts and groans, and to sum it up in two words it is <u>horrible</u>." A friend noted that Private Heber Wells, 13th New Jersey, had endured "a very bad attack of nightmare" in September 1862. "All who had taken part in the battle of Antietam were still thinking of the horrible sights during the day and dreaming of it at night," he added. Today, we tend to focus on the psychological roots of trauma, but Victorians too often looked for a more tangible, physical root cause. Nurse Hannah Ropes, working at a Union hospital in Georgetown, near D.C., recorded a patient enduring habitual nightmares. She recorded that "as they all are, he was on the battlefield, struggling to get away from the enemy." But she did not diagnose the condition as originating in emotional trauma, citing instead a lung wound that she thought had lessened blood circulation to the brain. In fact, the soldier's intellect even more than his body had been wounded. Future explorer and Confederate soldier Henry Morton Stanley wrote of Shiloh's butcher's bill: "I can never forget the impression that those wide-open dead eyes made on me." It became for Stanley a haunting common to many veterans.[39]

The descent into combat exhaustion could be gradual, akin to clockwork winding down. On the other hand, one traumatic event might trigger total collapse, like a tight spring snapping. One Union soldier served well until he saw his father killed in the ranks beside him at Fredericksburg. Then, his nerve failed. Although sentenced to die, the soldier received a pardon from the president. In another episode, Union Private Albert Frank had just offered his canteen to a friend when a shell splattered the man's brains everywhere. In shock, Frank ran about, screaming. Comrades calmed him, but by evening he was making whining shell sounds and repeating, "Frank is killed." When he showed no improvement, the surgeon declared him insane, and commitment to a government asylum followed. We cannot say why another man might manage to hold onto his sanity under such conditions. Private Sam Watkins, 1st Tennessee (C.S.A.), breakfasting when a shell hit Lieutenant Whittacker, standing nearby, retained self-control. Watkins later wrote of Whittacker's horrid death: "His brains fell in the plate from which we were sopping, and his head fell in my lap, deluging my face and clothes with his blood."[40]

Sam still did not crack, even when, after Murfreesboro, he witnessed the execution of a juvenile named Wright. The boy had to sit two hours on his coffin in a wagon while watching his grave being dug. "He had his hat pulled down over his eyes, and was busily picking at the ends of his fingers." Finally, the lad was tied to a post. As the volley hit him, he cried, "O, O, God." Sickened, Watkins "turned away and thought how long, how long will I have to witness these things." In the Army of Tennessee, quite often. But Watkins held onto his sanity, fighting steadily through bloodbaths like Shiloh, Murfreesboro, and Kennesaw Mountain. Only infrequently did he fall into a dream-like state, suffering mild dissociation. Nevertheless, he did show symptoms of PTSD after the war. By 1881, the butchery at Franklin remained so vivid that, he admitted, "My flesh trembles, and creeps, and crawls when I think of it today. My heart almost ceases to beat at the horrid recollection." Still, he had beaten the devil, managing to live a normal life.[41]

We can isolate some positive and negative coping factors. Youth could prove a liability. Eighteen-year-olds formed the largest single cohort in both armies, a crucial manpower pool, yet adolescents often lacked the emotional and intellectual maturity to cope with brute experience. They accounted for a disproportionate share of desertions and temporary absences. Religion offered many soldiers, young and old, a positive coping mechanism when confronting fear of death. Captain Thaddeus J. Hyatt, 12th Ohio, wrote home before the Third Battle of Winchester, 1864: "Sometimes, when I think how you will miss me at home it is hard to be entirely willing never to see you and the boys again but . . . we will meet again in the better land." Faith in God's will could help rationalize the slaughter. "I hope for the best and trust in Him who wields the destiny of all," wrote Sergeant Hamlin Alexander Coe, 19th Michigan.[42]

But, for many, the finality of sudden, unnatural death left small room for comfort. "I shall never forget how awfully I felt on seeing for the first time a man killed in battle," wrote Sergeant Leander Stillwell, 16th Illinois. "Only a few seconds ago that man was alive and well, and now he was lying on the ground, done for, forever." Prolonged butchery proved hard to reconcile with divine providence or benevolent human agency. "I long to go to some quiet place to rest body & mind," wrote Private James M. Bimford, 21st Virginia, reflecting on the August 1862 slaughter. "I am sick of seeing dead men, and men's limbs torn from their bodies." Killing hardly seemed sacred work. Captain Nathaniel Southgate Shaler, 5th Kentucky Artillery (U.S.), described a group of officers watching a sharpshooter take down a handsome young enemy officer sitting on a roof sketching their dispositions, noting weaknesses. The sniper drills the boy through the head: "As the face / Slips out of sight, we see the startled look / That comes upon it when the man knows death." This killing looks much like assassination, murder. The marksman stalks away, taking care "he does not look / Into our eyes," and the officers, too, "Keep eyes from others' faces and seek out / Some trifling thing to do." In Shaler's lexicon, fighting seems neither holy nor noble, but "Hard, brutal might, that bears the soul right down." War is hell's part, not heaven's, insists the captain: "Sherman was right—he knew."[43]

In the early stages of conflict, the chivalric ethic sanctified the cause, bracing men for combat. On the eve of Antietam, Colonel George Freeman Noyes, on the staff of General Abner Doubleday, could still depict a moonlit march as magically transforming the army: "No longer Yankee soldiers of the nineteenth century, we were for the nonce knights of the ancient chivalry, pledged to a holier cause and sworn to a nobler issue than Coeur de Lion [King Richard I of England] himself ever dreamed of." But muck and blood eventually blotted out Arthurian images. Only the most romantic, like Jeb Stuart, clung to rhetorical gallantry. When a young favorite, John Pelham, commanding his horse artillery, died in action, Stuart admitted to his wife, "You know how his death distresses me." Yet he could still rationalize the loss as transcendent: "He fell, the noblest of sacrifices, on the altar of his country, to whose glorious service he had dedicated his life from the beginning of the war."[44]

Loyalty to one's comrades could act as a cement holding a mentally ragged man together (even though, as we have seen, the glue might become unstuck when a whole group bolted). Joseph Hooker understood the importance of bonding. Inheriting the Army of the Potomac after the disastrous winter of 1862–63, he faced a continuous AWOL rate of 25 percent. The general borrowed a leaf from the British army's morale book. Small redcoat forces patrolled an immense empire by maintaining unit cohesion. They instilled regimental pride or esprit de corps through special badges and other unique regalia. Hooker followed suit, giving his corps and divisions their own distinctive insignia.[45]

He also regularized the furlough system, the arbitrary nature of which became a universal source of grievance in the armies. Ahead of his time, Hooker realized that prior intervention could prevent radical breakdowns. A limited rest proved efficacious in mentally rehabilitating men rendered temporarily exhausted by combat. The alternative, waiting until they needed permanent committal to a mental hospital, squandered manpower and meant personal disgrace in an era when mental illness equaled a shameful lack of character. (Some nurses observed that deserters on their wards tended to die, having lost self-respect and the will to live. Cornelia Hancock wrote with unusual perception: "The mind has such an effect upon the body, we cannot get them to rally a mite.") Unfortunately, Hooker's leadership confidence buckled at Chancellorsville and, after he left army command, unfairness in furloughing returned, leaves being used as a blunt instrument to reward reenlistment, while denied to men who refused to soldier another term.[46]

Desire not to let down the home folks, and fear of exposure if one failed, also kept some boys in the ranks. H. J. Hightower, 20th Georgia, serving under Longstreet, wrote, April 1863: "I had rather dye on the battle field than to disgrace my self & the hole family." Thus, when Private James Newton's company commander, 11th Connecticut, skulked in battle, men branded the officer a coward in letters home. After a lieutenant from a prominent family deserted his men in the storming of Fort Donelson, he received a knee wound as he bolted. His bitter father wrote the boy in hospital that he would be better dead, having publicly shamed the family. Cognizant of his disgrace and having no moral recourse, the son refused all medical treatment and died of septic poisoning. The surgeon speculated that the boy's stoic demonstration of character while in hospital redeemed him from the charge of cowardice. Combat had temporarily undone his resolution, a lapse for which he had now atoned. Feigning illness to avoid action also brought the offender into contempt with the service and the community. Captain Richard Lee, 8th Virginia (U.S.), described as "battle weary," used noxious substances to pretend violent nausea. Court-martial and local disgrace followed his exposure.[47]

Desperate men resorted to self-mutilation. After a soldier in Parson's Texas Cavalry Brigade shot his own hand off "to get to go back home," Sergeant Edwin Fay summed up the general feeling: he had not been "thought by most persons to be in his right mind." Usually, such acts resulted in dramatic consequences. A culprit might be paraded before his regiment and degraded, then turned away to face the censure at home. Sam Cobb of Illinois ran in his first battle and then allegedly wounded himself. His reputation lost, he moved west. By early 1863, deliberate self-mutilation became common enough to stop the Union from granting discharges. At the same time, sympathy among civilians for men resisting service actually began to increase as casualties ballooned and injustices in the recruiting system became apparent. In some communities, potential draftees might blow their trigger finger off without facing ostracism.[48]

Alcohol could help a "played out" soldier hang on, but this habit also fostered dependence and debilitation. Drink could be dangerous for men in the ranks, releasing violent currents running below the surface of angry and frustrated combat veterans. Private Dennis Lanaghan, 4th Pennsylvania, resented being ordered to march in the dust behind a wagon as punishment for intoxication. When he balked, a major ordered him roped to the vehicle. Later, still under the influence, Lanaghan killed the officer, a crime for which he received the death penalty. Finally, boozing to hold up under stress often proved to be a double-edged blade, turning into an agonizing form of suicide. Bob James, brother of Henry and William, served as an officer in the 55th Massachusetts. He saw hard fighting and ended as an alcoholic, unable to surmount his combat experience.[49]

Drawing enemy fire afforded a quicker end to the misery. Winslow Homer caught this in his 1864 painting *Defiance: Inviting a Shot before Petersburg, Virginia*. In the picture, a Rebel has climbed onto a trench parapet, exposing himself to a sniper. Such death-seeking acts became quite common in the trenches. Despite cultural and religious sanctions against self-murder, soldiers escaped through suicide. Men lay in front of trains or blew their heads off. On December 12, 1864, General Patrick recorded the death of a soldier in the 184th New York: "He seemed to have laid himself down, intentionally, about 50 feet in front of the locomotive—He was terribly mashed to pieces of course." A sergeant in Harker's Union brigade, ordered into the assault on Kennesaw, entered his tent and shot himself.[50]

———————•◦•———————

A commissioned officer who could stand no more might resign. Captain Oliver Wendell Holmes Jr. averred during the 1864 Virginia fighting that "many a man has gone crazy since this campaign begun from the terrible pressure on mind & body." He refused promotion and resigned, saying worry about his survival "demoralizes me as it does any nervous man—and now I honestly think the duty of fighting has ceased for me." Conversely, rankers had no such choice. They might not want to re-enlist when their terms expired, but their service could be arbitrarily extended, and they faced pressure to carry on from officers and community leaders. For many, then, running away appeared to offer the only escape from ongoing mental torture. But this could end badly as high commands, faced by steeply rising desertion rates, resorted to drastic measures.[51]

By February 1863, General Henry W. Halleck, at Union headquarters in D.C., calculated that one-third of all military personnel were absent, some on furlough but most without permission. By 1864, Grant estimated that 80 percent of recruits never made it to the front. Many who did arrive, he told Meade, quickly surrendered: "The ease with which our men of late fall into the hands of the enemy would indicate that they are willing prisoners." Confederates in the west began surrendering at least by Chattanooga, if not before. The hemorrhaging continued in all theaters. By May 1864, the Confederate Bureau of Conscription confessed it could no longer cope with the legions infesting the countryside; 10,000 had gone AWOL from Leonidas Polk's command alone. Finally, the Rebel forces melted like snow. After Cedar Creek in the east and Franklin in the west, Southern armies simply disintegrated.[52]

Authorities did what they could, inflicting carefully orchestrated rituals of humiliation and pain, grim theatricals to awe the troops. They lashed prisoners or branded them with the letter D. Private Benjamin Jackson, 33rd Alabama, wrote from Tupelo, Mississippi, in July 1862, about one punishment parade: "I saw three men who, after their shirts were taken off, were tied to a post with their hands stretched as high as they could reach, were given thirty-nine lashes on their naked backs with a leather strap tacked onto a stick. After their beating, the left side of their head was shaved and they were drummed out of the service to the tune of 'Yankee Doodle.' It was a bad looking sight. They had deserted and gone home."[53]

Increasingly, the punishment exacted became death by firing squad. As we have seen earlier, executions afforded grisly spectacles, open-air theaters of the macabre. There exist many descriptions of these occasions. Walt Whitman, for example, recorded the shooting of William Grover, a nineteen-year-old boy who ran after fighting through twelve battles had made him "simple." The killing, adjudged Whitman in a telling phrase, appeared a "horrid sarcasm."[54]

To understand official acts that appear to us as inhuman, we must remember the Victorians had no field of adolescent psychology: they thought juveniles should act as adults. Wearing the uniform imposed all the obligations of manhood. In 1842, Commander Alexander Slidell Mackenzie, on the U.S. training brig *Somers,* hanged from the yardarm Midshipman Philip Spencer, eighteen, son of the then Secretary of War, along with two seamen. After a peremptory drumhead court-martial found them guilty of mutiny because of their silly fantasy talk about piracy, the three stood atop cannons, there to be strung up to the mainmast and choked to death. Today, we might consider the victims' behavior merely sophomoric, meriting counseling and a stiff reprimand. In the Civil War, Sherman demonstrated a similarly harsh attitude to deserters and stragglers under his command, representing the common position of senior officers. In Special Field Order No. 17, the general asserted: "The only proper fate of such miscreants is that they be shot as common enemies to their profession and country." Sherman's own breakdown under pressure early in the war, requiring a period away from active duty, failed to make him sympathetic to those who could not get leave for emotional duress.[55]

Harsh punishment failed as a deterrent. Ella Lonn, an early analyst, noted in 1928 that severity of penalty and desertion rates increased concurrently. A 2003 study concurs. It notes that, of several hundred thousand deserters, authorities seized about a third. The capital punishment inflicted upon many of these had no practical effect on the desertion rate and may have fostered disaffection through inciting resentment. A separate analysis has examined the increased number of capital punishments in 1863. Desertion made up 147 of 267 capital cases. Yet the rate of running accelerated; the study conjectures that repetitive executions probably dulled the impact on witnesses.[56]

For boys who died tied to a stake or seated on a coffin, the road to war, often embarked on exuberantly and in hopes of earning distinction, ended in a dishonorable death none had anticipated. If news of their true fate reached home, the burden of family grief at their loss now bore an added incubus of dishonor, accompanied by bewilderment at what could have gone wrong in the soldier's course to warrant such harsh judicial retribution.

— CHAPTER SIX —

DEPRIVATIONS AND DISLOCATIONS

×

IN THE EARLY DAYS OF CONFLICT, AS THE SOLDIERS PREPARE to march off along the road to war, we hear bands playing jaunty melodies; we see boys grinning in their new uniforms; girls waving flags; and older relatives standing stiffly proud. Yet even in these heady times a subdued murmur of stress begins, as the dusty columns disappear into the distance, because families remain to face economic and emotional deprivation. The fighting will impose universal strains, even on comfortable middle-class households. For instance, college professor Joshua Lawrence Chamberlain fails to consult his wife about volunteering. In retaliation, she travels abroad while he fights. Lesser folk have more pragmatic reasons to resent war's interference. When, in July 1861, young Elisha Rhodes tells his mother he wants to enlist, she begs him not to go, arguing that he brings in the only family income. "My mother went about with tears in her eyes, while I felt disappointment that I could not express and therefore nursed my sorrow in silence." She finally breaks down and lets him go, a domestic drama acted out repeatedly in America's homes. In this chapter, we shall look at the many hardships inflicted by the war on civilians of all ages and classes, of both races and genders, in North and South.[1]

———◆———

War's allure diminished significantly for many when the fighting unexpectedly dragged on. In November 1863, Confederate government clerk John B. Jones wrote candidly: "How often have I and thousands in our youth expressed the wish to have lived during the first Revolution, or rather to have partaken of the excitements of war!" But reality had checkmated romance: "Now we see and feel the horrors of war, and we are unanimous in the wish, if we survive to behold again the balmy sunshine of peace, that neither we nor our posterity may ever more be spectators of or participants in another war."[2]

Wartime shortages and consequent price inflation quickly undercut the buying power of privates' pay, fixed by the prewar national government at a ceiling of $13 per month. One estimate suggests the Northern cost of living soared 200 percent just between April and December 1861. In November 1862, Governor Oliver P. Morton of Indiana unsuccessfully petitioned Congress to raise soldiers' wages, arguing that over the preceding fifteen months food prices had risen 60 percent and other necessities 120 percent. Black families found their predicament dire because soldiers of color initially earned about half that of whites.[3]

In both sections, chronic arrears in pay worsened want. One poor widow complained to President Lincoln: "I haint got no pay as was cummin toe him and none of his bounty munney." Confederate General Patrick Cleburne, serving in the Army of Tennessee, remonstrated with General Braxton Bragg, in September 1862, that his brigade had received no pay in nine months. Family distress weighed on soldiers. Herman Clarke, 117th New York, asserted that "men often after getting a letter from home go to the officers and enquire if there isn't some way to get pay. Their families write they are suffering for want of money; some are turned out of doors." State and local governments, along with private associations such as churches and women's groups, tried with differing success to help the destitute. Chronic inflation in the Confederacy drove Mississippi in 1862, for example, to appropriate $500,000 for soldiers' families, while Arkansas spent $62,000. Unfortunately, potential recipients often did not know they could get aid or how to apply for it. This problem particularly affected those in isolated rural counties with low literacy rates or areas cut off by the Yankees.[4]

Leading socialites in both sections frequently headed relief agencies. They unintentionally discouraged applications by patronizing the poor. Aristocratic lawyer George Strong, an officer of the civilian U.S. Sanitary Commission, working to keep soldiers in the field and their families above water, nevertheless blamed much of the want on soldiers' dissolute habits. Instead of sending money home, he said, wages got "expended in the purchase of bad pies and gut-rot whiskey." Strong, who had bought a substitute to avoid service, would not know how such small treats and consolations cheered up troops in the field. In fact, research suggests that most men with dependents did in fact send pay home. But, notes one study ominously, being without money meant soldiers "blithely relying on foraging and pillage to supply what extra comforts they hoped to enjoy." Since ancient times, armies had been obliged to plunder the populace to augment their pay, ironically adding to the people's misery.[5]

In a brief conflict such as most expected, deprivation would have been temporary. But in a long war of attrition, shortages cut deep, particularly in the Confederacy. Unlike the North, where economic hardship fell mainly on the poor, all Southern classes suffered materially. The South lacked an advanced industrial base, the region being primarily an exporter of agricultural products, importing manufactured goods in return from the North and Europe. The requirements of the military, together with the cutting off of supplies from outside markets, created civilian scarcity, driving up prices astronomically. Captain Robert Kean, a Richmond bureaucrat, calculated in 1863 that his $3,000 salary had the equivalent buying power to a $700 income in 1860. Fresh meat had leapt from 10 cents to $1.00; bacon 20 cents to $1.00; coal $1.00 a bucket, up from 20 cents. As early as May 1861, a prosperous Charleston girl noted that butter, usually imported from the North, had grown too expensive to purchase. Clothing fabric, along with much else, nearly left the shelves.[6]

Blockade runners made up some deficiencies, importing luxuries for consumers who could afford them, but many, even of the better classes, simply made do. Emma LeConte, daughter of a Columbia, South Carolina, chemistry professor, wrote that, as late as January 1865, bazaar "tables are loaded with fancy articles—brought through the blockade, or manufactured by the ladies." However, she kept her own dress modest: "My underclothing is of coarse unbleached homespun, such as we gave the negroes formerly, only much coarser." She knit stockings and wore calico dresses, save for two old silks, "carefully preserved for great occasions and which do not look shabby for the simple reason that all the other old silks that still survive the war are in the same state of decay."[7]

Shortages deepened when retreating Rebel soldiers cleaned out shops to deny the Yankees anything. Whatever they overlooked fell to the enemy. Private Thomas F. Dornblaser, 7th Pennsylvania cavalry, noted in Dalton, Georgia, in May 1864, that "a number of infantrymen, unrestrained by their officers, were bursting open stores and rifling them of their scanty contents." It might appear trivial for us to dwell on dress but many societies use fashion to define individual identity and class status. Although some citizens and soldiers made butternut and coarse cloth a proud symbol of endurance, to constantly wear threadbare and homespun became demoralizing.[8]

Scarcities of medicines, reserved first for the army, quickly became acute in the South. Only in 1864 did the Confederate government order blockade runners to devote 50 percent of cargo space to necessities, including pharmaceuticals. The Lincoln government listed medicines as contraband, their confiscation intensifying civilian deprivation. Emma Holmes, from a prominent Charleston family, endured, without anesthetic, the extraction of a rotten tooth that came away in fragments. She also talked frequently of child deaths from convulsions, probably brought on by malnutrition and a lack of prophylactics against disease. An anonymous woman complained that infants sick with fevers died for want of remedies, when twenty grams of quinine could save them.[9]

The diet of nonfarming households, like the Holmes family, quickly suffered. "Hominy, cornbread, & occasionally a little peas or eggs & still more rarely a scrap of bacon, is our ordinary bill of fare," wrote a girl in May 1864. "We live tolerably poorly. Two meals a day," recorded Miss LeConte, living through the last days of war. "Dinner consists of a very small piece of meat, generally beef, a few potatoes and a dish of hominy and a pone of corn bread." But, she added gamely, "We have no reason to complain, so many families are so much worse off." Country folk might fare better, but their produce became subject to government conscription, and soldiers ruthlessly plundered farmers. The primary victims lived in the major war zones, the South and

Border States. (Only rarely, as in Lee's 1863 invasion of Pennsylvania, did Northern citizens feel the full brunt of military scavenging.) For example, cavalry from both armies stripped Kentucky's horse farms to replace clapped-out mounts slaughtered each night like so much "night soil," in E. L. Doctorow's phrase. An anonymous Marylander in 1864 complained to Surgeon Thomas F. Wood, 3rd North Carolina, that "the Yankees come and take my horses and the Rebels come and take my wheat, and I do not know who is my friend." As sectional allegiance eroded, farmers tried to hide their stock from marauding soldiers of both governments, often unsuccessfully.[10]

In theory, military authorities instructed army units to pay for what they took and leave families enough to live on. But, despite chivalric rhetoric about protecting the weak and defenseless, soldiers often acted less like noble knights than callous mercenaries. Private Frank Wilkeson, 11th New York Battery, remembered, in spring 1864, a pale-faced Virginia woman "whose little children clung to her skirts as she stood in her kitchen door appealing to the Union soldiers not to strip her of stores as she had children to feed." Her plea fell on deaf ears. In spring 1862, Lucy Buck, nineteen-year-old daughter of a leading merchant and farmer, recorded her father's despair when Union forces stripped his Front Royal, Virginia, farm of food, fencing, and livestock. "He could only walk the pavement with folded arms and drooping head looking helplessly on the scene of desolation." Private William A. Fletcher, 5th Texas, in March 1864 witnessed a Southern woman trying to defend her larder of corn and bacon against soldiers from her own side. Wielding an axe gained her nothing: she lost every morsel.[11]

Civilians hated cavalry, deemed the worst predators because their mobility allowed them to sweep a whole region. Lieutenant Benjamin F. McIntyre, 19th Iowa, serving in Missouri, late in 1862, complained of the license allowed cavalry: "go in any direction you may for miles you will find their horses hitched near every dwelling. They scour the country in every direction and generally help themselves to anything they wish." James Brownlow, commanding the 1st Tennessee Cavalry (C.S.A.), operating around Chattahoochee, Georgia, in July

1864, admitted that his unit "live on the 'fat of the land.' We have potatoes, berries, honey, and chickens for nearly every meal." William Davidson, 5th Texas Mounted, said the troopers "ransack the whole country for ten miles around," taking pigs, poultry, "sheep, goats, and even old ganders."[12]

Sherman's "bummers" provided the most lasting images of licensed looting. Yankee foragers stripped a zone fifty miles wide after the general decided to live off the land during his march from Atlanta to the sea. Lieutenant Charles A. Booth, in Union General Peter J. Osterhaus's XV Corps, witnessed a bummer returning to camp, loaded with "first a bundle of fodder for his mule; second, three hams, a sack of meal, a peck of potatoes;" and then some household utensils. Union Soldiers took not only enemy property; they also stripped friendly black families of all they owned. The Rebels also denuded their own people. By an act of March 26, 1863, the Confederate government made all articles necessary for the war effort subject to impressment, overriding local objections. The victims usually received less than market value in compensation, if anything at all. Disillusioned Robert Patrick, 4th Louisiana, seeing a Southern woman stripped of her dairy and poultry products, May 21, 1864, wrote: "They talk about the ravages of the enemy in their marches through the country, but I do not think that the Yankees are any worse than our own army."[13]

Whether by deliberate policy, as during Sherman's western and Sheridan's eastern operations in 1864, or by simple attrition through repeated foraging, many areas in active theaters of operations became deserts, barren of resources. Soldiers impounded draught animals and their forage, then burned the barns and seed stocks. Famine stalked in the wake of armies. Major Thomas Osborn, chief of artillery, Union Army of the Tennessee, wrote on December 17, 1864, after Sherman reached the sea at Savannah, that the army had "cleaned up the country generally of almost every thing upon which the people could live." The march had ruined many previously prosperous planters, along with a host of ordinary people who had little to start with. Now, he concluded, "as we have left the country I do not see how the people can live for the next two years."[14]

Many noncombatants did die, starting with the old and very young. In March 1863, Sarah Morgan Dawson, a Southern girl, wrote that her mother had been ground down; a couple more months of "danger, difficulties, perplexities, and starvation will lay [her] in her grave." The family put the children to bed early, "to make them forget they were supperless." But a grown-up who "followed their example, could not sleep herself, for very hunger." Many people could not leave a ruined area, having no choice but to hang on where they lived. Others, who could travel and had relatives elsewhere, fled the countryside for the safety of towns and cities. But this also increased urban overcrowding, sanitation problems, and stress on food reserves, so that many refugees had to move on again. Such widespread social and geographic dislocation created a new class of Southern homeless migrants. A Confederate government policy of confiscating abandoned properties, intended to keep the population in place, actually made the situation worse, creating demoralization and war weariness.[15]

Often, refugees could not be sure of their reception. In April 1863, Kate Stone's family reluctantly left their plantation "Brokenburn" in Milliken's Bend, Louisiana, traveling to Tyler, Texas: "A year ago, would we have thought of going even to the house of a friend to spend some time without an invitation?" Now, seven of them set off, "to stay an indefinite time with a lady we have seen only once, and without any invitation, trusting only that, as she is a lady, she will be kind to us in our distress." Sarah Morgan, whose family refugeed from New Orleans to Clinton, Louisiana, September 1862, found they had jumped from frying pan to fire. The family had trouble obtaining basic supplies, such as soap, candles, matches, and wheat flour. Their daily diet consisted of a one-dish meal: "If any one had told me I could have lived off corn bread, a few months ago, I would have been incredulous."[16]

The unhygienic temporary shanties and extemporized shelters of refugees duplicated the miserable dwellings patched together by displaced persons all around the world, in all times, in major war zones. One Southern wife, named Kirksey, could not hold onto her home after Union troops captured her husband. But she obtained a roof over herself and her children in an abandoned car at the Augusta, Georgia, train depot, where her spouse had been a conductor. "My husband was such a good man," she sadly told Ella Thomas, a neighbor. "Every Christmas he filled the children's stockings with something for Santa Claus presents." Sad as her situation might appear, many fared even worse.[17]

In Vicksburg, 1863, citizens and fugitives from the surrounding area crowded into caves while Grant's shells pounded the city. The inhabitants dug a large and complex underground system, with living chambers connected by passages, but people hated trying to work or sleep in the damp, dark dugouts. Going out to get water, or for air and light, posed grave dangers. A young girl, tired of confinement, went outside, only to be hit by a shell fragment. She rushed back to her mother, dying. An anonymous diarist wrote that they had only a little spoiled bacon and musty pea flour for food. Butchers in Vicksburg and other overcrowded urban centers finally dressed cats, dogs, and rats to hang in meat markets. An omnipresent fear of famine and disease hung over all Confederate cities. John B. Jones, working in the Richmond bureaucracy, suffered constant anxiety about how to feed his family and find fuel. He wrote in March 1863 that the city verged on famine. The previous December he had recorded the onset of disease: "The small-pox is spreading in this city to an alarming extent."[18]

Folk who felt abandoned by their government and communities eventually resorted to a desperate expedient: they determined to get their soldiers home. Bureaucrat Robert Kean described women journeying to Richmond in September 1864, to petition the Conscription Bureau for release of their male kin: "appeal after appeal and all disallowed. Women come there and weep, wring their hands, scold, entreat, beg, and almost drive me mad. The iron is gone deep into the heart of society." Indeed, it had. Civilian desperation and official intransigence brought about a radical dislocation of civic relations, as noncombatants finally urged their men to desert. A provocative recent study argues the breakdown of the established order in the Confederacy represented a revolution in the political and social structure of the South, helping to bring about the downfall of the planter hegemony.[19]

Many soldiers' dependents no longer had the strength or the tools to plant and harvest a crop. Winter meant famine for a great number lacking salt to preserve their meager meat reserve. As early as 1862, with the Confederacy's infrastructure crumbling, the vital public salt ration failed in states like Georgia, Virginia, North Carolina, and Louisiana. Without men to hunt fresh game, families would die. A careful modern study of Georgia desertions suggests convincingly that the failure to distribute salt, along with crop losses, provoked a wave of desertions in the northern counties a year before Sherman's invasion. The people's desperation crystallized in their ache-filled language. Edward Cooper's wife wrote to him in the Army of Northern Virginia: "I would not have you do anything wrong for the world, but before God, Edward, unless you come home, we must die." The night before, their little boy cried out, "O Mamma! I am so hungry," and wept inconsolably. The North did not experience such widespread desperation, but the poor there often faced a similarly bleak prospect, forcing soldiers to seek discharges or desert. A case study of two New York townships determined that fewer soldiers absconded from the ranks when a tightly knit community offered support for their families; more frequent desertions indicated loose social bonds and a lack of public aid to soldiers' dependents.[20]

The plight of many noncombatants tore holes in the fabric of conventional patriotism, threatening the foundations of society. In the North, angry citizens fomented riots in urban areas like Detroit, Chicago, and New York. In the South, too, cities became flash points where soldiers' dependents collectively expressed their grievances, particularly in bread riots. In March 1863, in a wave of armed protest, women broke into food stores from Atlanta to Salisbury, North Carolina. The biggest mob gathered in Richmond in early April, where women evoked specters of the French Revolution, flooding the streets, crying "Bread or Blood." One historian dubs the riots "spectacular and numerous," going so far as to say, "It was truly a Confederate spring of soldiers' wives' discontent." In extremity, women in both sections rejected the cause. "What do I care for patriotism?" cried out a desperate Southern woman. "My husband is my country. What is country to me if he is killed?" The wife of Valentine Bechler, 8th New Jersey, urged him to bribe a surgeon to get a medical discharge: "If you will give one of the doctors a couple of dollars you can be home here with us."[21]

After the war, some Southern men blamed women's encouragement of desertion for Rebel defeat. Confederate veteran Robert Stiles asserted in 1893 that many a wife told her husband to desert, and "that if he come not at once, he need never come—that she will never see him more, never recognize him again as the husband of her heart or the father of her children." But, countered retired Confederate nurse Kate Cumming, "if the truth was wholly known, the rich people who remained at home and did nothing for the soldiers' families, are greatly to blame," not the soldiers' wives. Under necessity, women challenged conventional belief that working outside the home undermined their modesty. North and South, they applied for government clerking posts that, according to anxious male relatives, removed them from the safety of the home and placed them in danger of seduction. Susan Leigh Blackford, wife of Captain Charles Blackford, 2nd Virginia Cavalry, took in boarders for money, starting in 1862. He agreed but, by October 1863, demanded she go live with relatives instead: "The war has so demoralized the people that a woman as young as you are must be very careful to keep under the guardianship of her natural protectors." [22]

————•◦•————

The war did indeed produce breakdowns in the social code. The Reverend Thomas Girardeau, boarding with Mrs. Henry Lucas, the wife of a soldier, got her pregnant. Men in the ranks threatened vengeance. Orin West, a Berdan sharpshooter, about to go on furlough in April 1864, gave fair warning "that those men who were intimate with his wife had better look out." Children had to grow up fast, working to help family survival. In the country, young boys picked berries, cut wood, and trapped small game. Infant girls learned early to sew and cook. When, in rural Michigan, Anna Howard's father and brothers joined the army, she got drafted, too, helping with chores, serving boarders, even teaching other children to read and write to earn money. In cities, children did factory jobs, swept streets, and anything else that turned a coin. Comedian Eddie Foy recalled dancing and fiddling outside New York bars for pennies. [23]

The volume of female prostitution rose radically amid the social dislocation produced by war. Many women entered the trade reluctantly. But with male breadwinners distant or dead, pay and pensions in arrears, what asset finally did a poor woman have to use in trade beside herself? In this context, the word "whore" is unfairly pejorative. A city woman might take in sewing, but inflation hugely outpaced wages. What then? Or what when no food remained in a rural woman's pantry, her meager stores taken by soldiers? If charity failed, what awaited the plain, respectable widow with three young children, whose husband died in hospital the night she got there, and who "could not indulge in the luxury of Grief" because she must struggle to live? What options faced the widow of Private Fleming, 71st New York, who left her with five children when he succumbed to inflamed bowels in September 1861? As social historian Dixon Wecter observed, when Northern factories paid women under $2.50 a week, they inevitably "became prostitutes in considerable numbers," serving the barracks and camp.[24]

Soldiers happily made a trade. Mrs. Edward Jett, a rural Georgia woman, wrote her soldier husband on September 20, 1864, that Federals told her, "if I wod comedate them I never shold suffe for . . . the wod fetch me anything to eat I wanted." As an "onis woman," she refused, but several married neighbors were "horin" for food. A blue-coat reported from Sewanee, Tennessee, that for four grams of coffee "you could get a good diddle." Charles B. Haydon, 2nd Michigan, said in January 1863 that women in Tennessee would have sex for 5 cents to buy provisions. Further, "Capt. Poe told me he could seduce every woman in Tenn. with one haversack full of coffee." Most remarkable for candid cynicism, Lieutenant James Graham of the 80th Ohio, when Provost Marshal of any occupied town, demanded women have sex in his back office in exchange for permits and passes: "Before she left could well and truly say I knew her."[25]

It was easy for soldiers to rationalize the exploitation of women by labeling the victims morally loose. Yankees justified taking advantage of poor Southern rural women by falling back on the stereotype of "crackers," calling them backward creatures without sense or morals. Yet evidence from other wars supports the argument that women bartered sex primarily as an act of sacrifice to succor families, not wanton opportunism. During the German siege of Paris in the Franco-Prussian War, five years after Appomattox, the city endured famine. Milk shortages caused soaring infant mortality, especially among the poor.

Cats, dogs, even rats, became luxury dishes. In desperation, Parisian women bartered their bodies to feed their dependents.[26]

These facts help explain a startling statistic about Civil War prison populations. We have the most intact records for the North, since many Southern files got destroyed during invasions and governmental disintegration. One modern study contends that, despite the North's overall prosperity and a decline in male prison inmates, the number of poor women and children in jails and workhouses increased significantly. In 1860, women represented 20 percent of Massachusetts inmates; by 1864, 60 percent. During the war, the children in New York City's almshouses jumped 300 percent. Can we profile these unfortunates? In the mid-1920s, Edith Abbott undertook pioneering sociological analysis of this question, utilizing prison reports from the 1860s. Abbott found that homeless soldiers' widows and orphans comprised many of the incarcerated. A Massachusetts *Special Report on Prisons and Prison Discipline* (1865) noted that most female inmates fell into the categories of mothers, wives, or daughters of soldiers. Destitute, they had been taken into custody as vagrants.[27]

Prison officials reported a sharp wartime increase in juvenile delinquencies leading to incarcerations, the result of fathers at war and mothers at work, leaving adolescents unattended. One investigator noted in the Massachusetts special report, "I have talked with many boys in Jails and Houses of Correction who were either the sons or brothers of soldiers or sailors in the service. It may not be extravagant to say that one out of four of the many children in our prisons have near relatives in the army." The New York Prison Association reported that the increase in female internments partly reflected prosecutions for abortions, called the "female crime." "Wives, whose husbands had gone to the army, were left unprotected and exposed to the arts of the designing and the vicious of the other sex. Some of them—we are glad to believe they are the exception—have lapsed from virtue, and naturally desire to obliterate the evidence of their guilt." A more charitable explanation would have emphasized necessity over vice.[28]

Some of the small children in workhouses had committed no crime other than to be born out of wedlock, the offspring of girls servicing soldiers for remuneration, or the fruit of boys' desire to plant a seed of immortality before going off to be killed. Jeremiah Willits, a Quaker who represented the Philadelphia Society for Alleviating the Miseries of Public Prisons, concluded from his enquiries that there were in every public poor house "a number of little children, some the offspring of girls following the army." Embroidering the theme of fallen women, prison officials often averred that females had been justifiably detained for general delinquency, spending their dependents' pay and aid money on drink, this alcoholism then inducing them to commit graver offenses. Just as those in authority could not understand the behavior of psychologically damaged soldiers, they continued blind to the fact, as Abbott noted perceptively, "that some part of the delinquency of these women must also have been caused by the emotional disturbance, the anxiety, and the grief from which they suffered."[29]

It was evident from the start that hostilities would alter the dynamics of race relations, and no sector of the population experienced more turmoil than African Americans. In the free states, members of the black middle class saw opportunities to enhance their status as citizens. Northern women left home to nurse and teach with the Union forces. For example, Charlotte L. Forten, the educated daughter of a prominent black Philadelphia family, served in the South Carolina Sea Islands. African American male workers hoped to fill some of the slots vacated by white men recruited into the armed services. Their competition with whites made them bitterly resented. As discussed in chapter one, this factor helped to provoke the summer 1863 draft riots. Racist push-back went beyond the white working class. In New York, Marcia L. Daly, wife of a Democratic judge, said lynching blacks might be regrettable, but "it will give the Negroes a lesson, for since the war commenced, they have been so insolent as to be unbearable."[30]

The inferior compensation of black Union soldiers meant hardship for their families. One wife wrote her soldier husband, begging him to send home just fifty cents. But unfree African Americans in the Confederate states faced the hardest situation. At first, they remained property even in Federal eyes. However, the approach of Union armies sooner or later provided opportunities to escape from plantations, as the bonds holding Southern society together dislocated and fractured. Ironically, the option to flee put slaves on the horns of a dilemma. If they bolted, they might be intercepted and punished. Madison Kilpatrick, a slaveholding soldier, wrote from camp to his wife, August 12, 1864," saying "Tell the Negroes to stay at home and not be led into any difficulty, for there will apt to be hanging done." Mounted slave patrols hunted for runaways in Confederate-held territory. Colonel William Camm, 14th Illinois, on September 3, 1862, recorded an eighteen-year-old female slave making his lines, clutching her baby. She had outrun the hounds, despite struggling through tangling brush that lacerated her legs and feet. But reaching Union forces did not always guarantee sanctuary. As late as July 1862, the U.S. Navy's gunboat flotilla on the Mississippi received orders not to "promiscuously" harbor runaways.[31]

War's dislocation subtly changed and eroded the plantation power structure, freighting the lives of both races with instability and peril. Slaves who gave valuable military intelligence to Union forces entering their locales ran grave risks. Captain Charles Wright Wills, 103rd Illinois, campaigning in the western theater, recorded a black girl chasing down his unit to find safety. She had told a bluecoat patrol where to locate hidden livestock, for which her mistress "took half a rail and like to wore the wench out. Broke her arm and bruised her shamefully." Margaret Hughes, a young South Carolina slave, had to watch while her master hanged another girl who had revealed his hiding place to Union troops. On the other side, in limited instances, slaves killed masters in retribution for past wrongs, before running away. In June 1865, after Confederate policing had collapsed, former slaves chopped South Carolina planter William Allen to pieces in his barn. Some house servants, close to the white family, remained loyal throughout the conflict, but many workers without such ties chose to leave.[32]

Thousands of runaways pouring into Union lines ensured the eventual legal end of slavery. Their presence forced the government's hand, because such a multitude could not be returned to bondage. As historian Vincent Harding wrote: "The relentless movement of the self-liberated fugitives into the Union lines" became "an unavoidable military and political issue." This did not mean that "freedmen" received decent treatment, for the many racists in the Union army abused them. In Alexandria, Virginia, occupying Union soldiers shot blacks for amusement. Members of the 99th New York kidnapped persons of color to sell into slavery. Cornelia Hancock, a Union medical assistant, wrote that many contrabands came into hospital sick and injured. "It is not uncommon for a colored driver to be pounded nearly to death by some of the white soldiers."[33]

Some slaves, having already sampled Northern racism when Union soldiers ransacked their cabins, along with the big house, decided to stay put. Charlotte Forten, a middle-class black Northern volunteer in the Sea Islands, wrote disgustedly in February 1863 that white soldiers indiscriminately stole all plantation food stocks, "cheated the Negroes, and in some instances even burned their houses." Union generals could act disturbingly like slave oligarchs. General David Hunter tried to arbitrarily conscript all black males 18 to 45 into the army. Susan Walker, a Northern teacher, wept bitter tears as white officers ordered their men to shoot resisters. Also reminding her of slavery days, white Union soldiers made an "arrest if any negro is found away from home during working hours." Such treatment left the ex-slaves in a quandary as to whom they could trust. "One bright intelligent woman" told Walker "they had all been so 'confuse'; they did not know what to do; did not know where they belonged or anything about we!"[34]

Union armies that failed to feed and clothe their troops properly did not adequately provide for contraband families. Runaway camps became overcrowded and unhygienic. An unnamed visitor to the D.C. camp described some naked babies, together with another six children, all sleeping in a small cabin amid a sea of mud, in rags and without fuel. Another hut housed twelve, including a consumptive girl, an orphan with pneumonia, and an infant dying of malnutrition. Children often suffered most, as they rarely tasted any milk. G. N. Coan, a Northern teacher working in the occupied South in 1864, wrote that contraband "children have suffered a great deal from cold and hunger," often having as "their only garment an old brown tow-cloth frock, all rags and patches of different colors," sleeping in "wretched hovels, the cold wind piercing through every crevice, their beds the floor." After visiting the Washington camp in November 1862, Mary

Todd Lincoln told her husband that contrabands suffered terribly, with only a bit of carpet for cover in November cold. Malnutrition and filth encouraged disease, such as a yellow fever outbreak in the Memphis camp. Overall, the camp death rate reached a steep 25 percent.[35]

Male freedmen found work as mule drivers, trench and gravediggers, some of the worst tasks the army had to offer, grinding them down and making them sick. Even then, that they actually earned some pay from the public purse made them the target of white hostility, violently expressed. Females might find work as nurses, laundresses, or, finally, as camp followers. Union officers took them as flagrantly flaunted private concubines, traveling along with their commands. Esther Hawk, a physician from New Hampshire, charged that assistant surgeon Dr. Charles Meade and his steward, 112th New York, serving in her hospital, "had a pretty colored girl to minister to their private wants."[36]

Despite all these failings, the military formed a crucial initial springboard into free society. Black military service gave the slave-hut community a tangible, hitherto inconceivable, focus for pride. And, inadequate as provision for the dependents of black soldiers might be, the distribution of rudimentary food rations, clothing, medical treatment, and pay formed a lifeline (though, as Susie King Taylor, nurse and wife of a sergeant in the 1st South Carolina [U.S.], remarked, the regiment received no pay for eighteen months). The cooperation established between the military and Northern charitable groups proved to be a further important contribution toward progress, with hundreds of Northern teachers and aid workers setting up shop to help the ex-slaves prepare for citizenship.[37]

This endeavor dovetailed into assisting freedmen who continued tilling lands deserted by planters, with workers sharing in the profits. In the Sea Islands Port Royal Experiment alone, 10,000 slaves ran the plantations from November 1861 to March 1865. Whites mainly contributed moral support, explained Susan Walker. "All understand the planting better than we can teach them, but they need encouragement." Lesser-known instances of fruitful cooperation included the Department of Tennessee where, in 1862, Grant made General John Eaton Supervisor of Negro Affairs. He worked with aid groups to set up freedmen with farm plots and bring them basic education. By

1864, the department boasted sixty teachers with 3,000 students.[38]

Such success required a situation of stability and order in a region. In those parts of the seceded states where military control remained ambivalent, fear and anxiety prevailed. Dislocation of normal societal arrangements advanced to where large areas existed as virtual no-man's-land, the races living in a state of uneasy insecurity, alternating at times with naked terror. Confederate civilians, stunned by the dissolution of their world, suffered trauma when confronted by foraging parties of their former slaves, now in Federal uniforms or operating as guerrilla bands. Sidney Lanier recorded that, after one raiding party had been driven off by white militia, former slaveholder Mrs. Parven wailed, "God help us! It is but the beginning of the raids; next time, the raiders will be more infuriated, and we may have no friends at hand." Blacks still in the district could face savage retaliation. Amy Spain, a slave, was hanged in Darlington, South Carolina, in 1864, for reportedly shouting, "Bless the Lord, the Yankees have come!" as Sherman's troops marched by. Kate Stone described backwater Louisiana as being, by spring 1863, in a state of constant quasi-war, with black and white groups arming against each other. "We live on a mine," she said.[39]

While both black and white wondered what tomorrow might bring, praying for peace, there hung over all America a great cloud of grief that embraced all races and both genders as the casualty lists swelled. Walt Whitman "heard over the whole land, the last three years of the struggle, an unending, universal mourning—wail of woman, parents, orphans." He envisioned the country as one huge surgery: "it seemed sometimes as if the whole interest of the land, North and South, was one vast central Hospital," spreading out into countless graves, vast trenches serving as depositories of the slain, and creating a new national architecture of soldiers' cemeteries. Of all the deprivations visited on Civil War people, death loomed as the greatest, with people losing loved ones in numbers unimaginable before hostilities began. Grief touched all classes; even the Northern wealthy, who never felt an economic pinch, still had to cope with the vacant chair. Houses in every neighborhood showed door handles tied with black crepe.[40]

As soon as the boys started down the road to war, the anxiety of waiting began, an emotional stress akin to the strain of soldiers immobilized in trenches during bombardment. Charleston belle Emma Holmes wrote in April 1861 that General Joseph B. Kershaw's brigade had gone off: "How bravely they marched by, their bayonets glistening in the moonlight." Yet she already felt the obliterating presence of dark shrouds: "the shadows obscured their faces so that we could not distinguish them." Some appeared so young. "We turned away with mingled feelings of pride & sadness, the echo of the music fading in the distance, adding to the melancholy thoughts inspired by the sight."[41]

Civilians then settled into the deceptive calm of ordinary life that gave no outlet for release of pent-up worry. "Oh how often have I longed to battle with life as men do," wrote South Carolinian Grace Elmore in November 1862, "and expend in action those energies that work but to excite fretfulness because denied of the true outlet." As she waited for news from the front, she added: "How quiet our life is, and yet so much suffering, so much horror around us, and what a terrible uncertainty." Kate Stone cried, "Oh, this inactive life when there is such stir and excitement in the busy world outside." She continued: "My heart leaps to my lips and I turn sick with apprehension whenever I hear a quick step, see a stranger approaching, or note a grave look on the face of any of the boys." Her mother's frail health imposed a further need for pretended normality; Kate had to devour in secret the reports of her brother's brigade in action.[42]

Captain John William DeForest, 12th Connecticut, observed in retrospect that once it became clear the war would be drawn out, "Old persons and invalids sank into the grave that season under the oppression of straining suspense and preliminary horror." People became unbalanced by fretting, a medical condition known as "fright." They turned for relief to opium, alcohol, laudanum, and other drugs. Midwestern teacher and social activist Frances Willard grew appalled by Union blundering in 1862: "To think of our soldiers dying of exposure—without ever striking a blow for freedom—to think of two millions a day being spent for nothing." Though an erstwhile head of the Women's Christian Temperance Union, she resorted at times to "A little ether on a handkerchief," to escape the gloom, lifting "'the real Me' beyond the Himalayas and roseate hues gleam on me." When "dazedness" or depression became severe, she turned to electric shock treatments.[43]

For civilians, long periods of inactivity alternated with frantic news gathering whenever a big battle occurred. Then, the family would designate a relative or friend to join the crowd in front of government or editorial offices, there to await the published casualty lists before hurrying home to report. Virginian Susan Blackford, wife of Captain Charles Blackford, remembered watching for her father to bring the bulletin of casualties at Manassas. She deduced from his elastic step on the porch that they had been spared any loss, and there followed a general "shout of grateful joy when he caught his breath enough to say, with choking voice, 'All safe!'" Of course, some always heard the worst. Joel Chandler Harris stayed haunted by the memory of a woman finding out at his newspaper office that her husband was killed: "her screams when the editor told her of it, and the cries of her little daughter." The young wife of a Rebel officer described the bereaved as "stunned and stupefied," some even "died of grief." This double tragedy entered the war's poetry. In "After All," William Winter wrote of Grandpa following his soldier boy to the grave:

> But the grandsire's chair is empty,
> The cottage is dark and still;
> There's a nameless grave in the battle-field,
> And a new one under the hill.[44]

Individual grief often overshadowed news of victories. "Alas," wrote Emma Holmes after Lee's spring 1862 victories, "we have scarcely the heart to rejoice, for our land is filled with mourning for the heroes who had shed their life-blood for its liberty. . . ." The military custom of allowing clusters of hometown boys into one unit made the burden of loss worse, as a whole family or half a village might get wiped out in a day. After a skirmish in which Georgia militia tangled with the Federal 46th Ohio and 97th Indiana in November 1864, a bluecoat knelt by a badly-wounded fourteen-year-old Rebel who told him the adjacent corpses belonged to his father, two brothers, and an uncle. On the Prairie Grove field in December

1862, a Union officer watched a woman with children clinging to her skirts searching among the gray-coated dead. She found a brother, then another. When she reached her husband, she emitted a "wild unearthly shriek." He thought that "the suffering of that woman none but God can know."[45]

Grief often could not be contained or bottled up. Richmond socialite Thomas DeLeon described Mrs. Breck Parkman, a guest at an autumn 1862 wedding, trying to get through the ceremony in a church where only a year before she had married a soldier, now dead. She "tottered to a chancel pew, and threw herself prone upon the cushions, her slight frame racked with sobs." Louisiana diarist Sarah Morgan conjures for us, finally, the razor-sharp cut of devastating loss. On February 5, 1864, she recorded brother Gibbes' death and her initial denial: "Not dead! not dead! O my God! Gibbes is <u>not</u> dead. Where O dear God!" Just six days later, on February 11, she wrote of her other brother: "O God O God have mercy on us! George is dead! Both in a week! George our sole hope—our sole dependence." They had been killed in the same action.[46]

<hr>

In the depth of sorrow, three questions frequently stayed uppermost in people's minds. How and where had the loved one died; had the body been identified; and could it be retrieved? Often, three or four soldiers in a unit would agree that, should one survive an engagement, he would write to the others' families with basic details. Nurses performed the same function for patients. Commonly, correspondents included a lock of hair with the letter or, in a particularly meaningful gesture, the family received a planting from where the soldier fell—a growing, living memorial. James Weeks, a searcher after William Robinson of the 83rd New York, killed in the Cornfield at Antietam, wrote home to say, "I bought a rough coffin (the best I could get) and washed his face and combed his hair smooth and covered him round with a large clean sheet" before interring him. Still, this family was fortunate. Despite every effort, the disposition of about 50 percent of the dead remained unknown, identity or burial sites unaccounted for. The thought of a loved one simply disappearing intensified survivor pain, an emotion captured in verse by J. H. McNaughton:

My brave lad sleeps in his faded coat of blue;
In a lonely grave unknown lies the heart that beat so true;
He sank faint and hungry among the famished brave,
And they laid him sad and lonely within his nameless grave.

The emotional need for finite sites that provided some dignity to death led the Federal government in 1862 to develop national cemeteries. The South did the same on a local basis.[47]

Yearning to know about a soldier's last hours could be mixed with trepidation. Poor Sarah Morgan, after losing one of her brothers, said "I so sadly long to hear from living lips of his last days on earth," yet "It will be dreadful, dreadful, the first instant we look on one who saw his dead face." Photographs offered a link to the dead. By 1860, over 3,100 photographers worked in the United States, providing thousands of visiting-card-sized images that even those of modest means could afford. Thanks to the stereoscope devised by Oliver Wendell Holmes Sr., one might hope to look, in realistic three dimensions, at the place where the departed fell. Holmes thought everyone should see war's reality. Walt Whitman hesitated. Listening to the screams of the mangled boys hospitalized after Chancellorsville, he mused: "O well it is their mothers, their sisters cannot see them—cannot conceive, and never conceiv'd, these things." Indeed, looking at pictures of the dead could wrench more than comfort. Emma Holmes found it hurt "to gaze upon the features of these sad fated friends and how almost impossible to realize that their presence will never more bring a smile to the lip and a bright sparkle to the eye."[48]

Return of remains proved a mixed blessing. Decay often advanced so quickly that even loved ones felt repulsion. Families frequently received warnings not to open caskets. Union infantryman Newton Botts wrote his aunts in Boone County, Kentucky, about his brother Jasper's death at Murfreesboro in February 1865. A bullet hit him in the head while he reloaded behind a rail fence. The lieutenant propped him in a quiet corner to die. "I was sorry to learn," he added, "that the casket could not be opened." Embalming of recognizable remains could halt the rotting process, and firms offered this service near the lines. But only the rich could afford their rates. Receipt of the body could help bring closure or it could reopen the wound. When Sergeant Thomas Owen escorted Captain August Perkins' body to Pennsylvania, the outpouring of anguish unsettled him: "Up to this time I had not fully realized what war was. This was the first time I witnessed the great sorrow of friends at home over the loss of their sons and brothers killed in war, and it left an impression on my mind that I shall never forget."[49]

Religion offered consolation to many. There would be reunion in a better place according to God's ordained plan. And what better place to find community support in a bleak time than the church? At the same time, one influential recent argument suggests that the enormous butchery precipitated a critical questioning of faith, pointing toward a secularized spirituality. Undoubtedly, significant doubt welled up about the idea of a just and benevolent God overseeing the slaughter. But this religious skepticism probably became most accepted among the cultural elite. For example, some of the New England Brahmin caste, particularly young men in uniform, turned to a philosophy of blind stoicism, finding meaning only in how well one stood up to the hollowness of random fate. At the same time, we must be careful of over-intellectualizing the mood of many ordinary people, whose values surely changed less radically than those of leaders in ideas. Mainstream views seldom underwent a 180-degree revolution. Religion might be put aside as temporarily unhelpful without being absolutely eschewed. The deaths of Robert Gould Shaw and other family friends deeply affected Harriet Beecher Stowe. But, as the wife of a divinity professor, she did not renounce religion, turning instead for relief to "household merriment," the simple satisfactions of home and hearth. She began planning "House and Home Papers," "a sort of spicy sprightly writing that I feel I need to write in these days to keep from thinking of things that make me dizzy & blind & fill my eyes with tears."[50]

Many people typically treated religious rituals as somewhat a matter of proper form, of correct behavior, not particularly deeply felt. Good manners demanded that grief be expressed in conventional ways. For example, bereft relatives could buy a color print, suitable for framing, depicting a wife and daughter languishing on a dead soldier's grave. His name could be written in on the headstone. And,

at the end of the day, the frank fact remained that loss simply had
to be endured as best one could. For many, railing against God or
fate served no purpose. One just felt a pain in the heart that had to
be voiced and then endured. Susan Caldwell's two-year-old daughter
died of scarlet fever in September 1864. She neither cursed the Divinity nor talked of meeting the child as an angel in heaven. She simply
called out her grief, writing to her husband, Lycurgus, an official in
the Confederate government: "My darling babe—Mamma's heart
aches all day and night for you. I feel at times my heart will break
when I know I cannot get my baby back to me any more."[51]

—•—

Mary Boykin Chesnut had much to cope with in the war, and she did
not find faith a great support. Perhaps the finest diarist of her period,
she remains a fascinating personality, a woman of paradox who managed to get through somehow. Although of the slaveholding class, she
refused to be a virulent apologist for the Peculiar Institution. Despite
appearing a conventional Southern matron, she could be outspoken
to the point of violating convention. Strong in character, she yet
needed frequent opium doses to quiet her nerves. I find her wonder-
fully human, an old friend worth spending time with, whatever one's
viewpoint. We might imagine strolling with her along Charleston's
spacious Battery, fronting the Bay where Colonel Shaw and his brave
black soldiers perished in a gallant rush for freedom. Here, on the
promenade, we might briefly rest our eyes on the broad, sun-dappled
waters, a momentary respite from our investigation of war. And now,
let us walk on with her, trying through a thumbnail sketch of her
experience to provide the individual perspective that can sometimes
be an invaluable window into people and events.

Mary endured the conflict in two locations, the seat of government in Richmond and her South Carolina plantation. She witnessed
the terrible emotional deprivation Confederate losses brought and
experienced dislocation with the Confederacy's defeat and the end of
slavery. In her writings death became a constant caller. She quickly
learned not to romanticize battle injuries. Dr. Robert Gibbes, who
gazed on the Southern dead from Manassas, July 1861, told her,
"the faces of the dead are black and shining like charcoal." Later,

she viewed the corpse of a once-handsome soldier, Frank Hampton, killed at Brandy Station, in September 1863, now laid out in an open coffin. "How I wish I had not looked!" she moaned. "He died of a saber cut across the face and head and was utterly disfigured." In the same period, she witnessed horrid sights as a hospital volunteer, fainting on her first visit. On the ward, she watched "a poor wretch horribly maimed" struggling to walk, while other wounded soldiers laughed at him to cover their own anxieties. He collapsed on his cot, weeping hysterically. The suffering of the patients appalled her; their "eyes sunk in cavernous depths haunted me as they followed me from bed to bed." She felt badly for the men who slunk into hospital from their units before a battle. While medical officials berated them as cowards, she slipped away, "hanging my head for the poor devils so insulted."[52]

Mangled men became ubiquitous in Richmond, so close to the front. At an 1863 Christmas Eve dinner with the Prestons, a leading family, she noted the contrast between beautiful young belles and men "without arms, without legs," their throats smashed and eyes missing. She could laugh with one girl who joked darkly that the only men left were "a glorious assortment of noble martyrs and wrecks—heroes, I mean," and another belle who said that "I fear it will be my fate to marry one who has lost his head." But Mary also grieved for poor, physically wrecked John Bell Hood, doomed to lose Buck, the Prestons' beautiful daughter, because the family blocked her marriage to a cripple. After seeing the maimed, she would have nightmares and wake up screaming.[53]

Being within a war zone, men's deaths had a jolting immediacy. In church during the May 1863 Battle of Chancellorsville, she witnessed "a scene calculated to make the stoutest heart quail." A church official walked up discreetly to those "whose family had been brought down wounded, dying, or dead, and the pale-faced people following the sexton out." Just a few doors away, Captain Cheves McCord died in convulsions from brain damage incurred earlier at Fredericksburg, his pregnant wife and his mother arriving a day too late to kiss him goodbye. Mary suffered insomnia, so "unfortunate & miserable & wretched is it all." She retreated frequently to her room, there to embrace the cushion provided by opium and laudanum, a drug habit begun when she contracted gastric fever on the war's eve. Nervous fainting fits and violent hysterics also assailed her. She felt, like many women, that she had "no safety valves of any kind" for her pent-up need to act. But she held together through it all, even as others broke under the strain.[54]

After many funerals, she admitted, "I tremble when I hear the death march now." Yet she never screamed, although "I can understand now the women who do." Indeed, many houses echoed with screaming. Mary's niece let out a piercing wail when she confronted General Hood's new artificial leg standing in the corner of a closet; Mary was keeping it safe for him. The grief continued without end. Mary accompanied the widow of Colonel Francis Bartow when a military funeral passed by: "the first sound she heard of the dead march, she fainted!" Again: "Today a poor woman threw herself on her husband's coffin and kissed it. She was weeping bitterly. So did I, in sympathy." Mary knew some who simply could no longer carry on, such as the widow of Colonel Means, killed at Fredericksburg. She had already lost her daughter, Emma, to consumption. When news came that her son too had fallen, presumed killed, Mary reported the colonel's widow suffocated herself.[55]

A practical bent helped Mary Chesnut persevere. In addition to hospital work, she improvised military supplies: "To day, I have already picked to pieces some Moreen curtains—enough to make six shirts for the soldiers—4 counterpanes & some white stuff for bandages." In fall 1861, she set up her maid Molly in an egg and butter business on a profit-sharing basis. By the end of the war, the proceeds constituted the major family income. She showed no maudlin regret for having to sell a special pink gown to eke out the budget. She retreated to the rural asylum of the Chesnut plantation at the end of the war. Despite poverty and the threat that her husband, James, a leading secessionist, might be tried for treason and imprisoned, she kept the farm in operation, supervising the newly freed house servants and outdoor workers who wished to stay, finding remuneration for them and tending to the sick, showing a brave face even though she feared some of the field hands might "riot." She described her life as lonely and healthy, with books as comforting companions, though she frequently had trouble concentrating on them: "such a blow as we have survived does make one necessarily a little stupid the rest of their lives."[56]

Tart wit helped her cope, even though it got her into trouble. Thinking of the unstable, lawless condition of the state's rural interior in the wake of war, she remarked wryly: "happy land happy homes where foremost among the list of necessary house utensils rank Sharpe's rifle & Colts revolver." (An interesting perspective for Stowe's papers on domestic economy.) Mary never addressed head-on the conundrum of a just God allowing a cruel war. Instead, and perhaps more tellingly, she drew a sharp contrast between man's feeble efforts at mayhem, using rifle and cannon, and the all-powerful Divinity's much more spectacular slaughter inflicted through natural germ warfare (which she had observed in the hospitals). "Men murdering each other wholesale in these great battles—& sickness & disease God-sent, laughing their puny efforts to scorn. Ten men dying in hospitals where one dies on the battle field." Serving in hospitals, boiling her clothes when she got home, Mary knew the relative power of disease: "God shows he can make troubles."[57]

As the killing mounted and the South's cause floundered, Mary came to think the dead might be fortunate to have missed the final debacle. As early as February 1862, she wrote wistfully: "Men can find honorable graves—we do not see what is to become of the women and children." Mary's acerbic tongue, her acid political critiques, and her childlessness—in itself an offense to convention—made her resented in the South's exclusive social circles and thus a ready target for attack. At a social gathering in May 1865 she continued her earlier thought, remarking that the dead might be fortunate to be well out of harm's way. An acquaintance, Harriet Grant, attacked her viciously for this comment, accusing her of sentimentalizing the battlefield butchery. The unexpected attack reduced Mary, always more vulnerable than she admitted, to "strong hysterics." In fact, Harriet had misunderstood the point, perhaps on purpose. Mary did not intend to romanticize. Rather, she verbalized a common feeling among Civil War people that they who still lived had survived only to see their world, with all its former verities and safeguards, shattered by the invasive presence of war.[58]

CHAPTER SEVEN

INVASIONS AND VIOLATIONS

×

THE COMING OF FRATRICIDAL CONFLICT SHOCKED AND troubled many thoughtful Americans. Virginian Judith McGuire wrote, "Can it be that our country is to be carried on to the horrors of civil war?" When she thought of the coming time, "I shut my eyes and hold my breath." Those civilians closest to government circles often had the best opportunity to gauge the extent of the gathering storm. Varina Howell, wife of Jefferson Davis, recalled, "I felt like some poor creature circulating about a whirlpool helpless and drawing every moment nearer to the vortex."[1]

Yet, for many people, the possibility of being ruined or annihilated by war seemed remote. They might have boys in uniform to worry about, but the fighting would be short and limited to a few encounters between well-regulated armies that would respect the rights of property, along with the persons of noncombatants and prisoners. This vision of a "bandbox war" evaporated as it became evident that neither side would yield easily, and the contestants became locked in a bloody, grinding, slogging match. By spring of 1862, the conflict showed clear symptoms of moving from a limited to a total war, one in which not simply men in arms but the whole opposing society would be seen as a military resource to be ground down and broken. In this chapter, we will follow the road of war where it leads into ever more harshness and destruction, as the hearts of men harden and the defenseless pay accordingly.

Evidence of toughening attitudes included a series of general orders issued by John Pope to his Union Army in Virginia, July 1862. They authorized the expulsion from their homes of all who refused to take the oath of allegiance, along with seizure of their property and the summary execution of irregulars caught under arms. The Confederate government threatened retaliation, an example of escalating extremes of conduct. The situation in New Orleans, occupied by Union forces under General Benjamin F. Butler, provides a second illustration. Female residents persistently insulted bluecoats, culminating in a housewife throwing the contents of a chamber pot over Admiral David G. Farragut. "Such venom one must see to believe," asserted General Thomas Williams. "I look at them and think of fallen angels." Goaded into a response, on May 15, 1862, Butler ordered that a woman abusing the uniform "shall be regarded and held liable to be treated as a woman of the town plying her avocation" of prostitution. Inevitably, the South retaliated, targeting Yankee property for destruction.[2]

In fact, from the very beginning of the war, the conventions of proportionality that supposedly protected civilians from harm had been bent to the breaking point. In listing contraband of war subject to seizure, the Lincoln administration had in 1861 singled out medicines, a direct attack on the health of civilians and soldiers already rendered hors de combat by wounds or sickness. When opponents of this measure, such as Dr. W. H. Gardner, a Union army surgeon, tried to protest, they were shouted down. Partly because of this policy, chloroform and ether became scarce in Confederate hospitals. According to Southern nurse Fannie Beers, who served in both eastern and western theaters, "the surgeon relied on the manly fortitude of the patient" alone.[3]

Lincoln also claimed a special "war power" to take unilateral extralegal action against those he deemed a threat to public safety. "The Constitution," he argued, "invests its commander-in-chief with the law of war, in time of war," allowing for such radical measures as suspending the writ of habeas corpus in large areas of loyal territory. Through this method, Lincoln arbitrarily silenced much political opposition, imprisoning antiwar spokesmen in states with divided loyalties, such as Kentucky and Maryland. He also put constant irritants like Ohio Democrat Clement L. Vallandigham beyond the Union lines, to be taken in by embarrassed Confederates. Generals who widened hostilities to include civilians found increasing government support. In August 1863, General Quincy A. Gillmore received tacit approval to lob incendiary shells into Charleston, South Carolina, punishing the initiators of rebellion with fire. Once again, the action led to escalation, the Confederates positioning Union POWs near landmarks likely to be bombarded.[4]

Civilian or guerrilla violations of the conventions of war, requiring combatants to be regularly enlisted and in uniform, served as the pretext for ruthless reprisals. On May 2, 1862, for instance, Ohio troops sacked Athens, Alabama, in retribution for a raid by men out of uniform. And, on August 6, after irregulars wounded General Robert McCook, men of the 9th Ohio hanged a number of civilians and burned properties for miles around. In another 1862 incident, bushwhackers fired from the Mississippi shoreline at the gunboat *Cairo*. The frustrated captain, Lt. Commander Thomas O. Selfridge, retaliated by directing shellfire to demolish a neighboring plantation house.[5]

From the start, bad behavior by individual soldiers, who killed livestock for food or just to have fun, struck an ominous note for the future safety of vulnerable civilians. Gangs of soldiers quickly progressed to abusing noncombatants. Rebel Joshua Callaway confided to his wife that his comrades stole from the people. In the army, he admitted, "I learned more of human nature and deception than I ever cared to know." Junior officers joined their men in terrorizing the powerless. Violating one Baton Rouge home in August 1862, Union officers slashed women's underwear, shouting, "I have stuck the damned Secesh!" and "that's the time I cut her." Another put his revolver to the head of an old gentleman who protested their conduct, declaring, "I'll blow your damned brains out."[6]

Soldiers with higher professional standards, outraged by such behavior, blamed the army commanders for tacitly condoning the perpetrators. General Marsena Rudolph Patrick, Provost Marshal General of the Army of the Potomac, responsible for policing the troops, believed the rot had started early in the army's history. He fumed that Pope's orders had initiated the demoralization of men who "now believe they have a perfect right to rob, tyrannize, threaten & maltreat any one they please." On the other side, Rebel officer C. Franklin complained in November 1863 from Columbus County, Arkansas, "All here goes wrong." On every cavalry raid by Generals John S. Marmaduke and Joseph Shelby, troopers had been "beating, shooting at & otherwise putting in fear & dread" their own people.[7]

As it dawned on the population at large that the same roads that had taken their men to war now brought armed columns bent on hurting them, they could succumb to numbness born of shock and horror. When the Yankees approached Augusta, Georgia, Ella Thomas wrote that a strange kind of apathy crept over her, a helplessness in knowing "it must come." War correspondent Charles Carleton Coffin noted the same phenomenon in Pennsylvania in July 1863: people "were strangely apathetic," he recalled. Realizing their complete vulnerability, they begged the organized forces not to leave them, fearing Lee's troops and the mass of stragglers that lurked in the rear areas of both armies.[8] General Abner Doubleday remembered that, in the Gettysburg campaign, "pale and frightened women came out" of their houses and "implored us not to abandon them." Observers noted vacant expressions on the faces of Southern refugees. False hopes of rescue from the Yankee invaders often built up hopes that left people flat and lifeless when the bubble burst. And, like Northerners, Southerners begged and berated the soldiers who prepared to leave them. When John C. Pemberton's beaten troops retreated into the Vicksburg fortifications on May 17, 1863, witness Mary Ann Loughborough heard deserted rural women cry out, "Oh! shame on you!" One added bitterly, "and you running!"[9]

Anxiety and stark terror often followed initial shock. "The life we are leading now is a miserable, frightened one—living in constant dread of great danger, not knowing what form it may take, and utterly helpless to protect ourselves," wrote Kate Stone from Milliken's Bend, Louisiana, in March 1863. Fear fed on rumor and half-truth. "People are in an awful state of excitement," wrote Virginian Henrietta Burr in July 1862. "They are just about ready to believe anything they hear provided it is horrible." Unknown threats bred nightmares. Sallie Hunt, a Southern youngster, thought Northern troops would act like painted savages: "My hair 'stood on end' when I thought of the Yankees tying the children up in bags and knocking their brains out against a tree."[10]

The inexorable hardening of the conflict into total war heightened loathing of the enemy in an ever-intensifying spiral of bitter emotion. Angered by his impotence to prevent Yankee invasion of the sacred homeland, a Texas captain, Elijah P. Petty, in May 1863 urged his wife to inculcate in their children "a bitter and unrelating hatred to the Yankee race" that had "invaded our country and devastated it." There should be no quarter for an enemy that had placed "his unhallowed feet upon the soil of our sunny South." Many north of the Mason-Dixon Line reciprocated the animus. In 1863, visiting British writer Catherine Hopley registered shock when well-bred Northerners asserted during polite conversation that "we must annihilate them," meaning the Rebels. This was said "with as little remorse as they have before displayed in destroying the Indians." Toying with genocide had achieved respectability.[11]

———•••———

The decades before the war had seeded fertile ground for the escalation of sectional enmities, with all their destructive consequences. Ignorant of how other people lived beyond their own region, Americans' perceptions of each other crystallized in a series of stereotypes that filled the vacuum in knowledge. To begin with, the slave population largely lacked individual identity in white eyes. Popular images of the plantation people turned them into happy "sambos," putting up a smiling front for the master class, minstrels in blackface. However, on the rare occasions when they rose in defiance, they immediately became fiends incarnate, depraved savages just a step from the blood-drenched jungle. This scenario fomented nightmares of slave revolt in the beleaguered Confederacy. When, in September 1861, sixteen-year-old Clary Ann, a house servant, killed her mistress, Eveline Colbert, in Culpepper County, Virginia, the sister of the dead woman wrote to Governor Letcher, asking for release of her nephew from military service so he could protect the family from the expected servile rebellion.[12]

White Southerners in the antebellum period perceived Northern-ers largely as engaged in commerce and manufacturing, ignoring the huge belts of farmland in the rural free states. They gave Yankees credit for business acumen but also held them in contempt as capi-talist money-grubbers without ethics or higher values, and certainly not gentlemen. Southerners professed a Jeffersonian distaste for the industrial city with its factory workers, often typed as slum dwellers, immoral and brutalized denizens of bars and bordellos. The usually phlegmatic General Lee once remarked candidly that the killing off of these proletarians in the war signified no great loss, "as in all large cities there is a population which can well be spared." [13]

Southerners also branded Yankees as hypocrites who, prior to the war, denounced the Peculiar Institution while profiting from cot-ton manufacture and acting as factors for Southern planters. Worse, Northern radicals seemed bent on destabilizing plantation culture, calling for abolition that conjured up images of miscegenation. In 1864, Charleston diarist Emma Holmes wrote that a Mrs. Hunter of New York reported racial intermingling rife in the city: "One of the latest dances of Yankeedom, she says, is for two females to be har-nessed & driven around the room by a man, who whips them as they go. What a fearful picture of degradation and iniquity." [14]

Yankee spite and hypocrisy, said Southern critics, could be traced back to the Puritans who settled much of New England and became infamous for ruthless witch-hunting. This practice seemed to find a modern reincarnation in such zealous spirits as John Brown, who slaughtered proslavery settlers at Pottawatomie, Kansas, in 1856, and then tried to inaugurate a slave war by raiding the government arse-nal at Harpers Ferry, Virginia, in 1859. Union troops marched off to war singing that Brown's "soul goes marching on." Increasingly, to Rebel eyes, Union generals like Sheridan and Sherman incarnated the dead crusader's fierce avenging spirit, destroying all in their path and unleashing a depraved mob. Emma LeConte, expecting Sherman's advance on Columbia, South Carolina, in December 1864, wrote bit-terly, "All that is between us and our miserable fate is a handful of raw militia." According to rumor, "Sherman the brute avows his inten-tion of converting South Carolina into a wilderness. Not one house, he says, shall be left standing, and his licentious troops—whites and negroes—shall be turned loose to ravage and violate." Caricature magnified a very real threat into a cataclysm.[15]

For their part, Northerners usually acknowledged that the South had spawned an aristocracy of sorts, with surface manners. But the polish of plantation culture relied on the oppression of others. Surely, said Northern critics, this inherent violence must produce a vicious character in the master class. "Their civilization is a mermaid," editorialized *Harper's Weekly* in 1860, "lovely and languid above, but ending in bestial deformity." Some Northerners who spent time in the prewar plantation states agreed. General Sherman mainly liked the cadets he taught at a Louisiana military academy on the eve of war. But, in general, he had no time for the "young bloods" he had known since the 1840s, declaring their pretension to chivalry "all trash." This opinion paved the way for his late-war attitude that they might productively be swept from the earth. Preston Brooks, who in 1856 beat Charles Sumner senseless on the floor of the Senate for remarks critical of slavery, seemed to typify the breed.[16]

Plantation mistresses, though portrayed in much of American popular culture as delicate and charming, nevertheless struck some Northerners as Janus-faced because they shared in the cruel oppression of slaves. Consequently, the vituperation shown by Rebel women did not surprise all Union soldiers. Chaplain A. M. Stewart, 102nd Pennsylvania, wrote from Meade's army in 1864: "Fully, fiercely, terribly, malignantly have they entered into this conflict." Some Union officers held Confederate females equally responsible, along with their generals, for prolonging the war, because they shamed men into fighting. This accusation of warmongering set up a scenario of Federal officers winking at the abuse of women. During Sherman's 1864 campaign, Union General Smith D. Atkins told Virginia Wade of Lancaster, South Carolina: "You women keep up this war. We are fighting you." And New York lawyer George Templeton Strong, a leading figure in the humane U.S. Sanitary Commission, nevertheless wrote on November 28, 1864, that he could not sympathize with Southern women forced into prostitution to survive. Their pernicious role deserved such a just retribution.[17]

Outside observers generally failed to understand that the bulk of Southerners fit neither the simple category of planters nor poor white, belonging instead to the middling yeomen class. Union soldiers often depicted Dixie's ordinary folk as shiftless, illiterate, dirty, immoral trash, and clay eaters, a portrait that helped the invaders look callously on the plain people's sufferings. General Alpheus S. Williams, in November 1863, called the ordinary folk of Tennessee "disgusting; the mere scum of humanity, poor, half starved, ignorant, stupid, and treacherous." The stereotypes employed by both sides dehumanized whole categories of people and, once bereft of a shared identity, they could be brutalized with moral impunity.[18]

It has become commonplace to refer to the conflict as a "brothers' war," but perhaps a majority on both sides envisaged the struggle as one against foreigners, alien beings from another planet. "This is a queer country and queer people," wrote Sergeant Numa Barned, 73rd Pennsylvania, about Virginia. "I sometimes wonder if I am not in a foreign country," wrote another soldier, Edward Henry Courtney. Just as antagonists in the Pacific theater in World War II took body parts as trophies from the enemy they demonized, a trooper in the 10th Virginia cavalry dismembered the corpse of a Union soldier killed at Brandy Station, Virginia, in June 1863. According to his brother, John O. Collins, he "is now making a ring of Some portion of the leg bone of the dead yankee." Edward Burrus, 21st Mississippi, wrote to his parents in September 1862, "Tell Miss Anna that I thought of collecting her a peck of Yankee finger nails to make her a sewing basket of as she is ingenious at such things but I feared I could not get them to her."[19]

As the war lengthened, atrocities multiplied. Psychopaths committed some crimes, the military then as now containing on average about the same number of those violently disturbed as in civil society. But people we might consider normal also committed human rights violations. Often, they had become subject to a range of negative emotional phenomena that we may loosely cluster under the umbrella term "war psychosis." When a war, with all its loss and pain, drags on, rage grows against the enemy held responsible for all the extended suffering, the outrage building upon previously held negative caricatures already demonizing the opponent.

The continued loss of comrades and friends in the deepening slaughter becomes a frequent trigger of the rage that feeds war psychosis. We can see this factor at work as far back as the Trojan War described in Homer's epic poem *The Iliad*. Here, the Greek champion Achilles feels lukewarm toward the war until Hector slays his friend Patroklos. Homer depicts him then filled with towering rage: "Achilles the warrior was once gallant and chivalrous; since the death of Patroklos he is a different, murderous man." He pursues Hector with venom and abuse, stripping his mutilated body of armor and refusing even to give up the battered corpse for proper burial. Psychiatrist John Shay applies the same analysis to modern combat, noting that, in Vietnam, grunts' anger at the seeming unreasonableness of their predicament escalated rage at the enemy to an almost berserker state. One G.I. recalled, "Got worse as time went by. I really loved fucking killing, couldn't get enough. For every one that I killed I felt better."[20]

Roughly a century before, on October 5, 1863, Texas officer Thomas H. Coleman wrote to his parents, after inspecting "black and swollen" Union bodies at Chickamauga: "it actually done me good to see them lying dead, and every one else that I heard expressed [that] opinion." Maryland Colonel Osmund Latrobe, on General Longstreet's staff, said of the mutilated Union corpses at Fredericksburg, "Doing my soul good." On the other side, Indiana soldier William Bufton Miller wrote after a skirmish, "We captured about a hundred prisoners and killed about thirty of them. It was fun for us to see them Skip out." Wisconsin Lieutenant Frank Haskell, aide to General John Gibbon commanding Union I Corps, retained his humanity but worried about the escalation of passions generated by the slaughter. Contemplating a communal grave at Gettysburg with a chalk marker, "75 Rebils berid hear," he remarked sadly, "Oh, this damned rebellion will make brutes of us all, if it is not soon quelled."[21]

Not only traumatic individual battlefield experiences, but those policies of enemy authorities that appeared to violate accepted norms of conduct, could provoke the rage of war psychosis. Let us take two examples. First, the Lincoln government's Emancipation Proclamation of January 1863 declaring slaves in rebellious areas free, coupled with African American recruitment, made many Confederates see red because it appeared to invite servile insurrection, unleashing the jungle savage in the Southern black population. Southern soldiers went berserk, denying POW status to, and murdering, soldiers of color, along with their white officers. Rebels usually remanded into slavery those rank and file not executed out of hand. After the assault on Fort Wagner, July 1863, Confederates denied medical aid to the 54th Massachusetts' wounded, leaving them to die and burying them face down in insult. In gestures reminiscent of Achilles' treatment of Hector, Confederate authorities refused to return Colonel Robert Gould Shaw's body to his family, stripped off his uniform, and buried him anonymously "with his niggers."[22]

After engaging a black regiment near Monroe, Louisiana, a Texas officer wrote: "I never saw so many dead negroes in my life. We took no prisoners, except the white officers, fourteen in number; these were lined up and shot after the negroes were finished." Nathan Bedford Forrest's cavalry allegedly carried out one of the most ferocious massacres, at Fort Pillow, Tennessee, on April 12, 1864. Inevitably, atrocity bred atrocity. John Probst of the 25th Wisconsin told his sweetheart that, in fighting on May 23, 1864, "twenty-three of the rebs surrendered but the boys asked them if they remembered Fort Pillow and killed them all."[23]

Our second example begins with the perception of Northern generals that Rebel commanders prolonged the war inexcusably, long after they had any reasonable chance of winning independence. Thus, they bore the guilt of needlessly adding to the destruction. (Union generals dismissed as immaterial the Rebel leaders' conviction that they still had a legitimate shot at victory: how Union generals interpreted the case determined their actions.) Ulysses S. Grant, commanding general of the Union armies, contemplating the Confederacy's refusal to quit, determined that the Federal strategy in 1864 must be to use superiority in personnel and resources to grind the Rebels down in an unremitting war of attrition. This would entail constant contact with the enemy, denying him a breather to rest and replenish, and initiating some of the most concentrated slaughter in American history.

Also, in August 1864, Grant ordered General Benjamin Butler, now a special exchange agent, to suspend further prisoner exchanges. The commanding general cited the Confederacy's refusal to accord POW rights to black soldiers as the primary reason for this move.

But the end of captive swaps also served Grant's strategy of attrition, blocking Confederates' return to action. Grant later admitted he hoped to deny the enemy the services of 30,000 to 40,000 veteran troops. The intransigence of both sides regarding POWs condemned thousands of miserable victims to continuing mental and physical misery, resulting in debilitation and death.[24]

Grant authorized the downgrading of Virginia's infrastructure as part of the same attrition. The Shenandoah Valley became a particular target. The Valley's farmland had been a breadbasket for the famished Rebels. It also served as a corridor through which Confederate generals from Stonewall Jackson to Jubal A. Early could march to threaten the Union's lines of communications, and even the capital itself, Rebels penetrating Washington's outer fortifications in 1864. General David Hunter showed zeal in punishing rebellion in the Valley, burning Governor John Letcher's home and the Virginia Military Institute. This academy, said Hunter's aide, Colonel David Hunter Strother, had become "a most dangerous establishment where treason was systematically taught." But a conundrum arose: when you started to root out the cancer, where did you stop as your anger fomented? Hunter's appetite for burning disturbed Strother after the destruction even encompassed the home of a man called Leftwich, whose only crime was spreading pro-Confederate rumors.[25]

General Philip H. Sheridan, acting under Grant's authority, carried out the most thorough ravaging of Virginia. He systematically destroyed mills, farms, livestock, and crops, driving the inhabitants into exposure and starvation. The general reported, on October 7, 1864, that he had destroyed more than 2,000 barns filled with grain and seventy mills with their stocks of flour. His troops also killed or drove 4,000 cattle and 3,000 sheep. Sheridan boasted that "the Valley, from Winchester up to Staunton, ninety-two miles, will have but little in it for man or beast."[26]

As the Army of Northern Virginia fell back, yielding ground to the enemy and unable to protect the civilian population in occupied territory, the job of contesting the invaders fell to Partisan Rangers. Even though they were regularly enlisted troops, they provoked Federal ire, the high command categorizing them as guerrillas because they only wore uniforms on raids, disguising themselves as noncom-

batants when pursued. Thus, they became subject to summary execution under the usages of war. Colonel John Hunt Mosby's rangers had
the most impact in Virginia, engendering Union fear and hatred; they
therefore became the most hounded.[27]

Grant ordered Sheridan to execute Mosby's men without trial,
codifying a practice in use as early as April 1863, when one of General George Armstrong Custer's troopers, following a bushwhacking,
swore: "We take no prisoners after this." Custer, who had Southern
friends at West Point, nevertheless became vicious in hunting down
and killing rangers, even in front of their families, perhaps an example of psychotic fury. In an inevitable escalation, Lee announced in
November 1864: "I have directed Colonel Mosby to hang an equal
number of Custer's men in retaliation for those executed by him."
Still, some of this mutual savagery might have been avoided. In a
recent study, Daniel E. Sutherland argues that partisan and guerrilla
warfare became extremely vicious partly because the top authorities
on both sides failed to fully integrate unconventional forces into their
military establishments. Without clear guidelines defining their role,
troops on both sides in the shadow war became increasingly independent, ungovernable, and ruthless.[28]

Sherman remains perhaps the most controversial of the generals
who made hard war. He believed from early in the conflict that all of
Southern society had been complicit in rebellion, and that civilians
sustained continuation of the war through their moral and material
support of their troops. Therefore, he reasoned, the North needed to
break not only the will of the Rebel armies to fight, but the spirit of
the population as well. "We are not only fighting hostile armies, but a
hostile people, and must make old and young, rich and poor, feel the
hard hand of war," he wrote in 1864. As early as a year previously, he
had adopted the policy of cleaning a region out, creating famine in
the countryside to deny the produce of the area to the enemy.[29]

But he intensified the destruction in 1864, extending his policy to
removal of population clusters from farms and factories, even whole
cities in the war zone, such as Atlanta, Georgia, and Columbia, South
Carolina, that he intended to burn. His strategy of cutting free from
his line of communications and living off the land on the famous
march to the sea received official sanction. The march left a massive

trail of misery and ruin in its wake. Inevitably, in the mutual bitterness of the closing months of the war in the west, neither side gave
much quarter to opponents who fell into their hands; conventions of
proportionality were rubbed out.[30]

The extreme severity of Sherman's actions and the general's often
intemperate words have led some authors to question his sanity in the
latter stages of the conflict. The distinguished essayist and literary
critic Edmund Wilson, for example, suggested that Sherman exuded
a "manic elation." Evidence for this view occurs in comments such as
these, made in late 1863: "To secure the safety of the navigation of the
Mississippi I would slay millions. On that point I am not only insane
but mad." Professional chemist and controversial popular author Otto
Eisenschiml analyzing Sherman from a medical viewpoint, declared
him a war criminal with a split personality, a bon vivant and mania-
cal killer.[31]

We need not go quite so far. Let us say that, despite his latter success, the general had a stressful and painful war, at an early point
suffering a mental breakdown after the press mocked his anxious
predictions of a long and enormously costly war. He became increasingly angry at those he held accountable for his personal humiliation
and the collective pain of America. His grim pleasure in the suffering
of the enemy affords an example of war psychosis, but it seems no
different from that exhibited by countless thousands on both sides.
Watching South Carolina burn by night, for example, Federal Major
Thomas Osborn, chief of artillery in the Federal Army of the Tennessee, rhapsodized, "I wish I had the power of describing the grandeur
of this scene." The destruction struck him as "magnificently grand."[32]

Official hard war policies of the generals gave tacit encouragement to unofficial, individual acts of terror by soldiers preying upon
civilians. Depredations reached epic proportions in the last months of
hostilities. Provost Marshal General Patrick railed against Grant for
failing to condemn looting of the population: "Grant had expressed
himself strongly against protecting these people, and I learned that
his Staff, were, themselves, engaged in sheep stealing, fowl stealing
and the like." Patrick included Meade in his indictment, charging
that "this army is nearly demoralized." A minority of scholars challenge this view of limitless war, arguing that, despite some unauthor-

ized violations, official Union hard war policy did not go beyond a "directed severity" that sought to minimize civilian suffering. However, the bulk of evidence does not seem to support such a conclusion. We must also wonder about the efficiency of such a destructive policy: might the Confederacy have quit earlier if there had not been fear of total ravaging of the Southland? [33]

Besides official foragers, clouds of unauthorized stragglers fanned out from Sherman's marching columns to strip the countryside and harass the people. Corporal Harvey Reid, 22nd Wisconsin, wrote near the end of the march to the sea that "the cruelties practiced on the campaign towards citizens have been enough to blast a more sacred cause than ours." The huge extent of vandalism has led one historian to surmise that Sherman's severing of his communications freed the soldiery psychologically from the moral restraints of contact with home and community, giving them license to act outside the bounds of normally accepted behavior. [34]

The South's fierce intransigence and the North's ruthless determination resulted in thousands upon thousands of civilians being beaten, starved, economically ruined, their mental and physical health destroyed. Reports endlessly document the suffering. Thus, the *Cincinnati Daily Commercial*, July 20, 1864, noted the arrival of homeless Southern refugees: "Four hundred weeping and terrified Ellens, Susans, and Maggies," deprived of their factory employment by Sherman, driven "away from their lovers and brothers of the sunny South, and all for the offense of weaving tent-cloth and spinning stocking yarn!" John H. Hight, unit historian of the 58th Indiana, described civilians huddling together as Sherman's soldiers prepared to burn their homes: "Some of the women are crying, some wringing their hands in agony, some praying to the Almighty." [35]

In the wake of Sheridan's torching of the Valley, Confederate Major Henry Kyd Douglas witnessed the misery of the refugees there: "I saw mothers and maidens tearing their hair and shrieking to Heaven in their fright and despair," while a beautiful girl was "shrieking with wild laughter, for the horrors of the night had driven her mad." Terrified out of their wits by the invasive behavior of sol-

diers from both armies, pregnant women miscarried. "Poor Aunt Sallie suffered dreadfully, and her babe was born dead," wrote Emma
LeConte, January 1865, "the result of the fright she experienced when
the enemy passed through [Columbia, South Carolina]." Older people
succumbed to shock. Virginian Cornelia McVeigh described how her
mother died in 1864 when Yankee troopers "destroyed everything we
had." After their raid, "She lived only one week." Lucy Buck recorded
in her diary on November 15, 1864, that her Aunt Lizzie had died
after bluecoats burned their Front Royal farm in the Shenandoah
and destroyed the livestock. Lucy stopped writing, too numb for
words. "My diary was laid by. Those sad autumn days my heart was
too sad."[36]

Bad as conditions might be in the major theaters of war, none
suffered more than the people caught between contending parties
in the contested borderlands of the conflict, unstable zones where
guerrilla warfare predominated: the mountains of eastern Kentucky
and western Virginia, the ravaged communities of Kansas and Missouri, where violence had raged for most of a decade. One historian
of border warfare notes that grand strategies and notions of limited
engagement never drove the fighting there. The struggle "was instead
a very personal war, a war among neighbors, a war of theft and arson,
a war of midnight murder and torture—a vendetta."[37]

The bitter personal hatreds between contending parties in border
badlands, where divisions thrived, produced special cruelties, such
as the burning alive of enemy civilians thrown into flaming buildings, as well as random torturing and killings accompanied by taking grisly trophies, including ears, genitals, scalps. In exasperation at
their inability to prevent such atrocities and massacres, perpetrated
by guerrillas sheltered by proslavery settlers, Federal authorities
resorted to creating free-fire zones, necessitating forced population
removal and relocation, sometimes to unhygienic and crowded refugee camps where hungry people quickly sickened. After guerrillas
massacred the free-soil citizens of Lawrence, Kansas, Federal forces
cleared the border counties, driving the people away and destroying crops that sustained irregulars. Hard-bitten Union Colonel Bazel
Lazear, 1st Missouri Cavalry, who had summarily executed bushwhackers, nevertheless confessed, "It is heart sickening to see what

I have seen. A desolated country and women and children, some of them almost naked. Some on foot and some in old wagons. Oh God."[38]

Shooting men in front of their families became a common terrorist act of guerrilla bands. Several authors have suggested that, in this way, irregulars acted out a symbolic form of rape, demonstrating that wives and daughters could be violated at any time and with impunity. This argument seems persuasive. But, ironically, in trying to expose an underlying motive hidden in this murderous practice, writers have unintentionally contributed to the myth that mock rape largely took the place of actual sexual assault in the Civil War. We frequently hear that very little rape took place in any sector of the fighting at any time during the conflict. However, a wide range of sources suggests otherwise: women suffered sexual assault frequently throughout all theaters of the conflict.[39]

Cases occur, for example, in official documents such as the papers of the Adjutant General's office regarding the proceedings of military courts. Federal records yield most evidence, as many Confederate archives did not survive the chaos of the final weeks. Thus, we read that Union Sergeant Charles Sperry and members of his squad tried to rape fifteen-year-old Annie Nelson in Langley, Virginia, in the summer of 1864. Again, Private James Preble, 17th New York, attempted several sexual assaults, including the brutal rape of a fifty-eight-year-old spinster. Sergeant Arthur Nood, the arresting officer, testified to Preble's drunken state, "with his Privates hanging out, his pants and shirt in that region all covered with blood."[40]

Accounts of sexual attacks found their way into the newspapers. The *Missouri Democrat* reported on October 13, 1864, the attempted rape of a Mrs. Schmich by Rebel cavalry. A month later, on November 12, the paper noted the gang rape of three black servants by partisans. Correspondence also documents the brutal abuse of women. On January 3, 1865, an unidentified Rebel soldier wrote that, after the evacuation of Savannah, Georgia, by Confederate forces, you could hear the shrieks of women attacked by "the skulkers of our army who had commenced to pillage and destroy." Knowledge of violence to women became so commonplace that it could be talked about in official unit histories. In the narrative of the 72nd Indiana, Sergeant Benjamin Moge was quoted as saying that at Marietta, Georgia, on July 10,

1864, Union cavalry got liquored up and molested refugee female factory workers removed to that city on Sherman's orders. "Upon this occasion," the vet recalled of his fellow soldiers, "their delirium took the form of making love to the women."[41]

Individual memoirs also talked of the crimes committed. After the war, terrible memories haunted Philip Daingerfield Stephenson, a veteran of the 13th Arkansas (C.S.A.). He finally found healing by joining the Christian ministry. In his recollections, he wrote of many awful incidents. The following may particularly chill us: "one of the dark places of army life." He described a young woman, "once pretty no doubt, but now bedraggled and befouled, little more than a girl, and yet a hag in looks, with garments scant and ragged and filthy." This poor sick creature dragged herself along beside the column of marching Rebel soldiers. Her wits appeared addled, probably because of gross sexual abuse, either through prostitution or repeated rape. More than likely, she had contracted venereal disease. Bereft of sense, she shouted filth at the passing troops, "her mouth full of foul talk and ribaldry." That night, soldiers threw her off a bridge to her death in the gorge below. "It was the talk of a day among us and then forgotten."[42]

Many sexual assaults failed to be officially reported in part because junior officers colluded with their men in believing that taking advantage of women came as a perk of the uniform. Lieutenant George O'Malley, 115th Pennsylvania, assaulted a Mrs. Whippey, who was tending her wounded son in hospital. Union Major Thomas Jordan routinely threatened gang rape to cow Southern women into forced labor. He told a group in Sparta, Tennessee, that they must cook for six hundred troops or "he would turn his men loose upon them and would not be responsible for anything they might do." Later, at Selma, he warned women that if they failed to provide food for the soldiers, "they had better sew up the bottoms of their petticoats."[43]

Soldiers on both sides considered women of the slave cabins especially fair game. African Americans bore a large brunt of male lust, frequently diverting rapists' attention away from potential targets in white women. As early as August 1861, an official Union report from Missouri warned that General John Pope's men had become so habituated to "committing rapes on the negroes and such like things" that they stood in danger of permanently alienating free-soil sentiment. General Oliver Otis Howard wrote angrily from Beaufort, South Carolina, to one of his subordinate commanders, on January 10, 1865, expressing shock "that many depredations have been committed near this place, and certain things done that would disgrace us even in the enemy's country, e.g., the robbing of some negroes and abusing their women."[44]

Soldiers often sympathized with their comrades arrested and punished for sexual assault, indicating again that many in uniform did not consider taking advantage of women a crime. When, on June 28, 1864, General Patrick hanged two men for rape, he felt obliged to harangue the assembled troops on the seriousness of their offense because of "feeling expressed by some of the Troops in regard to the Sentence." He stood on the scaffold and uttered "such words of warning, of reproof & correction as seemed proper in the presence of . . . the dead hanging beneath my feet."[45]

The statistics for officially recorded rapes can sometimes mislead us, contributing to our underestimation of the incidence of sexual assault. Union military archives, for example, note only 350 trials for rape, and less than 10 percent of those convicted received the death penalty. But clearly many cases never went through formal channels, being dealt with summarily in the field, the incidents going unreported. Also, sexual assaults often lie buried under other categories of misbehavior—"conduct unbecoming" (1,506 convictions) or "conduct prejudicial to the service" (11,834). Thus, Captain F. M. Caldwell of the 157th Pennsylvania faced court-martial for drawing his pistol and accosting a woman at a train depot, insisting: "God damn you must sleep with me tonight." The service dismissed him for conduct unbecoming. A military court tried Lieutenant Francois Wallenus, New York Independent Battery, also accused of attempted rape. He faced the same charge as Caldwell and the service cashiered him.[46]

In a rage-filled war, rape allowed hostile men to exert power over categories of the most vulnerable and helpless. Sexual assault appears an overwhelmingly male on female crime; the evidence does not suggest widespread sodomy. Male on male abuse of the powerless tended to take the form of killing opponents, either wounded or captive, and in the brutal treatment of POWs. No military justification can be advanced for assault on the human rights of females or POWs. Both sides treated their military captives appallingly: 30,000 or 18 percent of 127,000 Union POWs died in Rebel captivity, 26,000 or 12 percent of 222,000 Confederates in Northern camps. At the worst prisons, such as Andersonville, Georgia, with a 30 percent death rate, and Elmira, New York, with 25 percent fatalities, the risk of dying proved worse than in battle.[47]

In extenuation, the argument can be made that military authorities proved unable to adequately provide for their active units in the field, so disease ravaged the armies also. It became particularly hard for Confederate authorities to get provisions and fuel to the prison camps as the Southern infrastructure and economy crumbled. But this offers only a partial excuse; many lives could have been saved on both sides through a modicum of effort. North and South practiced malignant neglect at best, callous inhumanity at worst.

The nightmare began when a soldier realized he would become a prisoner, subject to all the miseries of detainment. Expecting Pemberton's surrender of Vicksburg, Lieutenant William A. Drennan, 31st Tennessee (C.S.A.), wrote: "Oh! It is heart-sickening, for should Vicksburg be surrendered and we be taken prisoners, I have no idea that we shall see outside prison walls for months—perhaps not during the war." Captors usually stripped their charges of boots, watches, and other coveted belongings. Prisoners might then be abused on the way to confinement. A Union major named Potter, 40th New York, recalled that, after capture at Bull Run, the Rebels reduced him to his shirt, then marched him and other famished prisoners five miles under a burning sun, pushed forward by bayonets. "They were half starved, plundered of everything, and closely confined like hogs in a pen."[48]

Civilians tormented captives as they passed by. Major Abner Small, 16th Maine, recalled that, as he and fellow POWs passed through the streets of Petersburg, Virginia, in July 1864, "The sidewalks were lined with old men, boys, and decrepit women who vied with one another in flinging insults and venom. The women were the worst of the lot; they spat upon us, laughed at us and called us vile and filthy names." African American prisoners suffered further deliberate humiliation by being chained in a slave coffle. Charleston belle Emma Holmes wrote, on July 16, 1863, that black soldiers taken during the assault on Fort Wagner should be shot, for "it is revolting to our feelings to have them treated as prisoners of war as well as injurious in its effects upon our negroes." Still, she had the consolation that the prisoners "were brought to the city barefoot, hatless & coatless & tied in a gang like common runaways."[49]

Temporary accommodations on the road to permanent prison facilities invariably grew overcrowded and provided little shelter. John H. Brinton, a Union brigade surgeon, wrote candidly in 1864 that about 1,200 Rebels, penned behind railings in Winchester, Virginia, had little cover and meager rations because Mosby's men had wreaked havoc on the lines of communication, stopping supplies getting through. One stopover pen at Salisbury, North Carolina, a converted warehouse and yard, gave no shelter for the massive overspill of bodies. Thinly clad, barefoot Union prisoners suffered from exposure, not one in twenty possessing a blanket.[50]

The POWs received a further shock when they got to their ultimate destinations and found these enclosures no better, with gross overcrowding and lack of shelter from the elements. The claim, made by both sides, that manpower shortages prevented clearing further ground lacks credibility. Camps often could not boast even the most rudimentary sanitary arrangements. Men lived in giant cesspools, digging holes in the filth for living quarters. They also had to drink rainwater that collected in contaminated puddles. At Andersonville, where such conditions reached an extreme, one man died every ten minutes during the heat of August 1864; the death rate in the ill-equipped hospital climbed to 75 percent.[51]

Most camps had inadequate fuel supplies for heat and cooking. At the notorious Johnson's Island prison on frigid Lake Erie, two officers shared a thin blanket and huddled to keep warm. Even then, the coupled men would wake speechless with cold and had to break out of a covering of crackling ice. Still, officers largely fared better than enlisted men, who often had no cover and got worse rations. William A. Fletcher, 5th Texas, incarcerated in Chattanooga, Tennessee, swore that "the rack and stake of centuries passed were not more brutal than the confinement in the cold, slowly but surely starving."[52]

Food allowances often dropped beneath subsistence levels, dished out in filthy communal buckets, contaminated by legions of bacteria, insects, and rodents. At Elmira, Rebel prisoners discovered rodents in the well that provided their drinking water. On a December 1863 day in Richmond, Virginia, Union POWs, imprisoned in a tobacco warehouse used as an annex to Libby Prison, had to discard a boiled rat they found at the bottom of their pail of bean soup. Prisoners finally became so desperate they ate the vermin, along with feral cats they trapped. Virginia captain Isaac Coles recalled eating a feline while imprisoned at Hilton Head, South Carolina. "She was deliciously fat, she must have been a notoriously fine mouser."[53]

Evidence exists that, as the war went on, Union authorities deliberately reduced the ration allotted Southern captives so that, in the words of Commissioner of Prisons Colonel William Hoffman, "these prisoners might not be returned to the rebel army in better condition for service than when they were captured." By the end of 1863, food had on average been cut 10 to 20 percent from where the allowance had started, roughly on a par with military field rations. Prison officials also refused inmates permission to buy from civilian merchants extra food to eke out their diet. Issues of fresh vegetables dwindled, guaranteeing the outbreak of scurvy.[54]

Given the filth and excrement, battalions of flies thrived in prison as in army camp, alighting in clouds on waste, food, and bodies alike. They drowned in the water. Rebel Henry Rudasill, incarcerated at Fort Delaware, said he received two meals a day but "in summer too thick with flies for use." A Confederate medical officer inspecting conditions at Andersonville hospital had the integrity to report that "millions of flies crawled over everything and covered the faces of sleeping patients and crawled down their open mouths and deposited their maggots in the gangrenous wounds."[55]

The immune systems of men suffering from exposure and malnutrition, assaulted by millions of bacteria, succumbed to typhoid, dysentery, pneumonia, scurvy, and smallpox. Prison surgeons had too few medicines to combat the spread of disease. The environment degraded the spirit as well as the body. Again, enlisted men faced the worst situation. Officers often had yard space to exercise and play games; they could sometimes purchase pens and paper, even borrow books and journals from well-intentioned citizens, an understanding between gentlemen.[56]

Without intellectual stimulus, the rank and file could even lose the powers of speech and memory, or endure dementia. Sidney Lanier, imprisoned in Point Lookout, Maryland, described the harrowing antics of the insane: "A man would rise and start across the floor. Suddenly he would yell like a fiend, and, as if the inspiration of a howling dervish had rushed upon him, would set up a furious jig in which feet, arms, legs, and head strove in variety and wild energy of movement." Other sufferers withdrew into despair and expired, often victims of nostalgia.[57]

While the degradation of some led to their mental eclipse, others sank to an animalistic state, forming gangs to tyrannize their fellow prisoners, stealing what little others had in the way of shelter, clothing, and food. They beat up resisters, even committing murder. At Andersonville, bullyboys terrorized the camp for months. Finally, prisoners formed a vigilance committee and, in league with the prison authorities, brought the thugs to book, the ringleaders receiving the noose.[58]

The end of hostilities brought the steady repatriation of POWs. In late April 1865, Walt Whitman went down to a pier on the Potomac River in Washington to greet a boatload of several hundred returning prisoners. The state of the men appalled him. He estimated that, of the whole contingent, not more than three could disembark unassisted; most had to be carried ashore. "Can those be <u>men</u>?" asked the shocked former hospital attendant, who thought he had become accustomed to seeing the bodies of soldiers wasted by disease, mangled by wounds. The bloodiest battlefields, Whitman said, could not show worse sights: "those little livid-brown, ash-streak'd, monkey-looking dwarfs?—are they really not mummified dwindled corpses? They lay there, most of them quite still, but with a horrible look in their eyes and skinny lips, often with not enough flesh on the lips to cover their teeth."[59]

———————◆•❖•◆———————

At best, these shattered men faced a long road to physical and mental recovery after the brutal treatment meted out to them. Many would lead painful, demon-haunted, impoverished lives. Some would never make it back from the terrible war experience, their life path into the postwar world foreshortened, reminding us that the consequences of wars do not dissipate when generals proffer dress swords in surrender and statesmen sign official papers ending formal hostilities.

CHAPTER EIGHT

STATE OF THE UNION

×

THE ROAD THAT TOOK US THROUGH THE CONFLICT NOW brings us to the fretful postwar years. Not surprisingly, the texture of the peace echoes the complexity, even confusion, of the causes that inaugurated the fighting. Of the issues on the table, only one perhaps had been settled with certainty: the war had preserved the geographical integrity of the Union. Probably by the late 1880s, a fair majority of Americans would have said this had been a good thing. Periodically, others around the world have wondered if the United States became too big and clumsy for its own or anyone else's good. Domestically, we take occasional renewed calls for secession mainly as political rhetoric, intended for the ears of extremist voters, especially in Texas. The Union appears a fact, so that those who oppose allegedly radical social initiatives undertaken by the Federal government resort to demonizing the central authority, trying to undo it from within. Beyond this verity of national unity, the picture begins to resemble a kaleidoscope: some gains resulted, and a few groups became outright winners, but many suffered loss and setback. Much that mattered still remained undecided. In this chapter, we try to assess the war's outcomes, including its high human and material costs.

———◆◦◆◦◆———

By 1865, the ex-Confederacy, which had lost its bid for independence, lay in ruins and would take about a century to recover. The destruction wrought by invasion had created a shambles. New York journalist, John Townsend Trowbridge, touring the war zone in summer 1865, described the defeated states as a vast, stinking charnel house. A leading authority on the war estimates that, by war's end, Union forces had "destroyed two-thirds of the assessed value of Southern wealth, two-fifths of the South's livestock," and, perhaps most devastating, "one-quarter of her white men between the ages of twenty and forty." Further, "More than half the farm machinery was ruined, and the damage to railroads and industries was incalculable." The South's total wealth from all sources had probably dropped by 60 percent.[1]

Defeat had depleted the South's emotional resources. Losing the war, with all that entailed, left many initially too stunned for action, literally in a stupor. Northern journalist Whitelaw Reid said that many Rebel veterans "stared stupidly" and had a "played out manner." General Josiah Gorgas, formerly chief of Confederate ordnance, wrote: "I am as one walking in a dream, & expecting to awake. I cannot see its consequences, nor shape my own course, but am just moving along until I can see my way at some future day." At first, just eking out survival took maximum effort. According to his niece, Rose, one ruined Charleston aristocrat, Julius Pringle, sold off his library of rare books in order to eat. She recalled: "We could not understand why as each novel was sold Uncle Julius was so sad. It seemed to make him sick, ill."[2]

The ex-Confederacy became trapped in a colonial relationship to the victors, an internal American economic empire in which the South had to sell its raw materials and labor dirt cheap to attract Northern wealth into the capital-strapped region. Even those who tried to build a New South on a Yankee industrial-commercial model remained within the cycle of exploitation. Wages inevitably stayed depressed in mines and factories, while Northern owners rigged prices, so that Birmingham steel, for example, could not compete with the product of Pittsburgh mills.

Slave states that had remained loyal still suffered. By the 13th Amendment, slave property converted into free labor, a great human advance but a huge loss of capital when a prime field hand in 1860 cost around $1,300. Border state planters had cause to regret their blindness in rejecting earlier proposals for compensated voluntary emancipation. In Kentucky, the requisitioning of cavalry mounts by both sides ruined the Commonwealth's lucrative horse-breeding industry. The losses suffered by one leading horse-farm owner, R. A. Alexander, brought him to numb despair. He confessed, "I have become careless in almost everything that requires exertion," and "I feel little interest in any form of business." He died prematurely in December 1867.[3]

Rebel raiders destroyed much of Kentucky's developing infrastructure of roads and railways. Ironically, the perpetrators became local heroes as emancipation and the enforcement by U.S. troops of black civil rights through "Readjustment" turned whites into neo-Confederates. In 1860, the national census placed Kentucky in the top ten states by per capita income; since 1870, the state lists in the bottom ten. The resultant lack of funds showed up in every area of life. For example, in the 1850s the state had gone a long way toward completing a free universal basic education system. By 1865, over seven hundred school districts had closed; in 1861–62 alone, 130,000 pupils lost their classrooms. Lack of capital forced Kentuckians to sell off natural resources in minerals and timber cheaply to Northern buyers, ensuring disastrous strip mining and land erosion.[4]

As Southerners adjusted to their situation, some showed great ingenuity in overcoming difficulties and creating a new future. Emma LeConte, a young war widow in Columbia, South Carolina, successfully ran her own plantation, became a suffragette, and taught a Sunday school for black children. But the vastness of the South's problems foiled large-scale solutions. Trapped in abject poverty, much of the population subsisted close to the starvation point. Federal Major Thomas W. Osborn, stationed in South Carolina early in 1865, described ragged, filthy, and hungry poor whites living in shanties worse than pigsties. Later that summer, Albert Gallatin Browne Sr., wrote bitterly to New England progressive Wendell Phillips that in South Carolina and Georgia black freedmen went without food and clothing, "covering themselves with nothing but pieces of rags, held in front & rear as strangers approached."[5]

During Reconstruction, 1865–77, Northern "carpetbagger" and Southern "renegade" reformers tried to improve the situation of the poor of both races through social engineering. Conservatives North and South vilified this effort at public intervention as meddling in local affairs. Yet the nation needed to make a far greater investment in time and money than even progressives could accept to seriously improve the condition of poor Southern workers of both races, giving them a shot at economic independence. A model existed in the Union wartime agricultural experiments that allowed ex-slaves to run abandoned plantations on a profit-sharing basis. Large-scale redistribution of land, along with grants to buy seed and tools, conceivably might have produced a middle-class yeoman society encompassing both black and white. But President Andrew Johnson's 1865 amnesty proclamation returned most confiscated acres to their original owners. Northern policymakers had no taste for a radical reallocation of resources that smacked of communism.[6]

Many planters, cash short, could not pay wages, leasing out land to farm laborers in return for a share of the crop. Planters had to buy seed and tools from merchants by borrowing against the expected crop. A bad season locked planters and sharecroppers alike into a debt cycle. Also, ill-inclined planters deliberately cheated their workers, keeping them trapped in dependent poverty. In effect, the agricultural South returned to the stagnation of a feudal system.[7]

The army and the Freedmen's Bureau grasped the value of stability in these labor arrangements and so pressured African Americans to sign labor contracts that robbed them of geographic mobility and virtually returned them to slavery. We realize now that freeing the slaves without giving them an economic stake in society assured peonage. But the dominant "laissez-faire" theory of labor relations held that the right to bargain in the marketplace for the sale of one's labor guaranteed the rise of the thrifty and industrious. In a free society, you could pull yourself up by your bootstraps; that most Southern poor people of both races did not even own shoes, never mind laces, apparently seemed beside the point.[8]

Although it suited the ruling class to have the poor, especially blacks, once again tied to the land after the social chaos of the last war years, the sharecropping system evolved primarily as a matter of necessity rather than cynical repression. However, deliberate calculation underpinned the systematic robbing of civil rights from African Americans, a theft backed up by extralegal force. In theory, the 14th and 15th Amendments to the Constitution assured all Americans equal citizenship rights, including legal protection and the right to vote. But, as one commentator points out, many whites "never fully committed to that right," but instead "speak of voting as a privilege that should be granted to people capable of meeting minimal standards imposed to safeguard the electoral process."[9]

Steadily, such tactics as imposing a property qualification, requiring a written literacy test, or an annual tax receipt, disenfranchised most African Americans. The barriers also had an impact on many poor whites, but election officials "grandfathered" them into the system, waiving rules on their behalf. (Some observers find an echo in the modern push to demand a photo ID, a demand falling hardest on the poor who have the least opportunity and funds to meet the requirement. Proponents deny discrimination, saying the measure only aims to curtail supposed widespread voter fraud.)[10]

The postwar white South increasingly found sympathetic allies in the North as the thought of black equality sent shock waves through racist society. The late historian C. Vann Woodward pointed out long ago that Northerners took racial discrimination to a new depth, imposing "Jim Crow" segregation of housing, restaurants, theaters, restrooms, and public buildings. Enforced separation of the races had not characterized plantation society, emerging instead as a white urban response to blacks migrating into Northern cities.[11]

Even many whites that had officered black regiments abandoned the struggle for racial fairness once the technical legal issue of freedom had been decided in 1865. The liberally inclined rationalized their betrayal by arguing that the so-called law of natural selection, the inexorable operation of the survival of the fittest, doomed some species to inferior status and probable extinction. Walt Whitman felt comfortable in making the point bluntly, indicating the respectability of racist views at the time: "The nigger, like the Injun, will be eliminated: it is the law of history, races, what-not: always so far inexorable—always will be."[12]

White Southerners, particularly Rebel veterans, jolted out of their despondency by the threat of racial equality, decided to give natural selection a helping hand, using violence to intimidate African Americans from exercising their civil rights. Starting in 1867, paramilitary groups like the Ku Klux Klan and the Knights of the White Camelia sprang up, much like the Freikorps that would resist progressive tendencies in Germany after the Great War. General Nathan Bedford Forrest, whose cavalry had a particularly unsavory reputation for racial brutality in the war, became the first head of the Klan.[13]

The Liberator, mouthpiece for New England abolitionism, had warned as early as June 23, 1865: "The war is not ended as many fondly imagine." The paper charged that the planters comprised "a brutal and vicious class of persons, whose treatment of the negro is infamous. He is cruelly whipped and frequently shot down and the perpetrator often goes off with impunity." General, now college president, Robert E. Lee spoke out in 1867 against the war's violent legacy in the wild behavior of young Confederate veterans toward their professors as well as black people (an interesting pairing). But even so revered a figure as Lee could not prevent the aggressive "redeeming" of the South. Before long, the paramilitaries held parades and openly wore Rebel gray.[14]

By a political bargain struck in 1877, the Federal government ceased policing the South and admitted the failure of Reconstruction. Soldiers of color had expected much from their service. Sergeant Henry Maxwell put the case succinctly: "We want two more boxes besides the cartridge box—the ballot and the jury box." A meaningful relationship with the U.S. army and government continued into the peace through service in regular black regiments such as the 9th and 10th Cavalry, the famous "buffalo soldiers." The military had become a training ground for entry into public life, and the legacy runs straight to the desk of Colin Powell.[15]

But, in a broader social context, black veterans faced the marginalization of their history. Federal authorities banned African Americans from marching in the 1865 victory parades. The Grand Army of the Republic (GAR), the main Union veterans' organization, often excluded blacks or relegated them to segregated chapters. Few public memorials acknowledged their service. Augustus Saint-Gaudens' famous monument to Colonel Robert Gould Shaw and the 54th, unveiled in 1897 on Beacon Street, Boston, carried the names of the white officers inscribed on the base, but not those of the black other ranks. African American veteran George R. Williams lamented that "nowhere in all this free land is there a monument to brave negro soldiers" who "have had no champion, no one to chronicle their record." The neglect became palpable. As late as 1869, Union veteran Russell Conwell, correspondent for the *Boston Daily Evening Traveler,* expressed shock to see skulls of the men of the 54th still rolling in the surf of Charleston harbor. They "lay grinning, and filled us with sad sensations, which still haunt our dreams."[16]

Racists employed crude interpretations of the new science of evolution to demean the black soldier. In 1869, the Sanitary Commission published its conclusions from a study of the racial profiles of Civil War soldiers. The report argued that "full-blooded" Africans had elongated heels and arms, resembling apes. The implications could not be missed. Six years later, the provost marshal general's office published a massive study endorsing the earlier findings. Dr. Sanford B. Hunt wrote in his damaging contribution, "The Negro As a Soldier," that autopsies of Union dead showed white brains to be 10 percent larger than black, with direct implications for relative intelligence. Men of color did not make good officer material, Hunt asserted, only acceptable privates, smart in drill because of their imitative and rhythmic traits, able to march well on splayed feet.[17]

In December 1898, as black soldiers fought the Spanish, Representative John Sharp Williams of Mississippi reaffirmed on the floor of Congress the old jungle-savage caricature: if 10,000 blacks were put on an island, he said, "in less than three years, they would have retrograded governmentally, half of the men would have been killed, and the other half would have two wives apiece." Susie King Taylor, Union nurse and wife of Sergeant Edward King, wrote bitterly in 1902: "Was the war in vain? Has it brought freedom, in the full sense of the word or has it not made our condition more hopeless?" She charged: "we are burned, tortured, and denied a fair trial, murdered for any imaginary wrong conceived in the brain of the negro-hating white man." In his Harvard commencement address of 1904, Thomas Wentworth Higginson, who had commanded a black regiment, the First South Carolina (U.S.), begged his privileged white audience not to betray the men of color: "You built Shaw's statue: can you calmly doubt that those who marched with him should vote, like you?"[18]

The tide of discrimination rolled on. In 1915, leading filmmaker D. W. Griffith released his virulently racist *The Birth of a Nation*, lauding the KKK and leading to its resurgence, beginning in the Union state of Indiana. Pulling once more on the antebellum stereotype of the African animal lusting for white women, the movie depicted a bestial attempted rape and other vile conduct by black soldiers. Bigotry trumped history. Despite service in both world wars, the black soldier continued to face discrimination and received no positive notice save in scholarly works.

Then, in 1965, the poet Robert Lowell brought back the 54th and its black soldiers to popular attention. Shocked by TV pictures of the terrified faces of African American children, attacked by rabid whites while on their school bus, he wrote "For the Union Dead." Returning to Saint Gaudens' statue, he felt that the stiff-backed colonel, eternally leading his black soldiers into battle, no longer served as an appropriate American symbol: "The monument sticks like a fish bone in the city's throat." In 1989 came *Glory*, with Matthew Broderick's brilliant interpretation of the diffident, self-effacing Shaw. The movie revivified soldiers of color, even though some critics decried the use of African American stereotypes—the Uncle, the angry Buck, the uppity educated urban free black—when the film might have profiled real soldiers, such as Sergeant William Carney, who won the Congressional Medal of Honor for his conduct at Wagner.

In the 1990s, extralegal white militias proliferated, often sprouting in the old Confederate states. They revivified the paramilitary character of the KKK as they prepared to resist a Sherman-style blitzkrieg invasion by a sinister "new world order." This comprised an unholy alliance of the United States and the United Nations, both bent on robbing white Americans of their local sovereignty. The appeal of these militant organizations seemed to dissipate somewhat, however, as the new century dawned. But racial tensions heightened again in 2008, with the election as president of Barack Obama, a biracial candidate. Prominent whites continued to question whether this man of color really had been born in Hawaii and could possibly be a legitimate American.[19]

Despite this milestone election, for many members of the minority community not too much had changed. African Americans remained disproportionately represented in the ranks of the poor, the unemployed, the prison population, the dispossessed. Social commentator Jonathan Kozol reports that, from the 1990s on, America's public schools have been re-segregated. Peter Whoriskey adds that even Little Rock's schools, where desegregation began and equal attendance by both races had been achieved by 1980, now have an 80 percent black profile. Vouchers, charter, and parochial schools have drawn away white pupils. In a provocative article, March 2011, Darryl Pinckney, looking at the disparity in incarceration rates for blacks and whites throughout the country, argues that jails have become the new frontier of Jim Crow, authorities once again more concerned with the control of the dispossessed than with justice for all.[20]

Did America keep faith with the black regiments? *Harper's Magazine* reported in May 2012 a Federal government appropriation of $14.5 million to restore Confederate President Jefferson Davis' beach home, Beauvoir, in Biloxi, Mississippi. Tourists may take home souvenir pennies machine stamped with the head of Jefferson Davis, obliterating the bust of Lincoln, the "great emancipator." The gift shop plans to stock copies of *Little Black Sambo*.[21]

Many women who thought that war service as nurses, board members of volunteer organizations, propagandists, and bread-winning heads of households would bring them public recognition, found their aspirations thwarted. The Women's Loyal League collected 400,000 signatures in support of the 13th Amendment to free the slaves. Surely, they reasoned, the nation could do no less than lift legal restrictions based on gender as well? Some women, such as Mary A. Livermore, went from organizations like the Sanitary Commission into the suffragette movement, seeing a clear correlation. Progressive males, such as the Rev. Henry W. Bellows, supported them. War service, he asserted in 1867, "did more to advance the rights of woman by proving her gifts for public duties, than a whole library of arguments and protests." The U.S. Supreme Court would shortly disagree.[22]

The Fourteenth Amendment seemingly gave the franchise to all citizens. In 1872, activist Susan B. Anthony determined to test this proposition by casting her ballot in New York elections. Two weeks later police arrested her on a charge of "illegal voting." The court fined her $100, a substantial figure at that time. Three years later, the Supreme Court weighed in, decreeing that the Federal government could not bestow the franchise as a universal right; states allotted the privilege of voting to whom they wished. Thus, in a states' rights decision, the Court overrode the U.S. Constitution, declaring females not necessarily empowered citizens in the public arena. So women took their case to individual states, where they found a better reception. Western states began the trend, perhaps because men respected women's hard work on the farm, and fewer black females lived there to queer the political brew. Wyoming granted women the ballot in 1869. Still, it took until 1920, sixty years after Sumter, for Congress to pass the Nineteenth Amendment, making the female franchise universal.[23]

Conventional wisdom in the immediate post–Civil War period held that women should neither vote nor work outside the home. Yet, in fact, thousands of war widows and spouses of crippled vets needed paid work to eke out a living for themselves and their families. Women also sought employment if their marriages collapsed due to the violent and abusive behavior of husbands emotionally damaged by war service. Twenty-four-year-old Charlotte Cross applied for a Treasury Department job in 1866 because she had left her husband. He had enlisted from Buffalo, New York, in 1863. His spouse described him then as a good man, but he had returned alcoholic, "rendering him unfit for work, for society, and too soon unworthy of a wife's care, forgiveness, or endurance." Women (and children) earned slave wages in factories, department stores, or teaching school, leading Harriet Beecher Stowe to worry, in her *Atlantic* column, that women must sink into "vice," that is, prostitution, to survive.[24]

Government departments began hiring women in 1862. Elizabeth Custer, in D.C. during September 1864, already witnessed "an army of black [clad] and weary creatures who had lost their husbands or sons in the war and were working for themselves or their children." At quitting time, they could be seen "hurrying home to cook dinner for their children." By the early 1890s, women held nearly 33 percent of clerking jobs in the U.S. government's executive departments and by 1900 occupied 29 percent of clerking positions nationwide. They remained underrepresented at the senior levels in both private and public sectors.[25]

The United States has never had a female head of state. A common rationale for this anomaly cites women's lack of combat experience and a supposed want of the aggressiveness needed to be commander-in-chief. At the same time, until recently, the military deliberately denied women frontline assignments. Mary Walker won the Congressional Medal of Honor for duties performed as the first female surgeon in the U.S. Army, serving in the field throughout the Civil War. In 1917, Congress rescinded her award, saying she lacked "actual combat with an enemy," even though her life had been endangered many times. Only in 1977 did she again receive the honor, posthumously.[26]

———————

The labor movement in general hoped for improved working conditions as a result of a war seemingly fought to expand freedom. Some union leaders at the time, and historians since, have placed the conflict in the broad context of an ongoing struggle to improve the lives of ordinary people. Once again, the expectations remained unfulfilled, causing one historian of the period to conclude that "among the masses of Americans there were no victors, only the vanquished."[27]

Labor spokesmen reasoned that, having broken the slave oligarchy, the nation would support benefits for the working class, such as reduced hours per shift, child labor laws, safety regulations, workers' compensation, collective bargaining, and full employment. The first blow came with military demobilization in 1865–66, creating a flood of one million unemployed. This number failed to recede, creating a surplus labor pool that benefited bosses who could threaten militants with replacement.[28]

It quickly became apparent that workers' organizations had few allies in the establishment: owners, managers, and their political allies staunchly opposed reform. The *Rochester Daily Union and Advertiser* warned that the war had made wealth greater and more powerful; "the capital thus concentrated is to be used in a greater or lesser degree to defeat the objects sought by the working men." Even many former abolitionists opposed so-called "artificial" restraints on the free play of the labor market. When New England Brahmin radical Wendell Phillips told his friend, the poet James Russell Lowell, that he had a plan for an eight-hour working day, Lowell responded that he opposed this measure. He feared it would create a "material and unideal" (i.e., middle-class consumer) culture that the versifier "would not care to live in."[29]

To turn public sentiment against strident workers, opponents raised the specter of the communist menace. Washington, D.C.'s *National Republican*, July 21, 1877, pronounced in righteous anger "that communistic ideas are very widely entertained in America by the workmen employed in mines and factories and by the railroads. This poison was introduced into our social system by European laborers." The writings of Marx and Engels, along with the recent (1871) attempt of Paris, France, to form a separate, self-governing, egalitarian commune, poured gasoline on the flames.

Violence erupted as workers took the struggle to the streets, striking, picketing the worst employers, and roughing up scabs. The war made surplus guns readily available and many found their way into the hands of labor militants. Authorities, accustomed since 1861 to putting down sedition, struck back with force, using police and troops against even peaceful protesters. The *Independent*, a Congregationalist magazine, on August 2, 1877, editorialized: "If the club of the policeman, knocking out the brains of the rioter, will answer, then well and good; but if it does not meet the exigency, then bullets and bayonets, canister and grape . . . constitute the one remedy."

In the Great Strike of that year, lasting almost two weeks and leaving a hundred people dead, along with thousands wounded, ten governors called out the military against the workers. "The strikers have been put down by force," wrote President Hayes approvingly. In a twenty-five-year period, governors called out the National Guard, a force dominated by the prosperous and powerful, more than a hundred times against strikers. The authorities proved more willing to suppress industrial workers than to defend the civil rights of African Americans against Southern paramilitaries. The GAR overwhelmingly aided the establishment against labor, even turning out with arms. The old officer corps, defenders of class interests, dominated the chapters. But even many rank and file denigrated the common run of working men, associating them with wartime opposition to the Republican administration and fomenting the notorious draft riots.[30]

A cluster of corporate and fiscal leaders, whose careers often took off in the war, epitomized the class on behalf of whom the forces of the republic mobilized. The public funds businessmen received via huge defense contracts issued by the wartime government helped to build their fortunes, beginning a trend of redistributing wealth upward. In New York, by 1863 1 percent of the population owned 61 percent of the city's wealth. Nothing inherently unpatriotic exists in building up a business in wartime, but a whiff of profiteering clung to some of the era's prominent capitalists. J. P. Morgan sold guns to the Union at six times the price he paid to acquire them. It also seems striking how many of these men forged ahead by not bearing arms while others remained away fighting. Morgan paid $300 for a substitute when facing the 1863 draft. Others who opted out of service included Jay Gould, Andrew Carnegie, John D. Rockefeller, Jim Fisk, and the railroad magnate James J. Hill.[31]

If the war proved an unalloyed success for any one group, it comprised these captains of industry, commerce, and banking. The industrial revolution would have generated great assets anyway, but the war acted as a vital catalyst. Philip Armour made his first two million selling pork to the army; Clement Studebaker began amassing a vast fortune manufacturing army wagons. Benefiting from the strife while not making a personal sacrifice seemed fair to these men of capital and their supporters. Apologists argued they possessed unique expertise vital to outbuilding and outgunning the Confederacy. If this resulted in a vast inequality of wealth between the upper tier and ordinary folk, it simply reflected the inevitable "survival of the fittest" projected by the newly popular Social Darwinism, a bowdlerization of the British naturalist's hypotheses.[32]

Corporate leaders learned in the war how to lobby for government contracts, preferments, tax loopholes, and subsidies. The fiscal ties of business to government carried over into peacetime, giving to the capitalist hegemony the unsavory title Robber Barons. So flagrant became the buying of influence in Congress that even President Hayes, a robust exponent of free enterprise, felt moved to inquire, "Shall the railroads govern the country, or shall the people govern the railroads?" Playing off Lincoln's famous Gettysburg address, he dubbed D.C. "a government of corporations, by corporations, and for corporations."[33]

For many, the Grant administration typified the depths to which the tone of public life had sunk. Though Grant did not personally take part in illegal acts, he surrounded himself with old war comrades who mired the president in scandal, as they greedily feasted at the public trough, arm in arm with their business cronies. Popular essayist John Burroughs, provoked by the corruption, speculated that Grant had a split personality, "a very great man, a hero, covered over, or wrapped about, by a common, ordinary man." Burroughs reasoned that "during his Presidency the vulgar, commonplace man shows himself frequently—the hero subsides again, sinks back out of sight." But perhaps these seeming personality changes do not require so dramatic an explanation. Many successful Union soldiers, like Grant, came from modest backgrounds and had known want in their early years. They now had no desire to serve out their lives on half-pay, contending instead that their proven leadership qualities fitted them for the highest offices. They had earned a place in the sun by risking their lives and, if this put opportunities to make fast money in their way, so much the better.[34]

The massive wealth produced by the booming industrial revolution fermented an era of ostentatious consumption, a reckless greed at the top unsurpassed before the twenty-first century. Not only at home, but abroad, observers looked askance at the lavish, frivolous expenditures of America's plutocracy. Diplomat and journalist John Russell Young, who accompanied Grant on his 1877–79 world tour, found Europeans amazed by America's "shoddy lords" and "petroleum aristocracy" that "overran Paris and amazed the frugal French mind by extravagance and want of culture." They provided a bonanza for restauranteurs, jewelers, and art dealers, who could not charge them too much. One recent writer says of the period: "As a people we practiced excess. Excess in everything—pleasure, gaudy display, endless toil, and death. Vagrant children slept in the alleys. Rag picking was a profession."[35]

Walt Whitman, disgusted by the war's afterbirth, wrote: "Never was there, perhaps, more hollowness at heart than at present," in all spheres of life. "The depravity of the business classes of our country is not less than has been supposed, but infinitely greater," because "the one sole object is, by any means, pecuniary gain." The crassness of the period led Mark Twain and Charles Dudley Warner to coin a phrase that would stick: "The Gilded Age." In their novel of that name, they wrote that the war had, "changed the politics of a people . . . and wrought so profoundly upon the national character that the influence cannot be measured short of two or three generations."[36]

Some Northern gentlemen, pushed out of politics by machine politicians like Boss Tweed of New York, began to empathize with their old antagonists of the planter class (a shift in loyalties that boded ill for African Americans). Whatever their faults, Southern gentlemen did not seem wedded to "the bottom line," and increasingly the claim that they had not fought for slavery but for honor appealed also above the Mason-Dixon Line. Even before the fighting ended, Colonel Theodore Lyman of Meade's staff, embroiled in the 1864 slaughter, watching Rebel officers mowed down, conceded that they "are a valuable people, capable of a heroism that is too rare to be lost."[37]

Henry Adams, a Northern aristocrat, registered bitter disappointment in Grant as a peacetime leader. Intimates of the president, he claimed, said the man followed no fixed principles and some were not sure he was capable of rigorous mental activity. "They could never follow a mental process in his thought. They were not sure that he did think." When, in 1882, Adams wrote a didactic novel about political life, he made the central Northern character, Senator Silas P. Ratcliffe of Illinois, a corrupt figure. By contrast, the hero, a Virginian, had gone to war on principle, even though "he had seen from the first that, whatever issue the war took, Virginia and he must be ruined."[38]

Southerners proved more than happy to accept the role of national critic, picking up the threads of their antebellum attacks on Yankee corruption and greed. In 1930, twelve prominent Southern men of letters published *I'll Take My Stand*, a critique from the agrarian perspective of the failings of business-industrial capitalism. Their numbers included the poet Allen Tate, the historian Frank Owsley, and the novelist Robert Penn Warren. Then, in 1939, millions heard Rhett tell Scarlett, at the end of *Gone with the Wind*, that he was leaving her and Atlanta, showcase of the New South with its gaudy mansions built on chain-gang labor. He would return to Charleston, no longer considered the national pariah as the home of sedition, but a haven where he hoped to find "something left in life of charm and grace." Yet the Southerner could not serve as a good foil for the capitalist, when racist cruelty still marred Dixie's escutcheon. The Southern white did not hold the moral high ground. Between 1882 and 1968, 4,743 lynchings occurred in the United States; blacks accounted for 75 percent of victims and the killings concentrated heavily in the ex-Confederacy.[39]

———•◦•———

Many people hoped that the war would purify character, bringing out qualities of comradeship, heroism, self-sacrifice. This it did in many cases. But some observers felt that the massive violent destruction had coarsened the national identity. As early as 1863, Lincoln had worried about the degrading of personality through violence: "Actual war coming, blood grows hot, and blood is spilled. Thought is forced from old channels into confusion. Deception breeds and thrives." He went on: "Each man feels an impulse to kill his neighbor, lest he first be killed by him. Revenge and retaliation follow." In short, "Every foul bird comes abroad, and every dirty reptile rises up."[40]

Henry James mulled on this theme in a fascinating little ghost story, "The Jolly Corner," published in 1908. James had sat out the Civil War through residence in Europe. In his tale, he speculates on the man he might have become had he stayed, seen combat, and sought power in postwar America. At night, in his ancestral home, he meets the shadow of the man he would have been, someone more imposing, decisive, yet also coarser, brutal, aggressive, and mutilated, a sad and sorry soul. Garth, Henry's brother, had been an officer in the 54th Massachusetts. He became a war hero, wounded in the side and foot at Wagner. But he suffered constant pain, was nearly crippled, and became alcoholic. Disinherited finally, he died in poverty.[41]

James' story may have been somewhat self-serving, but he had a point. The war undoubtedly had a brutalizing effect on many of those who fought, introducing a period of heightened social violence and lawlessness. By 1865, arms manufacturers produced a million guns per year, and the nation bristled with army surplus weapons. One historian of gun violence argues that the war and its aftermath created the modern American gun culture. This may be a little overstated: American belief in the regenerative power of the gun in the hands of the worthy citizen enjoys a long history. When on Lexington Green, April 19, 1775, Major John Pitcairn of the Royal Marines shouted, "Disperse, ye rebels," he also ordered them to "Lay down your arms, damn you!" The militia scattered but took their guns with them, and the attachment to firearms has grown ever since.[42]

To keep up demand in the 1870s and 1880s, the gun makers fed the fear of lawbreakers spawned by the war, citing a string of urban bank robberies and burglaries, plus theft and other crimes committed by tramps who infested the rural highways. In 1875, the industry put out a little book entitled *The Pistol in Its Home and on the Road*, encouraging all citizens to tote a revolver for their safety. By 1877, the *Chicago Tribune* estimated that one-tenth of their city's residents carried concealed weapons. The next year, social activist William Graham Sumner, writing in *Scribner's Monthly*, warned that arms manufacturers now targeted youths as future gun owners. Boys' stories, he charged, increasingly exuded violence, and "it is always mixed with the code of the revolver, and in many of the stories, the latter is taught in its fullness. These youngsters generally carry revolvers and use them at their good discretion. Every youth who aspires to manliness [suggested the stories] ought to get and carry a revolver."[43]

Violent crime became a legacy of the war. From the 1860s through the 90s, population rose 170 percent, but violent crime increased 445 percent. Much mayhem came at the hands of veterans. In 1940, criminologist Betty Rosenbaum calculated that, in 1866, for example, two-thirds of all those committed to state prisons for violent crimes had been soldiers. Why? A modern army psychologist explains that we have been much better at overcoming soldiers' repugnance to taking life than we have been at deprogramming their violent impulses when the killing is over.[44]

The huge demobilization of 1865–1866 left large numbers unemployed. Veterans, used to appropriating what they needed, might go on doing just that. Some treated this as a temporary expedient, but others had acquired a taste for violent adventure that became incurable. The James and Younger boys, "Bloody Bill" Anderson, all got their training as guerrillas in the war. Sue Mundy, another hoodlum, had been a captain in John Hunt Morgan's cavalry. He found death at the hands of a peace officer, as did most of the others. Veteran Sam Hildebrand, for example, ended a career of violence gunned down by a constable in Illinois, March 1872.[45]

Border areas that had been contested by the two sides, Kansas, Missouri, West Virginia, and the eastern Kentucky mountains, remained areas of bitter personal division, often resulting in long-lasting blood feuds, such as the famous Hatfield and McCoy clan war of 1873 to 1878. As in other times and places around the globe that have seen decades of violence, casual brutality became a norm of life. Witness the death of Rebel private John Patterson, as reported by Lucy Maxfield from Randolph County, Missouri. Released from service, July 1865, "He started home and had got but a short distance from the army when he was murdered by two robbers," just for his horse and saddle.[46]

Drug abuse encouraged unpredictable, unruly behavior. The use of opium derivatives as anesthetics, and pain and stress relievers, led to a huge increase in consumption. Between 1860 and 1870, use in the northeast alone rose from 105,000 lbs. to 500,000 lbs. Opium-based patent medicines and tonics also soared in popularity. Veterans by no means accounted for all those with a drug habit, and not all veteran users became criminals. But, at the very least, overuse of mood-altering substances by veterans produced theft, violent and erratic behavior, and often a state of criminal indigence.[47]

Connecticut Captain John William DeForest thought the war made a man of the volunteer: "He has the patience of a soldier, and a soldier's fortitude under discouragement. He is a better and stronger man for having fought three years, out-facing death and suffering. Like the nation, he has developed and learned his powers." True, many thousands of vets adjusted well to home life, moving on to lead productive lives in business and the public sphere. Many others, however, shattered mentally or physically, struggled to assume a normal life, and not all made it. One medical historian estimates that, if the war killed about 600,000, it debilitated and disfigured an equal number.[48]

To give some idea of the scope of mutilation, in 1867 alone Federal medical authorities purchased 4,095 prosthetic legs, 2,391 arms, 61 hands, and 14 feet. In the first postwar year, Mississippi spent half its budget on artificial limbs. Looking at the same picture from the aspect of the microcosm, a study of the muster rolls of one unit, Co. I, 30th Georgia, suggests that as many men were crippled as killed. Disabling wounds leading to discharge included shots through the arms, legs, side, ankles, and hands, with amputations in the worst cases. Disease also left men wasted and subject to recurring bouts of sickness. W. H. Belknap, of the 15th Iowa, wrote in 1887 of the long-term effects on the constitution: "More fatal than bullets, its poison-ous effects upon the blood continued with many long after the smoke of battle had cleared away, producing other disease which made life a burden."[49]

Heroic remedies and opium-based pain relievers had radical side effects. Morphine created a sense of vertigo, with walls and inani-mate objects seeming to spin. Patients experienced the impression of massive electric shock in the trunk and limbs, giving way to tor-por. Hallucinations, headaches, and stomach pains also commonly occurred. Of the drug's addictive qualities, one medical researcher writes: "habitual users of opiates require increasing quantities of the drug to satisfy the craving and suffer severe withdrawal symptoms after removal of the drug." In 1879, U.S. army surgeon Joseph Wood-ward estimated that 45,000 Union vets had reached this condition. People so identified use of the hypodermic with veterans that shoot-ing up became known as "the soldier's disease."[50]

Disabled veterans encountered discrimination in the workplace. The Federal government provided some openings to amputees. For example, Private Decker, a double amputee, became doorkeeper of the House of Representatives. Others became clerks. But those hired represented a minority of the needy. Disfigured veterans also evoked embarrassment at home, their relatives often tucking them away out of sight. Humiliation added to the physical stress of wound pain. One psychiatric study suggests that the amputation of a limb, for example, may produce a sense of loss and subsequent grieving equivalent to the death of a loved one, and may last as long.[51]

Veterans suffered nightmare reliving of traumatic events or PTSD, a frequent and debilitating complaint that most civilians failed to understand. The quartermaster of the 5th Indiana Cavalry never recovered mentally from his incarceration in Andersonville. Repatriated, he worked obsessively on building a model of the prison in his backyard, then spent the last twenty-five years of his life in the Indiana Hospital for the Insane. Major John McMurray, 6th United States Colored Troops, recalled in 1916 that when he entered the army "I was young and strong, and had never suffered from any sort of dissipation." But he had relived the horror of combat "every year of my life since," concluding bitterly that he had "borne it all with a mighty small amount of sympathy from those about me."[52]

When mentally unstable and violent veterans could no longer be coped with at home, they frequently ended in asylums. Thus, relatives requested that Lucas Hoffman be committed to the Government Hospital for the Insane after he demonstrated acute delirium and had become dangerous. At the start of the war, about 8,500 patients existed in mental homes. By the end of the conflict, that number had doubled, and did so again by 1870. The GAR attempted to serve as a halfway house for the transition back to civilian life, allowing vets to "domesticate" the war experience. But many fell through the cracks or remained too damaged to seek assistance.[53]

Then, as now, many emotionally damaged veterans failed to make the mental journey back from the battlefield and became homeless. For twenty years after the war, the roads that had taken boys to war now filled with battalions of shiftless tramps, moving from place to place, scrounging what they could to stay alive. Police moved tramps on or picked them up as vagrants. Undoubtedly, many had been skulkers who dropped out of the armies because they could not cope, living off the countryside. Still unable to function, they found no way out of the tunnel of misery into which the war had pitched them. The Chief Detective of Massachusetts reported in 1878: "This tramp system is undoubtedly an outgrowth of the war; the bummers of our armies could not give up their habits of roving and marauding, and settle down to the honest and industrious duties of the citizen, as did most of our volunteer soldiers, but preferred a life of vagrancy." The tone is typically unsympathetic to those who had lost their bearings on the firing line.[54]

The deaths of soldiers in the war, the suffering of vets in the postwar, created long-term anguish and practical problems for relatives and friends. Domestic violence and drug abuse broke up homes. Captain George Carse, 40th New York, had been hit in the face and leg three times at Chancellorsville. Disfigured and in lasting pain, he drank whiskey heavily, also taking chloroform and absinthe. Unable to cope with her husband's disintegration, his wife divorced him in 1876. The absence of a father in war, or his failure as a parent in the postwar, could lead neglected offspring into juvenile delinquency. Writing in 1918 about the Civil War, the legal scholar H. C. Parsons concluded: "There was a marked increase in juvenile delinquency and it was found to be due to the disturbance of home conditions, the absence of the father and elder brother, the employment of the mother in other than domestic pursuits and the interruption of school attendance."[55]

Civil War people understood that children's emotional problems often began with news of the father's death. Chauncey Burr had written in 1865 that the youngster "Too young to know sorrow, Or life's woes to borrow, / Must learn some to-morrow, Its father is dead." War death could inflict permanent depression on young and old alike. Ada Bacot had been pregnant when her husband died in the Confederate service, January 1864. After the war, she struggled with chronic bouts of depression as she fought to raise her son alone, at times neglecting both herself and the child.[56]

Mary Todd Lincoln, having witnessed her husband's assassination, became unnerved by the trauma. Her health slid precariously, symptoms including chills and migraines. Incessant weeping made her temples pound, her eyes burn and swell. Words she used to describe her condition included desolation, misery, agony, and affliction. She confessed to Simon Cameron, her husband's first Secretary of War, that, "Such a fearful life, has injured my health, to such an extent, that at least 3 days, of each week, I am unable to sit up, with my severe head-aches."[57]

Historians have not done an outstanding job of tracing the consequences of wartime loss over generations. A fascinating exception is Prof. Don Fehrenbacher, who writes about his own family. George Outman, a forebear, was mortally wounded at Stones River, December 1862. The death brought grief and poverty to the family. Seven years later, the widow died while trying to relocate the family to Kansas. She left behind an eleven-year-old daughter, the historian's grandmother. This grim scenario limited the young girl's life choices and horizons. Her grandson speculates that, if Outman had survived, his daughter would have grown up differently and married differently, perhaps leading a richer and fuller life. "My very existence, it seems, is connected to a single deadly moment in Tennessee on the last day of 1862."[58]

The wartime inability of relatives to find emotional closure, when the fate and resting place of so many thousands remained unknown, continued into the postwar years, prolonging anguish and exacerbating grief. Walt Whitman noted that the War Department estimated at least 25,000 Union dead had never received burial, 5,000 drowned could not be recovered, 15,000 lay buried in hastily dug, unmarked graves, and 2,000 corpses had been unearthed by erosion or animals. Whitman acknowledged the government's efforts to collect remains into National Cemeteries to give as much recognition to the fallen as possible, but he thought officialdom underestimated the number of unidentified: "ages yet may see, on monuments and gravestones, singly or in masses, to thousands or tens of thousands, the significant word UNKNOWN."[59]

By 1870, Federal authorities calculated that 309,225 Union dead had been reinterred, at a cost of $3,112,209. The Southern states tried to create Confederate cemeteries, but this proved a challenging task with meager public budgets. It helped that most fighting had been on home ground so that local and private groups could fill the place of government. Henry Bottom, whose land had been a battleground during Perryville, October 1862, created a Confederate cemetery on his property where he reinterred 347. But he could not identify 30. The same held true in the North. Clara Barton estimated the headstones of 45 percent in the National Cemeteries bore the legend, Unknown.[60]

To help comfort the bereaved, the GAR began sponsoring Memorial Day observance in 1868, building on periodic ceremonies at the national cemeteries. A similar event started informally in the South in 1866. It helped a little to know that loved ones lived on in memory, although remembrance day quickly morphed into an all-purpose holiday. Those who had suffered no personal bereavement soon forgot the dead; the unlucky families bore the full burden of grief. As a New York woman predicted during the war: "for everyone that falls on the battlefield or suffers a languishing death in the hospitals, some friends mourn and weep their lives away."[61]

If the human consequences of the war proved long-lasting, so did the fiscal costs. We commonly think that wars always boost the economy. This may be true for war-related industries and businesses, but conflicts in general bear down hard on the taxpayer. Emory Upton, Victorian soldier and military theorist, estimated the Mexican War cost the U.S. Treasury $100 million. By comparison, the immediate cost of the Civil War to the Federal government reached $3 billion, with a further incalculable loss to the ex-Confederate states, whose treasury and banking system ceased to exist.[62]

To pay for the war effort, the United States in 1861 introduced the first Federal income tax, followed by an inheritance tax in 1862, with the Internal Revenue Service to police the system. Thaddeus Stevens, chair of the House Ways and Means Committee, stated the underlying principle: "While the rich and the thrifty will be obliged to contribute largely from the abundance of their means . . . no burdens have been imposed on the industrious laborer and mechanic." Following this rationale, the government imposed luxury taxes on such commodities as carriages, yachts, and jewelry. Only one measure caused real hardship for working people, a sin tax on tobacco, introduced in 1862. Despite these measures, the government still had to borrow money, financing two-thirds of the war through loans. Paying off such debt provides one reason why the cost of wars does not peak until two generations later.[63]

State and local governments also needed to raise taxes and take out war loans to pay for equipping troops and supporting the families of men at the front. For example, Claremont, New Hampshire, raised the property tax rate from $.39 per $100 of real estate value to $1.58, but still ended the war $71,000 in the red. Neighboring Newport found itself $56,000 in the hole. The bill to the states included the costs of maintaining asylums and orphanages. Pennsylvania for years supported 2,000 war orphans at an annual cost of $150 per child plus clothing.[64]

A further major cost to the national and state governments accrued in the provision of prosthetic limbs. Ultimately, pensions to soldiers, notably the disabled and their dependents, made up the largest postwar price tag. Adjutant Anthony McDermott, 69th Pennsylvania, applied for a pension due to the problems that developed as he aged, following a kick delivered in 1865 by an army horse. He drew the pension, granted in 1885, until his death in 1916. After that, his widow continued to receive a benefit.[65]

Pension disbursements ate up over 50 percent of many Southern state budgets and, by 1893, more than 40 percent of Federal allocations. The total cost to the U.S. taxpayer for military pensions from the Civil War may have crossed the $8 billion mark. It is not unreasonable to estimate that the final bill for the war, all costs to North and South, including destruction to infrastructure, fiscal, and economic resources, topped $20 billion.[66]

History never becomes simply a thing of the past. The consequences of wars, their impact on all areas of human life, remain with us long after the textbooks close the chapter on this or that armed conflict. The national government made pension disbursements for Civil War dependents into the late 1980s. Alabama holds the distinction of being the last government authority to make a pension payment to a Civil War dependent, Alberta Martin, aged eighty-nine. At twenty-one, she had married Jasper Martin, then eighty-one. As a boy soldier, he served with the 4th Alabama in Virginia, 1864–65. Alberta received her final distribution in October 1996. Bill Clinton occupied the White House.[67]

———— •◆• ————

Only one question remains. Given the huge costs of the war years, 1861–65, how long did Americans take before once again embracing armed conflict as one of the highest expressions of national character and values, pushing aside—if not entirely forgetting—the blood and muck of their recent experience? We can approach our question by eavesdropping on General Robert E. Lee.

GENERAL LEE AND
THE GRAY LADIES

×

ON DECEMBER 13, 1862, GENERAL LEE WATCHED TRIUM-
phantly as his troops threw back a determined Yankee attempt
to break his lines at Fredericksburg. Caught up in the thrill of the
moment, Lee turned to his colleague, General James Longstreet, and
said: "It is well that war is so terrible—[or] we should grow too fond
of it!" Success in combat could trigger the exuberant adrenaline flow
that gripped Lee. But, as a wise and experienced soldier, the general
understood that the heady rush came with a huge human price tag.[1]

By 1865, many on both sides agreed with the general that the price
of war's stimulating excitement might be exorbitantly high. Earlier,
we met John B. Jones, who fought his war from behind a desk in
Richmond. At first, he hoped to experience vicariously the excitement of war. By 1863, he understood the horror of fighting, and spent
much of his time worrying about how to keep his family warm and
fed. And by 1865, two years later, he no longer even cared about winning; he just wanted peace. "Sitting by our cheerless fires, we sum-
mon up countless blessings that we could enjoy, if this war was only
over." Jones could not believe that the survivors of the conflict might
someday be brought to embrace fighting again. "Will this generation,
with their eyes open, and their memories fresh, ever, ever, go to war
again?" he asked.[2]

The South had every reason to be sick of war, with its harvest
of death, ruin, and crippled men, its forests and wilderness areas
infested with deserters and outlaws. In the North, despite early

enthusiasm for the boys in blue, the unsavory reputation of soldiers had never quite dissipated. Now, as they came home in thousands, stories of their bad behavior went the rounds again. Popular repute stigmatized veterans as unreliable in habits, prone to substance abuse and sexual license (as indeed some had been). Bars and chop houses still posted signs prohibiting Irish, dogs, and soldiers. A police officer ordered men of the 10th Illinois, strolling a Chicago sidewalk, June 1865, into the gutter, as he would bums or vagrants. "Could a greater insult have been offered us?" asked Corporal James A. Congleton.[3]

The Soldier's Friend, a Union veterans' magazine, reported in its November 1865 issue that ex-soldiers met trouble getting hired, and so felt obliged to "conceal the fact of their having been in the army." A grievous war wound might not be seen as a romantic red badge of courage so much as a burden upon the public. *The Soldier's Friend* also related an anecdote of a man who had lost both arms, reduced to begging on a sidewalk. A passerby, angered at being panhandled, snarled at the cripple, "with an oath, 'he was a —— fool for going to the war!'" Gratitude to the brave hero, maimed in his country's cause, could prove short-lived.[4]

Boys who had not been in the war soon got tired of ex-soldiers acting as though military service had initiated them into another, special world whose secrets remained closed to all others. The veterans' emotional inability to leave the war behind, their constant recurrence to marches and battles, bewildered adolescents. Edward Moore, of Poague's Battery (C.S.A.), wrote that the younger generation "cannot comprehend, and express surprise that the old soldiers never forget and are so wrought up by the recollections of their war experiences." How do we explain that Grant, a soldier, won the presidency in 1869? Simply, his appeal reflected his executive experience and presumed devotion to public service, rather than any enthusiasm for his military record, his doctrine of brutal total war. The president himself candidly remarked to John Russell Young during his world tour that "I never went into a battle willingly or with enthusiasm. I was always glad when a battle was over. I never want to command another army."[5]

Yet by 1876, toward the end of Grant's term, we may discern already a perceptible shift in the public mood, back toward a more favorable view of war and soldiering. Gluttony in the marketplace and corruption in government began to rekindle the myth of combat as ennobling, a cleansing of the selfish individualism of peace. Graft had reached as far as the western frontier, where unprincipled agents cheated reservation tribes out of government disbursements promised them by treaty. The Civil War's boy general, George Armstrong Custer, travelled east to give evidence before Congress, testifying that unfair treatment drove the tribes toward war. Custer infuriated Grant, as his and others' revelations about the scandal appeared to implicate some of the president's intimate circle in the tawdry dealings. The chief executive almost refused to let Custer return to his command. This would have been a grave public humiliation when the 7th Cavalry would shortly be ordered to join other units charged with herding disgruntled Sioux and Cheyenne warriors back onto their reservations.

As events unfolded, Custer took the field to lead his regiment into a debacle, losing his own life along with those of most of his troopers. Public reaction to his death indicates the sea change occurring in attitudes to the military. The shift may be charted in the thinking of Walt Whitman. While not quite saying, "as Whitman goes, so goes the nation," he does act as a barometer of the changing cultural climate. To set the scene, we need to appreciate, as the late Stephen E. Ambrose pointed out, that Custer did not rank as a great general. Ambrose's succinct summation of Custer deserves quoting in full: "His undoubted audacity and courage were offset by a criminal lack of good judgment, a refusal to gather intelligence about the enemy, an insistence on attacking at the earliest possible opportunity, a petty jealousy toward his fellow officers, a monumental ambition, and a total disregard for the lives of his men."[6]

In the Civil War, Custer adhered to the school that operated by blind faith in the moral superiority of the reckless offense. He failed to carry out effective reconnaissances or to maneuver for better tactical position before heavily engaging the enemy. Ambrose calculated that the general's turnover in casualties became so high in his Michigan command that, "as a brigade commander, Custer suffered 100 percent losses." Subsequently, Custer rushed into action on the Little

Big Horn, ignoring warnings from his native scouts who believed the hostiles severely outnumbered the cavalry.[7]

The bodies of many troopers, found clustered around Custer's corpse, superficially suggested a gallant last stand. Commentators quickly drew parallels to such epics as the Spartans holding the pass at Thermopylae or Charlemagne's knights under Roland dying in the rearguard at Roncevaux. In fact, to the trained eye, as several officers studying the field after the action noted, the grouping of bodies did not suggest a heroic, well-fought, last action. The clustering suggested that the troopers had panicked, lost cohesion, deserted their posts, and bunched together in terror.[8]

How so? The development of fast-action, breech-loading rifles forced commanders at last to open up the battlefield, because densely packed bodies of troops now served as lambs to the slaughter. Soldiers in 1876 deployed on an extended picket line in squads of four. However, soldiers might lack the comforting shoulder-to-shoulder contact of the earlier close-order formations. To compensate for the sense of aloneness, squads needed to be made up of trusted comrades, welded together by the buddy system.[9]

Unfortunately, officers experimenting with the revised tactics did not yet understand the importance of small-unit bonding. The first four men to dismount formed an impromptu squad that might not know each other, particularly as many troopers had only just joined the regiment. Some recent immigrants barely understood the officers' orders. When the companies came under heavy and unexpected pressure from hostiles, the skirmish lines buckled, losing vital control of the extended perimeter, the men herding back upon each other. Archaeological digs reveal a lack of shell cases on the skirmish line where we would expect to find them if the soldiers had put up a stern defense. Also, native accounts depict many troopers acting so frightened that they looked like drunken men, throwing down their weapons and waiting hopelessly to die. This paralysis often typifies units that have lost their confidence and cohesion.[10]

Whitman had not worn a uniform. Yet, in the Civil War, he enjoyed thinking of himself as a quasi-military man; he dressed like a soldier in a blue suit and army boots, sporting a black hat with gold acorns. He liked it when the guards at hospitals saluted him. He had gained insight into the human aspects of the war. But he had little grasp of military tactics and no understanding of their evolution since the war. Hence, he read into the bunched bodies on the Little Big Horn the makings of a great American epic of sacrifice. He had hoped the Civil War would be America's "Iliad," but it proved too bloody, mucky, sordid, and brutal. The vulgarity and venality of the postwar era disgusted him further. So he welcomed the sacrificial devotion to duty of Custer's 7th. In the *New York Herald,* on July 12, 1876, he acclaimed "The cavalry companies fighting to the last in sternest heroism," and saluted their demonstration of "the utter consecration of one's life to his duty, the sublimest thing a man can do."[11]

Shortly after, he penned "A Death Sonnet for Custer," announcing that America now had its national epic:

> Continues yet the old, old legend of our race,
> The loftiest of life upheld by death.
> The ancient banner perfectly maintain'd,
> O lesson opportune, O how I welcome thee!

Here Whitman subscribes to the myth that war ennobles mankind; that death in battle is the finest act one can undertake for one's country. The poet had already forgotten his musing of a decade earlier on the bleak darkness in men's souls revealed by the cruelty of armed conflict.[12]

———•◆•———

As veterans aged, they, too, distanced the horrors of the Civil War in nostalgia for their passing youth. Could dentures and rheumatics pills ever make a fair substitute for the glow of the campfire on the mountainside, where young men had camped, and for the adventure of marching ranks? Memory became highly selective under the influence of sentiment. As time passed, a survivor of Stuart's cavalry wrote that "the memory of those days seems like a beautiful dream—seen through the mists of the rolling years." Pining for youth also pervaded a poem written in 1895 for the U.S. 1st Cavalry's reunion: "Backward, turn backward, oh, time in your flight, / Make me a soldier boy just for tonight."[13]

Even being a college president or Supreme Court justice failed to stop an old soldier from donning rose-colored spectacles as he journeyed through middle age. Joshua Lawrence Chamberlain, severely wounded in the war, by 1865 entered "an emotional abyss." In 1868, his wife Fannie revealed that he emotionally and physically abused her, almost driving her to divorce. Yet, despite the trauma, Chamberlain came to romanticize military service. He enjoyed returning to Gettysburg, hailed as the hero of Little Round Top, who had saved the Union left flank. He made his last trip in 1913. Toward the end of his life, Chamberlain wrote that Sherman got it wrong about war being hell: it had destructive elements, yes, but it also called forth the best of manhood, eliciting courage, self-discipline, fortitude, and comradeship.[14]

Perhaps the most vivid turnabout occurred in the thinking of Oliver Wendell Holmes Jr. Badly wounded several times during the conflict, he resigned his commission in 1864, fearing that the slaughter in Virginia would drive him mad. But, twenty years later, in a Memorial Day address, on May 30, 1884, he pronounced that his generation had been specially privileged to fight in the war. "Through our great good fortune," he asserted, "in our youth our hearts were touched with fire." Allowing the rhetoric to soar, he proclaimed, "We have seen with our own eyes the snowy heights of honor."[15]

The psychologist William James did not fight in the war. He appreciated some of the selfless and courageous qualities elicited by military service, but he had also witnessed what combat did to his brothers Garth and Robinson, both of whom became dramatic postwar failures. William did not see bloody mayhem working out as a great tonic for the human condition. Instead, in a 1910 essay entitled "The Moral Equivalent of War," he proposed useful but pacific public service outlets for the energy and enthusiasm of youth. These, as much as military service, could be structured to inculcate values of hardihood, civic responsibility, and self-discipline. James' concept became an important inspiration for President John F. Kennedy's Peace Corps. To the same end, some Civil War veterans promoted football as a mock war game, hoping to encourage the muscular values demanded by soldiering.

But nothing could substitute for the real thing. Watching the American attack go in at San Juan Hill, Cuba, 1898, Stephen Crane declared it to be "the best moment in anyone's life." Here he reprised Lee's exultant sentiment at Fredericksburg, but without the more mature man's added caution. Crane's comment might seem odd, coming from an author generally reputed to have written the first fully realistic, perhaps even antiwar, American combat novel. But the authentic settings of *The Red Badge* may make it too easy to misread the novel's ambiguity toward war.[16]

Crane skillfully sketches the character of soldiers, he deftly renders his images of wounded men struggling down the road to the rear, and he demonstrates a real feel for the chaos of battle. Yet the final message of the book fits a time-honored romantic model: the ultimate test, combat, makes men out of boys. We have the climactic moment, right out of chivalric adventure stories, when Henry and his friend Wilson seize the enemy standard, the most knightly of all feats in battle. As Crane says of Henry's rehabilitation, his running away put safely behind him, "He had slept and, awakening, found himself a knight." As often as not, *The Red Badge* would encourage, not deter, adolescent desire to experience the mysterious elevation of combat.[17]

To read a truly stark depiction of the destruction wrought by war, we might compare *The Red Badge* (1895) to a contemporaneous French novel, Émile Zola's *The Debacle* (1892). Breathtaking in scope, Zola's story depicts in excruciating detail the 1870–71 demolition of France's armies by Prussia. We see a defeated and demoralized army descend into a mob, herding behind the defenses of Sedan, trapped like sheep surrounded by wolves. In the rear of the armies masses of looters congregate, and human vultures rob the dead, "pockets jingling with watches and silver coins stolen from pockets."[18]

Zola vividly describes the ghastly wounds of men smashed by modern weapons: "a Zouave with his entrails exposed," an artilleryman on fire from an incoming round, whose "back must have been broken for he was unable to move and was crying bitterly," an officer "with his left forearm gone and his right side slit down to the thigh," who was "imploring somebody, in a dreadful high-pitched voice, to finish him off." The book unflinchingly catalogs the many horrors of field hospitals. Here we read about some head wounds: "smashed jaws with tongue and teeth a bleeding mess, eye-sockets driven in and eyes half out, skulls split open with brains visible." Injuries do not heal but continue to seep pus and secrete bone chips. Flies drink the blood of wounds, while crows pick at tender morsels.[19]

In a particularly chilling scene, peasant partisans tie a captured German soldier to a kitchen table and bleed him slowly to death, like a butchered pig. The partisan who cuts the enemy's throat ensures the end will be drawn-out, lasting hours: he "had taken care with the cut and only a few drops pumped out with the heartbeats." The victim could neither speak nor move. "The only way the march of death could be followed was on the face, a mask distorted by terror." In Zola's final, bleak climax, during the civil war following the Emperor Napoleon III's abdication, two comrades find each other on opposite sides of a barricade as the Paris Commune suffers its death throes. Without realizing who he faces, Jean, a stoical peasant noncom, bayonets Maurice, a headstrong bourgeois idealist who left the army to join the Communards. Jean will live on to help rebuild a broken nation, but this ending has none of the transcendence of Henry Fleming's rebirth as a hero at Chancellorsville. Zola died in 1902, before he could witness the next debacle begin in 1914.[20]

American journalist Richard Harding Davis called the Chicago Exposition of 1893 "the greatest event in the history of the country since the Civil War," unwittingly suggesting that both were magnificent shows. By this time, promoters advertised vacation trips to renovated battle sites, encouraging a growing tourist trade that treated once-bloody fields as picnics for the family. Panoramic dioramas of the great contests, now as famous as Homer's Troy, toured the country. Inevitably, as the accuracy of memory faded with time, myth-making embellished the popular drama of the war. *The Confederate Veteran* lavished praise on the *Gettysburg Cyclorama*, a panoramic painting of the climactic Pickett's charge. Having paid the 50 cents entrance fee, the viewer could stand in rapt fascination: "General Armistead, who led the forlorn hopes of the Confederates, is seen falling from his horse desperately wounded, his horse rearing and plunging, mad with terror." Actually, of Pickett's three brigadiers, Armistead had been the only one to go forward on foot.[21]

The Civil War now made an appealing game for children. Margaret Preston, as a mother, worried about boys' aping of combat: "Almost their entire set of plays have reference to a state of war," she complained. Her five-year old staged marches and battles with his chums, and commanded an army of paper soldiers he made, even building a toy field hospital for the wounded. Most disturbing to his mother, "He gets sticks and hobbles about, saying that he lost a leg at the Second Battle of Manassas." The lasting agony of amputation now forgotten, mutilation became in imagination a red badge of courage, not a grim debilitation.[22]

Reconciliation between white North and South served as a necessary precursor to the renewal of American faith in the positive benefits of military endeavor. The immediate postwar years witnessed great bitterness between the antagonists, whose actions in the latter stages of the conflict had gone well beyond the recognized conventions of war. Mutual recrimination kept the memory of the horror alive. But, at least by the 1880s, anger had mellowed. Recognition of the need to present a united racial front against the possibility of blacks achieving civic and social equality made forgiveness imperative.

In the 1890s, Memorial Day observances at sites such as Gettysburg featured both white Confederate and Union veterans, coming together in fellowship. Speakers increasingly insisted that preservation of slavery had never been the South's primary war aim, nor had the Northern cause encompassed racial equality. Researchers have studied the role of selective memory in reconfiguring the nature of the conflict. One authority concludes that a storyline developed "in which devotion alone made everyone right, and no one truly wrong in the remembered Civil War." Northerners could afford magnanimity because, after all, they had won, breaking the South's economic and political power.[23]

Northerners allowed Southerners to claim they had produced the better soldiers, and had been borne down by sheer numbers only, defending a Lost Cause fought to defend nothing save honor. As late as 1995, novelist Sharyn McCrumb could still use this myth as an effective plot device in one of her ballad books, *She Walks These Hills*.

A character, mulling on the making of a Southern identity, focuses on "the Southern warrior, who prided himself on his bravery and shooting skill, [and] had lost a war to a bureaucratic foe, who won by having more supplies and a vast expendable population of immigrants to throw in the path of Southern gun barrels." The myth remained potent precisely because it grossly simplified what had actually occurred.[24]

Not quite all Northerners proved willing to embrace Confederate myths and heroes. In 1896, the Yale graduating class planted ivy from the grave of Robert E. Lee on the university campus as part of the commencement ceremonies. A Yale alumnus, Joseph Twichell, who had served as a chaplain in the Union Excelsior Brigade, spoke out in opposition. He deemed it wrong to plant in Northern soil "ivy from the grave of Robert Lee, a good man, but the representative of an infamous cause." A huge controversy ensued. Leonard W. Bacon, also from a clerical background, supported Twichell, saying "it can not be too positively impressed on the ingenuous undergraduate mind that, whatever they may think, we old folks have not yet come to the point of looking upon the Civil War as a football game upon a grand scale."[25]

What of the great Confederate general himself? Lee stood by his belief that war's essential nature makes it too terrible to sentimentalize or institutionalize as a high national value. He refused to write an extended memoir of the kind that became popular among other leading figures from the war period, an exercise that helped to make interaction with the war's memory a pleasurable intellectual exercise to be enjoyed in a study chair. Lee urged his countrymen to put the conflict behind them and concentrate, like Zola's Jean, on building the peace. In refusing an invitation to help raise memorials at Gettysburg, Lee explained his motivation: "I think it wiser moreover not to keep open the sores of war, but to follow the example of those nations who endeavored to obliterate the marks of civil strife and to commit to oblivion the feelings it engendered."[26]

Such pacific sentiments failed to dominate the national discourse. Lee's Army of Northern Virginia had already entered the realm of legend, and he himself held a conspicuous position in the pantheon of great American heroes. Charles Francis Adams Jr. from the distinguished family that had given America two presidents and many public servants, found that the more he came to know about Lee, the more he admired the Rebel general: "a great man,—great in defeat, a noble, moral character."[27]

Southern boys would long feel badly that they had missed the subliminal experience, marching with "Marse Robert" into the pages of history, before the butchery of the last months smothered the glory. William Faulkner famously captured the martial daydream of youth when he wrote: "For every Southern boy fourteen years old, not once but whenever he wants it, there is the instant when it's still not yet two o'clock on that July afternoon in 1863, the brigades are in position behind the rail fence, the guns are laid and ready in the woods and the furled flags are already loosened to break out."[28]

No time machine could turn the clock back to Seminary Ridge, but other opportunities to cheer for war appeared on the horizon. In 1898, the nation declared war on Spain, making the Pacific a sphere of influence and embarking upon the long road to confrontation with imperial Japan. In an ultimate gesture of reunification, Rebel General Joseph Wheeler received command of the dismounted cavalry brigade in Cuba. Future reliance on war as a first-priority tool of policy appeared inevitable. In some ways, America's road to world power through vast territorial expansion, brought about by military action, had been quietly advancing all along.[29]

At the close of the War between the States, the United States threatened Emperor Napoleon III of France with force if he did not withdraw his troops occupying Mexico. This assertion of the Monroe Doctrine led France to abort an attempt to add America's neighbor to its colonial possessions while Uncle Sam had other business. In a remarkable foreshadowing of the concept of "nation building," the *New York Herald*, May 24, 1865, expanded upon this muscle-flexing. The paper envisaged the victorious Federal armies marching on to establish republics all across the globe, "on—till the soldiers of Grant, Sherman and Sheridan have saved the world as they have saved the Union."

The army steadily pushed the Native Americans westward, depriving them of their ancestral lands, and forcing them onto often barren, bleak reservations of poor land. This culminated a process that had begun in the antebellum period and continued apace. A senior military historian has made the thoughtful assessment that Sherman and Sheridan's method of waging hard war on civilians entered permanently into American strategic and tactical thinking: "making war against non-combatants emerged from the American Civil War as a strategy that American leaders generally regarded as acceptable. Once that acceptance existed, the door was opened enough that a further opening into more ruthless attacks on civilians came at least within the boundaries of contemplation."[30]

Thoroughly exasperated by the vexing relations with the Amerindians, Sherman once swore that "we must act with vindictive earnestness against the Sioux, even to their extermination, men, women, and children." That road led to the massacre at Wounded Knee. The so-called "Filipino Insurrection" followed the driving of Spain from the Philippines in 1898, when the United States reneged on its promise to give the islanders full independence: in the fierce unconventional warfare that subdued the people, 220,000 Filipinos died. Some prominent American cultural icons, notably Mark Twain and William Dean Howells, bitterly opposed going to war in 1898. But the public at large showed general enthusiasm for what one of Lincoln's private secretaries, John Hay, now Secretary of State, labeled "a splendid little war." American character had been regenerated by a little bloodletting, and the road to major power status had been opened at comparatively little cost.[31]

We have almost ended our journey together. But, before we part, the time has come to take one last walk together, this time down a dusty road in Texas. It leads us to the railroad tracks. A train has just passed this way. It takes the 1st United States Volunteer Cavalry, the famous Rough Riders, from their training camp in the west to their embarkation point for Cuba at Tampa, Florida. Lieutenant Colonel Theodore Roosevelt, in acting command of the regiment, confides to us in his memoir what he saw from the observation platform of his rail car. "Everywhere," he recalls, "the people came out to greet us and cheer us." At depot stops, they brought flowers and food, watermelons and jugs of milk to succor the soldiers."

This had been Confederate territory, noted Roosevelt, where legendary tales of Forrest and Morgan, Jackson and Hood, told by old soldiers, still held audiences hushed in courthouse squares. Rebel veterans came down to the tracks in their suits of cadet gray to salute the train, and lads came to wave flags and admire the older boys in their blue and khaki uniforms, lucky enough to be going off on a great adventure. "The blood of the old men stirred to the distant breath of battle; the blood of the young men leaped with eager desire to accompany us." Young girls, too, flocked to the roadbed, thrilled to be sending knights away on romantic quests. They "drove down in bevies, arrayed in their finery, to wave flags in farewell to the troopers and to beg cartridges and buttons as mementos."

The gray-haired old ladies, too, came down to the tracks to stand and watch. But (and it is a large but) they showed no animation; they did not wave and cheer along with the others. They looked on sadly and kept silent. Long ago, they had waved and blown kisses to other boys, dressed in butternut and gray, as they went off down this same road to another, bigger war. So many had not come back; they had wasted away from disease in hospitals or taken minnie balls, dying in agony on far distant fields. Often, their graves remained unknown. Many others who had come back did so crippled and different, distracted and with a faraway look. The girls had cried and cried then, for the boys they had lost and for the shrunken lives they themselves would lead.[32]

By 1898, those missing boys had become a faded memory, their corpses buried in rags of uniform, crumbled to dust. And the women's tears had dried long ago, their pain wrapped away in a deep and abiding sense of emptiness and loneliness. Now, all the heartbreak would happen again. A new generation of boys had donned uniforms, hell-bent on going off to see the elephant and win mighty war laurels. The old women knew that many would die of sickness and wounds, or return distant and abstracted. But that would be later. In this moment, the gray-haired ladies could only stand quietly by the tracks and watch. For what could they possibly say?

— Notes —

OPENING. JIM CONKLIN AND GENERAL SHERMAN

1. Michael C. C. Adams, *Our Masters the Rebels: A Speculation on Union Military Failure in the East, 1861–1865* (Cambridge, MA: Harvard University Press, 1978). The book won the 1978 Jefferson Davis Prize, awarded by the Museum of the Confederacy. Lillian Ross, *Picture* (New York: Limelight, 1984), pp. 26, 28.

2. *Ohio State Journal*, August 12, 1880. Also, Lloyd Lewis, *Sherman: Fighting Prophet* (1932, repr. New York: Harcourt, Brace & World, 1960), p. 635.

3. Allan Nevins, "The Glorious and the Terrible," in Nicholas Cords and Patrick Gerster, eds., *Myth and the American Experience* (New York: Glencoe, 1973), vol. 2, p. 365.

4. Fanny Fern, *Ruth Hall: A Domestic Tale of the Present* (1855, repr. New York: Penguin, 1997), p. 87; Joan Hedrick, *Harriet Beecher Stowe: A Life* (New York: Oxford University Press, 1994), p. 169.

5. Charles East, ed., *Sarah Morgan: The Civil War Diary of a Southern Woman* (New York: Touchstone, 1992), pp. 335, 345, 406; Jean V. Berlin, ed., *A Confederate Nurse: The Diary of Ada W. Bacot, 1860–1863* (Columbia: University of South Carolina Press, 1994), p. 172, on the child's death.

6. For sanitation problems in New Orleans and New York, Otto L. Bettmann, *The Good Old Days—They Were Terrible* (New York: Random House, 1974), pp. 138, 35; Robert K. Krick, "The Parallel Lives of Two Virginia Soldiers: Armistead and Garnett," in Gary W. Gallagher, ed., *The Third Day at Gettysburg & Beyond* (Chapel Hill: University of North Carolina Press, 1994), p. 105, on Fort Riley.

7. Charles Dickens, *American Notes* (Philadelphia: Peterson, n.d.), p. 45; Alan Huffman, *Sultana: Surviving Civil War, Prison, and the Worst Maritime Disaster in American History* (New York: HarperCollins-Smithsonian Books, 2009), pp. 1–4.

8. Mary E. Walker, *HIT: Essays on Women's Rights* (Amherst, NY: Humanity,

2003), pp. 103, 107 on tobacco use and homes ruined by alcohol; Stephen W. Berry II, *All That Makes a Man: Love and Ambition in the Civil War South* (New York: Oxford University Press, 2003), p. 47, for congressional brawling.

9. Alonzo Calkins, *Opium and the Opium-Appetite* (1871, repr. New York: Arno Press, 1981), p. 36 on opium consumption Theodore Zeldin, *An Intimate History of Humanity* (New York: HarperCollins, 1994), p. 231, considers escape from pain and boredom via drug use; Leon Edel, ed., *The Diary of Alice James* (New York: Penguin, 1982), pp. 5–6, 149; C. Vann Woodward, ed., *Mary Chesnut's Civil War* (New Haven, CT: Yale University Press, 1981), e.g., pp. 247, 286, 291.

10. Margaret Armstrong, *Fanny Kemble: A Passionate Victorian* (New York: Macmillan, 1938), p. 88, on Victorian stardom; James A. Ramage, *Rebel Raider: The Life of General John Hunt Morgan* (Lexington: University Press of Kentucky, 1986), pp. 1–7, for example, describes idolization of a popular soldier.

11. Carol Bleser, ed., *The Hammonds of Redcliffe* (New York: Oxford University Press, 1981), p. 68.

12. Thomas P. Lowry, *The Story the Soldiers Wouldn't Tell: Sex in the Civil War* (Mechanicsburg, PA: Stackpole, 1994), p. 97, abortion statistics.

13. George Templeton Strong, *Diary of the Civil War, 1860–1865* (New York: Macmillan, 1962), p. 4.

14. James M. McPherson, "Was It More Restrained Than You Think?," *New York Review of Books*, February 14, 2008, p. 44. Demographic historian J. David Hacker, by careful analysis of census data to establish male deaths 1860–1870, believes that losses have been underestimated by at least 20 percent. Between 750,000 and 850,000 probably died, an even grimmer percentage of the population than previously thought. Cited in Guy Gugliotta, "New Estimate Raises Civil War Death Toll," *New York Times*, April 3, 2012.

CHAPTER ONE. GONE FOR A SOLDIER

1. Virginia Ingraham Burr, ed., *The Secret Eye: The Journal of Ella Gertrude Clanton Thomas, 1848–1889* (Chapel Hill: University of North Carolina Press, 1990), p. 184.

2. Frank Moore, ed., *The Rebellion Record* (New York: G. P. Putnam, 1861) 1, "Poetry & Incidents," p. 31; "Rumors & Incidents," pp. 123–24.

3. Daniel E. Sutherland, *The Expansion of Everyday Life, 1860–1876* (New York: Harper & Row, 1989), p. 3; Stephen W. Berry II, *All That Makes a Man: Love and Ambition in the Civil War South* (New York: Oxford University Press, 2003), p. 170; Theodore Winthrop, "Washington as a Camp," *Atlantic Monthly* 8 (July 1861): pp. 106, 109.

4. Peter Burchard, *One Gallant Rush: Robert Gould Shaw and His Brave Black Regiment* (New York: St. Martin's Press, 1965), p. 21; Bliss Perry, *Life and Letters of Henry Lee Higginson* (Boston: Atlantic Monthly Press, 1921), p. 142.

5. Emry E. Werner, *Reluctant Witnesses: Children's Voices from the Civil War* (Boulder, CO: Westview, 1998), p. 10; J. G. deRoulhac Hamilton, ed., *The Papers of Randolph Abbott Shotwell* (Raleigh: North Carolina Historical Commission, 1929), p. 40.

6. Gwynne Dyer, *War* (Homewood, IL: Dorsey, 1985), p. 108; Joseph E. Crowell, *The Young Volunteer: The Everyday Experiences of a Soldier Boy in the Civil War* (Paterson, NJ: Joseph E. Crowell, 1906), p. 10.

7. Bell Irvin Wiley, *The Life of Billy Yank: The Common Soldier of the Union* (New York: Bobbs-Merrill, 1952), p. 38; Sutherland, *Expansion of Everyday Life*, pp. 1–2; Michael J. Varhola, *Everyday Life during the Civil War* (Cincinnati, OH: Writer's Digest Books, 1999), p. 119.

8. Charles Royster, *The Destructive War: William Tecumseh Sherman, Stonewall Jackson, and the Americans* (New York: Vintage, 1993), p. 274; Werner, *Reluctant Witnesses*, p. 23.

9. Spencer B. King Jr., ed., *Rebel Lawyer: Letters of Theodorick W. Montfort, 1861–1862* (Athens: University of Georgia Press, 1965), pp. 71–72.

10. William H. Hastings, *Letters from a Sharpshooter: The Civil War Letters of Private William B. Greene, Co. G 2nd United States Sharpshooters (Berdan's) Army of the Potomac, 1861–1865* (Belleville, WI: Historic Publications, 1993), pp. 146, 172, 184, 198, 75.

11. Milo M. Quaife, ed., *From the Cannon's Mouth: The Civil War Letters of General Alpheus S. Williams* (Detroit, MI: Wayne State University Press & Detroit Historical Society, 1959), p. 221; Mills Lane, ed., *"Dear Mother: Don't Grieve about Me; If I Get Killed I'll Only Be Dead"; Letters from Georgia Soldiers in the Civil War* (Savannah, GA: Beehive, 1977), p. 260; Robert W. Johannsen, *The "Wicked Rebellion" and the Republic: Henry Tuckerman's Civil War* (Milwaukee, WI: Marquette University Press, 1994), pp. 31–32.

12. Susan Leigh Blackford, *Letters from Lee's Army* (New York: A. S. Barnes, 1962), p. 144; Stephen W. Sears, ed., *For Country, Cause & Leader: The Civil War Journal of Charles B. Haydon* (New York: Ticknor & Fields, 1993), p. 300.

13. Thomas P. Lowry, *Don't Shoot That Boy! Abraham Lincoln and Military Justice* (Mason City, IA: Savas, 1999), p. 23; Burr, *Secret Eye*, p. 209; William T. Lusk, *War Letters of William Thompson Lusk* (New York, 1911), p. 189.

14. Crowell, *Young Volunteer*, pp. 59–60; Robert F. Harris and John Niflot, eds., *Dear Sister: The Civil War Letters of the Brothers Gould* (Westport, CT: Praeger, 1998), p. 2; Martin Hardwick Hall, ed., "The Taylor Letters: Correspondence from Fort Bliss, 1861," *Military History of Texas and the Southwest* 15 (Fall 1980): p. 56.

15. Lane, *Dear Mother*, p. 40; John H. Brinton, *Personal Memoirs of John H. Brinton, Civil War Surgeon, 1861–1865* (1914, repr. Carbondale: Southern Illinois University Press, 1996), pp. 43–44.

16. Joshua Kendall, "A Minor Exception," *The Nation*, April 4, 2011, pp. 32–33.

17. Robert Knox Sneden, *Eye of the Storm: A Civil War Odyssey* (New York: Free

Press, 2000), p. 121; Frank Wilkeson, *Recollections of a Private Soldier in the Army of the Potomac* (1886, repr. Freeport, NY: Books for Libraries, 1972), p. 33; Allan Nevins, ed., *A Diary of Battle: The Personal Journals of Colonel Charles S. Wainwright 1861–1865* (New York: Harcourt, Brace & World, 1962), p. 116.

18. Gerald J. Prokopowicz, *All for the Regiment: The Army of the Ohio, 1861–1862* (Chapel Hill: University of North Carolina Press, 2001), p. 139; Sneden, *Eye of the Storm*, p. 4.

19. Clifford Dowdey and Louis H. Manarin, eds., *The Wartime Papers of Robert E. Lee* (Boston: Little, Brown, 1961), p. 73; Lowry, *Don't Shoot That Boy*, p. 24; Nathaniel Southgate Shaler, *From Old Fields: Poems of the Civil War* (Boston: Houghton Mifflin, 1906), pp. 20–26.

20. R. Gregory Laude, *Madness, Malingering, and Malfeasance: The Transformation of Psychiatry and the Law in the Civil War Era* (Washington, DC: Brassey's, 2003), p. 60; Hedrick, *Stowe*, p. 299.

21. C. F. Boyd, "The Civil War Diary of C. F. Boyd," *Iowa Journal of History* 50 (1952): pp. 59, 66. Louisa May Alcott, *Hospital Sketches* (1863, repr. Bedford, MA: Applewood, 1993), p. 65.

22. Fred J. Hood, *Kentucky: Its History and Heritage* (St. Louis, MO: Forum, 1978), p. 135; Kenneth Radley, *Rebel Watchdog: The Confederate States Army Provost Guard* (Baton Rouge: Louisiana State University Press, 1989), pp. 56, 182.

23. Henrietta Stratton Jaquette, ed., *South after Gettysburg: Letters of Cornelia Hancock from the Army of the Potomac, 1863–1865* (1937, repr. Freeport, NY: Books for Libraries, 1971), p. 141.

24. Alfred Jay Bollet, *Civil War Medicine: Challenges and Triumphs* (Tucson, AZ: Galen, 2002), pp. 313, 292–93, 315.

25. Varhola, *Everyday Life during the Civil War*, p. 110; David Herbert Donald, ed., *Gone for a Soldier: The Civil War Memoirs of Private Alfred Bellard* (Boston: Little, Brown, 1975), p. 256; Blackford, *Letters from Lee's Army*, p. 23.

26. Emil Rosenblatt and Ruth Rosenblatt, eds., *Hard Marching Every Day: The Civil War Letters of Private Wilbur Fisk, 1861–1865* (Lawrence: University Press of Kansas, 1992), pp. 213–14; Sears, *Country, Cause & Leader*, p. 4.

27. Larry M. Logue, *To Appomattox and Beyond: The Civil War Soldier in War and Peace* (Chicago: Ivan R. Dee, 1996), p. 39; Thomas P. Lowry, *The Story the Soldiers Wouldn't Tell: Sex in the Civil War* (Mechanicsburg, PA: Stackpole, 1994), pp. 104–6; James I. Robertson Jr., *General A. P. Hill: The Story of a Confederate Warrior* (New York: Random House, 1987), pp. 11–12; David Evans, *Sherman's Horsemen: Union Cavalry Operations in the Atlanta Campaign* (Bloomington: Indiana University Press, 1996), p. 35.

28. Reid Mitchell, *The Vacant Chair: The Northern Soldier Leaves Home* (New York: Oxford University Press, 1993), p. 6; Peter Messent and Steve Courtney, eds., *The Civil War Letters of Joseph Hopkins Twichell: A Chaplain's Story* (Athens: University of Georgia Press, 2006), p. 299.

29. Richard Holmes, *Redcoat: The British Soldier in the Age of Horse and Musket*

(London: HarperCollins, 2002), pp. 249–50; Bollet, *Civil War Medicine*, p. 17; Byron Farwell, *Stonewall: A Biography of General Thomas J. Jackson* (New York: W. W. Norton, 1992), p. 276.

30. Boyd, "Civil War Diary," p. 56; Donald, *Gone for a Soldier*, p. 5.

31. John S. D. Eisenhower, *So Far from God: The War with Mexico, 1846-1848* (New York: Anchor Doubleday, 1990), pp. xviii, xxii; Ann R. Gabbert, "'They Die Like Dogs': Disease Mortality among U.S. Forces during the U.S.-Mexican War," *Military History of the West* 31, no. 1 (Spring 2001): pp. 27–28; Ira M. Rutkow, *Bleeding Blue and Gray: Civil War Surgery and the Evolution of American Medicine* (New York: Random House, 2005), pp. 8, 14; K. Jack Bauer, ed., *Soldiering: The Civil War Diary of Rice C. Bull, 123rd New York Volunteer Infantry* (San Rafael, CA: Presidio, 1977), p. 8.

32. Prokopowicz, *All for the Regiment*, p. 64.

33. J. B. Gordon, *Reminiscences of the Civil War* (New York: C. Scribner's Sons, 1905), p. 49.

34. Bollet, *Civil War Medicine*, p. 283; Rutkow, *Bleeding Blue and Gray*, pp. 8, 14; Stewart Brooks, *Civil War Medicine* (Springfield, IL: Charles C Thomas, 1966), pp. 114–15; Brinton, *Personal Memoirs*, p. 61.

35. Harris and Niflot, eds., *Dear Sister*, pp. 4, 14; Bollet, *Civil War Medicine*, p. 233; Prokopowicz, *All for the Regiment*, p. 64.

36. Eric T. Dean Jr., *Shook over Hell: Post Traumatic Stress, Vietnam, and the Civil War* (Cambridge, MA: Harvard University Press, 1997), p. 52.

37. Berlin, *Confederate Nurse*, pp. 83–87; Alcott, *Hospital Sketches*, pp. 77–78; George Templeton Strong, *Diary of the Civil War, 1860-1865* (New York: Macmillian, 1962), pp. 467–68.

38. Richard A. Gabriel, *No More Heroes: Madness & Psychiatry in War* (New York: Hill and Wang, 1987), p. 58; Franklin D. Jones, "Future Directions of Military Psychiatry," in Richard A. Gabriel, ed., *Military Psychiatry: A Comparative Perspective* (New York: Greenwood, 1986), pp. 181–89; George Rosen, "Nostalgia: A 'Forgotten' Psychological Disorder," *Psychological Medicine* 5 (1975): pp. 340–54; *The Medical and Surgical History of the War of the Rebellion* (Washington, DC: Government Printing Office, 1888), vol. 1, pt. 3, p. 885.

39. Werner, *Reluctant Witnesses*, p. 12.

40. Guy R. Everson and Edward W. Simpson Jr., eds., *"Far, Far from Home"*: *The Wartime Letters of Dick and Tally Simpson, Third South Carolina Volunteers* (New York: Oxford University Press, 1994), pp. 24–25; Wiley, *Life of Billy Yank*, p. 331.

41. De Witt C. Peters, "The Evils of Youthful Enlistments, and Nostalgia," *American Medical Times*, February 14, 1863, pp. 75–76.

42. Messent and Courtney, *Civil War Letters*, p. 80.

43. Boyd, "Civil War Diary," p. 53; Crowell, *Young Volunteer*, p. 309; Werner, *Reluctant Witnesses*, pp. 120–21.

44. D'Ann Campbell and Richard Jensen, "Gendering Two Wars," in Gabor Boritt,

ed., *War Comes Again: Comparative Vistas on the Civil War and World War II* (New York: Oxford University Press, 1995), p. 107.

45. Varhola, *Everyday Life during the Civil War*, p. 123.

46. James M. McPherson, *What They Fought For, 1861–1865* (New York: Anchor, 1995), p. 16; Mark A. Weitz, *A Higher Duty: Desertion among Georgia Troops during the Civil War* (Lincoln: University of Nebraska Press, 2000), pp. 122, 163.

47. James W. Geary, *We Need Men: The Union Draft in the Civil War* (DeKalb: Northern Illinois University Press, 1991), esp. pp. 4, 29–30; Iver Bernstein, *The New York City Draft Riots: Their Significance for American Society and Politics in the Age of the Civil War* (New York: Oxford University Press, 1990), p. 7.

48. *New York Times*, June 30, 1864.

49. John Michael Priest, ed., *Captain James Wren's Civil War Diary* (New York: Berkley, 1991), p. 129.

50. Sneden, *Eye of the Storm*, p. 5.

51. Laude, *Madness, Malingering, and Malfeasance*, pp. 134–35.

52. Ella Lonn, *Desertion during the Civil War* (1928, repr. Gloucester, MA: Peter Smith, 1966), pp. 3, 13–14; Radley, *Rebel Watchdog*, p. 30.

53. Barnet Schecter, *The Devil's Own Work: The Civil War Draft Riots and the Fight to Reconstruct America* (New York: Walker, 2005), pp. 1, 180, 134; Sutherland, *Expansion of Everyday Life*, pp. 220–21.

54. Edward K. Spann, *Gotham at War: New York City, 1860–1865* (Wilmington, DE: Scholarly Resources, 2002), pp. 96–97.

55. Bernstein, *New York City Draft Riots*, pp. 23–24, 28–30; Spann, *Gotham at War*, p. 96.

56. S. Smith, *Doctor in Medicine, and Other Papers on Professional Subjects* (New York: William Wood, 1872), p. 192; Also S. Smith, *The City That Was* (New York: Frank Allaben, 1911), p. 36. Schecter, *Devil's Own Work*, p. 203.

57. Schecter, *Devil's Own Work*, pp. 166–67, 177, 157.

58. Schecter, *Devil's Own Work*, pp. 251–52. Spann, *Gotham at War*, p. 101.

59. Schecter, *Devil's Own Work*, pp. 210–11, 255–56; Bernstein, *New York City Draft Riots*, p. 65; Lonn, *Desertion during the Civil War*, p. 151.

60. Walter Lowenfels, ed., *Walt Whitman's Civil War* (New York: Alfred A. Knopf, 1971), p. 208; Radley, *Rebel Watchdog*, p. 204.

61. John David Smith and William Cooper Jr., eds., *A Union Woman in Civil War Kentucky: The Diary of Frances Peter* (Lexington: University Press of Kentucky, 2000), p. 44.

62. Gerald F. Linderman, *Embattled Courage: The Experience of Combat in the American Civil War* (New York: Free Press, 1987), p. 173.

63. Dudley Taylor Cornish, *The Sable Arm: Negro Troops in the Union Army, 1861–1865* (New York: W. W. Norton, 1966), pp. 46, 80; Joseph T. Glatthaar, *Forged in Battle: The Civil War Alliance of Black Soldiers and White Officers* (New York: Meridian, 1991), p. 7.

64. Cornish, *Sable Arm*, pp. iv, 24, 29, 230.
65. Geary, *We Need Men*, pp. 18–19, 76; Jim Cullen, *The Civil War in Popular Culture: A Reusable Past* (Washington, DC: Smithsonian Institution, 1995), p. 147.
66. Virginia Matzke Adams, ed., *On the Altar of Freedom: A Black Soldier's Civil War Letters from the Front* (Amherst: University of Massachusetts Press, 1991), p. 19; Geary, *We Need Men*, pp. 29–30; Burchard, *One Gallant Rush*, p. 151.
67. Lonnie R. Speer, *War of Vengeance: Acts of Retaliation against Civil War POWs* (Mechanicsburg, PA: Stackpole, 2002), p. 58; Daniel E. Sutherland, *Seasons of War: The Ordeal of a Confederate Community, 1861–1865* (New York: Free Press, 1995), p. 360.
68. Brooks D. Simpson, *Let Us Have Peace: Ulysses S. Grant and the Politics of War and Reconstruction, 1861–1868* (Chapel Hill: University of North Carolina Press, 1991), p. 44; John R. Neff, *Honoring the Civil War Dead: Commemoration and the Problem of Reconciliation* (Lawrence: University Press of Kansas, 2005), p. 185; Bollet, *Civil War Medicine*, pp. 287–89; Cullen, *Civil War in Popular Culture*, p. 147; Donald Yacovone, ed., *A Voice of Thunder: A Black Soldier's Civil War* (Urbana: University of Illinois Press, 1998), p. 277.
69. Cullen, *Civil War in Popular Culture*, p. 147; Cornish, *Sable Arm*, pp. 46, 183, 194–95; Ira Berlin, "Fighting on Two Fronts: War and the Struggle for Racial Equality in Two Centuries," in Gabor Boritt, ed., *War Comes Again: Comparative Vistas on the Civil War and World War II* (New York: Oxford University Press, 1995), pp. 134–35.
70. Gerald Schwartz, ed., *A Woman Doctor's Civil War: Esther Hill Hawk's Diary* (Columbia: University of South Carolina Press, 1986), p. 61.
71. Stephen B. Oates, *A Woman of Valor: Clara Barton and the Civil War* (New York: Free Press, 1994), p. 174.

CHAPTER TWO. ON THE MARCH

1. F. Colburn Adams, *The Story of a Trooper* (1865), quoted in Richard Wheeler, *Voices of the Civil War* (New York: Thomas Y. Crowell, 1976), p. 121.
2. Milo M. Quaife, ed., *From the Cannon's Mouth: The Civil War Letters of General Alpheus S. Williams* (Detroit, MI: Wayne State University Press & Detroit Historical Society, 1959), p. 159; Albert Castel, *Tom Taylor's Civil War* (Lawrence: University Press of Kansas, 2000), p. 67; C. E. Wood, *Mud: A Military History* (Washington, DC: Potomac Books, 2006), p. 117; Alfred Jay Bollet, *Civil War Medicine: Challenges and Triumphs* (Tucson, AZ: Galen, 2002), p. 285.
3. William H. Hastings, *Letters from a Sharpshooter: The Civil War Letters of Private William B. Greene, Co. G 2nd United States Sharpshooters (Berdan's) Army of the Potomac, 1861–1865* (Belleville, WI: Historical Publications, 1993), p. 101; Edward K. Spann, *Gotham at War: New York City, 1860–1865* (Washington, DC: Scholarly Resources, 2002), p. 53; Alan Huffman, *Sultana: Surviv-*

ing Civil War, Prison, and the Worst Maritime Disaster in American History (New York: HarperCollins-Smithsonian Books, 2009), pp. 51–52; William W. Hassler, ed., *The General to His Lady: The Civil War Letters of William Dorsey Pender to Fanny Pender* (Chapel Hill: University of North Carolina Press, 1965), p. 173.

4. W. C. Holbrook, *A Narrative of the Service of the Officers and Enlisted Men of the 7th Regiment of Vermont Volunteers* (New York: American Bank Note Co., 1882), p. 219; Gary W. Gallagher, ed., *The Second Day at Gettysburg: Essays on Confederate and Union Leadership* (Kent, OH: Kent State University Press, 1993), p. 128.

5. C. F. Boyd, "The Civil War Diary of C. F. Boyd," *Iowa Journal of History* 50 (1952): p. 58; Geoffrey Regan, *Great Military Disasters: A Historical Survey of Military Incompetence* (New York: M. Evans, 1987), p. 102; Quaife, *From the Cannon's Mouth*, p. 69.

6. Robert Perry, "Colonel Andrew Jackson May and the Battle of Ivy Mountain," *Journal of Kentucky Studies* 13 (September 1996): p. 75; Moxley G. Sorrel, *At the Right Hand of Longstreet: Recollections of a Confederate Staff Officer* (1905, repr. Lincoln: University of Nebraska Press, 1999), pp. 133–34.

7. *The War of the Rebellion: A Compilation of the Official Records of the Union and Confederate Armies* (Washington, DC: Government Printing Office, 1880–1901), series III, vol. 1, p. 399; John W. Haley, *The Rebel Yell & the Yankee Hurrah: The Civil War Journal of a Maine Volunteer* (Camden, ME: Down East Books, 1985), p. 96.

8. William Camm, "Diary of Colonel William Camm, 1861 to 1865," *Journal of the Illinois State Historical Society* 18, nos. 3–4 (October 1925–January 1926): pp. 808–9; Lawrence Van Alstyne, *Diary of an Enlisted Man* (New Haven, CT: Morehouse & Taylor, 1910), pp. 327, 331.

9. Nathaniel Cheairs Hughes Jr., *The Pride of the Confederate Artillery: The Washington Artillery in the Army of Tennessee* (Baton Rouge: Louisiana State University Press, 1997), p. 151; Gerald J. Prokopowicz, *All for the Regiment: The Army of the Ohio, 1861–1862* (Chapel Hill: University of North Carolina Press, 2001), p. 148; Susan Williams Benson, ed., *Berry Benson's Civil War Book: Memoirs of a Confederate Scout and Sharpshooter* (Athens: University of Georgia Press, 1992), p. 36, on the pleasures of eating squirrel; Richard Wheeler, *Voices of the Civil War* (New York: Thomas Y. Crowell, 1976), p. 390.

10. Patricia B. Mitchell, *Cooking for the Cause* (Chatham, VA, 1988), p. 6; Alto Loftin Jackson, ed., *So Mourns the Dove: Letters of a Confederate Infantryman and His Family* (New York: Exposition, 1965), pp. 25–26; Gerald Schwartz, ed., *A Woman Doctor's Civil War: Esther Hill Hawk's Diary* (Columbia: University of South Carolina Press, 1986), p. 62; W. J. Joyce, *The Life of W. J. Joyce, Written by Himself* (San Marcos, TX: San Marcos Printing Co., 1913), p. 3.

11. Joseph E. Crowell, *The Young Volunteer: The Everyday Experiences of a Soldier Boy in the Civil War* (Paterson, NJ: Joseph E. Crowell, 1906), p. 285; J. I. Rob-

ertson, *Soldiers Blue and Grey* (Columbia: University of South Carolina Press, 1988), p. 70.

12. George M. Blackburn, ed., *"Dear Carrie—" The Civil War Letters of Thomas N. Stevens* (Mount Pleasant: Central Michigan University Press, 1984), pp. 89–90; Peter Messent and Steve Courtney, eds., *The Civil War Letters of Joseph Hopkins Twichell: A Chaplain's Story* (Athens: University of Georgia Press, 2006), p. 206.

13. Bollet, *Civil War Medicine*, pp. 337–52.

14. Michael A. Palmer, *Lee Moves North: Robert E. Lee on the Offensive* (New York: John Wiley, 1998), p. 25; Mary B. Mitchell, "A Woman's Recollections of Antietam," in Robert Underwood Johnson and Clarence C. Buel, eds., *Battles and Leaders of the Civil War* (New York: Century, 1884–1888), vol. 2, pp. 687–88.

15. Thomas B. Buell, *The Warrior Generals: Combat Leadership in the Civil War* (New York: Three Rivers Press, 1997), p. 115; Bernard Potter, "All about the Beef," *London Review of Books*, July 14, 2011, p. 31.

16. Timothy B. Smith, *Champion Hill: Decisive Battle for Vicksburg* (New York: Savas Beatie, 2006), p. 361. Stephens belonged to General William H. Loring's division.

17. Prokopowicz, *All for the Regiment*, p. 161; Eric T. Dean Jr., *Shook over Hell: Post-Traumatic Stress, Vietnam, and the Civil War* (Cambridge, MA: Harvard University Press, 1997), p. 52; Noah Andre Trudeau, *Bloody Roads South: The Wilderness to Cold Harbor, May–June 1864* (Boston: Little, Brown, 1989), p. 33.

18. Camm, "Diary of Colonel William Camm," p. 885; C. W. Kepler, *History of the Three Months' and Three Years' Service* (Cleveland, OH: Leader Printing, 1886), p. 287.

19. Lee Kennett, *Marching through Georgia: The Story of Soldiers and Civilians during Sherman's Campaign* (New York: Harper, 1996), p. 153; Paul E. Steiner, *Disease in the Civil War: Natural Biological Warfare in 1861–1865* (Springfield, IL: Charles C Thomas, 1968), p. 10; Jerry Thompson, ed., *From Desert to Bayou: The Civil War Journal of Morgan Wolfe Merrick* (El Paso: Texas Western Press, 1991), pp. 30–31.

20. Emil Rosenblatt and Ruth Rosenblatt, eds., *Hard Marching Every Day: The Civil War Letters of Private Wilbur Fisk, 1861–1865* (Lawrence: University Press of Kansas, 1992), p. 227; Henrietta Stratton Jaquette, ed., *South after Gettysburg: Letters of Cornelia Hancock from the Army of the Potomac, 1863–1865* (1937, repr. Freeport, NY: Books for Libraries, 1971), pp. 114–15.

21. Mills Lane, ed., *"Dear Mother: Don't Grieve about Me; If I Get Killed I'll Only Be Dead"; Letters from Georgia Soldiers in the Civil War* (Savannah, GA: Beehive, 1977), p. 215; Robert Hunt Rhodes, ed., *All for the Union: The Civil War Diary and Letters of Elisha Hunt Rhodes* (New York: Vintage, 1992), p. 125; Messent and Courtney, *Civil War Letters*, p. 79.

22. Susan Leigh Blackford, *Letters from Lee's Army* (New York: A. S. Barnes, 1962), p. 220. Guy R. Everson and Edward W. Simpson Jr., eds., *"Far, Far from Home":*

The Wartime Letters of Dick and Tally Simpson, Third South Carolina Volunteers (New York: Oxford University Press, 1994), p. 163.

23. Woodward, *Mary Chesnut's Civil War*, p. 90; John William DeForest, *Miss Ravenel's Conversion from Secession to Loyalty* (1867, repr. Columbus, OH: Charles E. Merrill, 1969), p. 276.

24. Gary W. Gallagher, *Lee and His Army in Confederate History* (Chapel Hill: University of North Carolina Press, 2001), p. 29; John David Smith and William Cooper Jr., eds., *A Union Woman in Civil War Kentucky: The Diary of Frances Peter* (Lexington: University Press of Kentucky, 2000), p. 30; Joseph L. Harsh, *Taken at the Flood: Robert E. Lee and Confederate Strategy in the Maryland Campaign of 1862* (Kent, OH: Kent State University Press, 1999), p. 171; Bauer, ed., *Soldiering*, p. 143.

25. Allan Nevins, ed., *A Diary of Battle: The Personal Journals of Colonel Charles S. Wainwright, 1861–1865* (New York: Harcourt, Brace & World, 1962), p. 33; Stewart Brooks, *Civil War Medicine* (Springfield, IL: Charles C Thomas, 1966), p. 31.

26. Mary E. Kellogg, ed., *Army Life of an Illinois Soldier: Letters and Diary of Charles W. Wills* (Carbondale: Southern Illinois University Press, 1996), p. 232; Evans, *Horsemen*, p. 378.

27. William A. Fletcher, *Rebel Private, Front and Rear: Memoirs of a Confederate Soldier* (1908, repr. New York: Meridian, 1997), pp. 8, 19; Nathaniel Southgate Shaler, *From Old Fields: Poems of the Civil War* (Boston: Houghton Mifflin, 1906), "Near the Front," p. 3.

28. Donald S. Frazier, *Blood & Treasure: Confederate Empire in the Southwest* (College Station: Texas A&M University Press, 1995), p. 142; Sam R. Watkins, *"Co. Aytch": A Side Show of the Big Show* (1881, repr. New York: Collier, 1962), p. 55.

29. W. C. Ford, *A Cycle of Adams Letters, 1861–1865* (Boston: Houghton Mifflin, 1920), vol. 1, pp. 171, 247; vol. 2, pp. 78–79; Otto L. Bettmann, *The Good Old Days—They Were Terrible* (New York: Random House, 1974), p. 3.

30. S. Walkley, *History of the Seventh Connecticut Volunteer Infantry* (1905), p. 226; Everson and Simpson, *Far from Home*, p. 134; Evans, *Sherman's Horsemen*, p. 189.

31. Watkins, *"Co. Aytch,"* p. 114.

32. Bollet, *Civil War Medicine*, pp. 272–78.

33. Wood, *Mud: A Military History*, pp. 95–96. Steiner, *Disease in the Civil War*, pp. 6, 73–74, 139, 143–44; Molly Caldwell Crosby, *The American Plague: The Untold Story of Yellow Fever, the Epidemic That Shaped Our History* (New York: Berkley Books, 2006), pp. 2, 38–39, 70–72.

34. Fiammetta Rocco, *The Miraculous Fever-Tree: Malaria and the Quest for a Cure That Changed the World* (New York: HarperCollins, 2006), pp. 18, 35, 171, 174–75, 178–79, 206; Bollet, *Civil War Medicine*, p. 289. See also the recent comprehensive study, Andrew McIlwaine Bell, *Mosquito Soldiers: Malaria, Yel-*

low Fever, and the Course of the American Civil War (Baton Rouge: Louisiana State University Press, 2010).

35. Kellogg, ed., *Army Life of an Illinois Soldier*, p. 275; A. D. Albert, *History of the Forty-Fifth Regiment Pennsylvania Volunteer Infantry* (Williamsport, PA: Grit Publishing, 1912), p. 530; W. Dwight, *Life and Letters of Wilder Dwight* (Boston: Ticknor & Fields, 1868), p. 349; J. R. C. Ward, *History of the One Hundred and Sixth Regiment Pennsylvania Volunteers* (Philadelphia: McManus, 1906), p. 455; Alan S. Brown, ed., *A Soldier's Life: Civil War Experiences of Ben C. Johnson* (Kalamazoo: Western Michigan University Press, 1962), pp. 48–49.

36. Harry Barnard, *Rutherford B. Hayes and His America* (Indianapolis, IN: Bobbs-Merrill, 1954), p. 216; DeForest, *Miss Ravenel's Conversion*, p. 276.

37. Carol Reardon, *Pickett's Charge in History and Memory* (Chapel Hill: University of North Carolina Press, 1997), p. 19; Everson and Simpson, *Far from Home*, pp. 61–62; Priest, *Diary*, pp. 109–10.

38. Watkins, *"Co. Aytch,"* p. 38; J. B. Jones, *A Rebel War Clerk's Diary, at the Confederate States Capital* (Philadelphia: J. B. Lippincott, 1866), vol. 2, p. 393; Blackford, *Letters from Lee's Army*, p. 220.

39. Boyd, "Civil War Diary," p. 59; Bollet, *Civil War Medicine*, p. 308; Jean V. Berlin, ed., *A Confederate Nurse: The Diary of Ada W. Bacot, 1860–1863* (Columbia: University of South Carolina Press, 1994), pp. 104–5, 117; R. Gregory Laude, *Madness, Malingering, and Malfeasance: The Transformation of Psychiatry and the Law in the Civil War Era* (Washington, DC: Brassey's, 2003), pp. 137–38; Steiner, *Disease*, p. 10.

40. Francis Augustín O'Reilly, *The Fredericksburg Campaign: Winter War on the Rappahannock* (Baton Rouge: Louisiana State University Press, 2003), p. 293; Kellogg, *Army Life of an Illinois Soldier*, p. 328.

41. David S. Sparks, ed., *Inside Lincoln's Army: The Diary of Marsena Rudolph Patrick* (New York: Yoseloff, 1964), e.g., pp. 22–23, 34, 125, 140, 154, 414, 423, 432, 453. On the therapeutic effects of electrical treatments, Andy Dougan, *Raising the Dead: The Men Who Created Frankenstein* (Edinburgh: Birlinn, 2008).

42. Hal Bridges, *Lee's Maverick General: Daniel Harvey Hill* (New York: McGraw-Hill, 1961), pp. 15, 162, 227; Jack D. Welsh, *Medical Histories of Confederate Generals* (Kent, OH: Kent State University Press, 1995), pp. 100–101.

43. Welsh, *Medical Histories of Confederate Generals*, p. 23; Judith Lee Hallock, *Braxton Bragg and Confederate Defeat* (Tuscaloosa: University of Alabama Press, 1991), vol. 2, p. 271.

44. Jeffry D. Wert, *The Controversial Life of George Armstrong Custer* (New York: Simon & Schuster, 1996), pp. 34–35; Evans, *Sherman's Horsemen*, p. 383.

45. Evans, *Sherman's Horsemen*, pp. 48, 325–26; Welsh, *Medical Histories of Confederate Generals*, pp. xii, 76–77.

46. Edward G. Longacre, *Pickett: Leader of the Charge* (Chambersburg, PA: White Mane Publishing, 1995), pp. 4, 18, 160–61.

47. Thomas Wentworth Higginson, *Army Life in a Black Regiment* (New York: Norton, 1984), pp. 214, 248; Welsh, *Medical Histories of Confederate Generals*, pp. 239–40; William C. Davis, *The Battle of New Market* (Garden City, NY: Doubleday, 1975), p. 38; Steiner, *Disease*, p. 73.

48. Welsh, *Medical Histories of Confederate Generals*, p. 196; Frazier, *Blood & Treasure*, p. 149; Gallagher, *Lee and His Army*, p. 128; Joseph Lancaster Brent, *Memoirs of the War between the States* (New Orleans, LA: Fontana, 1940), p. 192.

49. Clifford Dowdey, *Robert E. Lee* (London: Gollancz, 1970), p. 238; Regan, *Disasters*, p. 42; William C. Davis, *The Cause Lost: Myths and Realities of the Confederacy* (Lawrence: University Press of Kansas, 1996), p. 170; Paul D. Casdorph, *Lee and Jackson: Confederate Chieftains* (New York: Paragon House, 1992), p. 283.

50. Charles Royster, *The Destructive War: William Tecumseh Sherman, Stonewall Jackson, and the Americans* (New York: Vintage, 1993), pp. 49–50; Davis, *The Cause Lost*, p. 167; Earl Schenck Miers, *A Rebel War Clerk's Diary* (New York: Sagamore, 1958), p. 92.

51. Emory M. Thomas, *Robert E. Lee* (New York: Norton, 1995), pp. 148, 184–85, 241, 277–78; John D. McKenzie, *Uncertain Glory: Lee's Generalship Re-examined* (New York: Hippocrene, 1997), pp. 24–25, 155; John M. Taylor, *Duty Faithfully Performed: Robert E. Lee and His Critics* (Dulles, VA: Brassey's, 1999), p. 161; Michael Fellman, *The Making of Robert E. Lee* (New York: Random House, 2000), pp. 152, 165.

52. Edward H. Bonekemper III, *How Robert E. Lee Lost the Civil War* (Fredericksburg, VA: Sergeant Kirkland's Press, 1998), p. 139; Palmer, *Lee Moves North*, pp. 99, 116; Gallagher, *Lee and His Army*, p. 212.

53. O.R., series I, vol. 5, "McClellan's Report," p. 26; Rocco, "Malaria," pp. 176–78.

54. F. D. Williams, *The Wild Life of the Army: The Civil War Letters of James A. Garfield* (East Lansing: Michigan State University Press, 1964), p. 325; T. C. Smith, *The Life and Letters of James Abram Garfield* (New Haven, CT: Yale University Press, 1925), vol. 1, p. 650; Robert Stiles, *Four Years under Marse Robert* (New York: Neale, 1903), p. 232.

55. Joseph T. Durkin, ed., *John Dooley, Confederate Soldier: His War Journal* (1945, repr. Notre Dame, IN: University of Notre Dame Press, 1965), p. 96. Blackford, *Letters from Lee's Army*, p. 177; Rosenblatt and Rosenblatt, *Hard Marching Every Day*, pp. 105–6; Jaquette, ed., *South after Gettysburg*, p. 146.

56. Rosenblatt and Rosenblatt, *Hard Marching Every Day*, p. 41; A. J. Long, *Memoirs of Robert E. Lee* (New York: Stoddart, 1887), p. 205; John H. Worsham, *One of Jackson's Foot Cavalry* (New York: Neale, 1912), p. 243.

57. Smith and Cooper, eds., *A Union Woman in Civil War Kentucky*, p. 77; Prokopowicz, *All for the Regiment*, p. 77; Glenn LaFantasie, *Gettysburg: Colonel William C. Oates and Lieutenant Frank A. Haskell* (New York: Bantam, 1992), p. 87; Craig L. Symonds, *Stonewall of the West: Patrick Cleburne and the Civil*

War (Lawrence: University Press of Kansas, 1997), p. 228; Watkins, *"Co. Aytch,"* p. 43.

58. Abner Doubleday, *Chancellorsville and Gettysburg* (1882, repr. New York: Da Capo, 1994), p. 73.

59. Marli F. Weiner, ed., *Heritage of Woe: The Civil War Diary of Grace Brown Elmore, 1861–1868* (Athens: University of Georgia Press, 1997), p. 34.

60. John R. Neff, *Honoring the Civil War Dead: Commemoration and the Problem of Reconciliation* (Lawrence: University Press of Kansas, 2005), pp. 22–24. Neff is excellent on Victorian commemoration conventions.

61. Blackford, *Letters from Lee's Army*, pp. 167–68; Lane, *Dear Mother*, p. 51.

62. Berlin, *A Confederate Nurse*, p. 71.

63. Louise Porter Daly, *Alexander Cheves Haskell: The Portrait of a Man* (Norwood, MA: Plimpton, 1934), p. 76; also, George Michael Neese, *Three Years in the Confederate Horse Artillery* (New York: Neale, 1911), p. 112.

64. Camm, "Diary of Colonel William Camm," p. 825.

65. Jackson, *So Mourns the Dove*, p. 39.

66. Castel, *Tom Taylor's Civil War*, p. 19.

CHAPTER THREE. CLOSE-ORDER COMBAT

1. Paddy Griffith, *Forward into Battle: Fighting Tactics from Waterloo to the Near Future*, rev. ed. (Novato, CA: Presidio, 1992), p. 78.

2. Michael C. C. Adams, *Echoes of War: A Thousand Years of Military History in Popular Culture* (Lexington: University Press of Kentucky, 2002), pp. 161–62.

3. *The War of the Rebellion: A Compilation of the Official Records of the Union and Confederate Armies* (Washington, DC: Government Printing Office, 1880–1901), series 1, vol. 4, chap. 7, pp. 228–30; Gary W. Gallagher, ed., *The First Day at Gettysburg: Essays on Confederate and Union Leadership* (Kent, OH: Kent State University Press, 1992), p. 133.

4. Richard Harwell, *Lee* (New York: Scribner, 1961), p. 340.

5. Carol Reardon, *Pickett's Charge in History and Memory* (Chapel Hill: University of North Carolina Press, 1997), p. 5.

6. Edward Porter Alexander, *Fighting for the Confederacy: The Personal Recollections of Gen. Edward Porter Alexander* (Chapel Hill: University of North Carolina Press, 1989), p. 111.

7. *O.R.* series 1, vol. 47, pt. 2, p. 910. Sherman may seem here at odds with his view of civilian suffering.

8. Richard M. McMurry, *John Bell Hood and the War for Southern Independence* (Lexington: University Press of Kentucky, 1982), pp. 196, 50, 55, 139, 152, 176; J. B. Hood, *Advance and Retreat* (1880, repr. Secaucus, NJ: Blue and Grey Press, 1985), pp. 130–31.

9. Paddy Griffith, "Packs Down—Charge! The Frontal Attack," in Robert Cowley, ed., *With My Face to the Enemy: Perspectives on the Civil War* (New York: G. P.

Putnam's Sons, 2001), pp. 239–41; Stephen B. Oates, *A Woman of Valor: Clara Barton and the Civil War* (New York: Free Press, 1994), pp. 172, 175.

10. Joshua Lawrence Chamberlain, *The Passing of the Armies: An Account of the Final Campaign of the Army of the Potomac, Based upon Personal Reminiscences of the Fifth Army Corps* (1915, repr. New York: Bantam, 1993), p. 102; Lee Kennett, *Marching through Georgia: The Story of Soldiers and Civilians during Sherman's Campaign* (New York: Harper, 1996), pp. 151–52; Samuel G. French, *Two Wars: An Autobiography of Gen. Samuel G. French, an Officer in the Armies of the United States and the Confederate States* (Nashville, TN: Confederate Veteran, 1901), pp. 221–22.

11. Raleigh E. Colston, "Address before the Ladies' Memorial Association," *Southern Historical Society Papers* 21 (1893): pp. 44–45; C. F. Boyd, "The Civil War Diary of C. F. Boyd," *Iowa Journal of History* 50 (1952): pp. 75, 79.

12. Earl J. Hess, *The Union Soldier in Battle: Enduring the Ordeal of Combat* (Lawrence: University Press of Kansas, 1997), pp. 69–70; Edward E. Leslie, *The Devil Knows How to Ride: The True Story of William Clarke Quantrill and His Confederate Raiders* (New York: Random House, 1996), p. 275; Lucien B. Crooker et al., *The Story of the 55th Regiment Illinois Infantry in the Civil War, 1861–1865* (Clinton, MA: W. J. Coulter, 1887), p. 124; Timothy B. Smith, *Champion Hill: Decisive Battle for Vicksburg* (New York: Savas Beatie, 2006), p. 227; John Myers, "'Dear and Mutch Loved One'—An Iowan's Vicksburg Letters," *Annals of Iowa* 43, no. 1 (Summer 1975): p. 53.

13. William A. Fletcher, *Rebel Private, Front and Rear: Memoirs of a Confederate Soldier* (New York: Meridian, 1997), p. 28; Milo M. Quaife, ed., *From the Cannon's Mouth: The Civil War Letters of General Alpheus S. Williams* (Detroit, MI: Wayne State University Press and Detroit Historical Society, 1959), pp. 129–30; Richard Wheeler, *Voices of the Civil War* (New York: Thomas Y. Crowell, 1976), p. 153; Noah Andre Trudeau, *Bloody Roads South: The Wilderness to Cold Harbor, May–June 1864* (Boston: Little, Brown, 1989), p. 72.

14. Robert Hicks, *The Widow of the South* (New York: Warner, 2005), p. 406; McKenzie, *Glory*, pp. 233–34; Henrietta Stratton Jaquette, ed., *South after Gettysburg: Letters of Cornelia Hancock from the Army of the Potomac, 1863–1865* (1937, repr. Freeport, NY: Books for Libraries, 1971), p. 11; Charles Royster, *The Destructive War: William Tecumseh Sherman, Stonewall Jackson, and the Americans* (New York: Vintage, 1993), p. 308; Daniel E. Sutherland, *Seasons of War: The Ordeal of a Confederate Community, 1861–1865* (New York: Free Press, 1995), p. 64; Stephen W. Sears, *Landscape Turned Red: The Battle of Antietam* (Boston: Houghton Mifflin, 1983), p. 211; *O.R.*, vol. 10, pt. 1, p. 583; Richard A. Baumgartner, *Buckeye Blood: Ohio at Gettysburg* (Huntington, WV: Blue Acorn Press, 2003), pp. 9, 57.

15. Alan T. Nolan, *Lee Considered: General Robert E. Lee and Civil War History* (Chapel Hill: University of North Carolina Press, 1991), pp. 80–81; Hal Bridges, *Lee's Maverick General: Daniel Harvey Hill* (New York: McGraw-Hill, 1961),

p. 226; Henry Woodhead, ed., *The Illustrated Atlas of the Civil War* (Alexandria, VA: Time-Life, 1991), pp. 205, 132; James M. McPherson, *Battle Cry of Freedom: The Civil War Era* (New York: Ballantine, 1989), p. 582; Edward H. Bonekemper III, *How Robert E. Lee Lost the Civil War* (Fredericksburg, VA: Sergeant Kirkland's Press, 1998), p. 158.

16. Peter Messent and Steve Courtney, eds., *The Civil War Letters of Joseph Hopkins Twichell: A Chaplain's Story* (Athens: University of Georgia Press, 2006), p. 127. There were many smoothbore wounds, particularly in the first years of the war. These did great damage to the body. Adam Nicolson, who has carefully studied arms and projectiles of the Napoleonic era, describes the career of a ball through the body as follows. As the ball penetrated the flesh and organs, a high-pressure shock wave developed, spreading out from the path of the bullet. A cavity formed behind the ball track, the flesh or muscle then snapping back into place, starting a pulsing repetition of collapse and re-expansion. This had the effect of a series of explosions within the tissue, like repeated blows of a fist. Finally, blood was drawn into the ruptured body areas, preventing proper cardiac circulation. The victim's blood pressure dropped because of the internal hemorrhaging, and shock resulted, the combination often proving fatal. See Adam Nicolson, *Seize the Fire: Heroism, Duty, and Nelson's Battle of Trafalgar* (New York: Harper Perennial, 2006), pp. 255–56.

17. Brooks, *Medicine*, p. 75.

18. Nathaniel Cheairs Hughes Jr., ed., *The Civil War Memoir of Philip Daingerfield Stephenson, D.D.* (Conway, AR: UCA Press, 1995), p. 234; Mark De Wolfe Howe, *Touched with Fire: Civil War Letters and Diary of Oliver Wendell Holmes, Jr., 1861–1864* (New York: Da Capo, 1969), pp. 13–24.

19. Wilkeson, *Recollections*, pp. 202–3; Mills Lane, ed., *"Dear Mother: Don't Grieve about Me; If I Get Killed I'll Only Be Dead"; Letters from Georgia Soldiers in the Civil War* (Savannah, GA: Beehive, 1977), p. 124; Abner Doubleday, *Chancellorsville and Gettysburg* (1882, repr. New York: Da Capo, 1994), p. 147; Gerald J. Prokopowicz, *All for the Regiment: The Army of the Ohio, 1861–1862* (Chapel Hill: University of North Carolina Press, 2001), p. 131; Don E. Alberts, ed., *Rebels on the Rio Grande: The Civil War Journal of A. B. Peticolas* (Albuquerque: University of New Mexico Press, 1984), p. 86; Sneden, *Storm*, p. 128.

20. James A. Mulligan, "The Siege of Lexington," in Johnson and Buel, eds., *Battles*, vol. 1, pp. 307, 311; Sutherland, *Seasons of War*, p. 146, notes the urination in rifle barrels.

21. We encountered the following soldiers on our virtual tour of the firing line: Corporal James Quick, 38th New York, shot at Fredericksburg, December 1862; Lieutenant William N. Taylor, aide to Union General Oliver Otis Howard, hit at Whippy Swamp Creek, South Carolina, February 1, 1865; Private Keils, 15th Alabama, mortally wounded on July 2 at Gettysburg, dying on the 3rd; Private George W. Walker, 148th Pennsylvania, whose artery was severed

at Spotsylvania, 1864; also at Spotsylvania, an unidentified Federal officer blinded in both eyes.

Their stories are in Ira M. Rutkow, *Bleeding Blue and Gray: Civil War Surgery and the Evolution of American Medicine* (New York: Random House, 2005), p. 210; Richard Harwell and Philip N. Racine, eds., *The Fiery Trial: A Union Officer's Account of Sherman's Last Campaigns* (Knoxville: University of Tennessee Press, 1986), p. 210; Glenn LaFantasie, ed., *Gettysburg: Colonel William C. Oates and Lieutenant Frank A. Haskell* (New York: Bantam, 1992), p. 100; Trudeau, *Bloody Roads South*, pp. 147, 174.

22. Continuing along the firing line, we also met an unidentified Rebel shot at Belmont, Missouri, 1862, seen by Union surgeon John H. Brinton; an unidentified private, 48th Pennsylvania, shot in the knee at Fredericksburg, December 1862; Frank Hersey and Henry Stockwell, both New Hampshire soldiers from Newport; and an unidentified Union 12th Corps enlisted man observed lying with his brains oozing out, Chancellorsville, May 1863.

For their stories, see John H. Brinton, *Personal Memoirs of John H. Brinton, Civil War Surgeon, 1861–1865* (1914, repr. Carbondale: Southern Illinois University Press, 1996), p. 80; John Michael Priest, ed., *Captain James Wren's Civil War Diary* (New York: Berkley, 1991), p. 122; Maris A. Vinovskis, ed., *Toward a Social History of the American Civil War: Exploratory Essays* (Cambridge: Cambridge University Press, 1990), p. 43; David Herbert Donald, ed., *Gone for a Soldier: The Civil War Memoirs of Private Alfred Bellard* (Boston: Little, Brown, 1975), p. 214.

23. Rufus R. Dawes, *Service with the Sixth Wisconsin Volunteers* (Marietta, OH: Alderman & Sons, 1890), p. 88; Terrence Winschel, "The Gettysburg Diary of Lieutenant William Peel," *Gettysburg Magazine*, no. 9 (July 1993): p. 105.

24. Fletcher, *Rebel Private, Front and Rear*, p. 55; Wheeler, *Voices of the Civil War*, p. 216; Ernest B. Furgurson, *Chancellorsville 1863: The Souls of the Brave* (New York: Knopf, 1992), p. 230.

25. J. G. D. Hamilton and Rebecca Cameron, eds., *The Papers of Randolph Abbott Shotwell* (Raleigh: North Carolina Historical Commission, 1929–31), vol. 1, pp. 193–95; H. F. Christy, "The 'Reserves' at Fredericksburg," *National Tribune*, September 19, 1901; Priest, *Wren's Civil War Diary*, p. 121; Joseph T. Durkin, ed., *John Dooley, Confederate Soldier: His War Journal* (1945, repr. Notre Dame, IN: University of Notre Dame Press, 1965), p. 102.

26. Joseph E. Crowell, *The Young Volunteer: The Everyday Experiences of a Soldier Boy in the Civil War* (Paterson, NJ: Joseph E. Crowell, 1906), pp. 130–31, 402, 372.

27. Crowell, *Young Volunteer*, p. 421.

28. Boyd, "Civil War Diary," p. 81; Nathaniel Cheairs Hughes, ed., *The Civil War Memoir of Philip Daingerfield Stephenson, D.D.* (Conway, AR: UCA Press, 1995), pp. 214–15.

29. William Wheeler, *Letters of William Wheeler of the Class of 1855, Yale College*

(Cambridge, MA: H. O. Houghton, 1875), pp. 409–11; Boyd, "Diary," p. 80.

30. John H. Worsham, *One of Jackson's Foot Cavalry* (1912, repr. New York: Random House, 1992), pp. 112–13; Hess, *Union Soldier in Battle*, p. 28; Trudeau, *Bloody Roads South*, p. 66.

31. Nathaniel Southgate Shaler, *From Old Fields: Poems of the Civil War* (Boston: Houghton Mifflin, 1906), pp. 61–62; John Gibbon, *Personal Recollections of the Civil War* (New York: G. P. Putnam's, 1928), pp. 83–84.

32. McPherson, *Battle Cry of Freedom*, p. 330. Doubleday, *Chancellorsville and Gettysburg*, p. 210.

33. McPherson, *Battle Cry of Freedom*, p. 662; Nolan, *Lee Considered*, p. 85; John R. Neff, *Honoring the Civil War Dead: Commemoration and the Problem of Reconciliation* (Lawrence: University Press of Kansas, 1997), p. 157.

34. Griffith, "Packs Down—Charge!," p. 240.

35. William C. Davis, *The Battle of New Market* (Garden City, NY: Doubleday, 1975), p. 112; Bridges, *Lee's Maverick General*, p. 108.

36. John D. Welsh, *Medical Histories of Confederate Generals* (Kent, OH: Kent State University Press 1995), pp. 13–14, 44.

37. John B. Gordon, *Reminiscences of the Civil War* (New York: Scribner, 1903), pp. 89–92; Welsh, *Medical Histories of Confederate Generals*, pp. 83, 40–41; Craig L. Symonds, *Stonewall of the West: Patrick Cleburne and the Civil War* (Lawrence: University Press of Kansas, 1997), p. 93.

38. Thomas B. Buell, *The Warrior Generals: Combat Leadership in the Civil War* (New York: Three Rivers Press, 1997), pp. 120, 229, 303; Alfred Jay Bollet, *Civil War Medicine: Challenges and Triumphs* (Tucson, AZ: Galen, 2002), p. xviii.

39. Welsh, *Medical Histories of Confederate Generals*, pp. 63–65; *O.R.*, vol. 33, pp. 1095–96. Donald C. Pfanz, a Ewell biographer and editor of the general's letters, defends him against charges of being incompetent and psychotic. Unfortunately, Ewell's correspondence for critical periods in 1863, which might have proved helpful in the case, appears sporadic. Pfanz, *Richard S. Ewell: A Soldier's Life* (Chapel Hill: University of North Carolina Press, 1998); and Pfanz, ed., *The Letters of General Richard S. Ewell, Stonewall Jackson's Successor* (Knoxville: University of Tennessee Press, 2012).

40. Hood, *Advance and Retreat*, pp. 59–61, 64; McMurry, *John Bell Hood*, p. 132; Symonds, *Cleburne*, p. 254.

41. Bollet, *Civil War Medicine*, p. 354; Arthur Herman, *To Rule the Waves: How the British Navy Shaped the Modern World* (New York: HarperCollins, 2004), pp. 163–64, 260; Russell Duncan, ed., *Blue-Eyed Child of Fortune: The Civil War Letters of Robert Gould Shaw* (Athens: University of Georgia Press, 1992), p. 377.

42. Herman Melville, *White-Jacket, or the World in a Man-of-War* (1850, repr. Oxford: Oxford University Press, 1990), pp. 178, 319; Alvah Folsom Hunter, *A Year on a Monitor and the Destruction of Fort Sumter* (Columbia: University of South Carolina Press, 1991), p. 20.

43. Philip Van Doren Stern, *The Confederate Navy: A Pictorial History* (New York: Da Capo, 1992), p. 180; Wheeler, *Voices of the Civil War*, p. 65.

44. Melville, *White-Jacket*, p. 21; Stern, *Confederate Navy*, pp. 25, 83.

45. Hunter, *A Year on a Monitor*, p. 53; Stern, *Confederate Navy*, p. 139.

46. Stern, *Confederate Navy*, pp. 104, 219.

47. Stern, *Confederate Navy*, pp. 205, 102; Edwin C. Bearss, *Hardluck Ironclad: The Sinking and Salvage of the Cairo*, rev. ed. (Baton Rouge: Louisiana State University Press, 1980), p. 99.

48. James Tertius deKay, *Monitor: The Story of the Legendary Civil War Ironclad and the Man Whose Invention Changed the Course of History* (New York: Walker, 1997), pp. 162–63; Wheeler, *Voices of the Civil War*, pp. 67–69, 411.

49. Melville, *White-Jacket*, pp. 72–73, 320.

50. Melville, *White-Jacket*, p. 320.

CHAPTER FOUR. CLEARING THE BATTLEFIELD

1. Richard Slotkin, *The Crater* (New York: Atheneum, 1981), p. xiv.

2. Henry Kyd Douglas, *I Rode with Stonewall* (1940, repr. Greenwich, CT: Fawcett, 1961), p. 173; John Keegan, *Fields of Battle: The Wars for North America* (New York: Knopf, 1996), pp. 242–43; Alfred Jay Bollet, *Civil War Medicine: Challenges and Triumphs* (Tucson, AZ: Galen, 2002), p. 7.

3. Bollet, *Civil War Medicine*, p. 103; Robert Knox Sneden, *Eye of the Storm: A Civil War Odyssey* (New York: Free Press, 2000), p. 69.

4. Sidney Lanier, *Tiger-Lilies* (1867, repr. Chapel Hill: University of North Carolina Press, 1969), p. 169; Sneden, *Eye of the Storm*, p. 138.

5. Mark H. Dunkelman, "Key to a Mystery," *American History* 32, no. 2 (May–June 1997): p. 18; Charles J. Stillé, *History of the United States Sanitary Commission* (New York: Hurd and Houghton, 1868), pp. 146–47; George Templeton Strong, *Diary of the Civil War, 1860–1865* (New York: Macmillan, 1963), p. 230; Walt Whitman, *Memoranda during the War: Civil War Journals, 1863–1865* (1875, repr. Mineola, NY: Dover, 2010), p. 6.

6. Bollet, *Civil War Medicine*, pp. 3, 103.

7. Samuel H. Hurst, *Journal-History of the Seventy-Third Ohio Volunteer Infantry* (Chillicothe, OH, 1866), pp. 72–73; Wilbur F. Crummer, *With Grant at Fort Donelson, Shiloh, and Vicksburg* (1915, repr. Whitefish, MT: Kessinger, 2008), pp. 69–70.

8. *The War of the Rebellion: A Compilation of the Official Records of the Union and Confederate Armies* (Washington, DC: Government Printing Office, 1880–1901), series 1, vol. 36, pt. 3, pp. 600, 638–39, 666–67.

9. Ulysses S. Grant, *Personal Memoirs of U. S. Grant* (New York: C. L. Webster, 1885), p. 425.

10. Jonathan P. Stowe Diary, 15th Massachusetts, Antietam National Battlefield Park, quoted in Stephen W. Sears, *Landscape Turned Red: The Battle of Antietam*

(Boston: Houghton Mifflin, 1983), p. 231; Nathaniel Southgate Shaler, *From Old Fields: Poems of the Civil War* (Boston: Houghton Mifflin, 1906), pp. 19–20.

11. *Report of the Proceedings of the Society of the Army of the Tennessee*, Second Annual Meeting, November 13–14, 1867 (Cincinnati, OH: By the Society, 1868), p. 102; John N. Edwards, *Shelby and His Men* (Cincinnati, OH: Miami Printing Co., 1867), pp. 94–104, 125–27.

12. R. L. Dabney, *Life and Campaigns of Lieut.-Gen. Thomas J. Jackson* (1865), quoted in Peter Svenson, *Battlefield: Farming a Civil War Battleground* (Boston: Faber and Faber, 1992), p. 196; Wirt Armistead Cate, ed., *Two Soldiers: The Campaign Diaries of Thomas J. Key, C.S.A., December 7, 1863–May 17, 1865 and Robert J. Campbell, U.S.A., January 1, 1864–July 21, 1864* (Chapel Hill: University of North Carolina Press, 1938), p. 182; Albert Castel, *Tom Taylor's Civil War* (Lawrence: University Press of Kansas, 2000), p. 90.

13. Peter Messent and Steve Courtney, eds., *The Civil War Letters of Joseph Hopkins Twichell: A Chaplain's Story* (Athens: University of Georgia Press, 2006), p. 144; C. F. Boyd, "The Civil War Diary of C. F. Boyd," *Iowa Journal of History* 50 (1952): p. 80.

14. Milo M. Quaife, ed., *From the Cannon's Mouth: The Civil War Letters of General Alpheus S. Williams* (Detroit, MI: Wayne State University Press and Detroit Historical Society, 1959), p. 219.

15. Sneden, *Eye of the Storm*, p. 72; Henrietta Stratton Jaquette, ed., *South after Gettysburg: Letters of Cornelia Hancock from the Army of the Potomac, 1863–1865* (1937, repr. Freeport, NY: Books for Libraries, 1971), p. 10.

16. Henry Wilburn Stuckenberg, *I'm Surrounded by Methodists: Diary of John H. W. Stuckenberg* (Gettysburg, PA: Thomas, 1995), pp. 83–84.

17. Ira M. Rutkow, *Bleeding Blue and Gray: Civil War Surgery and the Evolution of American Medicine* (New York: Random House, 2005), p. 8; Larry M. Logue, *To Appomattox and Beyond: The Civil War Soldier in War and Peace* (Chicago: Ivan R. Dee, 1996), p. 69; W. W. Keen, "Surgical Reminiscences of the Civil War," *Transactions of the College of Physicians of Philadelphia*, series 3, vol. 27 (1905): pp. 95–114.

18. Joseph E. Crowell, *The Young Volunteer: The Everyday Experiences of a Soldier Boy in the Civil War* (Paterson, NJ: Joseph E. Crowell, 1906), pp. 414, 417, 432.

19. Timothy B. Smith, *Champion Hill: Decisive Battle for Vicksburg* (New York: Savas Beatie, 2006), p. 371.

20. F. Llewellyn, "Limbs Made and Unmade by War," *America's Civil War* 8 (September 1995): p. 40.

21. J. J. Chisolm, *A Manual of Military Surgery for Use of the Surgeons in the Confederate Army*, 3rd. ed. (1861, repr. Dayton, OH: Morningside, 1992), pp. 358–60.

22. Bollet, *Civil War Medicine*, pp. 192, 153; Jonathan Shay, *Achilles in Vietnam: Combat Trauma and the Undoing of Character* (New York: Touchstone, 1995), p. 128; Allie Patricia Wall, "The Letters of Mary Boykin Chesnut," Master's thesis, University of South Carolina, 1977, p. 24.

23. Steven E. Woodworth, ed., *The Loyal, True, and Brave: America's Civil War Soldiers* (Wilmington, DE: Scholarly Resources, 2002), p. 39; Whitman, *Memoranda during the War*, p. 5; Bell Irvin Wiley, *The Life of Billy Yank: The Common Soldier of the Union* (New York: Bobbs-Merrill, 1952), p. 83; Crowell, *Young Volunteer*, p. 150.

24. James A. Mulligan, "The Siege of Lexington," in Robert Underwood Johnson and Clarence C. Buel, eds., *Battles and Leaders of the Civil War* (New York: Century, 1884–1888), vol. 1, p. 311.

25. S. Weir Mitchell, *Injuries of Nerves and Their Consequences* (1872, repr. New York: Dover, 1965), p. 309; Jacquette, ed., *South after Gettysburg*, p. 85; Strong, *Diary of the Civil War*, p. 462.

26. William L. Barney, *The Making of a Confederate: Walter Lenoir's Civil War* (New York: Oxford University Press, 2009), p. 93; John D. Imboden, "The Confederate Retreat from Gettysburg," in Johnson and Buel, eds., *Battles*, vol. 3, p. 424.

27. Louisa May Alcott, *Hospital Sketches* (1863, repr. Bedford, MA: Applewood, 1993), pp. 27–29; Richard Barksdale Harwell, ed., *Kate: The Journal of a Confederate Nurse* (Baton Rouge: Louisiana State University Press, 1959), pp. 14–16, 36.

28. Gerald Schwartz, ed., *A Woman Doctor's Civil War: Esther Hill Hawk's Diary* (Columbia: University of South Carolina Press, 1986), pp. 50–51; John H. Brinton, *Personal Memoirs of John H. Brinton: Civil War Surgeon, 1861–1865* (Carbondale: Southern Illinois University Press, 1996), p. 328; Stephen B. Oates, *A Woman of Valor: Clara Barton and the Civil War* (New York: Free Press, 1994), p. 176; Bollet, *Civil War Medicine*, pp. 4, 217.

29. Charles Royster, *The Destructive War: William Tecumseh Sherman, Stonewall Jackson, and the Americans* (New York: Vintage, 1993), pp. 219–25; Whitman, *Memoranda during the War*, pp. 10–11; F. H. Hamilton, *A Treatise on Military Surgery and Hygiene* (New York: Belliere Brothers, 1865), p. 80.

30. Mills Lane, ed., *"Dear Mother: Don't Grieve about Me; If I Get Killed I'll Only Be Dead"; Letters from Georgia Soldiers in the Civil War* (Savannah, GA: Beehive, 1977), p. 331.

31. *Medical and Surgical History of the War of the Rebellion* (Washington, DC: Government Printing Office, 1870–1888), vol. 2, pt. 3, case 1106, p. 767.

32. C. Vann Woodward, *Mary Chesnut's Civil War* (New Haven, CT: Yale University Press, 1981), p. 668; Joseph T. Durkin, ed., *John Dooley, Confederate Soldier: His War Journal* (1945, repr. Notre Dame, IN: University of Notre Dame Press, 1965), p. 114.

33. Mitchell, *Injuries of Nerves*, pp. 200–201.

34. Mitchell, *Injuries of Nerves*, pp. 207–8.

35. Mitchell, *Injuries of Nerves*, pp. 230–31, 268–70, 273–74.

36. Mitchell, *Injuries of Nerves*, pp. 292–94, 298–300.

37. Mitchell, *Injuries of Nerves*, pp. 302–7, 319–20, 331–33.

38. Richard Barksdale Harwell, ed., *Kate a Confederate Nurse* (1866, repr. Baton

Rouge: Louisiana State University Press, 1959), pp. 99, 20–21.

39. Burr, *Thomas*, pp. 229–30; John R. Brumgardt, ed., *Civil War Nurse: The Diary and Letters of Hannah Ropes* (Knoxville: University of Tennessee Press, 1980), p. 119; Jane Stuart Woolsey, *Hospital Days* (New York: Van Nostrand, 1870), p. 27; Schwartz, *Woman Doctor's Civil War*, pp. 51, 71.

40. Cecil D. Eby Jr., ed., *A Virginia Yankee in the Civil War: The Diaries of David Hunter Strother* (Chapel Hill: University of North Carolina Press, 1961), p. 113.

41. David H. Strother, "Personal Recollections of the War," *Harper's Magazine* 35 (August 1867): p. 289.

42. Carol Reardon, *Pickett's Charge in History and Memory* (Chapel Hill: University of North Carolina Press, 1997), p. 28; Sherman R. Norris, "Ohio at Gettysburg: The Regiments That Participated in the Great Battle," *National Tribune*, June 9, 1887; *O.R.*, vol. 24, pt. 1, p. 715.

43. William C. Davis, *The Battle of New Market* (Garden City, NY: Doubleday, 1975), p. 43.

44. Russell Duncan, ed., *Blue-Eyed Child of Fortune: The Civil War Letters of Colonel Robert Gould Shaw* (Athens: University of Georgia Press, 1992), p. 231; Joshua Lawrence Chamberlain, *The Passing of the Armies: An Account of the Final Campaign of the Army of the Potomac, Based upon Personal Reminiscences of the Fifth Army Corps* (1915, repr. New York: Bantam, 1993), p. 233.

45. William Martin, *Out and Forward, or Recollections of the War of 1861–1865* (n.p., 1941), p. 39; T. F. Dornblaser, *Sabre Strokes of the Pennsylvania Dragoons in the War of 1861–1865* (Philadelphia: Lutheran Publication Society, 1864), p. 164.

46. Richard Wheeler, *Voices of the Civil War* (New York: Thomas Y. Crowell, 1976), p. 395. Steven R. Stotelmyer, *The Bivouacs of the Dead: The Story of Those Who Died at Antietam and South Mountain* (Baltimore: Toomey, 1992), p. 5.

47. John R. Neff, *Honoring the Civil War Dead: Commemoration and the Problem of Reconciliation* (Lawrence: University Press of Kansas, 2005), p. 35. Guy R. Everson and Edward W. Simpson Jr., eds., *"Far, Far from Home": The Wartime Letters of Dick and Tally Simpson, Third South Carolina Volunteers* (New York: Oxford University Press, 1994), p. 49.

48. Susan William Benson, ed., *Berry Benson's Civil War Book: Memoirs of a Confederate Scout and Sharpshooter* (Athens: University of Georgia Press, 1992), pp. 13–14. Ernest B. Furgurson, *Chancellorsville 1863: The Souls of the Brave* (New York: Knopf, 1992), p. 75.

49. K. Jack Bauer, ed., *Soldiering: The Civil War Diary of Rice C. Bull, 123rd New York Volunteer Infantry* (San Rafael, CA: Presidio, 1977), p. 244; David Herbert Donald, ed., *Gone for a Soldier: The Civil War Memoirs of Private Alfred Bellard* (Boston: Little, Brown, 1975), p. 86.

50. J. W. Ames, "In Front of the Stone Wall at Fredericksburg," in Johnson and Buel, eds., *Battles*, vol. 3, p. 122.

51. Robert Hunt Rhodes, ed., *All for the Union: The Civil War Diary of Elisha*

Hunt Rhodes (New York: Vintage, 1992), p. 73; William W. Blackford, *War Years with Jeb Stuart* (New York: Scribner's, 1945), pp. 150–51.

52. J. S. C. Abbott, *The History of the Civil War in America* (New York: Ledyard Bill, 1865), vol. 2, p. 494.

53. Robert Hicks, *The Widow of the South* (New York: Warner, 2005), pp. 407, 409–10; Charles Carleton Coffin, *The Boys of '61, or Four Years of Fighting*, rev. ed. (Boston: Dana Estes, 1896), pp. 91–92. Coffin worked for the *Boston Journal*.

54. S. A. Putnam, *Richmond during the War* (New York: G. W. Carleton, 1867), p. 389; Fannie A. Beers, *Memories: A Record of Personal Experiences and Adventures during Four Years of War* (Philadelphia: Lippincott, 1888), pp. 152–55.

55. Sneden, *Eye of the Storm*, p. 54.

56. Sneden, *Eye of the Storm*, pp. 121–22; Stotelmyer, *Bivouacs of the Dead*, p. 10.

57. Edward E. Leslie, *The Devil Knows How to Ride: The True Story of William Clarke Quantrill and His Confederate Raiders* (New York: Random House, 1996), p. 289; Svenson, *Battlefield*, pp. 157–58; Louis N. Chapin, *A Brief History of the Thirty-Fourth Regiment N.Y.S.V.* (New York, 1903), p. 80.

58. Charles East, ed., *Sarah Morgan: The Civil War Diary of a Southern Woman* (New York: Touchstone, 1992), p. 238; Clifton Johnson, *Battlefield Adventures: The Story of the Dwellers on the Scenes of Conflict in Some of the Most Notable Battles of the Civil War* (Boston: Houghton Mifflin, 1915), p. 101.

59. Hicks, *Widow of the South*, p. 415.

CHAPTER FIVE. THE EDGE OF SANITY

1. Richard A. Gabriel, *No More Heroes: Madness and Psychiatry in War* (New York: Hill and Wang, 1987), pp. 61, 67–68; Arthur M. Smith, "Fear, Courage, and Cohesion," *Naval Institute Proceedings*, 120/11/1, 101 (November 1994): p. 65.

2. C. G. Moore-Smith, *The Life of John Colborne: Field Marshal Lord Seaton* (1903), in Richard Holmes, *Redcoat: The British Soldier in the Age of Horse and Musket* (London: HarperCollins, 2002), p. 260; Elizabeth Longford, *Wellington: The Years of the Sword* (New York: Harper & Row, 1975), p. 400.

3. John Talbott, "Combat Trauma in the American Civil War," *History Today*, March 1996, pp. 41–47, repr. in *Annual Editions: American History*, 14th ed. (Guilford, CT: Dushkin, 1997), vol. 1, pp. 208–12. McEntire is quoted on p. 208. In December 1864, Leeds was committed to St. Elizabeths Hospital, a government insane asylum in D.C. Susan Leigh Blackford, *Letters from Lee's Army* (New York: A. S. Barnes, 1962), pp. 261–62.

4. S. Weir Mitchell, W. W. Keen, and George R. Morehouse, "On Malingering, Especially in Regard to Simulation of Diseases of the Nervous System," *American Journal of Medical Science* 48 (1864): pp. 367–94; Earl J. Hess, *The Union*

Soldier in Battle: Enduring the Ordeal of Combat (Lawrence: University Press of Kansas, 1997), p. 82. On somatic indicators of combat stress, Larry H. Ingraham and Frederick J. Manning, "Psychiatric Battle Casualties: The Missing Column in a War without Replacements," *Military Review*, August 1980, p. 23; Horace Porter, "The Philosophy of Courage," *Century Illustrated Monthly Magazine* 36 (May 1888–October 1888): pp. 249, 253.

5. Ella Lonn, *Desertion during the Civil War* (1928, repr. Gloucester, MA: Peter Smith, 1966), pp. 231–34.

6. Mary Livermore, *My Story of the War* (Hartford, CT: Worthington, 1890), p. 185. Charles East, ed., *Sarah Morgan: The Civil War Diary of a Southern Woman* (New York: Touchstone, 1992), pp. 52–53.

7. Edward King Wightman and Edward G. Longacre, *From Antietam to Fort Fisher: The Civil War Letters of Edward King Wightman, 1862–1865* (Rutherford, NJ: Fairleigh Dickinson University Press, 1985), p. 99; Nathaniel Cheairs Hughes, ed., *The Civil War Memoir of Philip Daingerfield Stephenson, D.D.* (Conway, AR: UCA Press, 1995), p. 88.

8. Frank Wilkeson, *Recollections of a Private Soldier in the Army of the Potomac* (1886, repr. Freeport, NY: Books for Libraries, 1972), pp. 188–89; Gary W. Gallagher, ed., *Two Witnesses at Gettysburg: The Personal Accounts of Whitelaw Reid and A. J. L. Fremantle* (St. James, NY: Brandywine, 1994), p. 14.

9. Peter Messent and Steve Courtney, eds., *The Civil War Letters of Joseph Hopkins Twichell: A Chaplain's Story* (Athens: University of Georgia Press, 2006), p. 71; Oscar Haas, ed., "The Diary of Julius Gieseke, 1861–1862," *Military History of Texas and the Southwest* 18 (1988): p. 52; *The War of the Rebellion: A Compilation of the Official Records of the Union and Confederate Armies* (Washington, DC: Government Printing Office, 1880–1901), vol. 10, pt. 2, pp. 340–41. Crittenden was demoted to colonel; Carroll resigned the service. C. F. Boyd, "The Civil War Diary of C. F. Boyd," *Iowa Journal of History* 50 (1952): p. 72; Francis Augustín O'Reilly, *The Fredericksburg Campaign: Winter War on the Rappahannock* (Baton Rouge: Louisiana State University Press, 2003), p. 502; David S. Sparks, ed., *Inside Lincoln's Army: The Diary of Marsena Rudolph Patrick* (New York: Thomas Yoseloff, 1964), p. 414.

10. S. H. M. Byers, "How Men Feel in Battle: Recollections of a Private at Champion Hill," *Annals of Iowa* 2, no. 6 (July 1896): p. 441.

11. Ardant Du Picq, *Battle Studies* (1870, repr. Harrisburg, PA: Military Service Publishing Co., 1947), p. 118; Joseph E. Crowell, *The Young Volunteer: Everyday Experiences of a Soldier Boy in the Civil War* (Paterson, NJ: Joseph E. Crowell, 1906), pp. 83, 91.

12. John Ellis, *Eye-Deep in Hell: Trench Warfare in World War I* (1976), on shell shock; William Nathaniel Wood, *Reminiscences of Big I* (1909, repr. Jackson, TN: McCowat-Mercer, 1956), p. 39; Noah Andre Trudeau, *The Last Citadel: Petersburg, Virginia, June 1864–April 1865* (Boston: Little, Brown, 1991), p. 240; Emil and Ruth Rosenblatt, eds., *Hard Marching Every Day: The Civil*

War Letters of Private Wilbur Fisk, 1861–1865 (Lawrence: University Press of Kansas, 1992), p. 78.

13. Carol Rainey, *A Fine Morning: Stories of a Cincinnati Childhood* (Cincinnati, OH: Cyndell, 2009), p. 78; Jacob Roemer, *Reminiscences of the War of the Rebellion* (Flushing, NY, 1897), p. 79; Louisa May Alcott, *Hospital Sketches* (1863, repr. Bedford, MA: Applewood, 1993), p. 45; Nathaniel Cheairs Hughes Jr., *The Pride of the Confederate Artillery: The Washington Artillery in the Army of Tennessee* (Baton Rouge: Louisiana State University Press, 1997), p. 190.

14. John William DeForest, *Miss Ravenel's Conversion from Secession to Loyalty* (1867, repr. Columbus, OH: Charles E. Merrill, 1969), p. 334; Alfred Jay Bollet, *Civil War Medicine: Challenges and Triumphs* (Tucson, AZ: Galen, 2002), pp. 321–23; Peter Svenson, *Battlefield: Farming a Civil War Battleground* (Boston: Faber and Faber, 1992), p. 25.

15. John W. Thomason Jr., *Jeb Stuart* (1930, repr. New York: Konecky & Konecky, 1958), pp. 456–57; Mark De Wolfe Howe, ed., *Touched with Fire: Civil War Letters and Diary of Oliver Wendell Holmes, Jr., 1861–1864* (New York: Da Capo, 1969), pp. 50–51.

16. Wilkeson, *Recollections of a Private Soldier*, p. 95; John G. Biel, ed., "The Battle of Shiloh: From the Letters and Diary of Joseph Dimmit Thompson," *Tennessee Historical Quarterly* 18, no. 3 (September 1958): p. 271.

17. Talbott, "Combat Trauma in the American Civil War," p. 210. Discussion of Samuel A. Stouffer, *The American Soldier*, vol. 2, *Combat and Its Aftermath* (1949), and S. L. A. Marshall, *Men against Fire* (1947), in Michael C. C. Adams, *The Best War Ever: America and World War II* (Baltimore: Johns Hopkins University Press, 1994), esp. pp. 101, 175; Joseph T. Durkin, ed., *John Dooley, Confederate Soldier: His War Journal* (1945, repr. Notre Dame, IN: University of Notre Dame Press, 1965), p. 99; Hughes, ed., *Philip Daingerfield Stephenson*, p. 193.

18. Captain Wilberforce Nevin, 79th Pennsylvania, quoted in Gerald J. Prokopowicz, *All for the Regiment: The Army of the Ohio, 1861–1862* (Chapel Hill: University of North Carolina Press, 2001), p. 177; E. and R. Rosenblatt, eds., *Hard Marching Every Day*, p. 217.

19. T. Harry Williams, ed., "The Reluctant Warrior: The Diary of N. K. Nichols," *Civil War History* 3 (1957): p. 36; Hal Bridges, *Lee's Maverick General: Daniel Harvey Hill* (New York: McGraw-Hill, 1961), p. 118; John Laffin, *Americans in Battle* (New York: Crown, 1973), p. 253; Cecil D. Eby Jr., ed., *A Virginia Yankee in the Civil War: The Diaries of David Hunter Strother* (Chapel Hill: University of North Carolina Press, 1961), p. 281.

20. Ambrose Bierce, "What I Saw of Shiloh," June 1864, repr. in *Bierce's Civil War* (Washington, DC: Regnery Gateway, 1956), p. 17; Henry Villard, *Memoirs* (Boston: Houghton Mifflin, 1904), vol. 1, p. 246; Ulysses S. Grant, "The Battle of Shiloh," in Robert Underwood Johnson and Clarence C. Buel, eds., *Battles and*

Leaders of the Civil War (New York: Century, 1884–1888), vol. 1, p. 474.

21. Abner R. Small, *The Road to Richmond: The Civil War Memoirs of Major Abner R. Small of the Sixteenth Maine Volunteers* (1939, repr. New York: Fordham University Press, 2000), pp. 70–71; Albert Theodore Goodloe, *Some Rebel Relics from the Seat of War* (Nashville, TN, 1893), p. 174.

22. J. E. Brant, *History of the Eighty-fifth Indiana Volunteer Infantry, Its Organization, Campaigns and Battles* (Bloomington, IN: Craven Bros., 1902), pp. 56–57; Sparks, ed., *Inside Lincoln's Army*, pp. 388, 417.

23. Joseph Allan Frank and George A. Reaves, *"Seeing the Elephant": Raw Recruits at the Battle of Shiloh* (Westport, CT: Greenwood, 1989), cited in Larry M. Logue, *To Appomattox and Beyond: The Civil War Soldier in War and Peace* (Chicago: Ivan R. Dee, 1996), p. 68.

24. Robert Garth Scott, ed., *Fallen Leaves: The Civil War Letters of Major Henry Livermore Abbott* (Kent, OH: Kent State University Press, 1991), p. 143.

25. Joan D. Hedrick, *Harriet Beecher Stowe: A Life* (New York: Oxford University Press, 1994), pp. 307, 324, 382–83; Mills Lane, ed., *"Dear Mother: Don't Grieve about Me; If I Get Killed, I'll Only Be Dead": Letters from Georgia Soldiers in the Civil War* (Savannah, GA: Beehive, 1977), p. 144; Richard A. Baumgartner, *Buckeye Blood: Ohio at Gettysburg* (Huntington, WV: Blue Acorn Press, 2003), p. 140; Eric T. Dean Jr., "'Dangled over Hell': The Trauma of the Civil War," in Michael Barton and Larry M. Logue, eds., *The Civil War Soldier: A Historical Reader* (New York: New York University Press, 2002), p. 411.

26. David Herbert Donald, ed., *Gone for a Soldier: The Civil War Memoirs of Private Alfred Bellard* (Boston: Little, Brown, 1975), p. 198; Charles Carleton Coffin, *The Boys of '61, or Four Years of Fighting*, rev. ed. (Boston: Dana Estes, 1896), p. 173; Charles Winder Squires, "'Boy Officer' of the Washington Artillery—Part 1," *Civil War Times Illustrated* 14 (1975): p. 19; Lynda Lasswell Crist and Mary Seaton Dix, eds., *The Papers of Jefferson Davis* (Baton Rouge: Louisiana State University Press, 1971–1995), vol. 8, p. 404; Joseph L. Harsh, *Confederate Tide Rising: Robert E. Lee and the Making of Southern Strategy, 1861–1862* (Kent, OH: Kent State University Press, 1998), pp. 102–3; Douglass Southall Freeman and Grady McWhiney, eds., *Lee's Dispatches: Unpublished Letters of General Robert E. Lee* (Baton Rouge: Louisiana State University Press, 1994), pp. 122–23; *O.R.*, series 1, vol. 27, pt. 3, pp. 1040–41, 1048; Douglass Southall Freeman, *Lee's Lieutenants* (New York: Scribner's, 1942–1944), vol. 3, pp. 217–19; also, Frederick Maurice, *Robert E. Lee the Soldier* (1925, repr. New York: Bonanza, 1976), pp. 159–60; Sparks, *Inside Lincoln's Army*, p. 274.

27. Thomas B. Buell, *The Warrior Generals: Combat Leadership in the Civil War* (New York: Three Rivers, 1997), pp. 87–88; William W. Hassler, ed., *The General to His Lady: The Civil War Letters of William Dorsey Pender to Fanny Pender* (Chapel Hill: University of North Carolina Press, 1965), pp. 175–76, 179; Donald B. Koonce, ed., *Doctor to the Front: The Recollections of Confederate*

Surgeon Thomas Fanning Wood, 1861–1865 (Knoxville: University of Tennessee Press, 2000), pp. 109–10.

28. Adams, *Best War Ever*, p. 98; Richard Wheeler, *Voices of the Civil War* (New York: Thomas Y. Crowell, 1976), pp. 193–94.

29. Helen Epstein, "Life & Death on the Social Ladder," *New York Review of Books*, July 16, 1998, p. 28.

30. Wightman and Longacre, *From Antietam to Fort Fisher*, p. 32; Noah Andre Trudeau, *Bloody Roads South: The Wilderness to Cold Harbor, May–June 1864* (Boston: Little, Brown, 1989), p. 191; Allan Nevins, ed., *A Diary of Battle: The Personal Journals of Colonel Charles S. Wainwright, 1861–1865* (New York: Harcourt, Brace & World, 1962), p. 422.

31. Shirley A. Leckie, *Elizabeth Bacon Custer and the Making of a Myth* (Norman: University of Oklahoma Press, 1993), p. 60; Basil Duke, *History of Morgan's Cavalry* (Cincinnati, OH: Miami Printing and Publishing, 1867), p. 532.

32. Buell, *The Warrior Generals*, p. 90; Daniel H. Hill, "McClellan's Change of Base and Malvern Hill," in Johnson and Buel, eds., *Battles and Leaders*, vol. 2, p. 394.

33. Arthur James Lyon Fremantle, *Three Months in the Southern States, April–June 1863* (1864, repr. Lincoln: University of Nebraska Press, 1991), p. 277; Richard B. McCaslin, *Lee in the Shadow of Washington* (Baton Rouge: Louisiana State University Press, 2001), p. 170; Gordon C. Rhea, *The Battles for Spotsylvania Court House and the Road to Yellow Tavern, May 7–12, 1864* (Baton Rouge: Louisiana State University Press, 1997), pp. 255–56; William Allen, "Memoranda of Conversations with General Robert E. Lee," in Gary W. Gallagher, ed., *Lee the Soldier* (Lincoln: University of Nebraska Press, 1996), p. 11.

34. Stephen W. Sears, *George B. McClellan: The Young Napoleon* (New York: Ticknor & Fields, 1988), pp. 196, 218–19, 305, 319–22; George B. McClellan, *McClellan's Own Story* (New York: C. L. Webster, 1887), p. 354.

35. Carol K. Bleser and Lesley J. Gordon, eds., *Intimate Strategies of the Civil War: Military Commanders and Their Wives* (New York: Oxford University Press, 2001), pp. 73–77; Robert A. Bright, "Pickett's Charge," *Southern Historical Society Papers* 31 (1903): p. 234; Lesley J. Gordon, *General George E. Pickett in Life and Legend* (Chapel Hill: University of North Carolina Press, 1998), pp. 110–12; Henrietta Stratton Jaquette, ed., *South after Gettysburg: Letters of Cornelia Hancock from the Army of the Potomac, 1863–1865* (1937, repr. Freeport, NY: Books for Libraries, 1971), pp. 55, 58; Nevins, ed., *Diary of Battle*, pp. 409, 476, 508–9, 513.

36. Joshua Lawrence Chamberlain, *The Passing of the Armies: An Account of the Final Campaign of the Army of the Potomac, Based upon Personal Reminiscences of the Fifth Army Corps* (1915, repr. New York: Bantam, 1993), pp. 104–5; Bleser and Gordon, *Intimate Strategies of the Civil War*, p. 170.

37. C. Vann Woodward and Elisabeth Muhlenfeld, *The Private Mary Chesnut: The Unpublished Civil War Diaries* (New York: Oxford University Press, 1984), p. 222; Lee Kennett, *Marching through Georgia: The Story of Soldiers and Civil-*

ians during Sherman's Campaign (New York: Harper, 1996), p. 58; Donald, *Gone for a Soldier*, p. 166; E. Porter Alexander, "Sketch of Longstreet's Division," *Southern Historical Society Papers* 9 (1881): p. 515; Harsh, *Confederate Tide Rising*, p. 124.

38. Fletcher Pratt, *Ordeal By Fire: An Informal History of the Civil War*, rev. ed. (New York: William Sloane, 1948), p. 321; Sparks, ed., *Inside Lincoln's Army*, p. 415; Shelby Foote, *The Civil War: A Narrative* (New York: Random House, 1958), pp. 536–37.

39. David W. Blight, ed., *When This Cruel War Is Over: The Civil War Letters of Charles Harvey Brewster* (Amherst: University of Massachusetts Press, 1992), p. 145; Crowell, *Young Volunteer*, pp. 210–11; John R. Brumgardt, ed., *Civil War Nurse: The Diary and Letters of Hannah Ropes* (Knoxville: University of Tennessee Press, 1980), p. 67; Richard Hall, *Stanley: An Adventurer Explored* (London: Collins, 1974), p. 128.

40. William C. Davis, *Lincoln's Men: How President Lincoln Became Father to an Army and a Nation* (New York: Simon & Schuster, 2000), p. 186; Eric T. Dean Jr., *Shook over Hell: Post-Traumatic Stress, Vietnam, and the Civil War* (Cambridge, MA: Harvard University Press, 1997), pp. 65–66; Sam R. Watkins, *"Co. Aytch": A Side Show of the Big Show* (1881, repr. New York: Collier, 1962), p. 209.

41. Watkins, *"Co. Aytch,"* pp. 84–85, 211, 232.

42. A. G. Hart, *The Surgeon and the Hospital in the Civil War* (1902, repr. Gaithersburg, MD: Olde Soldier Books, 1987), p. 9; Lonn, *Desertion during the Civil War*, p. 6; Ohioan Thaddeus Hyatt in James M. McPherson, *For Cause and Comrades: Why Men Fought in the Civil War* (New York: Oxford University Press, 1997), p. 71; Daniel Coe, ed., *Mine Eyes Have Seen the Glory: Combat Diaries of Union Sergeant Hamilton Alexander Coe* (Rutherford, NJ: Fairleigh Dickinson University Press, 1975), p. 123.

43. Leander Stillwell, *The Story of a Common Soldier of Army Life in the Civil War, 1861–1865*, 2nd ed. (Eire, KS: Hudson, 1920), p. 56; Daniel E. Sutherland, *Seasons of War: The Ordeal of a Confederate Community, 1861–1865* (New York: Free Press, 1995), p. 163. Nathaniel Southgate Shaler, *From Old Fields: Poems of the Civil War* (Boston: Houghton Mifflin, 1906), "The Marksman's Work," pp. 5–8, and "The Way with Mutineers," p. 26.

44. George Freeman Noyes, *The Bivouac and the Battle-field* (New York: Harper & Brothers, 1863), p. 66. On Victorian chivalric attitudes to war, Michael C. C. Adams, *The Great Adventure: Male Desire and the Coming of World War I* (Bloomington: Indiana University Press, 1990), chap. 5, "Knights and Their Dragons," pp. 62–72; Thomason, *Jeb Stuart*, pp. 209–10, 360–61.

45. Lonn, *Desertion during the Civil War*, p. 145. O.R., series 1, vol. 25, pt. 2, p. 78.

46. Richard Wheeler, *Voices of the Civil War* (New York: Thomas Y. Crowell, 1976), p. 249; Jaquette, *South after Gettysburg*, p. 163; on intervention before hospitalization, Ingraham and Manning, "Psychiatric Battle Casualties," pp.

23–24. For more on Hooker's mental eclipse at Chancellorsville, see Michael C. C. Adams, *Our Masters the Rebels: A Speculation on Union Military Failure in the East, 1861–1865* (Cambridge, MA: Harvard University Press, 1978), pp. 141–42.

47. Dewey W. Grantham, ed., "Letters from H. J. Hightower, a Confederate Soldier, 1861–1864," *Georgia Historical Quarterly* 40 (1956): p. 183; Reid Mitchell, *The Vacant Chair: The Northern Soldier Leaves Home* (New York: Oxford University Press, 1993), pp. 27–28; John H. Brinton, *Personal Memoirs of John H. Brinton: Civil War Surgeon, 1861–1865* (Carbondale: Southern Illinois University Press, 1996), pp. 141–42; R. Gregory Laude, *Madness, Malingering, and Malfeasance: The Transformation of Psychiatry and the Law in the Civil War Era* (Washington, DC: Brassey's, 2003), pp. 106–7.

48. Bell I. Wiley, ed., *"This Infernal War": The Confederate Letters of Sgt. Edwin H. Fay* (Austin: University of Texas Press, 1958), p. 32; Stillwell, *Common Soldier of the Army*, pp. 119–20; Bell Irvin Wiley, *The Life of Billy Yank: The Common Soldier of the Union* (New York: Bobbs-Merrill, 1952), p. 278; Ann K. Blomquist and Robert A. Taylor, eds., *This Cruel War: The Civil War Letters of Grant and Malinda Taylor, 1862–1865* (Macon, GA: Mercer University Press, 2000), pp. 14–15.

49. Milo M. Quaife, ed., *From the Cannon's Mouth: The Civil War Letters of General Alpheus S. Williams* (Detroit, MI: Wayne State University Press & Detroit Historical Society, 1959), p. 44; Leon Edel, *Henry James: A Life* (New York: Harper & Row, 1985), pp. 62–63.

50. Julian Grossman, *Echo of a Distant Drum: Winslow Homer and the Civil War* (New York: Harry N. Abrams, 1974), pp. 176–77; Henry Woodhead, ed., *The Illustrated Atlas of the Civil War* (Alexandria, VA: Time-Life, 1991), p. 182; Sparks, *Inside Lincoln's Army*, p. 449; David P. Conyngham, *Sherman's March through the South* (New York: Sheldon, 1865), p. 108.

51. Howe, *Touched with Fire*, pp. 141–42, 149–50, 151–52.

52. Lonn, *Desertion during the Civil War*, p. 151; Michael C. C. Adams, "Retelling the Tale: Wars in Common Memory," in Gabor Boritt, ed., *War Comes Again: Comparative Vistas on the Civil War and World War II* (New York: Oxford University Press, 1995), p. 221; William S. McFeely, *Grant: A Biography* (New York: Norton, 1982), p. 189; John R. Jones, in *Battles and Leaders*, "Extra Illustrated," vol. 8, quoted in Stephen W. Sears, *Landscape Turned Red: The Battle of Antietam* (Boston: Houghton Mifflin, 1983), p. 307; *O.R.*, vol. 19, pt. 2, p. 627; Kenneth Radley, *Rebel Watchdog: The Confederate State Army Provost Guard* (Baton Rouge: Louisiana State University Press, 1989), pp. 10, 83; Craig L. Symonds, *Stonewall of the West: Patrick Cleburne and the Civil War* (Lawrence: University Press of Kansas, 1997), p. 158.

53. William Carey Dodson, ed., *Campaigns of Wheeler and His Cavalry, 1862–1865* (Atlanta, GA: Hudgins, 1899), bucking and gagging, pp. 393–94, 426; Watkins, *"Co. Aytch,"* for branding and lashing, p. 48; Alto Loftin Jackson, ed., *So*

Mourns the Dove: Letters of a Confederate Infantryman and His Family (New York: Exposition, 1965), p. 29.

54. Walter Lowenfels, ed., *Walt Whitman's Civil War* (New York: Knopf, 1971), pp. 215–16.

55. Buckner F. Melton, *A Hanging Offense: The Strange Affair of the Warship Somers* (New York: Free Press, 2003). Documentary record in Harrison Hayford, ed., *The Somers Mutiny Affair* (Englewood Cliffs, NJ: Prentice-Hall, 1959); Lee Kennett, *Sherman: A Soldier's Life* (New York: HarperCollins, 2001), p. 226.

56. Lonn, *Desertion during the Civil War*, p. 91; Laude, *Madness, Malingering, and Malfeasance*, p. 70; Gerald F. Linderman, *Embattled Courage: The Experience of Combat in the American Civil War* (New York: Free Press, 1987), pp. 174–75.

CHAPTER SIX. DEPRIVATIONS AND DISLOCATIONS

1. Carol K. Bleser and Lesley J. Gordon, eds., *Intimate Strategies of the Civil War: Military Commanders and Their Wives* (New York: Oxford University Press, 2001), p. 170; Robert Hunt Rhodes, ed., *All for the Union: The Civil War Diary and Letters of Elisha Hunt Rhodes* (New York: Random House, 1992), pp. 3, 7.

2. J. B. Jones, *A Rebel War Clerk's Diary at the Confederate States Capital* (Philadelphia: J. B. Lippincott, 1866), vol. 2, p. 88.

3. Patricia B. Mitchell, *Union Army Camp Cooking*, rev. ed. (Chatham, VA, 1991), p. 2; James W. Geary, *We Need Men: The Union Draft in the Civil War* (DeKalb: Northern Illinois University Press, 1991), pp. 44–45.

4. Harold Holzer, ed., *Dear Mr. Lincoln: Letters to the President* (Reading, MA: Addison-Wesley, 1993), p. 107; Craig L. Symonds, *Stonewall of the West: Patrick Cleburne and the Civil War* (Lawrence: University Press of Kansas, 1997), p. 93; Harry F. Jackson and Thomas F. O'Donnell, *Back Home in Oneida: Herman Clarke and His Letters* (Syracuse, NY: Syracuse University Press, 1965), p. 158; Ella Lonn, *Desertion during the Civil War* (1928, repr. Gloucester, MA: Peter Smith, 1966), p. 115.

5. George Templeton Strong, *Diary of the Civil War, 1860–1865* (New York: Macmillan, 1962), pp. 184–85; Alvin F. Harlow, *Old Waybills: The Romance of the Express Companies* (New York: Appleton-Century, 1934), p. 291.

6. Edward Younger, ed., *Inside the Confederate Government: The Diary of Robert Garlick Hill Kean* (Baton Rouge: Louisiana State University Press, 1993), p. 43; John F. Marszalek, ed., *The Diary of Miss Emma Holmes, 1861–1866* (Baton Rouge: Louisiana State University Press, 1994), p. 43.

7. Earl Schenck Miers, ed., *When the World Ended: The Diary of Emma LeConte* (New York: Oxford University Press, 1957), pp. 12, 16.

8. T. F. Dornblaser, *Sabre Strokes of the Pennsylvania Dragoons in the War of 1861–1865* (Philadelphia: Lutheran Publication Society, 1864), p. 186.

9. Alfred Jay Bollet, *Civil War Medicine: Challenges and Triumphs* (Tucson, AZ:

Galen 2002), p. 246; Marszalek, *Diary of Emma Holmes*, pp. 193–94, 312, 326; Katharine M. Jones, *Heroines of Dixie: Confederate Women Tell Their Story of the War* (1955, repr. New York: Smithmark, 1995), p. 285.

10. Marszalek, *Diary of Emma Holmes*, p. 352; Miers, *When the World Ended*, p. 17; James A. Ramage, *Rebel Raider: The Life of General John Hunt Morgan* (Lexington: University Press of Kentucky, 1986), p. 175; E. L. Doctorow, *The March* (New York: Random House, 2005), p. 267; Donald B. Koonce, ed., *Doctor to the Front: The Recollections of Confederate Surgeon Thomas Fanning Wood, 1861–1865* (Knoxville: University of Tennessee Press, 2000), p. 170; "Horse Cove," near Highlands, NC, is an example of a stock hideaway that the reader may still visit; see Allen De Hart, *North Carolina Hiking Trails*, 3rd ed. (Boston, MA: Appalachian Mountain Club Books, 1996), p. 154.

11. Frank Wilkeson, *Recollections of a Private Soldier in the Army of the Potomac* (1886, repr. Freeport, NY: Books for Libraries, 1972), p. 103; William Andrew Fletcher, *Rebel Private, Front and Rear: Memoirs of a Confederate Soldier* (1908, repr. Austin: University of Texas Press, 1954), pp. 110–11; William P. Buck, ed., *Sad Earth, Sweet Heaven: The Diary of Lucy Rebecca Buck during the War between the States, December 25, 1861–April 5, 1865*, 2nd ed. (Birmingham, AL: Buck Publishing, 1992), pp. 65–66.

12. Nannie M. Tilley, ed., *Federals on the Frontier: The Diary of Benjamin F. McIntyre, 1862–1864* (Austin: University of Texas Press, 1963), pp. 75–76; *The War of the Rebellion: A Compilation of the Official Records of the Union and Confederate Armies* (Washington, DC: Government Printing Office, 1880–1901), vol. 38, pt. 5, pp. 75, 77–78; Donald S. Frazier, *Blood & Treasure: Confederate Empire in the Southwest* (College Station: Texas A&M University Press, 1995), p. 131.

13. G. S. Bradley, *The Star Corps; or, Notes of an Army Chaplain during Sherman's Famous "March to the Sea"* (Milwaukee, WI: Jermain & Brightman, 1865), pp. 274–76; Lonn, *Desertion during the Civil War*, p. 13; F. Jay Taylor, ed., *Reluctant Rebel: The Secret Diary of Robert Patrick, 1861–1865* (Baton Rouge: Louisiana State University Press, 1959), p. 168.

14. Richard Harwell and Philip N. Racine, eds., *The Fiery Trial: A Union Officer's Account of Sherman's Last Campaigns* (Knoxville: University of Tennessee Press, 1986), p. 55.

15. Sarah Morgan Dawson, *A Confederate Girl's Diary* (Bloomington: Indiana University Press, 1960), p. 343; Mary Elizabeth Massey, *Refugee Life in the Confederacy* (Baton Rouge: Louisiana State University Press, 1964), pp. 4, 231.

16. John Q. Anderson, ed., *Brokenburn: The Journal of Kate Stone, 1861–1868* (Baton Rouge: Louisiana State University Press, 1955), p. 189; Charles East, ed., *Sarah Morgan: The Civil War Diary of a Southern Woman* (New York: Touchstone, 1992), p. 251.

17. Virginia Ingraham Burr, ed., *The Secret Eye: The Journal of Ella Gertrude*

Clanton Thomas, 1848–1889 (Chapel Hill: University of North Carolina Press, 1990), p. 251.

18. Richard Wheeler, *Voices of the Civil War* (New York: Thomas Y. Crowell, 1976), pp. 341–48; Miers, ed., *When the World Ended*, pp. 102, 105, 126, 182, 131.

19. Younger, ed., *Inside the Confederate Government*, p. 174; Stephanie McCurry, *Confederate Reckoning: Power and Politics in the Civil War South* (Cambridge, MA: Harvard University Press, 2010). In her Prologue, pp. 1–10, McCurry argues that the planters' overreach, in trying to found a proslavery nation, brought down their powerful regime, empowering Southern women and blacks for the first time.

20. Michael J. Varhola, *Everyday Life during the Civil War* (Cincinnati, OH: Writer's Digest Books, 1999), p. 85; Mark A. Weitz, *A Higher Duty: Desertion among Georgia Troops during the Civil War* (Lincoln: University of Nebraska Press, 2000), pp. 3, 107–11, analyses the salt shortage; Kenneth Radley, *Rebel Watchdog: The Confederate States Army Provost Guard* (Baton Rouge: Louisiana State University Press, 1989), p. 148; Judith Lee Hallock, "The Role of the Community in Civil War Desertion," *Civil War History* 29 (1983): pp. 123–34.

21. Edward K. Spann, *Gotham at War: New York City, 1860–1865* (Wilmington, DE: Scholarly Resources, 2002), pp. 58–60; Stephanie McCurry, "Bread or Blood!" *Civil War Times* 49, no. 3 (June 2011): pp. 37–41; McCurry, *Confederate Reckoning*, p. 178; Drew Gilpin Faust, "Altars of Sacrifice: Confederate Women and the Narratives of War," *Journal of American History* 76 (1990): p. 1222; Robert C. Goodell and P. A. M. Taylor, eds., "A German Immigrant in the Union Army: Selected Letters of Valentine Bechler," *Journal of American Studies* 4 (1971): p. 159.

22. Robert Stiles, "Dedication of the Monument to the Confederate Dead of the University of Virginia, June 7, 1893," in *Southern Historical Society Papers* 21 (1893): p. 32; Richard Barksdale Harwell, ed., *Kate: The Journal of a Confederate Nurse* (Baton Rouge: Louisiana State University Press, 1959), p. 296; Susan Leigh Blackford, *Letters from Lee's Army* (New York: A. S. Barnes, 1962), pp. 81, 214.

23. Marszalek, ed., *Diary of Emma Holmes*, p. 194; William H. Hastings, *Letters from a Berdan Sharpshooter: The Civil War Letters of Private William B. Greene, Co. G. 2nd United States Sharpshooters (Berdan's) Army of the Potomac, 1861–1865* (Belleville, WI: Historic Publications, 1993), p. 199; Anna Howard Shaw, *The Story of a Pioneer* (New York: Harper & Brothers, 1915), p. 34; James Marten, ed., *Lessons of War: The Civil War in Children's Magazines* (Wilmington, DE: Scholarly Resources, 1998), p. 155.

24. Burr, ed., *Secret Eye*, p. 203, also p. 227; Peter Messent and Steve Courtney, eds., *The Civil War Letters of Joseph Hopkins Twichell: A Chaplain's Story* (Athens: University of Georgia Press, 2006), p. 62; Dixon Wecter, *When Johnny Comes Marching Home* (1944, repr. Westport, CT: Greenwood, 1976), pp. 191–92.

25. Bell Irvin Wiley, *Confederate Women* (Westport, CT: Greenwood, 1975), pp. 162–63; Reid Mitchell, *The Vacant Chair: The Northern Soldier Leaves Home*

(New York: Oxford University Press, 1993), p. 90; Stephen W. Sears, ed., *For Country, Cause & Leader: The Civil War Journal of Charles B. Haydon* (New York: Ticknor & Fields, 1993), p. 354; "James E. Graham Diary," July–August 1864, Ohio Historical Society, Columbus.

26. Alistair Horne, *The Fall of Paris: The Siege and the Commune, 1870–71* (1965, repr. London: Reprint Society, 1967), p. 185.

27. J. Matthew Gallman, *The North Fights the Civil* War: *The Home Front* (Chicago: Ivan R. Dee, 1994), p. 107; Edith Abbott, "The Civil War and the Crime Wave of 1865–70," *Social Service Review* 1 (1927): pp. 215–16.

28. Abbott, "Crime Wave of 1865–70," pp. 220–22; also, *Twenty-First Annual Report of the Prison Association of New York* (1866), p. 173.

29. Abbott, "Crime Wave of 1865–70," pp. 232, 220.

30. Iver Bernstein, *The New York City Draft Riots: Their Significance for American Society and Politics in the Age of the Civil War* (New York: Oxford University Press, 1990), p. 53.

31. Donald Yacovone, ed., *A Voice of Thunder: A Black Soldier's Civil War* (Urbana: University of Illinois Press, 1998), p. 73; Mills Lane, ed., *"Dear Mother: Don't Grieve about Me; If I Get Killed, I'll Only Be Dead"; Letters from Georgia Soldiers in the Civil War* (Savannah, GA: Beehive, 1977), p. 329; William Camm, "Diary of Colonel William Camm, 1861–1865," *Journal of the Illinois State Historical Society* 18, nos. 3–4 (October 1925–January 1926): p. 902; *Official Records of the Union and Confederate Navies in the War of the Rebellion*, 31 vols. (Washington, DC: Government Printing Office, 1895–1929), series 1, vol. 23, pp. 255–57.

32. Charles Wright Wills, *Army Life of an Illinois Soldier: Including a Day by Day Record of Sherman's March to the Sea* (Washington, DC: Globe, 1906), p. 332; Frank Leslie's *Illustrated Newspaper*, September 30, 1865, quoted in Edward D. C. Campbell Jr. and Kym S. Rice, eds., *A Woman's War: Southern Women, Civil War, and the Confederate Legacy* (Richmond, VA: Museum of the Confederacy; Charlottesville: University Press of Virginia, 1996), p. 63; Marszalek, *Diary of Emma Holmes*, p. 455.

33. Vincent Harding, *There Is a River: The Black Struggle for Freedom in America* (New York: Harcourt Brace Jovanovich, 1981), pp. 225–35; Reid Mitchell, *Civil War Soldiers: Their Expectations and Their Experiences* (New York: Simon & Schuster, 1998), pp. 120–23; Henrietta Stratton Jaquette, ed., *South after Gettysburg: The Letters of Cornelia Hancock from the Army of the Potomac, 1863–1865* (1937, repr. Freeport, NY: Books for Libraries, 1971), p. 31.

34. Lee Kennett, *Marching through Georgia: The Story of Soldiers and Civilians during Sherman's Campaign* (New York: Harper, 1996), pp. 289–90; Ray Allen Billington, *The Journal of Charlotte L. Forten* (New York: Dryden, 1953), p. 167; Susan Walker, "Journal of Miss Susan Walker, Mar. 3–June 6, 1862," *Quarterly Publication of the Historical and Philosophical Society of Ohio* (Jan.–Mar. 1912): pp. 38, 39, 35.

35. James Marten, ed., *Lessons of War: The Civil War in Children's Magazines* (Wilmington, DE: Scholarly Resources, 1998), p. 9; G. N. Coan, *The Little Pilgrim* 2 (June 1864): p. 82; Justin G. Turner and Linda Levitt Turner, *Mary Todd Lincoln: Her Life and Letters* (New York: Knopf, 1972), p. 141; Molly Caldwell Crosby, *The American Plague: The Untold Story of Yellow Fever, the Epidemic That Shaped Our History* (New York: Berkley, 2006), p. 22.

36. Gerald Schwartz, ed., *A Woman Doctor's Civil War: Esther Hill Hawk's Diary* (Columbia: University of South Carolina Press, 1986), p. 55.

37. John Cimprich, *Slavery's End in Tennessee* (University: University of Alabama Press, 1985), p. 90; also, Leon P. Litwack, *Been in the Storm So Long: The Aftermath of Slavery* (New York: Knopf, 1979), p. 101.

38. The seminal work on the Sea Islands is Willie Lee Rose, *Rehearsal for Reconstruction: The Port Royal Experiment* (New York: Bobbs-Merrill, 1964); Walker, "Journal of Miss Susan Walker," p. 30; John W. Blassingame, "The Union Army as an Educational Institution for Negroes, 1862–1865," *Journal of Negro Education* 34, no. 2 (1965): pp. 152–59.

39. Sidney Lanier, *Tiger-Lilies* (1867, repr. Chapel Hill: University of North Carolina Press, 1969), pp. 136–37; Campbell and Rice, *A Woman's War*, p. 63; Anderson, ed., *Brokenburn*, pp. 28, 174–75, 195–96.

40. Walt Whitman, *Memoranda during the War: Civil War Journals, 1863–1865* (1875, repr. Mineola, NY: Dover, 2010), p. 4.

41. Marszalek, *Diary of Emma Holmes*, pp. 36–37.

42. Marli F. Weiner, ed., *Heritage of Woe: The Civil War Diary of Grace Brown Elmore, 1861–1868* (Athens: University of Georgia Press, 1997), 1, 14; 2, 71; Anderson, *Brokenburn*, pp. 87, 133.

43. DeForest, *Miss Ravenel's Conversion*, p. 80; Carolyn De Swarte Gifford, ed., *Writing Out My Heart: Selections from the Journal of Frances E. Willard, 1855–96* (Urbana: University of Illinois Press, 1995), pp. 166, 210, 251.

44. Blackford, *Letters from Lee's Army*, p. 37; Joel Chandler Harris, *On the Plantation: A Story of a Georgia Boy's Adventures during the War* (Athens: University of Georgia Press, 1980), p. 49; Myrta Lockett Avary, ed., *A Virginia Girl in the Civil War, 1861–1865* (New York: Appleton, 1903), p. 41; Lois Hill, ed., *Poems and Songs of the Civil War* (New York: Barnes & Noble, 1990), pp. 133–34.

45. Marszalek, *Diary of Emma Holmes*, pp. 178–79; Stanley Weintraub, *General Sherman's Christmas: Savannah, 1864* (Washington, DC: Smithsonian Books; New York: Harper, 2009), pp. 62–63; Tilley, ed., *Federals on the Frontier*, pp. 72–74.

46. Thomas C. DeLeon, *Belles, Beaux and Brains of the 60's* (1909, repr. New York: Arno, 1974), p. 158; East, *Sarah Morgan*, p. 597.

47. John W. Schildt, *Drums along the Antietam* (Parsons, WV: McClain, 1972), p. 231; Lois Hill, *Poems and Songs of the Civil War* (New York: Barnes & Noble, 1990), p. 227; Neil Hanson, *Unknown Soldiers: The Story of the Missing of the First World War* (New York: Knopf, 2006), p. 241.

48. East, *Sarah Morgan*, p. 610; William C. Darrah, *Cartes de Visite in Nineteenth Century Photography* (Gettysburg, PA: W. C. Darrah, 1981), pp. 4, 12, 14, 19; Bob Zeller, *The Civil War in Depth: History in 3-D* (San Francisco, CA: Chronicle, 1997), pp. 14, 18, 38; Whitman, *Memoranda during the War*, p. 17; Marszalek, *Diary of Emma Holmes*, pp. 191–92.

49. Harlow, *Old Waybills*, p. 299; Susan S. Kissel and Margery T. Rouse, eds., *The Story of the Pewter Basin and Other Occasional Writings: Collected in Southern Ohio and Northern Kentucky* (Bloomington, IN: T.I.S. Publications, 1981), pp. 59–61; Thomas Owen, "Back in War Times," *Athens Gazette* (PA), March 11, 1897.

50. Drew Gilpin Faust, *This Republic of Suffering: Death and the American Civil War* (New York: Knopf, 2008), p. 210. Also, reviews of Faust: Adam Gopnik, "In the Mourning Store," *The New Yorker*, January 21, 2008; James M. McPherson, "Dark Victories," *New York Review of Books*, April 17, 2008; Joan D. Hedrick, *Harriet Beecher Stowe: A Life* (New York: Oxford University Press, 1994), p. 312; Stowe, "The New Year," *Household Papers and Stories* (1865, repr. Boston: Houghton Mifflin, 1896), pp. 425–37.

51. Print in the Behringer Crawford Museum collection, Park Hills, KY; J. Michael Welton, ed., *"My Heart Is So Rebellious": The Caldwell Letters, 1861–1865* (Warrenton, VA, 1990), p. 19.

52. C. Vann Woodward and Elisabeth Muhlenfeld, *The Private Mary Chesnut: The Unpublished Civil War Diaries* (New York: Oxford University Press, 1984), p. 106; C. Vann Woodward, *Mary Chesnut's Civil War* (New Haven, CT: Yale University Press, 1981), pp. 452, 474–75, 155.

53. Woodward, *Mary Chesnut's Civil War*, pp. 515, 588–89; Woodward and Muhlenfeld, *Private Mary Chesnut*, pp. 223–24, 206.

54. Woodward, *Mary Chesnut's Civil War*, pp. 477, 247, 286; Allie Patricia Wall, ed., "The Letters of Mary Boykin Chesnut," M.A. thesis, University of South Carolina, 1977, p. 67; Woodward and Muhlenfeld, *Private Mary Chesnut*, pp. 105, 138–39, 191, 208; Elisabeth Muhlenfeld, *Mary Boykin Chesnut: A Biography* (Baton Rouge: Louisiana State University Press, 1981), p. 128.

55. Elisabeth Showalter Muhlenfeld, "Mary Boykin Chesnut: The Writer and Her Work," Ph.D. diss., 2 vols., University of South Carolina, 1978, 1:394; Muhlenfeld, *Mary Boykin Chesnut*, p. 123; Woodward and Muhlenfeld, *Private Mary Chesnut*, p. 101; Woodward, *Mary Chesnut's Civil War*, pp. 500, 426.

56. Muhlenfeld, *Mary Boykin Chesnut*, pp. 115, 129; Woodward and Muhlenfeld, *Private Mary Chesnut*, p. 177; Woodward, *Mary Chesnut's Civil War*, p. 643; Wall, "Letters of Mary Boykin Chesnut," p. 71.

57. Wall, "Letters of Mary Boykin Chesnut," p. 72; Woodward and Muhlenfeld, *Private Mary Chesnut*, p. 161; Woodward, *Mary Chesnut's Civil War*, p. 637.

58. Woodward, *Mary Chesnut's Civil War*, pp. 291, 716; Woodward and Muhlenfeld, *Private Mary Chesnut*, p. 252.

CHAPTER SEVEN. INVASIONS AND VIOLATIONS

1. Joan Cashin, ed., *Our Common Affairs: Texts from Women in the Old South* (Baltimore: Johns Hopkins University Press, 1996), p. 281; Carol K. Bleser and Lesley J. Gordon, eds., *Intimate Strategies of the Civil War: Military Commanders and Their Wives* (New York: Oxford University Press, 2001), p. 14.

2. James M. McPherson, *Battle Cry of Freedom: The Civil War Era* (New York: Ballantine, 1988), p. 501; Thomas Williams, "Letters," *American Historical Review* 14 (January 1909): p. 320; Robert S. Holzman, *Stormy Ben Butler* (New York: Macmillan, 1954), pp. 84–85; Donald B. Koonce, ed., *Doctor to the Front: The Recollections of Confederate Surgeon Thomas Fanning Wood, 1861–1865* (Knoxville: University of Tennessee Press, 2000), p. 103.

3. Lonnie R. Speer, *War of Vengeance: Acts of Retribution against Civil War POWs* (Mechanicsburg, PA: Stackpole, 2002), pp. 137–38; also, Walt Whitman in the *New York Times,* December 27, 1864; Fannie Beers, *Memories: A Record of Personal Experiences and Adventures during Four Years of War* (Philadelphia: Lippincott, 1888), p. 156.

4. Arthur M. Schlesinger Jr., "War and the Constitution: Abraham Lincoln and Franklin D. Roosevelt," in Gabor Boritt, ed., *War Comes Again: Comparative Vistas on the Civil War and World War II* (New York: Oxford University Press, 1995), pp. 151–63; also, Roy P. Basler et al., eds., *The Collected Works of Abraham Lincoln,* 9 vols. (New Brunswick, NJ: Rutgers University Press, 1953–55), 6:408, 5:421, 6:29–30, 428; Stephen R. Wise, *Gate of Hell: Campaign for Charleston Harbor, 1863* (Columbia: University of South Carolina Press, 1994), pp. 148, 169; Speer, *War of Vengeance,* pp. 96–97.

5. Gerald J. Prokopowicz, *All for the Regiment: The Army of the Ohio, 1861–1862* (Chapel Hill: University of North Carolina Press, 2001), pp. 122, 133; Edwin C. Bearss, *Hardluck Ironclad: The Sinking and Salvage of the Cairo,* rev. ed. (Baton Rouge: Louisiana State University Press, 1980), p. 94.

6. Charles Carleton Coffin, *The Boys of '61, or Four Years of Fighting,* rev. ed. (Boston: Dana Estes, 1896), p. 59; William Andrew Fletcher, *Rebel Private, Front and Rear: Memoirs of a Confederate Soldier* (1908, repr. Austin: University of Texas Press, 1954), p. 140; Judith Lee Hallock, ed., *The Civil War Letters of Joshua K. Callaway* (Athens: University of Georgia Press, 1997), p. 157; Charles East, ed., *Sarah Morgan: The Civil War Diary of a Southern Woman* (New York: Touchstone, 1992), p. 233.

7. David S. Sparks, ed., *Inside Lincoln's Army: The Diary of Marsena Rudolph Patrick* (New York: Thomas Yoseloff, 1964), p. 110; Bell Irvin Wiley, *Confederate Women* (Westport, CT: Greenwood, 1975), p. 149.

8. Virginia Ingraham Burr, ed., *The Secret Eye: The Journal of Ella Gertrude Clanton Thomas, 1848–1889* (Chapel Hill: University of North Carolina Press, 1990), p. 230; Coffin, *The Boys of '61,* p. 218.

9. Abner Doubleday, *Chancellorsville and Gettysburg* (1882, repr. New York:

Da Capo, 1994), p. 149; David Evans, *Sherman's Horsemen: Union Cavalry Operations in the Atlanta Campaign* (Bloomington: Indiana University Press, 1996), p. 139; Richard Wheeler, *Voices of the Civil War* (New York: Thomas Y. Crowell, 1976), p. 344; Katharine M. Jones, *Heroines of Dixie: Confederate Women Tell Their Story of the War* (1955, repr. New York: Smithmark, 1995), pp. 225–26.

10. John Q. Anderson, ed., *Brokenburn: The Journal of Kate Stone, 1861–1868* (Baton Rouge: Louisiana State University Press, 1955), p. 185; Marilyn Mayer Culpepper, *Trials and Triumphs: Women of the American Civil War* (East Lansing: Michigan State University Press, 1991), p. 97; Sallie Hunt, "Boys and Girls in the War," in News and Courier, eds., *Our Women in the War: The Lives They Lived, The Deaths They Died* (Charleston, SC: News and Courier Book Presses, 1885), p. 45.

11. Norman D. Brown, ed., *Journey to Pleasant Hill: The Civil War Letters of Captain Elijah P. Petty* (San Antonio: University of Texas, 1982), pp. 78–79, 223, 215; Catherine Hopley, *Life in the South from the Commencement of the War* (London: Chapman and Hall, 1863), vol. 2, p. 396.

12. Daniel E. Sutherland, *Seasons of War: The Ordeal of a Confederate Community, 1861–1865* (New York: Free Press, 1995), p. 73.

13. William R. Taylor, *Cavalier & Yankee: The Old South and American National Character* (Garden City, NY: Doubleday, 1963) on prewar stereotypes. Michael C. C. Adams, *Our Masters the Rebels: A Speculation on Union Military Failure in the East, 1861–1865* (Cambridge, MA: Harvard University Press, 1978), chaps. 1 and 2 for their military significance; John Leyburn, "An Interview with Gen. Robert E. Lee," *Century Illustrated Monthly Magazine* 30 (May 1885): pp. 166–67.

14. John F. Marszalek, ed., *The Diary of Miss Emma Holmes, 1861–1866* (Baton Rouge: Louisiana State University Press, 1994), p. 362.

15. Earl Schenck Miers, ed., *When the World Ended: The Diary of Emma LeConte* (New York: Oxford University Press, 1957), p. 4.

16. Michael Fellman, *Citizen Sherman* (New York: Random House, 1995), p. 19; Willamjames Hull Hoffer, *The Caning of Charles Sumner: Honor, Idealism and the Origins of the Civil War* (Baltimore: Johns Hopkins University Press, 2010).

17. A. M. Stewart, *Camp, March and Battle-Field* (Philadelphia: Jas. B. Rodgers, 1865), quoted in Wheeler, *Voices of the Civil War*, p. 397; Charles Royster, *The Destructive War: Sherman, Stonewall Jackson, and the Americans* (New York: Vintage, 1993), p. 87; George Templeton Strong, *Diary of the Civil War, 1860–1865* (New York: Macmillan, 1962), p. 521.

18. Milo M. Quaife, ed., *From the Cannon's Mouth: The Civil War Letters of General Alpheus S. Williams* (Detroit: Wayne State University Press and Detroit Historical Society, 1959), p. 276.

19. Reid Mitchell, *Civil War Soldiers* (New York: Viking, 1988), p. 107; James M. McPherson, *What They Fought For, 1861–1865* (New York: Anchor, 1995), pp.

23–24; John W. Dower, *War without Mercy: Race and Power in the Pacific War* (New York: Pantheon, 1986) on mutual savagery in the Pacific.

20. Caroline Alexander, *The War That Killed Achilles: The True Story of Homer's Iliad and the Trojan War* (New York: Viking, 2009), p. 168; Jonathan Shay, *Achilles in Vietnam: Combat Trauma and the Undoing of Character* (New York: Touchstone, 1995), p. 78.

21. McPherson, *What They Fought For*, p. 23; Alan Huffman, *Sultana: Surviving Civil War, Prison, and the Worst Maritime Disaster in American History* (New York: HarperCollins-Smithsonian Books, 2009), pp. 38–39; Glenn LaFantasie, ed., *Gettysburg: Colonel William Oates and Lieutenant Frank A. Haskell* (New York: Bantam, 1992), p. 251.

22. Donald Yacovone, ed., *A Voice of Thunder: A Black Soldier's Civil War* (Urbana: University of Illinois Press, 1998), p. 45. On Shaw's symbolism, Michael C. C. Adams, "Seeking Glory: Our Continuing Involvement with the 54th Massachusetts," *Studies in Popular Culture* 14, no. 2 (1992): pp. 11–19. Chandra Manning argues that the fight over slavery increasingly became the single most important driving force in both armies. See *What This Cruel War Was Over: Soldiers, Slavery, and the Civil War* (New York: Alfred A. Knopf, 2007).

23. George Gautier, *Harder Than Death: The Life of George Gautier, an Old Texan* (Austin, TX, 1902), pp. 10–11; Mary Brobst Roth, ed., *"Well, Mary": Civil War Letters of a Wisconsin Volunteer* (Madison: University of Wisconsin Press, 1960), p. 57.

24. *The War of the Rebellion: A Compilation of the Official Records of the Union and Confederate Armies* (Washington, DC: Government Printing Office, 1880–1991), series 2, vol. 7, pp. 607, 615, 687–91; Ulysses S. Grant, "The Treatment of Prisoners during the War Between the States," *Southern Historical Society Papers* 1, no. 4 (April 1876): p. 317.

25. Cecil D. Eby, ed., *A Virginia Yankee in the Civil War: The Diaries of David Hunter Strother* (Chapel Hill: University of North Carolina Press, 1961), pp. 254–56, 263, 280.

26. *O.R.*, series 1, vol. 43, pt. 1, pp. 30–31.

27. James A. Ramage, *Gray Ghost: The Life of Col. John Singleton Mosby* (Lexington: University Press of Kentucky, 1999) provides a balanced treatment of the partisans.

28. *O.R.*, series 1, vol. 43, pp. 822, 910; Helen Everett Wood, ed., *A Kalamazoo Volunteer in the Civil War* (Kalamazoo, MI: Kalamazoo Public Museum, 1962), p. 22; Daniel E. Sutherland, *A Savage Conflict: The Decisive Role of Guerrillas in the American Civil War* (Chapel Hill: University of North Carolina Press, 2009). Sutherland argues that partisans and guerrillas played a vital role in, for example, defending the homeland and harassing enemy forces. But they were not seen as quite respectable by the top brass and so were not brought fully into the military fold where there could have been better oversight and control of their activities. See, for instance, pp. ix–xii, 68–70, 89–90, 97–98.

29. *O.R.*, series 1, vol. 44, p. 799; Lee Kennett, *Sherman: A Soldier's Life* (New York: HarperCollins, 2001), p. 228; and Lee Kennett, *Marching through Georgia: The Story of Soldiers and Civilians during Sherman's Campaign* (New York: Harper, 1996), p. 94.

30. *O.R.*, series 1, vol. 47, pt. 2, p. 533.

31. Edmund Wilson, *Patriotic Gore: Studies in the Literature of the American Civil War* (New York: Oxford University Press, 1966), pp. 181, 188; *O.R.*, series 1, vol. 31, pt. 3, p. 459; Otto Eisenschiml, "Sherman: Hero or War Criminal?," *Civil War Times Illustrated* 2, no. 9 (January 1964): pp. 7, 29. Two authors compare Sherman's conduct to the Vietnam My Lai massacre of 1968: see John Bennett Walters, *Merchant of Terror: General Sherman and Total War* (Indianapolis, IN: Bobb-Merrill, 1973); and James Reston Jr., *Sherman's March and Vietnam* (New York: Macmillan, 1984).

32. Richard Harwell and Philip N. Racine, eds., *The Fiery Trial: A Union Officer's Account of Sherman's Last Campaigns* (Knoxville: University of Tennessee Press, 1986), pp. 119–20, 129–30.

33. Sparks, *Inside Lincoln's Army*, pp. 376, 400. A leading defender of the "directed severity" position is Mark Grimsley, who argues the case well in *The Hard Hand of War: Union Military Policy toward Southern Civilians, 1861–1865* (New York: Cambridge University Press, 1995), e.g., pp. 6, 157. However, in defending Sherman, Grimsley notes approvingly that the general urged leniency toward Southern civilians who took the Oath of Allegiance, while saying "death is a mercy" for those who remained "persistent secessionists," hardly a ringing endorsement of Sherman's humanity (p. 174). On the potentially counterproductive military results of total war, note that the Pentagon's 1946 report on Allied unrestricted or carpet bombing of civilian targets showed that German morale and industrial production had actually gone up under ruthless attack.

34. Wiley, *Confederate Women*, p. 150; Reid Mitchell, *The Vacant Chair: The Northern Soldier Leaves Home* (New York: Oxford University Press, 1993), p. 36.

35. John H. Hight, *History of the Fifty-Eighth Regiment of Indiana Volunteer Infantry* (Princeton, IN: Clarion Press, 1895), p. 410.

36. Henry Kyd Douglas, *I Rode with Stonewall* (1940, repr. Greenwich, CT: Fawcett, 1961), p. 302; Miers, ed., *When the World Ended*, p. 5; Susan S. Kissel and Margery T. Rouse, eds., *The Story of the Pewter Basin and Other Occasional Writings: Collected in Southern Ohio and Northern Kentucky* (Bloomington, IN: T.I.S. Publications, 1981), pp. 66–68; William P. Buck, ed., *Sad Earth, Sweet Heaven: The Diary of Lucy Rebecca Buck during the War Between the States, December 25, 1861–April 15, 1865*, 2nd. ed. (Birmingham, AL: Buck Publishing, 1992), pp. 287–89.

37. Thomas Goodrich, *Bloody Dawn: The Story of the Lawrence Massacre* (Kent, OH: Kent State University Press, 1991), p. 4.

38. Goodrich, *Bloody Dawn*, p. 153; Vivian K. McLarty, ed., "The Civil War Letters of Colonel Bazel Lazear," *Missouri Historical Review* 45, pt. 2 (July 1950): p. 390.

39. Michael Fellman, "Women and Guerrilla Warfare," in Catherine Clinton and Nina Silber, eds., *Divided Houses: Gender and the Civil War* (New York: Oxford University Press, 1992), p. 151.

40. National Archives, RG 94: Records of the Adjutant General's Office (List of U.S. soldiers executed by United States military authorities during the late war, 1861–1866). Case of Charles Sperry, file no. NN 2427; Case of James Preble, file no. MM 1774.

41. Burr, *Secret Eye*, p. 252; William R. Jevell, ed., *History of the 72d Indiana Volunteer Infantry* (Lafayette, IN: S. Vater, 1882), pp. 337–38.

42. Nathaniel Cheairs Hughes, *The Pride of the Confederate Artillery: The Washington Artillery in the Army of Tennessee* (Baton Rouge: Louisiana State University Press, 1997), pp. 250–51.

43. National Archives, RG 153, case of George W. O'Malley, file no. MM 402; *O.R.*, series 2, vol. 4, pp. 876–77, 885, 915.

44. *O.R.*, series 1, vol. 3, pp. 457–59, 433–35; Richard S. Brownlee, *Gray Ghosts of the Confederacy: Guerrilla Warfare in the West, 1861–1865* (Baton Rouge: Louisiana State University Press, 1986), p. 35; *O.R.*, series 1, vol. 47, pt. 2, p. 33.

45. Sparks, *Inside Lincoln's Army*, pp. 388–99.

46. Thomas P. Lowry, "Research Note: New Access to a Civil War Resource," *Civil War History* 49, no. 1 (March 2003): pp. 56, 58; R. Gregory Laude, *Madness, Malingering, and Malfeasance: The Transformation of Psychiatry and the Law in the Civil War Era* (Washington, DC: Brassey's, 2003), p. 44; National Archives, RG 153, case of F. M. Caldwell, file no. MM 890; case of Francois Wallenus, file no. MM 1054.

47. Alfred Jay Bollet, *Civil War Medicine: Challenges and Triumphs* (Tucson, AZ: Galen, 2002), p. 377. Philip Burnham, "The Andersonvilles of the North," in Robert Cowley, ed., *With My Face to the Enemy: Perspectives on the Civil War* (New York: Putnam's, 2001), pp. 367–81, esp. 367; Larry M. Logue, *To Appomattox and Beyond: The Civil War Soldier in War and Peace* (Chicago: Ivan R. Dee, 1996), p. 71.

48. Terry Winschel, "The Siege of Vicksburg," *Blue & Gray Magazine* 20, no. 4 (Spring 2003): p. 48; Robert Knox Sneden, *Eye of the Storm: A Civil War Odyssey* (New York: Free Press, 2000), p. 4.

49. Abner R. Small, *The Road to Richmond: The Civil War Memoirs of Major Abner R. Small of the Sixteenth Maine Volunteers* (1939, repr. New York: Fordham University Press, 2000), p. 157; Marszalek, ed., *Diary of Emma Holmes*, p. 282.

50. John H. Brinton, *Personal Memoirs of John H. Brinton: Civil War Surgeon, 1861–1865* (Carbondale: Southern Illinois University Press, 1996), p. 301; Sneden, *Eye of the Storm*, pp. 197–98.

51. Emmy E. Werner, *Reluctant Witnesses: Children's Voices from the Civil War*

(Boulder, CO: Westview, 1998), p. 99.

52. Douglas, *I Rode with Stonewall,* pp. 251–52; Fletcher, *Rebel Private, Front and Rear,* p. 153.

53. Susan Williams Benson, ed., *Berry Benson's Civil War Book: Memoirs of a Confederate Scout and Sharpshooter* (Athens: University of Georgia Press, 1992), p. 135; Sneden, *Eye of the Storm,* p. 172; Maud Carter Clement, *Writings of Maud Carter Clement* (Chatham, VA: Pittsylvania Historical Society, 1982), pp. 61–63.

54. M. C. Gillet, *The United States Army Medical Department, 1818–1865* (Washington, DC: Army Center of Military History, 1987), p. 267; *O.R.,* series 2, vol. 6, pp. 158, 218; Speer, *War of Vengeance,* pp. 114–21.

55. Clarence Poe, ed., *True Tales of the South at War* (Chapel Hill: University of North Carolina Press, 1961), p. 143; J. K. Barnes, *Medical and Surgical History of the War of the Rebellion* (Washington, DC: Government Printing Office, 1870–88), vol. 3, medical section, pp. 33, 42.

56. Eric T. Dean Jr., *Shook over Hell: Post-Traumatic Stress, Vietnam, and the Civil War* (Cambridge, MA: Harvard University Press, 1997), p. 83.

57. Sidney Lanier, *Tiger-Lilies* (1867, repr. Chapel Hill: University of North Carolina Press, 1969), pp. 182–83.

58. Though accused of some intentional dramatization, John L. Ransom, *John Ransom's Andersonville Diary* (1881, repr. New York: Berkley, 1988), still gives a good account of the gangs and their breakup.

59. Walt Whitman, *Memoranda during the Civil War: Civil War Journals, 1863–1865* (1875, repr. Mineola, NY: Dover, 2012), pp. 65–66.

CHAPTER EIGHT. STATE OF THE UNION

1. Earl J. Hess, *The Union Soldier in Battle: Enduring the Ordeal of Combat* (Lawrence: University Press of Kansas, 1997), p. 186; James M. McPherson, *Ordeal By Fire: The Civil War and Reconstruction* (New York: Knopf, 1982), p. 476; Larry M. Logue, *To Appomattox and Beyond: The Civil War Soldier in War and Peace* (Chicago: Ivan R. Dee, 1996), p. 107.

2. Whitelaw Reid, *After the War* (New York: Moore, Wilstach & Baldwin, 1866), pp. 224, 360; Sarah Woolfolk Wiggins, ed., *The Journals of Josiah Gorgas, 1857–1878* (Tuscaloosa: University of Alabama Press, 1995), p. 167; Elizabeth Ravenel Harrigan, *Charleston Recollections and Recipes: Rose P. Ravenel's Cookbook* (Columbia: University of South Carolina Press, 1983), p. 68.

3. William Preston Magnum II, "Disaster at Woodburn Farm: R. A. Alexander and the Confederate Guerrilla Raids of 1864–1865," *Filson Club Historical Quarterly* 70, no. 2 (April 1996): pp. 177, 182.

4. Lowell H. Harrison and James C. Klotter, *A New History of Kentucky* (Lexington: University Press of Kentucky, 1997), pp. 150, 379–80; E. Merton Coulter, *The Civil War and Readjustment in Kentucky* (Chapel Hill: University of North Carolina Press, 1926), esp. pp. 400–401.

5. Emmy E. Werner, *Reluctant Witnesses: Children's Voices from the Civil War* (Boulder, CO: Westview, 1998), p. 148; Richard Harwell and Philip N. Racine, eds., *The Fiery Trial: A Union Officer's Account of Sherman's Last Campaigns* (Knoxville: University of Tennessee Press, 1986), p. 102; Donald Yacovone, ed., *A Voice of Thunder: A Black Soldier's Civil War* (Urbana: University of Illinois Press, 1998), pp. 84–85.

6. Richard Nelson Current, *Those Terrible Carpetbaggers* (New York: Oxford University Press, 1988), analyses the much-maligned agents of reform through the biographies of ten participants; John R. Neff, *Honoring the Civil War Dead: Commemoration and the Problem of Reconciliation* (Lawrence: University Press of Kansas, 2005), p. 105.

7. See Edward Royce, *The Origins of Southern Sharecropping* (Philadelphia: Temple University Press, 2003), a nuanced analysis, and Kyle G. Wilkinson, *Yeomen, Sharecroppers, and Socialists: Plain Folk Protest in Texas, 1870–1914* (College Station: Texas A&M University Press, 2008), a case study of attempts to change peonage.

8. Jackson Lears, "Divinely Ordained," *London Review of Books*, May 19, 2011, p. 3; Neff, *Honoring the Civil War Dead*, p. 145.

9. Andrew Hacker, writing in the *New York Review of Books*, September 27, 2012, p. 39.

10. Hacker, *New York Review*, p. 39; Elizabeth Drew, "Determined to Vote!," *New York Review of Books*, December 20, 2012.

11. C. Vann Woodward, *The Strange Career of Jim Crow* (New York: Oxford University Press, 1974).

12. Joseph T. Glatthaar, *Forged in Battle: The Civil War Alliance of Black Soldiers and White Officers* (New York: Meridian, 1991), p. 209; Mark Ford, "Petty Grotesques," *London Review of Books*, March 17, 2011, p. 27.

13. Logue, *To Appomattox and Beyond*, pp. 112, 115–16; Also, Wyn Craig Wade, *The Fiery Cross: The Ku Klux Klan in America* (New York: Simon & Schuster, 1987). On the Freikorps mentality, Klaus Theweleit, *Male Fantasies*, vol. 1: *Women, Floods, Bodies, History* (Minneapolis: University of Minnesota Press, 1987).

14. Michael Fellman, *The Making of Robert E. Lee* (New York: Random House, 2000), p. xiii.

15. Bobby L. Lovett, "Memphis Riots: White Reaction to Blacks in Memphis, May 1865–July 1866," *Tennessee Historical Quarterly* 38 (Spring 1979): p. 12.

16. Maris A. Vinovskis, ed., *Toward a Social History of the American Civil War: Exploratory Essays* (Cambridge: Cambridge University Press, 1990), p. 144; George W. Williams, *A History of the Negro Troops in the War of the Rebellion, 1861–1865* (New York: Negro Universities Press, 1969), p. 328; G. Kurt Piehler, *Remembering War the American Way* (Washington, DC: Smithsonian Institution Press, 1995), p. 69; also, Albert Boime, *The Art of Exclusion: Representing Blacks in the Nineteenth Century* (Washington, DC: Smithsonian

Institution Press, 1990); *Boston Daily Evening Traveler*, quoted in David W. Blight, *Beyond the Battlefield: Memory and the American Civil War* (Amherst: University of Massachusetts Press, 2002), pp. 176–77.

17. Glatthaar, *Forged in Battle*, p. 253.

18. R. W. Logan, *The Betrayal of the Negro from Rutherford B. Hayes to Woodrow Wilson* (New York: Collier, 1965), p. 99; Susie King Taylor, *A Black Woman's Civil War Memoirs* (1902, repr. New York: Marcus Wiener, 1988), p. 135; Tilden G. Edelstein, *Strange Enthusiasm: A Life of Thomas Wentworth Higginson* (New Haven, CT: Yale University Press, 1968), p. 391.

19. See Kenneth S. Stern, *A Force upon the Plain: The American Militia Movement and the Politics of Hate* (New York: Simon & Schuster, 1996); James William Gibson, *Warrior Dreams: Paramilitary Culture in Post-Vietnam America* (New York: Hill & Wang, 1994); James Ridgeway, *Blood in the Face: The Ku Klux Klan, Aryan Nations, Nazis, Skinheads and the Rise of a New White Culture*, 2nd. ed. (New York: Thunder's Mouth Press, 1995).

20. Jonathan Kozol, *Shame of the Nation: The Restoration of Apartheid Schooling in America* (New York: Crown, 2005), pp. 18–19, 21–25; Peter Whoriskey, "On 50th Anniversary 'Little Rock Nine' Get a Hero's Welcome," *Washington Post*, September 26, 2007; Darryl Pinckney, "Invisible Black America," *New York Review of Books*, March 10, 2011, pp. 33–35.

21. Daniel Brook, "Unreconstructed: The Federal Government Builds a Shrine to Its Archenemy," *Harper's Magazine* (May 2012): pp. 40–41.

22. Stephen B. Oates, *A Woman of Valor: Clara Barton and the Civil War* (New York: Free Press, 1994), p. 376; Carl R. Fish, "Back to Peace in 1865," *American Historical Review* 24 (1919): p. 440; Catherine Clinton and Nina Silber, *Divided Houses: Gender and the Civil War* (New York: Oxford University Press, 1992), p. 257.

23. David Williams, *A People's History of the Civil War: Struggles for the Meaning of Freedom* (London: New Press, 2005), pp. 487–89.

24. Cindy S. Aron, "'To Barter Their Souls for Gold': Female Clerks in Federal Government Offices, 1862–1890," *Journal of American History* 67 (March 1981): p. 847. Stowe, "The Chimney Corner," pt. 1, *Atlantic* 15 (January 1865): p. 113.

25. Shirley A. Leckie, *Elizabeth Bacon Custer and the Making of a Myth* (Norman: University of Oklahoma Press, 1993), p. 52; Aron, "Barter Their Souls for Gold," p. 836.

26. Mary E. Walker, *HIT: Essays on Women's Rights* (Amherst, NY: Humanity, 2003), p. 6.

27. Williams, *A People's History of the Civil War*, pp. 1, 484–85; Kenneth M. Stampp, *And the War Came: The North and the Secession Crisis, 1860–61* (Chicago: University of Chicago Press, 1950), p. 298.

28. Fred A. Shannon, "The Homestead Act and the Labor Surplus," *American Historical Review* 41 (1936): pp. 650–51.

29. Philip S. Foner, *Business and Slavery: The New York Merchants and the Irre-*

pressible Conflict (New York: Russell and Russell, 1986), p. 370; John G. Sproat, *"The Best Men": Liberal Reformers in the Gilded Age* (New York: Oxford University Press, 1968), p. 211.

30. Barnet Schecter, *The Devil's Own Work: The Civil War Draft Riots and the Fight to Reconstruct America* (New York: Walker, 2005), pp. 368–69; Robert V. Bruce, *1877: Year of Violence* (1959, repr. Chicago: Ivan R. Dee, 1989), pp. 91–92, 200; Vinovskis, ed., *Toward a Social History*, p. 169; Richard Severo and Lewis Milford, *The Wages of War: When America's Soldiers Came Home—from Valley Forge to Vietnam* (New York: Touchstone, 1990), p. 177.

31. Schecter, *Devil's Own Work*, pp. 109–10; Vinovskis, ed., *Toward a Social History*, p. 132; Ben Macintyre, *The Napoleon of Crime: The Life and Times of Adam Worth, Master Thief* (New York: Farrar, Straus and Giroux, 1997), p. 259; Matthew Josephson, *The Robber Barons: The Great American Capitalists, 1861–1901* (New York: Harcourt, Brace and World, 1962), pp. 4, 32.

32. J. Matthew Gallman, *The North Fights the Civil War: The Home Front* (Chicago: Ivan R. Dee, 1994), pp. 101–3; also Ray Ginger, *Age of Excess: The United States from 1877–1914*, 2nd. ed. (New York: Macmillan, 1975); and Richard Hofstadter, *Social Darwinism in American Thought* (Boston: Beacon, 1955).

33. Sproat, *"The Best Men,"* p. 246; Charles R. Williams, ed., *Diary and Letters of Rutherford Birchard Hayes*, 5 vols. (Columbus: Ohio State Archaeological and Historical Society, 1922–1926), vol. 4, pp. 278, 374, 383.

34. Clara Barrus, ed., *The Heart of Burroughs's Journals* (1928, repr. Port Washington, NY: Kennikat Press, 1967), p. 166; Brooks D. Simpson, *Let Us Have Peace: Ulysses S. Grant and the Politics of War and Reconstruction, 1861–1868* (Chapel Hill: University of North Carolina Press, 1991), p. 262.

35. John Russell Young, *Around the World with General Grant* (New York: American News Company, 1879), vol. 1, pp. 158–59; E. L. Doctorow, *The Waterworks* (New York: Random House, 1994), pp. 14–15.

36. Walt Whitman, *Democratic Vistas, and Other Papers* (1888, repr. St. Clair Shores, MI: Scholarly Press, 1970), p. 11; Mark Twain and Charles Dudley Warner, *The Gilded Age* (1873, repr. New York: New American Library, 1969), pp. 137–38.

37. George R. Agassiz, ed., *Meade's Headquarters, 1863–1865: Letters of Colonel Theodore Lyman from the Wilderness to Appomattox* (Boston: Atlantic Monthly Press, 1922), pp. 152, 186–87, 207.

38. Henry Adams, *The Education of Henry Adams: An Autobiography* (1918, repr. Boston: Houghton Mifflin, 1961), p. 264; Henry Adams, *Democracy: An American Novel* (Leipzig: Bernhard Tauchnitz, 1882), pp. 20, 273; also, George M. Fredrickson, *The Inner Civil War: Northern Intellectuals and the Crisis of the Union* (New York: Harper and Row, 1965).

39. Twelve Southerners, *I'll Take My Stand: The South and the Agrarian Tradition* (1930, repr. Baton Rouge: Louisiana State University Press, 2006); David Cole, "Thirty-Five States to Go," *London Review of Books*, March 3, 2011, pp. 15–16.

40. Roy P. Basler, et al., eds., *The Collected Works of Abraham Lincoln,* 9 vols. (New Brunswick, NJ: Rutgers University Press, 1953–55), vol. 6, p. 500; also, Brian R. Dirck, *Lincoln & Davis: Imagining America, 1809-1865* (Lawrence: University Press of Kansas, 2001), p. 212.

41. Jackson Lears, *Rebirth of a Nation: The Making of Modern America, 1877-1920* (New York: Harper, 2009), pp. 15–16.

42. Michael A. Bellesiles, *Arming America: The Origins of a National Gun Culture* (New York: Knopf, 2000), pp. 406, 434; Michael C. C. Adams, "A Note on the Military Engagement at Lexington, Massachusetts, on April 19, 1775," *Perspectives in History* 14 (1998–99): pp. 26–39; also Richard Slotkin, *Regeneration through Violence: The Mythology of the American Frontier, 1600-1860* (Norman: University of Oklahoma Press, 2000).

43. Bellesiles, *Arming America,* pp. 436–37, 440; William Graham Sumner, "What Our Boys Are Reading," *Scribner's Monthly,* March 1878, pp. 681–84.

44. Otto L. Bettmann, *The Good Old Days—They Were Terrible* (New York: Random House, 1974), p. 87; Betty Rosenbaum, "The Relationship between War and Crime in the U.S.," *Journal of Criminal Law and Criminology* 30 (1940): pp. 725–26. Abbott, "Crime Wave of 1865–70," p. 215; Dave Grossman, *On Killing: The Psychological Cost of Learning to Kill in War and Society* (Boston: Little, Brown, 1995).

45. Logue, *To Appomattox and Beyond,* pp. 87–88; Abbott, "Crime Wave of 1865–70," pp. 225, 227; William C. Davis, *The Cause Lost: Myths and Realities of the Confederacy* (Lawrence: University Press of Kansas, 1996), p. 91; Richard S. Brownlee, *Gray Ghosts of the Confederacy: Guerrilla Warfare in the West 1861-1865* (Baton Rouge: Louisiana State University Press, 1986), pp. 240–44; James A. Ramage, *Rebel Raider: The Life of General John Hunt Morgan* (Lexington: University Press of Kentucky, 1986), pp. 238–39; Carl W. Breichan, *Sam Hildebrand: Guerrilla* (Wauwatosa, WI: Pine Mountain Press, 1984), p. 154.

46. Daniel E. Sutherland, *The Expansion of Everyday Life 1860-1876* (New York: Harper & Row, 1989), pp. 219–20; Susan S. Kissel and Margery T. Rouse, eds., *The Story of the Pewter Basin and Other Occasional Writings: Collected in Southern Ohio and Northern Kentucky* (Bloomington, IN: T.I.S. Publications, 1981), pp. 62–63.

47. Dean Latimer and Jeff Goldberg, *Flowers in the Blood: The Story of Opium* (New York: Franklin Watts, 1981), p. 180; Theodore Zeldin, *An Intimate History of Humanity* (New York: HarperCollins, 1994), p. 231.

48. John William DeForest, *Miss Ravenel's Conversion from Secession to Loyalty* (1867, repr. Columbus, OH: Charles E. Merrill, 1969), pp. 520–21; Ira M. Rutkow, *Bleeding Blue and Gray: Civil War Surgery and the Evolution of American Medicine* (New York: Random House, 2005), p. 317.

49. Alfred Jay Bollet, *Civil War Medicine: Challenges and Triumphs* (Tucson, AZ: Galen, 2002), p. 160; Maggie Davis, *The Far Side of Home* (New York: Mac-

millan, 1963), pp. 305–14; W. H. Belknap, *History of the Fifteenth Regiment, Iowa Veteran Volunteer Infantry* (Keokuk, IA: R. B. Ogden & Son, 1887), p. 644; Fiammetta Rocco, *The Miraculous Fever-Tree: Malaria and the Quest for a Cure That Changed the World* (New York: HarperCollins, 2003), p. 186.

50. Joselyne Rey, *The History of Pain* (Cambridge, MA: Harvard University Press, 1995), p. 151. For the quotation on addiction, John Mann, *Murder, Magic, and Medicine* (New York: Oxford University Press, 1992), p. 182; Rudolf Schmitz, "Friedrich Wilhelm Serturner and the Discovery of Morphine," *Pharmacy in History* 27, no. 2 (1985): pp. 67–68; Joseph J. Woodward, in *Medical and Surgical History of the War of the Rebellion* (Washington, DC: Government Printing Office, 1870–88), vol. 1, pt. 2, p. 750.

51. Bollet, *Civil War Medicine*, pp. 159–60; William L. Barney, *The Making of a Confederate: Walter Lenoir's Civil War* (New York: Oxford University Press, 2009), p. 88; Colin Murray Parkes, "Psycho-Social Transitions: Comparison between Reactions to Loss of a Limb and Loss of a Spouse," *British Journal of Psychiatry* 127 (1975): pp. 204–10.

52. Scott Allen, "The Enduring Cost of War," *Boston Globe,* February 13, 2006; John McMurray, *Recollections of a Colored Troop* (Brookville, PA, 1916), p. 62.

53. Eric T. Dean Jr., *Shook over Hell: Post-Traumatic Stress, Vietnam, and the Civil War* (Cambridge, MA: Harvard University Press, 1997), p. 137; R. Gregory Laude, *Madness, Malingering, and Malfeasance: The Transformation of Psychiatry and the Law in the Civil War Era* (Washington, DC: Brassey's, 2003), pp. 187–88; Albert Deutsch, *The Mentally Ill in America: A History of Their Care and Treatment from Colonial Times,* 2nd rev. ed. (New York: Columbia University Press, 1949), pp. 229–45; Vinovskis, *Toward a Social History,* p. 170.

54. John D. Seelye, "The American Tramp: A Version of the Picaresque," *American Quarterly* 15 (1963): p. 543.

55. Thomas P. Lowry, *The Story the Soldiers Wouldn't Tell: Sex in the Civil War* (Mechanicsburg, PA: Stackpole, 1994), p. 174; Rosenbaum, "War and Crime in the U.S.," p. 729.

56. Chauncey E. Burr, "The Soldier's Baby," in *The Student and Schoolmate* 12 (August 1865): p. 239; Jean V. Berlin, ed., *A Confederate Nurse: The Diary of Ada W. Bacot, 1860–1863* (Columbia: University of South Carolina Press, 1994), pp. 182–83.

57. Justin G. Turner and Linda Levitt Turner, *Mary Todd Lincoln: Her Life and Letters* (New York: Knopf, 1972), pp. 238, 240, 366.

58. Don E. Fehrenbacher, "Epilogue: Two Casualties of War," in Gabor Boritt, ed., *War Comes Again: Comparative Vistas on the Civil War and World War II* (New York: Oxford University Press, 1995), pp. 245–46.

59. Walt Whitman, *Memoranda during the Civil War: Journals, 1863–1865* (1875, repr. Mineola, NY: Dover, 2010), pp. 75–76.

60. Neff, *Honoring the Civil War Dead,* pp. 108, 128, 134; see also, Ric Burns, dir., *Death and the Civil War,* in the PBS American Experience series, 2012. Though

a trifle sentimentalized, this program has excellent visuals. Harry Smeltzer, "'Squire' Bottom Founds a Confederate Cemetery," *Civil War Times* 49, no. 3 (June 2011): pp. 27–28; Ishbel Ross, *Angel of the Battlefield: The Life of Clara Barton* (New York: Harper, 1956), p. 87.

61. Michael Kammen, *Mystic Chords of Memory: The Transformation of Tradition in American Culture* (New York: Random House, 1993), pp. 103, 105; J. Matthew Gallman, *The North Fights the Civil War: The Home Front* (Chicago: Ivan R. Dee, 1994), p. 76.

62. Emory Upton, *The Military Policy of the United States* (Washington, DC: Government Printing Office, 1917), pp. 216–18; Sproat, *"The Best Men,"* p. 171; James M. McPherson, *Battle Cry of Freedom: The Civil War Era* (New York: Ballantine, 1988), pp. 443, 447.

63. McPherson, *Battle Cry of Freedom,* p. 447; Varhola, *Everyday Life during the Civil War,* p. 108.

64. Vinovskis, ed., *Toward a Social History,* p. 74; Dixon Wecter, *When Johnny Comes Marching Home* (1944, repr. Westport, CT: Greenwood, 1976), p. 163.

65. Frank A. Boyle, "Common Soldier: Adjutant Anthony McDermott, 69th Pennsylvania Infantry," *Blue & Gray Magazine* 20, no. 4 (Spring 2003): p. 46.

66. Vinovskis, *Toward a Social History,* pp. viii, 23; Gallman, *North Fights the Civil War,* p. 183.

67. Werner, *Reluctant Witnesses,* p. 149.

CLOSING. GENERAL LEE AND THE GRAY LADIES

1. Douglas Southall Freeman, *R. E. Lee: A Biography* (New York: Scribner's, 1934), vol. 2, p. 462.

2. J. B. Jones, *A Rebel War Clerk's Diary, at the Confederate States Capital* (Philadelphia: J. B. Lippincott, 1866), vol. 2, pp. 88, 183, 214, 235, 424.

3. Reid Mitchell, *Civil War Soldiers* (New York: Viking, 1988), p. 207.

4. See also Dixon Wecter, *When Johnny Comes Marching Home* (1944, repr. Westport, CT: Greenwood, 1976), pp. 183–89.

5. Edward A. Moore, *The Story of a Cannoneer under Stonewall Jackson* (1907, repr. New York: Time-Life, 1983), p. 254. John Russell Young, *Around the World with General Grant* (New York: American News Company, 1879), vol. 2, p. 451.

6. Stephen E. Ambrose, *Americans at War* (New York: Berkley, 1998), p. 60.

7. Ambrose, *Americans at War,* pp. 65, 69.

8. Michael C. C. Adams, *Echoes of War: A Thousand Years of Military History in Popular Culture* (Lexington: University Press of Kentucky, 2002), p. 152.

9. See Richard Allan Fox Jr., *Archaeology, History, and Custer's Last Battle: The Little Big Horn Reexamined* (Norman: University of Oklahoma Press, 1993).

10. Adams, *Echoes of War,* pp. 160–62.

11. Esther Shephard, *Walt Whitman's Pose* (New York: Harcourt, Brace, 1938), p. 109.

12. Michael C. C. Adams, "Poet Whitman and General Custer," *Studies in Popular Culture* 18, no. 2 (April 1996): pp. 1–17.

13. Thomas L. Connelly, *The Marble Man: Robert E. Lee and His Image in American Society* (New York: Knopf, 1977), p. 101; Michael Kammen, *Mystic Chords of Memory: The Transformation of Tradition in American Culture* (New York: Random House, 1993), p. 102.

14. Carol K. Bleser and Lesley J. Gordon, eds., *Intimate Strategies of the Civil War: Military Commanders and Their Wives* (New York: Oxford University Press, 2001), pp. 172, 174, 176–77; Alice Rains Trulock, *In the Hands of Providence: Joshua L. Chamberlain and the American Civil War* (Chapel Hill: University of North Carolina Press, 1992), p. 374; Joshua Lawrence Chamberlain, *The Passing of the Armies: An Account of the Final Campaigns of the Army of the Potomac, Based upon Personal Reminiscences of the Fifth Army Corps* (1915, repr. New York: Bantam, 1993), p. 295.

15. G. Edward White, *Oliver Wendell Holmes, Jr.* (New York: Oxford University Press, 2006), p. 19; Also, Earl J. Hess, *The Union Soldier in Battle: Enduring the Ordeal of Combat* (Lawrence: University Press of Kansas, 1997), p. 179.

16. Gerald F. Linderman, *The Mirror of War: American Society and the Spanish-American War* (Ann Arbor: University of Michigan Press, 1974), p. 106.

17. Michael C. C. Adams, *The Great Adventure: Male Desire and the Coming of World War I* (Bloomington: Indiana University Press, 1990), pp. 47–49; Michael C. C. Adams, "'Anti-War' Isn't Always Anti-War," *Midwest Quarterly* 31 (Spring 1990): pp. 297–313.

18. Émile Zola, *The Debacle*, trans. Leonard Tancock (1892, repr. New York: Penguin, 1972), pp. 150–54, 347–49.

19. Zola, *The Debacle*, pp. 300, 279–80, 347, 405.

20. Zola, *The Debacle*, pp. 434, 481.

21. Erik Larson, *The Devil in the White City: Murder, Magic, and Madness at the Fair That Changed America* (New York: Vintage, 2004), p. 5; Hess, *Union Soldier in Battle*, p. 186; Connelly, *The Marble Man*, p. 111.

22. Elizabeth Preston Allan, ed., *The Life and Letters of Margaret Junkin Preston* (Boston: Houghton Mifflin, 1903), pp. 158–59.

23. G. Kurt Piehler, *Remembering War the American Way* (Washington, DC: Smithsonian Institution Press, 1995), pp. 65–66; David Blight, *Beyond the Battlefield: Race, Memory, and the American Civil War* (Amherst: University of Massachusetts Press, 2002), p. 173.

24. Marcus Cunliffe effectively challenged the martial South myth in *Soldiers & Civilians: The Martial Spirit in America 1775–1865* (Boston: Little, Brown, 1968), chap. 10; Sharyn McCrumb, *She Walks These Hills* (New York: Signet, 1995), p. 239.

25. Peter Messent and Steve Courtney, eds., *The Civil War Letters of Joseph Hopkins Twichell: A Chaplain's Story* (Athens: University of Georgia Press, 2006), pp. 316–17.

26. Thomas, *The Marble Man,* p. 392.

27. Kammen, *Mystic Chords of Memory,* p. 109.

28. William Faulkner, *Intruder in the Dust* (1948, repr. New York: Vintage, 1972), pp. 194–95.

29. On the Spanish-American War as an invigorating masculine endeavor, see Kristin L. Hoganson, *Fighting for American Manhood: How Gender Politics Provoked the Spanish-American and Philippine-American Wars* (New Haven, CT: Yale University Press, 1998).

30. Russell F. Weigley, "The Necessity of Force: The Civil War, World War II, and the American View of War," in Gabor Boritt, ed., *War Comes Again: Comparative Vistas on the Civil War and World War II* (New York: Oxford University Press, 1995), pp. 232–33.

31. Robert G. Athearn, *William Tecumseh Sherman and the Settlement of the West* (Norman: University of Oklahoma Press, 1956), p. 99.

32. Theodore Roosevelt, *The Rough Riders* (1902, repr. New York: Da Capo, 1990), pp. 52–53.

— *Suggested Further Reading* —

LIVING HELL DEALS IN DEPTH WITH MILITARY CONFLICT during the Civil War era. For readers who would like to explore further the broad nature of war, including combat, many helpful sources are available. I recommend Gwynne Dyer, *War* (Homewood, IL: Dorsey, 1985) and Richard Holmes, *Acts of War: The Behavior of Men in Battle* (New York: Free Press, 1985). John Keegan's *The Face of Battle* (New York: Viking, 1976) set a new standard for exacting analysis of the character of combat, focusing on three periods: the high medieval (Agincourt), the horse and musket (Waterloo), and the advanced industrial (the Somme). Stephen E. Ambrose's *Americans at War* (New York: Berkley, 1998) is both provocative and entertaining.

The Civil War occurred at a transitional moment when advances in weaponry were shifting the tactical advantage from the offense to defense. A succinct analysis of this shift is found in Paddy Griffith, *Forward into Battle: Fighting Tactics from Waterloo to the Near Future*, rev. ed. (Novato, CA: Presidio, 1992). Also see Thomas B. Buell, *The Warrior Generals: Combat Leadership in the Civil War* (New York: Three Rivers, 1997) and Herman Hattaway and Archer Jones, *How the North Won: A Military History of the Civil War* (Urbana: University of Illinois Press, 1983). Richard Allan Fox charts the belated transition to tactics appropriate to the new fast-firing weapons, and George Armstrong Custer's failure to implement them properly, in *Archaeology, History, and Custer's Last Battle: The Little Big Horn Reexamined* (Norman: University of Oklahoma Press, 1993).

People sometimes assume that historians are in agreement on all that has gone before, their task being simply to relate the past through a generally agreed-upon narrative. In fact, history is a continuing conversation with no definitive answers or conclusions. One debate particularly concerns us as we look at the dark side of the Civil War— the extent to which the conflict went beyond acceptable boundaries of military behavior, both because of war psychosis (a rising anger at the enemy) and as a result of deliberate "hard war" policy aimed at breaking the opponents' will to fight. Harry S. Stout assesses the gap between the claims of both sides to be fighting a just war with God on their sides and the actual conduct of hostilities in *Upon the Altar of the Nation: A Moral History of the Civil War* (New York: Penguin, 2007). George R. Burkhardt looks at the intensifying savagery of the conflict in *Confederate Rage, Yankee Wrath: No Quarter in the Civil War* (Carbondale: Southern Illinois University Press, 2007). Charles Royster's *The Destructive War: William Tecumseh Sherman, Stonewall Jackson, and the Americans* (New York: Vintage, 1993) takes a close look at two men who advocated a ruthless attitude toward enemy people.

How successful were such strategies that violated just war conventions? We addressed this issue in the text, but readers might want to explore further facets of the subject. After examining Union firebombing of Charleston, South Carolina, August 1863, the result of deploying a weapon of mass destruction against civilians, Stephen R. Wise concluded that the tactic actually raised Rebel morale by increasing hatred of the Yankees. See *Gate of Hell: Campaign for Charleston Harbor, 1863* (Columbia: University of South Carolina Press, 1994). This finding is consistent with conclusions from studies of recent tactics that harm civilians, from World War II carpet bombing to current unmanned drones; they also suggest that resistance to the enemy increases when people are subjected to attacks deemed unreasonable and unfair. It was long assumed that Sherman's highly destructive march to the sea broke the backbone of Rebel resistance in the heartland. But in a brilliantly original analysis, Mark A. Weitz showed that the loyalty of many ordinary Georgia civilians and soldiers dissipated a year before Sherman's invasion, due to the failure of the salt ration and congruent agricultural failures. Thus, a preservative rather than a blitzkrieg started the erosion of morale: *A Higher Duty: Desertion among Georgia Troops during the Civil War* (Lincoln: University of Nebraska Press, 2000).

The psychological consequences of combat have received increasing attention since the Great War of 1914–18. Two American contributions from the World War II era stand out: S. L. A. Marshall, *Men against Fire: The Problem of Battle Command in Future War* (Washington, DC: Infantry Journal, 1947), and Samuel A. Stouffer et al., *The American Soldier* (Princeton, NJ: Princeton University Press, 1949). More recently, Jonathan Shay studied the psychological cost of modern warfare in *Achilles in Vietnam: Combat Trauma and the Undoing of Character* (New York: Simon & Schuster, 1995). Dave Grossman argues we are more successful at overcoming soldiers' initial repugnance to killing than we are at reinstalling moral sanctions against violence once the slaughter officially stops (hence, we may extrapolate, the wild behavior of some Civil War veterans). See *On Killing: The Psychological Cost of Learning to Kill in War and Society* (Boston: Little, Brown, 1996). John Talbott applies recent psychological insights to the experiences of Billy Yank and Johnny Reb in "Combat Trauma in the American Civil War," *History Today* (March 1996).

Medicine in general has tended to be neglected in mainstream histories of the Civil War. For those who wish to know more about diseases, wounds, and their treatment, a good, balanced introduction is provided by Alfred Jay Bollet, *Civil War Medicine: Challenges and Triumphs* (Tucson: Galen, 2002). For an interesting study of medical concerns affecting the African American soldier, see Margaret Humphreys, *Intensely Human: The Health of the Black Soldier in the American Civil War* (Baltimore: Johns Hopkins University Press, 2008). To understand how a simple natural phenomenon can affect military operations and undermine soldiers' health, take a look at C. E. Wood, *Mud: A Military History* (Washington, DC: Potomac Books, 2006).

For those who would like to read more of the words written by participants in the conflict, the chapter endnotes provide a comprehensive guide to the letters, diaries, reports, and memoirs of eyewitnesses. We are fortunate that both parties to the conflict spoke English, were relatively literate, and there was no official censorship.

Consequently, our access to the thoughts of the 1860s generation is almost limitless. A huge number of sources have been printed. Many may now be read on-line, while volumes printed in the nineteenth century remain relatively easy to obtain from public and academic libraries. For starters, try sampling Bell Irvin Wiley's two magnificent compendiums, *The Life of Johnny Reb* (Indianapolis, IN: Bobbs-Merrill, 1943) and *The Life of Billy Yank* (Indianapolis, IN: Bobbs-Merrill, 1952).

We all have our favorite sources. Mine include Joseph E. Crowell, *The Young Volunteer: The Everyday Experiences of a Soldier Boy in the Civil War* (Paterson, NJ: Joseph E. Crowell, 1906); Peter Messent and Steve Courtney, eds., *The Civil War Letters of Joseph Hopkins Twichell: A Chaplain's Story* (Athens: University of Georgia Press, 2006); and Sam R. Watkins, *"Co. Aytch": A Side Show of the Big Show* (1881, repr. New York: Collier, 1962), all of which give candid insights into soldier life. Perhaps because their destinies were so profoundly affected by the collapse of their society, Southern civilians have left us particularly arresting accounts of the war's impact on ordinary lives. Good examples include Charles East, ed., *Sarah Morgan: The Civil War Diary of a Southern Woman* (New York: Simon & Schuster, 1992) and John Q. Anderson, ed., *Brokenburn: The Journal of Kate Stone, 1861–1868* (Baton Rouge: Louisiana State University Press, 1955). John B. Jones, *A Rebel War Clerk's Diary*, ed. Earl Schenck Miers (New York: Sagamore, 1958), is a mine of information on life in the beleaguered Confederate capital. From the other side, Charlotte Forten, a well-educated African American, left her cogent thoughts on North and South in Ray Allen Billington, *The Journal of Charlotte L. Forten* (New York: Dryden, 1953).

Late in the process of producing *Living Hell*, we made a decision not to illustrate the book. However, many collections of contemporary pictures are available. Hirst D. Milhollen and Milton Kaplan, picture eds., *Divided We Fought: A Pictorial History of the War, 1861–1865* (New York: Macmillan, 1961) contains a fine selection of photographs and sketches from the Library of Congress collection. An excellent text by David Donald, General Editor, accompanies the illustrations. For more of the war artists' work, see Earl Schenck Miers, *The American Civil War: A Popular Illustrated History of the Years 1861–1865 as Seen by the Artist-Correspondents Who Were There* (New York: Golden Press, 1961).

We did not illustrate *Living Hell* because none of the pictures seemed to match the stark honesty of written eyewitness accounts. This leads to the question: how truly revelatory were pictures from the front? The 1860s were an age of public engagement with camera use as intense as that of today's cell phones and other popular communications technology. See, for instance, William C. Darrah, *Cartes de Visite in Nineteenth Century Photography* (Gettysburg, PA: W. C. Darrah, 1981). Also, Ronald S. Coddington's three volumes, *Faces of the Civil War: An Album of Union Soldiers and Their Stories; Faces of the Confederacy: An Album of Southern Soldiers and Their Stories;* and *African American Faces of the Civil War: An Album*. All are published in Baltimore by the Johns Hopkins University Press, 2004, 2008, and 2012, respectively. Moreover, war pictures, including those of the dead, could be seen in three dimensions thanks to the Holmes Stereoscope. See Bob Zeller, *The Civil War in Depth: History in 3-D* (San Francisco, CA: Chronicle Books, 1997).

But perhaps the photographers only partially pulled aside the veil that covered the sights of the killing fields. We see bloated corpses, but we do not witness charred bodies, dismembered carcasses, guts hanging out, decapitated heads in close-up, shredded flesh hanging from trees. Some of the corpses were even artfully posed by the cameramen to appear as if in repose, with muskets arranged neatly nearby. Perhaps battle photography did not go much beyond what civilians might have learned from being unable to get Uncle Fred under ground quickly enough in high summer, or from fishing out of the village pond a reeking, decomposing body. And is it possible that visual repetition of similar battlescapes blunted the impact on the sensibilities?

A scholar who studied the work of the war artists, W. Fletcher Thompson Jr. argued in *The Image of War: The Pictorial Reporting of the American Civil War* (New York: Thomas Yoseloff, 1960) that renditions of men at war became more realistic as the war went on. But this judgment seems to have applied mainly to such matters as showing dirt, crumbling uniforms, dejected countenances. Artists largely continued to draw a line at too candid a rendering of smashed flesh, crippled and maimed bodies, the hopelessly insane. In short, we may wish to conclude that photographers and artists colluded in stopping short of the complete disclosure of combat's brutal truths.

Film has not been particularly helpful in providing audiences with a visual sense of the carnage. *Gone with the Wind* (1939) showed terrified refugees fleeing Atlanta, giving a good sense of their panic and desperation. The panoramic view of Confederate wounded lying out on the railroad tracks waiting for attention has never been equaled in its depiction of acres of prolonged suffering. But, through the amputation scene, the movie also promoted the myth of surgeons sawing away, as if at the woodpile, while the unanesthetized patient screams and begs for the hacking to stop. *Glory* (1989) showed us a burst of blood (it should have included bone fragments and gray matter) as an officer's head explodes. And there is a nice touch when Robert Gould Shaw jumps and spills his drink as a servant slams a window. But the movie copies the "please don't cut" moment from *Gone with the Wind*, an instance of film imitating film purveying a myth.

TNT's 1994 miniseries *Gettysburg*, based on Michael Shaara's *The Killer Angels: A Novel* (New York: McKay, 1974), received viewer kudos for the realism of the battle scenes, such as infantry being blown back by close-range canister fire. But these men would have been blown to pieces, not pushed backward. And, for safety reasons, the guns were not loaded with a heavy enough charge to show recoil, a difficult and dangerous feature facing gunners. Given moviemakers' ability to produce special effects (such as spacecraft, storm troopers, and alien creatures being blown apart), we must wonder if we see again a reluctance to fully rend the curtain covering what happens when flesh and metal collide on the battlefield.

Often, film is best at exposing not the physical but the emotional cost of war. In *Gettysburg*, Richard Jordan gives a heart-breaking rendition of the ghastly scenario confronting General Lew Armistead on the third day, when he must lead his brigade in a suicidal frontal assault against a position held by his oldest friend. *Shenandoah* (1965) achieved critical and popular acclaim for its unwavering depiction of the sufferings experienced by peace-craving civilians (in Virginia) caught between the contending armies. Two short films treat the psychological impact of the war. The 1962 French movie

An Occurrence at Owl Creek Bridge brought to the screen one of the twisted Gothic nightmares from the haunted imagination of Civil War veteran Ambrose Bierce. And *The Jolly Corner* (1975) faithfully retold Henry James' ghost story about the apparition of a cruel and brutal veteran, maimed physically and mentally by the war.

By stretching a little beyond our immediate subject, we can add to our visual understanding of war. Tony Richardson's 1968 film, *The Charge of the Light Brigade*, based on Cecil Woodham-Smith's classic *The Reason Why* (New York: McGraw Hill, 1954), shows in graphic detail the result of ignoring the power of modern defensive weaponry. Although often seen as a unique blunder, the charge was actually representative of officers' refusal to surrender belief in inevitable offensive superiority. In *The Gallant Six Hundred: A Tragedy of Obsessions* (New York: Mason & Lipscomb, 1974), John Harris argues that Captain Louis Nolan, who carried the order for the charge, deliberately misled General Lord Cardigan into attacking the wrong position in order to prove a theory that light cavalry, with neither artillery nor infantry support, could carry a heavily fortified position. Nolan did not live long enough into the attack to learn that he was wrong. General Custer, another exponent of the reckless offense without reconnaissance or support, named two of his hunting dogs Cardigan and Nolan.

Stretch a little further to David Lean's 1970 film of Ireland in the aftermath of the failed 1916 Rebellion, *Ryan's Daughter*. Here you will see a quite startling movie recreation of what soldiers meant by the Civil War term "shook over hell." In an Irish pub, the village idiot sits beating his boot on the wainscoting. The rhythmic thumps reproduce the pulsing of shells bursting over trenches on the western front. A British soldier, Major Doryan, a decorated officer who also happens to have chronic post-traumatic stress disorder, starts to shake, the tremors becoming so uncontrollable that glasses and bottles on the counter rattle and bounce.

Ken Burns' ambitious nine-episode documentary miniseries, *The Civil War* (1990), occupies a category of its own. When the program aired on PBS, it was seen by approximately 40,000,000 viewers, and the series has remained popular. It has netted some forty major TV and film honors. Nevertheless, Burns has been variously criticized:

for over-emphasizing slavery as a cause of conflict, for sentimentalizing the participants, for presenting a textbook view of the war, and for giving too much air time to the views of author Shelby Foote. Whatever the case, Burns deserves credit for doing an enormous amount to educate the public about the war.

Reenactors claim to realistically reproduce the mayhem and slaughter of the Civil War battlefield. Journalist Tony Horwitz spent several days with "hard core" reeanactors who assert that by living rough they reproduce the Civil War field experience. Horwitz wrote up his reportage in *Confederates in the Attic: Dispatches from the Unfinished Civil War* (New York: Vintage, 1999). According to Horwitz, one particularly colorful character, Robert Lee Hodge, was able to flawlessly imitate the bloat that afflicted corpses left out on the battlefield. This is not an informed judgment, as Hodge's spectators will see no shattered bone, no pools of black clotted blood, no stink, no putrescent melting facial features. Brian Pohanka, a reenactor in the 5th New York, told *USA Weekend* (June 29, 1990) that his activities supply "the guts of the Civil War." But they can't, metaphorically or physically: reenactors don't load with ball ammunition.

An unintended potential consequence of reenacting is that it may give the impression a visit to the battlefield provides a fun outing for the whole family, much like a visit to the circus, and that combat was probably an exciting undertaking. This undermines our attempt to grasp the dark side of the war. As poet Kent Gramm pointed out in *Gettysburg: A Meditation on War and Values* (Bloomington: Indiana University Press, 1994), Civil War sites are killing fields that we should approach with all the solemnity and sobriety we would reserve for a chapel or a cemetery, not as recreation areas. At the end of the day, one of the best ways to begin fully appreciating what soldiers endured in the great conflicts is to read a first-rate study. I suggest for starters, Stephen W. Sears, *Landscape Turned Red: The Battle of Antietam* (New Haven, CT: Ticknor & Fields, 1983) and James Lee McDonough, *Shiloh: In Hell before Night* (Knoxville; University of Tennessee Press, 1977).

Civil War fiction has not fared well at the hands of critics. Stephen Crane's *The Red Badge of Courage* (1895) and Margaret Mitchell's *Gone with the Wind* (1936) are considered classics, but most novels about the conflict have been ephemeral, failing to evoke the essence of the struggle. An example might be Ross Lockridge Jr.'s *Raintree County* (Boston: Houghton Mifflin: 1948). The plot about an Indiana family experiencing all facets of the war is perhaps interesting in itself but somehow too convoluted and distanced from the guts of the struggle to work as a good war novel.

Possibly the most successful branch of the genre has focused on stories of ordinary Rebel soldiers trying to find their way home as the Confederacy crumbles. Good older examples include Ray Grant Toepfer, *The Scarlet Guidon* (New York: Coward-McCann, 1958) and Maggie Davis, *The Far Side of Home* (New York: Macmillan, 1963). The most wrenching story of a soldier determined to get home, even at the price of desertion, is Charles Frazier's splendid *Cold Mountain* (New York: Atlantic Monthly Press, 1997), brought to the screen in 2003. Readers might want to consider this tale in conjunction with Kenneth Radley's *Rebel Watchdog: The Confederate States Army Provost Guard* (Baton Rouge: Louisiana State University Press, 1989). Also, stories of ordinary Southerners challenging the accepted social hierarchy might encourage one to read Stephanie McCurry's challenging argument that the war had revolutionary effects on the Southern power structure. See *Confederate Reckoning: Power and Politics in the Civil War South* (Cambridge, MA: Harvard University Press, 2010).

If, while reading *Living Hell*, you have wondered why you were not more informed about the dark side of the conflict, you might wish to explore how we have dominantly remembered our wars. See, for instance, G. Kurt Piehler, *Remembering War the American Way* (Washington, DC: Smithsonian Institution Press, 1995); Jim Cullen, *The Civil War in Popular Culture: A Reusable Past* (Washington, DC: Smithsonian Institution Press, 1995); Edward Tabor Linenthal, *Changing Images of the Warrior Hero in America: A History of Popular Symbolism* (New York: Mellen, 1982); Linenthal, *Sacred Ground: Americans and Their Battlefields* (Urbana: University of Illinois Press, 1991); David W. Blight, *Beyond the Battlefield: Race, Memory and the American Civil War* (Amherst: University of Massachusetts Press, 2002); Albert Boime, *The Art of Exclusion: Representing Blacks in the Nineteenth Century* (Washington, DC: Smithsonian

Institution Press, 1990); John Limon, *Writing after War: American War Fiction from Realism to Postmodernism* (New York: Oxford University Press, 1994); and Mark C. Carnes, ed., *Past Imperfect: History According to the Movies* (New York: Henry Holt, 1995).

Finally, in a perceptive recent study, Evan Thomas documents how quickly the Civil War was mythologized as a great adventure paving the way for America's leap into international power: *The War Lovers: Roosevelt, Lodge, Hearst, and the Rush to Empire, 1898* (New York: Little, Brown, 2010).

— Index —

Abbott, Edith, 144, 145
Abbott, Henry Livermore, 118
abortion, 10
Adams, Charles Francis, Jr., 48, 215–16
Adams, F. Colburn, 39
Adams, Henry, 196
African American soldiers, 13, 27–28, 31, 33–36, 148–49; burial duty assigned to, 101; conscription of, 147; execution of, 35–36; medical treatment for, 94–95; as prisoners of war, 177–78; racial discrimination experienced by, 34–36; unfair treatment of, after the war, 187–89
African Americans: children of, 147–48; desperate circumstances of, 147–48; disenfranchisement of, 186; incarceration rates for, 190; lynching of, 197; racism experienced by, 6, 13, 186–90; sexual assaults on, 175–76; stereotypes of, 163, 188, 189. *See also* freedmen; race relations; slaves
agrarianism, Southern, 6–7, 196
Alabama (ship), 81
Albemarle (ship), 81
alcohol abuse: by civilians, 150–51; by officers, 112–13, 124; by soldiers, 20–21, 22, 53, 80, 129

alcohol consumption, 9–10
Alcott, Louisa May, 20, 25, 94, 114
Alexander II, Tsar, 7
Alexander, Porter E., 64
Alexander, R. A., 184
Allen, William, 146
Ambrose, Stephen E., 208
ambulances, 85, 86
ammunition, 66, 68–69, 73–74
amputations, 68, 89–90, 91–92, 95; aftermath of, 200
Anderson, "Bloody Bill," 198
Anderson, Richard H., 74
Andersonville, Georgia, prison at, 177, 178, 180, 201
anesthesia, 91, 92–93, 97–98; scarcity of, 160
animals: inadequate care of, 39; injuries to, 105. *See also* hogs
Anthony, Susan B., 191
anthrax, 49
Antietam, Battle of (Sharpsburg, Battle of), 43, 67, 71–72, 74, 77, 78, 87–88, 100, 104, 106, 115, 116, 118, 120, 127, 152
Armistead, Lewis A., 74, 76–77, 213
Armory Square Hospital, 95
Armour, Philip, 194

Scoring the Record

In this chapter we will assume that (as suggested in Chapters 4 and 5) you have built or selected an adequate, structured, observation system which contains a number of behavior items relevant to whatever dimensions of classroom behavior you wish to measure. We will also assume that, following the procedures described in Chapter 7, you have collected records of behavior in the classrooms of a substantial number of teachers; and that you have records of the performance of each teacher on two or more occasions.

Finally, we will assume that the competencies or dimensions of performance you propose to measure relate to the teachers' skill in maintaining the learning environments in their classrooms rather than in implementing instructional plans, as suggested in Chapter 6. Our reason for making this assumption is that the only empirical base we (the authors) can draw upon in dealing with scoring problems is experience in measuring teacher behavior accumulated in doing research on teacher effectiveness. This research has dealt almost entirely with the relationship between the learning environment the teacher maintains and pupil outcomes; accordingly, most of the discussion that follows will deal with scoring records on dimensions of the classroom learning environment.

The question with which this chapter is concerned is: How should the records be scored? How should you go about the task of deriving reliable and valid measures of meaningful dimensions of classroom behavior from the behavior records you have collected?

If you were using a rating scale instead of a structured observation system, this problem would not arise, since your raters would already have scored the performances they observed. Each rater would have attached whatever weights he thought were appropriate to whatever behaviors he had observed in each teacher's classroom, and arrived at a rating of each teacher on each dimension. In using ratings as if they were measurements you would be operating in blissful ignorance of the problems with which this chapter is concerned, and none of them would be solved.

The basic task that faces you is to specify precisely what you mean when you speak of something like *teacher warmth* or *enthusiasm*, to specify exactly how the behavior of a teacher who is warm or enthusiastic differs from the behavior of a teacher who is not warm or enthusiastic. You will, of course, have made substantial progress already if you have followed the procedures described in Chapter 4. As we noted there, the task is both difficult and challenging, and far too important to be left to the observer to be performed as part of the rating process. One of the great strengths of measurement-based teacher evaluation is that this critical task is given the careful attention it deserves and this attention ensures that (1) exactly the same definition of the dimension is used to evaluate every teacher and that (2) the definition is both clear and public.

CREATING PERFORMANCE MEASURES

This is done by constructing a *scoring key* which may be applied to a record of behavior just as a scoring key is applied to the answer sheet on an objective test. Such a key specifies a positive, negative, or zero weight that is to be applied to the frequency of each item or category of behavior on a record in arriving at a score for that record. As we learned in Chapter 2, applying such a scoring key to a performance record is the third and last of the three essential steps in the process of measuring human performance.

Using Individual Items

The simplest way to define a scoring key for a dimension of performance is to use the frequency on a single item or category of behavior. *Giving feedback on pupil conduct*, for example, might be an item on your instrument that you regard as important for teachers to display. You might, therefore, consider basing your evaluation of a teacher in part on the frequency of this one behavior in a teacher's record. Teachers scoring low on this measure could be given feedback, remedial action could be planned to help them add this behavior to their repertoire, and so on. We do not recommend this approach for general use, however, because one-item keys tend to have a number of serious limitations, including those that follow.

Number of Measures. The typical observation record shows frequencies on so many different items that it becomes difficult to use all (or even most) of the information available in a record when each item is treated as a separate competency. This can be especially troublesome when (as is sure to happen) there is a good deal of redundancy. Even as parsimonious a system as Flanders' (10 categories), yields freqencies on 100 distinct events. Sign systems with 200 or more items are not unusual. Giving feedback to a teacher on so many distinct measures is difficult, and it is even more difficult for a teacher to absorb and retain so much information.

One way of dealing with this would be to interpret only those items that meet some criterion of statistical significance, such as a significant departure from a norm or standard, a significant change over time, or a significant relationship to some desired outcome of instruction. One problem with this strategy arises from the number of spurious results generated when the number of items is large. When the 5 percent level of significance is used, for example, we expect 5 percent of the items to show significant results by chance. Thus if 12 items on a 100-item instrument were significant, you could be fairly certain that 5 of the 12 were meaningless, but would be unable to tell which they were. If you took remedial action on all of them, almost half of your effort would be wasted.

Low Reliability. This is, perhaps, the most serious drawback to single-item scores: like scores on individual test items, they tend to have very low reliabilities. You will be wise not to put any more faith in the frequency recorded on a single behavior item than you would have in a score on one test item.

Low Validity. If you attempt to establish the validity of scores based on a single-item key by correlating them with a criterion, the correlation you get is likely to be very low, if for no other reason than because of the low reliability of a single-item score, which greatly attenuates its correlation with any other measure.

The basic reason why one-item keys have low validities, however, is the fact that they usually measure aspects of behavior that are intrinsically unimportant, or meaningless, or both. Different teachers often use the identical behavior to serve very different purposes. As an example, take the item, *teacher calls on a pupil whose hand is not raised.* One teacher may do this because the pupil is shy and needs to participate more. Another does it to get the correct answer, which only that pupil knows. Another may do the same thing because the pupil's attention is wandering, in order to keep him on task. There may even be instances when the teacher does it in an effort to humiliate the pupil. How could you expect how often a teacher calls on a pupil whose hand is not raised to correlate with anything, when it can measure any one of so many different things?

Item Distributions.   One final problem with one-item keys is that scores (i.e., frequencies) on single items are not normally distributed in most cases. The frequency of an item like *teacher levitates*, for example, would certainly be zero on most teachers' records; but there just might be a teacher somewhere, or perhaps more than one, who has mastered the art of levitation. Chances are that the frequency of this item in the record of such a teacher would be greater than zero; it might even be high. But in most teachers' records it would be zero. Scores (frequencies) on this item would therefore follow what is called a *J-shaped distribution*. In such a distribution, most of the scores will be piled up at one end of their range (in this case the lower end), and there would only be a few scores toward the other end.

Many behavior items are like this; items like *teacher shouts at a child* or *pupil defies teacher* which rarely occur in most classrooms, but may be rather common in a few. Such items tend to be important when they do occur. There are also items like *pupil asks for help* which happen often in most classrooms, so that when we see a record on which this item is absent or rare, that seems important to know. Frequencies of both types of items follow J-distributions.

Why does this matter? For one thing, because (without realizing it) most of us automatically interpret any scores we see as though they were normally distributed; that is, we assume that most scores will normally be close to the middle of their range, and that there will be relatively few scores near either extreme. But frequencies of items on observational records tend not to behave this way. Among the anomalies you may encounter are having the best teacher in a group get no better than an average score; or having 95 percent or more of your teachers get identical scores.

Another problem is that J-shaped distributions also have strange, and often misleading effects on the results of statistical analyses, especially on intercorrelations between items. Unless you are on the alert, you can be seriously misled by some of the results you get.

These are some of the reasons why we recommend that you make a practice of combining all of the items that seem to reflect the same aspect of teacher performance to a greater or lesser degree into a single composite scoring key. When you do this, this aspect of performance acts as a *common factor* in the items; that is, it tends to take over, and the total score on the composite reflects that aspect of performance much more accurately and reliably than the score on any one item.

Before you perform this or any other statistical operation on the item scores, however, we recommend that you normalize the distribution of frequencies on each item in the set of data you are working with.

Normalization. We recommend that you normalize them as a matter of routine, using an *area transformation*. An area transformation first converts each frequency to a percentile rank, and then replaces each frequency with a standard score that would have the same percentile rank in a normal distribution of standard scores. In our own work we use T scores, which have a mean of 50 and a standard deviation of 10. Such a transformation preserves the rank order of the scores (frequencies) but changes the distances between adjacent scores, lengthening some and shortening others, to make them approximate what they would have been if the original frequencies had been distributed normally.

The usual procedure statisticians use for normalizing distributions is to convert them to squares, square roots, logarithms, or some other function, depending on the nature of the original distribution. We prefer an area transformation because the transformed scores are intuitively easier to understand. It seems to us rather difficult to visualize what the square root or the logarithm of a frequency might mean, but like most educators we have some familiarity with standard scores, especially when they are normally distributed.

Item Variabilities. Another characteristic of item frequencies which you need to consider is their variability, the range of frequencies on each item. Frequencies on one item may range from 0 to 5; those on another may range as high as 25 or 50. When items with different variabilities are combined in the same composite key with nominally equal weights, the actual weight any one item has in the composite score will depend on the variability of the item. Items with large variabilities will make much larger contributions to the total score than items with small variabilities. If the variability of an item is close to 0, its actual weight will approach 0, and if there are other items on the key with large variabilities, the effect will be the same as if the item were eliminatd from the key entirely.

The normalizing transformation of item frequencies that we recommended as a cure for abnormalities in item distributions also takes care of this problem because the transformed scores on all the items, being standard scores, will have the same standard deviation; that is, they will all have equal variabilities. This puts you in control of the weights of the items in your composite: if you assign equal weights, they will have equal weights; if you assign larger weights to some items, they will have larger weights.

Item Means.   Finally, the transformed scores on all items will have the same mean. This can be useful if it is not possible for you to follow the recommendation we made in the last chapter, that you make sure that every observer you use sees every teacher who is to be evaluated. Sometimes, as when the number of teachers to be evaluated is large, it may be necessary to divide your teachers into two or more groups and have different observers observe the teachers in each group. In such cases, systematic observer errors can distort differences between teachers.

By a systematic observer error we mean a tendency for one observer to be more (or less) sensitive to occurrences of an item than another observer. For example one observer may see more instances of praise than another when they both observe the same teachers (especially after they have been observing in the field a while). The observers may agree quite closely on which teachers use the most or least praise, but not on the exact amount. In such instances, when you normalize the item distributions you should normalize the set of records made by each observer separately. This will remove the effects of systematic observer errors.

Rational Scoring Keys

In Chapter 4 we discussed procedures for identifying items or categories of behavior that indicate the presence or absence of a dimension of behavior or competency that you wish to measure, and taking steps to ensure that these behaviors will be recorded on the instrument you select or construct. If you have followed these procedures, the simplest and most direct way for you to develop a key that will yield scores that measure one of these dimensions is to develop a rational composite of these items. In other words, you should include in the same key those items that you think should go together, that seem to you to reflect the dimension you want to measure. If, in your judgment or that of whatever person or committee is responsible for planning the evaluation program, the presence of a particular item or category of behavior in a teacher's record is an indicator of the competency (or other dimension) you want to measure, that item would be included in the scoring key and given a positive weight. If the presence of a particular item of behavior in a record is judged to indicate the absence of the competency, it too should be included in the scoring key, but with a negative weight.

Measurement experts agree that all of the items on a key should be given equal weights unless there is strong evidence to support the use of differential weights. Dawes (1979) cites evidence that expert judgement can reliably indicate which items should have positive weights and which should have negative weights, but cannot reliably estimate how large the weights should be. We therefore recommend that all items on a key be weighted either plus or minus one. A score obtained with a rational scoring key will, then, consist of the simple total of the (normalized) scores on all items believed to indicate presence of the competency to be measured minus the simple total of the scores on all items believed to indicate absence of that competency.

One problem that can be quite troublesome arises when the same item seems to belong on more than one scoring key. In our experience in the project already referred to (Medley et al., 1981) there were a number of such items. One item that seemed to belong on several keys had to do with pupils' task involvement, which seemed to be related to effective communication by the teacher, to the teachers' selection and differential use of materials, and to classroom management, among others. If the same item is included on more than one key, those keys will measure the same thing to a degree, although they are supposed to measure different things, and there will be some spurious correlation between them. At this point, however, we suggest that when you are in doubt whether to assign an item to one or another of two keys, that you put it on both of them.

We have already noted that measurement-based teacher evaluation makes at least as good use of the wisdom and experience of professional educators as rating scales do, but it uses their expertise in a different way and at a different point in the evaluation process. The point under discussion is the point at which you can and should make use of all such wisdom you can. If you want to involve your teachers in your program, this is a good place for that, too. The important thing is to make your beliefs about competent teacher performance explicit enough so that they can be tested by using them. There is nothing more important we can do at this point than to begin the painful and laborious process of sorting out those things we believe about effective teaching that are true from those that are not. What we are talking about here is the first step in that process.

Testing a Scoring Key. When your set of rational keys has been assembled, your next step is to score a representative set of records and do a reliability analysis of each scoring key, using the method described in Appendix B. If a key discriminates satisfactorily in your population of teachers you have prima facie evidence that the competency or dimension of behavior you have defined exists in the real world, and that you are able to measure it reliably. If a scoring key discriminates satisfactorily you may decide to use it as it is. If a key fails to discriminate, it may be possible to refine the key enough so that it will discriminate, using methods we will describe below.

However, you will fail to exploit fully the power of the measurement-based approach to teacher evaluation unless you go one step further. The procedures for refining a scoring key that we are about to describe must be used to salvage keys that do not discriminate; but it is almost as important to apply them to keys that do discriminate. What we are saying is that the process should be routinely applied to every new scoring key that you construct.

REFINING A SCORING KEY

The process of refining a scoring key is really an extension of the process of internal consistency analysis that began with the reliability analysis just described. The size of the alpha coefficient obtained in the analysis depends on the average intercorrelation among the items on the key. If it is low, this may indicate that the competency or behavior dimension you have hypothesized does not exist, or that although the dimension does exist, some of the items you have chosen do not belong on the key. This problem of finding that an item or a subset of items within a key is inadequately related to the major set of items is not uncommon. We are sometimes inclined to be overly simplistic in our conceptualization of a dimension of teacher performance like classroom management; and sometimes we are simply mistaken in our concept of the nature of the dimension. For whatever reason, it is not unusual to find a few items on any rational scoring key that do not belong there.

Our main purpose in refining a key is to identify such items so that they can be removed and the reliability of the key, the power of scores on the key to discriminate, increased. Increasing the reliability of a score is important, but the refinement does something else which is probably more important: it clarifies the meaning of scores on the key and teaches us something about the nature of the dimension of behavior that we might never otherwise discover.

Consider, for example, the concept of *permissiveness* which was so common in the educational literature of a generation ago. The characteristic was seen as unidimensional and bipolar, with a warm, friendly, indulgent teacher who allowed pupils a maximum amount of freedom at one extreme, and a negative, critical teacher who ran a "taut ship" at the other extreme. Through the process we are discussing we have found that this conceptualization does not fit the real world.

In the real world of the classroom you will find warm, friendly teachers who share decision-making with pupils and whose classrooms may appear almost chaotic in some cases; you will also find teachers who use praise generously in a Skinnerian fashion to create rather tightly controlled conditions in a warm environment. You will also find teachers who maintain close control by being negative and critical; and teachers equally negative and critical who never succeed in establishing any control to speak of. It seems clear that what was thought to be a single bipolar dimension really reflects two dimensions, one of emotional climate and one of control, that are relatively independent of one another (Soar and Soar, 1979). The technique for studying the internal structure of a behavior measure that we have found to be generally most useful is factor analysis either of the items within the key or a set of such keys. A technical description of this method would fall outside the scope of this discussion; those interested in such a description should consult Appendix C. For those not familiar with the procedure, we will say only that it is a sophisticated statistical procedure for examining all of the intercorrelations in a set of scores and identifying a set of factors which convey the maximum amount of the information in those scores through the minimum number of subscores. If most of the differences between teachers measured by the items within a key reflect a single dimension or competency (as they are intended to), the analysis will reveal that fact. If the items reflect two or more different dimensions of behavior, the analysis will not only reveal this fact but will also tell us which items measure which dimension or factor. Thus factor analysis provides an excellent check on the accuracy of the expert judgments made in the development of the key.

An Alternative Approach.   Some readers may wonder whether the initial step of developing a rational scoring key might not be omitted entirely. If the procedures recommended in the last four chapters have been followed, you will have available a set of normalized records of the frequencies of occurrence of a substantial number of items of behavior believed to be relevant to competent teaching. Why not do one factor analysis of all of these items, and let the factor analysis identify a set of keys for you?

This purely empirical approach is a viable one, and the one that some researchers would recommend; we prefer the rational-empirical combination we have described for a number of reasons. Some of the limitations in a purely empirical approach are noted in Appendix C. In addition to these, we like to think that the opinions of experienced researchers or educators can supply information, however imperfect it may be, that no blind empirical process can uncover.

Some Examples.   The experience of submitting some cherished belief about the structure of teacher behavior to an empirical test and discovering that the belief was naive, simplistic, or just plain wrong is a chastening one, and one we as researchers have had many times. But it is a necessary part of the learning process; if you never change, you never learn. The evidence that teachers' expressions of positive and negative affect tend to be independent referred to earlier was discovered in just this way (Soar, 1966).

We also found evidence that verbal and nonverbal communication of positive affect by elementary-school teachers were also independent of each other (Soar and Soar, 1975). In developing measures of verbal and nonverbal communication of positive affect we naturally included items about teacher use of facial expression (smiling, nodding, frowning) in the same key with other nonverbal items; but a factor analysis indicated that they belonged on the key with the *verbal* items.

Although completely unexpected, this finding made good sense after the fact. We remember well one classroom in which the teacher frequently nodded, smiled, praised children, and expressed warmth verbally, but rarely touched a child. The aide in the same classroom never made a positive comment to a child that we observed, but she often patted or hugged a child, or ruffled his hair, and often held a child in her lap as she carried out a learning activity. In retrospect we realized that these were pure types of the two patterns identified in the factor analysis.

Another of these heuristic findings came from the unexpected emergence of a factor which has *extended teacher talk* at one end and *drill-type activity* at the other, a factor which we found to be more strongly related to pupil learning gains than any other in that study. Oddly enough, another factor, which had *extended teacher talk* at one end and *extended pupil talk* at the other, was unrelated to pupil learning gains. Examination of the protocols finally led us to conclude that the extended teacher talk reflected in the first factor tended to come in bursts of about 15 to 18 seconds, with bursts of pupil talk of similar duration interspersed among them. The indication was that teachers high on this factor were using cycles of optimal length for presenting information or structuring complex questions and for pupils to deal with the information or the question. Such a teacher seemed to be presenting information in the right-sized chunks. At about this time, Bellack and others (1966) hypothesized an optimal length of the cycle of interaction between teacher and pupils.

In a recent study we had an opportunity consciously to test the sequence of first constructing rational item sets or keys and then factor analyzing the scores (Soar and Soar, 1980). We began by proposing several behavior domains which we expected to be relatively independent and identifying separate sets of items or scoring keys which we thought belonged in each domain. Next we factored the item sets or keys in each of the domains to test for internal consistency. None of the sets was internally consistent. In every instance the items broke up into at least two distinct measures. And in each instance the distinctions, although unanticipated, made good sense. The complete set of scoring keys is included in the report cited.

As one example, we had assumed that the time the teacher devoted to interaction at a high cognitive level would fall along a single dimension, as Bloom's taxonomy suggests (Bloom, 1956), but the domain broke up into two parts, as shown in Figures 8.1 and 8.2. The factor measured by the items listed in Figure 8.1 is one in which the teacher encourages pupils to go beyond the information given to them and to suggest other ideas, guess and hypothesize; but there is no attempt to evaluate any of the ideas that are suggested. In brief, the factor suggests brainstorming.

The pattern which appears in Figure 8.2 resembles that in figure 8.1 in that the teacher also encourages the pupils to go beyond the data supplied them and suggest other ideas. But in this pattern the appropriateness or adequacy of the ideas suggested is tested. The pattern here is more one of problem solving than of brainstorming.

It is not difficult to see why teachers' scores on a rational key which mixes these two superficially similar patterns of behavior in a single score might fail to correlate with the results they get, since the two patterns differ so fundamentally in their intentions. The fact that

TPOR	Asks Q that is not readily answerable by study of lesson	.72
TPOR	Permits P to suggest additional or alternative answers	.69
TPOR	Encourages P to guess or hypothesize about unknown or untested	.59
TPOR	Emphasizes idealized, reassuring, or "pretty" aspects of a topic	.56
TPOR	Entertains even "wild" or farfetched sugg.	.53
TPOR	Emphasized realistic, disconcerting, or "ugly" aspects of topic	.48
TPOR	Steers P away from hard Q or problem	.41
TPOR	Motivates with intrinsic value of ideas or activity	.42
TPOR	Expects P to "know" rather than to guess answer to Q	−.64
TPOR	Asks Q that P can answer only if he studied the lession	−.46
TPOR	Accepts only one answer as being correct	−.45
	Eigenvalue	3.96

FIGURE 8.1   Factor 3: *guess or hypothesize*—no evaluation. (Adapted from Soar and Soar, 1980.)

TPOR	Involves P in uncertain or incomplete situation	.73
TPOR	Asks P to judge complete value of answers or questions	.62
TPOR	Asks P to support answers or opinions with evidence	.61
TPOR	Encourages P to put his ideas to the test	.58
TPOR	Helps P discover and correct factual errors and inaccuracies	.59
TPOR	Asks P to evaluate his own work	.56
TPOR	Leads P to Q or problem that stumps him	.53
TPOR	Questions misconceptions, faulty logic, unwarranted conclusions	.52
TPOR	Has P decided when Q has been answered satisfactorily	.49
TPOR	Motivates P with intrinsic values of ideas or activities	.44
TPOR	Permits P to suggest additional or alternative answers	.43
	Eigenvalue	4.05

FIGURE 8.2 Factor 1: *guided discovery backed up by facts*. (Adapted from Soar and Soar, 1980.)

previously used measures of high-cognitive interaction have not separated the two patterns may explain the perplexing finding that the more time a teacher spends in high-level interaction the less gains her pupils show, even on measures of high-level outcomes. One would expect that brainstorming activities (Figure 8.1) would not add to pupils' ability to perform on such tests while high-level problem-solving activities (Figure 8.2) would. But since both types of activities would earn the same score on the rational key, the scores would show zero relationship to pupil gains.

The Rational-Empirical Sequence. The main impression that the foregoing discussion is likely to leave with you is one of complexity. The impression is correct. But the process we are trying to measure, the teaching process, is as complex a process as any that man has ever attempted to study; and it is foolish to expect that it can be evaluated by any simple method. The examples we have cited clearly illustrate what is wrong with the simplistic procedures in use today.

But the second impression that you should retain is the important one: if one conclusion can be drawn from all of this it is that our opinions about the nature of effective teaching are extremely untrustworthy, and that *the blind faith in expert opinion that underlies present-day procedures for training and evaluating teachers is entirely unjustified.* Like any other complex problem this problem has no simple solution.

If you use measurement-based teacher evaluation with rational scoring keys, but do not refine them empirically, you will still reap many of the benefits it has over ratings-based evaluation, but not all of them. To fully exploit the power of this approach you must routinely submit each measure you develop, each rational scoring key, to the kind of empirical testing and refinement described in this chapter. This is partly due to the fact that you will be in a very real sense a pioneer breaking new ground. As the method comes into wider use, and, in consequence, our understanding of the structure of effective teacher behavior grows, our ability to put together rational keys that will stand up under empirical tests will increase to a point at which the empirical tests become much less important.

CONCLUDING REMARKS

As we noted at the beginning of this chapter, the scoring procedures described thus far are those that are appropriate for measures of teachers' competence in maintaining the classroom learning environment, which was identifed in Chapter 6 as the lowest or simplest level of teaching skill, and the easiest to measure. We also recommended (in Chapter 6) that your initial attempts at measurement-based teacher evaluation be confined to this level. We will conclude this section with some notes on measuring the higher levels of skill, those related to implementing instruction and maintaining individual pupil involvement.

Scoring Measures of Higher Levels of Skill

As we have seen, defining the teacher's task by controlling contextual factors becomes much more important when the focus of evaluation is on these higher-level skills. From the standpoint of scoring there are two distinct parts of the task definition problem. One part has to do with taking account of the kind of class characteristics that are often referred to as the *difficulty* of the class. The other has to do with the teacher's plan.

The fact that the kind of a class she has has a considerable impact on how the competent teacher behaves with that class is a fact that is widely recognized at the verbal level but generally ignored both in teacher evaluation and in research in teacher effectiveness. The practical consequence is the introduction of large errors of measurement that severely limit both the reliability and the validity of the measurements obtained.

We have a suggestion (as yet untried) for dealing with this part of the problem. We suggest that you measure the most important characteristics of the teacher's class and then regress (raw) item frequencies on these measures and use the regression equation to make statistical adjustments in the frequencies by analysis of covariance. This makes it possible to compare each teacher's performance with performances of other teachers with classes similar to her own. These adjusted frequencies would then be normalized and processed in the same way that unadjusted frequencies would.

It seems equally obvious that how the competent teacher behaves with a class also depends on her immediate goal and the strategy she has decided to use in achieving it. Since a particular category or item of behavior might indicate competence in using one strategy but not another, it would be appropriate to use different scoring keys for performances of teachers using different strategies.

But as was noted in Chapter 6, the day when we will be ready to measure these higher levels of teaching skill is still somewhere in the future, and we had best focus for the present on learning to measure environmental maintenance skills where the need is more urgent and success is more readily attainable.

BIBLIOGRAPHY

Bellack, A., H. M. Kliebard, R. T. Hyman, and F. L. Smith. *The Language of the Classroom.* New York: Teacher's College Press, 1966.

Bloom, B. S. *Taxonomy of Educational Objectives; The Classification of Educational Goals, Handbook I: Cognitive Domain.* New York: David McKay, 1956.

Dawes, R. M. "The Robust Beauty of Improper Linear Models in Decision Making." *American Psychologist*, 1979, 34, 571–582.

Medley, Donald M., Homer Coker, Joan G. Coker, Jeffery L. Lorentz, Robert S. Soar, and Robert L. Spaulding. "Assessing Teacher Performance from Observed Competency Indicators Defined by Classroom Teachers." *Journal of Educational Research*, 1981, 74, 197–216.

Soar, Robert S. "An Integrative Approach to Classroom Learning." Philadelphia: Temple University, 1966, ERIC document ED033749.

Soar, Robert S., and Ruth M. Soar. "Classroom Behavior, Pupil Characteristics and Pupil Growth for the School Year and the Summer." *JSAS Catalog of Selected Documents in Psychology*, 1975, 5(200), ms. no. 873.

———— "Emotional Climate and Management." In R. E. Peterson and J. H. Walberg, eds., *Research on Teaching.* Berkeley, CA: McCutchan, 1979.

———— "Setting Variables, Classroom Interaction and Multiple Pupil Outcomes." *JSAS Catalog of Selected Documents in Psychology*, 1980, 10, ms. no. 2110.

Part III

Evaluation: The Final Step

9

Measurement-Based Teacher
Evaluation in Operation

If you have followed the procedures described in Chapters 4 through 8 of this volume and implemented a measurement-based teacher evaluation program you have access to an amount of information about what is going on in the classrooms of your school system beyond anything you have ever experienced before. This information has many uses, some of which has little direct relation to teacher evaluation. In this chapter we will discuss ways of using this information.

We will assume that your primary interest is in using the information for teacher evaluation in ways that will improve the quality of teaching in your schools. One way of doing this is to use the information to improve personnel decisions related to the employment and utilization of teachers and the awarding of tenure and recognition of merit. Another way of using the information is to improve in-service training and other efforts to help teachers improve their own effectiveness.

Whether or not you share the rather dim view of the state of the art of teacher evaluation in general and supervisors' ratings of teachers in particular set forth in the first three chapters of this book, you must certainly agree on one point. You must agree on how important it is that any kind of teacher evaluation be based on the most complete, accurate, and relevant information about teacher performance that can be obtained. What we have described are procedures for obtaining the most accurate information possible through the use of (1) specially trained and disinterested observers, (2) carefully constructed schedules

159

to help them record what they observe accurately and objectively, and (3) the most sophisticated techniques and technology available for extracting all relevant information from the records.

You must also agree on the utter inadequacy of the information obtained from the relatively infrequent, casual, and brief observations that an administrator with little or no special training in classroom observation and many other more pressing tasks to perform is able to make. This is especially true when you know how difficult it is to make valid assessments of something as complex as interactive teaching, even under the most favorable conditions.

The reservation about measurement-based teacher evaluation most frequently expressed by educators has to do with how scores on observational records can possibly provide dependable information about something as complex as teacher performance, based as they are on frequency counts of bits of behavior so small that they must be intrinsically trivial in themselves. The best evidence that they can and do provide such information comes from the process-product research. Using these same methods, process-product research has established many more statistically significant relationships between these "trivia" and measures of pupil learning gains than were ever found between teacher ratings (or any other teacher characteristics) and pupil gains in 80 years of vain attempts. This, it seems to us, is strong prima facie evidence that data of this kind do in fact contain the valid information we need about teacher behavior.

If you want to be sure that your measurement-based teacher evaluation program is effective in improving instruction, you will need evidence that the specific measures of teacher competence, the competency indicators you are using, are valid in your situation and with your teachers and pupils. You need evidence that if you use the information you are getting in the ways we will describe, the effectiveness of your teachers and of your program will increase. A part of this chapter will therefore be devoted to a discussion of how to go about establishing that, in your setting, your scoring keys are valid predictors of the achievement gains produced by teachers.

SOME EXAMPLES

In order to give you a better idea of what a measurement-based evaluation of teacher performance program in operation is like, we will describe some brief examples of actual uses of observational measures. The examples will be drawn from experiences obtained with a single instrument, one that we have had occasion to cite before, the COKER (Coker and Coker, 1979a, b). As far as we can discover, the COKER is the only system that has actually been used in most of the ways we will be discussing.

The COKER is a relatively elaborate sign system, its items were adapted from five other observation schedules used in a single process-product study (Medley et al., 1981). The procedure used has already been described (see Chapter 4), but it may be worth emphasizing the point that, contrary to what we have recommended, the constructors of COKER had no particular competencies or dimensions of behavior in mind that the finished instrument was supposed to measure. The intent was to include such a broad variety of behavior items in the schedule that it would be possible to build a key for scoring almost any imaginable dimension of classroom behavior on a COKER record.

Sets of Competency Indicators

In various studies that have employed the COKER, several sets of competencies defined independently of the instrument have been operationalized by first having the definers identify items of behavior on the COKER that they believed to be relevant to each competency in the set, and then forming a composite key to measure that competency, in the manner described in Chapter 8.

The Toledo Competencies. Investigators at the University of Toledo, for example, developed the competency indicator keys shown in Figure 9.1, which were designed to measure 22 competencies in three areas, competencies that teacher education students were expected to exhibit during the student teaching experience.

The Georgia State Competencies. In a study of gains in competence of student teachers at Georgia State University, scoring keys for the somewhat different set of competencies shown in Figure 9.2 were developed.

The Medley Competencies. Using the results of process-product research as summarized by Medley (1977), we developed the 13 COKER keys shown in Figure 9.3. Each key was designed to measure one of 13 patterns of behavior found to be related to teacher effectiveness measured in terms of pupil achievement gains in the research summarized.

Reliability Problems. You should understand that not all of these keys proved to be reliable measures of differences between teachers in the groups studied. In the most recent study of the 22 Toledo competency indicators cited in the COKER technical manual, for instance, scores on two keys (numbers 7 and 11) based on eight visits per teacher had 0

AREA I: INSTRUCTIONAL STRATEGIES, TECHNIQUES AND/OR METHODS

1. Uses a variety of instructional strategies
2. Uses convergent and divergent inquiry strategies
3. Develops and demonstrates problem-solving skills
4. Establishes transitions and sequences in instruction which are varied, logical, and appropriate
5. Modifies instructional activities to accommodate identified learner needs
6. Demonstrates ability to work with individuals, small groups, and large groups
7. Structures the use of time to facilitate student learning
8. Uses a variety of resources and materials
9. Provides learning experiences which enable students to transfer principles and generalizations outside of school

AREA II: COMMUNICATION WITH LEARNERS

10. Provides group communication experiences for students
11. Uses a variety of functional verbal and nonverbal communication skills with students
12. Gives clear directions and explanations
13. Motivates students to ask questions
14. Uses questions that lead students to analyze, synthesize, and think critically
15. Accepts varied student viewpoints and/or asks students to extend or elaborate answers or ideas
16. Demonstrates proper listening skills
17. Provides feedback to learners on their cognitive performance

AREA III: LEARNER REINFORCEMENT-INVOLVEMENT

18. Maintains an environment in which students are actively involved, working on-task
19. Implements an effective classroom management system for positive student behaviour (discipline)
20. Uses positive reinforcement patterns with students
21. Assists students in discovering and correcting errors and inaccuracies
22. Develops student feedback, evaluation skills, and student self-evaluation

FIGURE 9.1   The 22 University of Toledo competency indicators.

1. *Demonstrates* enthusiasm for teaching and the topics being taught.
2. *Provides* opportunities for success experiences by students.
3. *Demonstrates* patience, empathy, and understanding.
4. *Identifies* learning styles, rates of learning, and capabilities of students.
5. *Demonstrates* understanding or processes involved in selection of learning content and methods.
6. *Specifies* teaching processes.
7. *Identifies* assessment processes.
8. *Maintains* student involvement in learning tasks.
9. *Uses* activities which call for pupil planning, observing, describing, experimenting and writing.
10. *Organizes* and uses a variety of appropriate instructional materials and equipment.
11. *Uses* a variety of cognitive levels in strategies of questioning.
12. *Gives* directions clearly.
13. *Manages* disruptive behaviour constructively.
14. *Helps* students recognize progress and achievements.

FIGURE 9.2   The 14 Georgia State University competency indicators.

reliabilities. The median reliability of all 22 keys was .466; seven keys had reliabilities above .600, and one (number 15) had a reliability of .801. Again, these measures of reliability treat variation due to differences between observers and visits as error, consequently are lower than estimates based on other procedures.

It is important to realize that, as has been the practice in most observational studies of teacher behavior, no attempt was made in this case to define the tasks the teachers were supposed to perform while the observations were being made. As a result, much of the apparent unreliability may have reflected purposeful variations in the teachers' behavior as the nature of the tasks varied from visit to visit rather than errors of measurement. The reliabilities would almost certainly have been higher if the tasks had been defined as recommended in Chapter 6.

The fact that some keys were unreliable may mean any one of a number of things. The unreliability may mean that the behavior of the teachers on these items is unstable. In that case, one would need to make more observations of each teacher to get more reliable measures. The unreliability may also mean that the instrument does not contain enough items relevant to the competency in question to supply a key to measure it. If, for example, you were using the COKER and you regarded competency indicator 11 as important enough to justify the effort, you could revise the instrument by adding items relevant to that competency. Taebel and Coker (1980), in a research study involving music teachers, added a 24-cell teacher by student matrix to the COKER

1. When teachers work with large groups rather than small groups student gain is more likely to occur.
2. When small groups work without adult supervision student gain is less likely to occur.
3. Seatwork by the student is more effective when there is an appropriate balance between teacher *focusing* and *structuring*, and student choice of either *what, how,* and *when.*
4. An increase in structured academic time is associated with greater student gain.
5. When students initiate verbal interactions, gain is less likely in lower grades but more likely in intermediate and higher grades.
6. Student correct substantive responses to teacher questions are related to greater student gain.
7. High cognitive level questions relate negatively to student gain and low cognitive level questions relate positively to student gain, even for complex learning outcomes.
8. When teachers amplify and discuss student responses, high-socioeconomic status students tend to show greater gain than do low-socioeconomic status students.
9. Teacher hostility and rebuking behavior relates negatively to student gain.
10. Disruptive student behavior is negatively associated with student gain.
11. Student involvement (time on task) is associated positively with student gain.
12. Non-substantive interaction between teacher and students relates negatively to student gain.
13. Unstructured student behavior is negatively related to student gain for a given learning task; a balance between teacher structuring and student freedom provides the optimal setting for student gain.

FIGURE 9.3   The 13 Medley competency indicators.

instrument. These items were used to increase the reliability of some keys and develop additional reliable keys unique to music teachers. You could use this same approach for other subject-matter areas, grade levels, or types of instructional programs to be studied. Alternatively, you could look for another instrument that already contains items applicable to a solution. There is a slight chance that observers are not making accurate records, in which case additional training would be warranted.

Finally, the unreliability of a key may mean that there are no detectable differences among your teachers in the competency you are trying to measure. In other words, they may all have equal amounts of the competency. When a key that has been found to be reliable in one group of teachers is unreliable in another group, this is almost certain to be the case. If norms are available, you may be able, by comparing the mean of your group with the norms, to decide whether everyone in the group already has the competency or whether they all need to work on the competency because they do not possess it.

Using Profiles of Competency Indicators

Let us assume for the moment that the primary purpose for which you will use the measurements you obtain will be for the improvement of instruction, and that the strategy you prefer to use involves staff development rather than personnel decisions. Let us also assume that you regard the teacher not as a mere employee or technician but as an autonomous practicing professional who is primarily responsible for her own professional growth. This implies, among other things, that the function of staff development is to support each teacher's own efforts to improve her performance and that staff development goals will be highly individualized.

The greatest potential of an observation system like the COKER lies in its ability to yield multiple scores, to measure several different competency indicators simultaneously. Obviously, no single measurement could ever adequately describe a complex process like teaching; what you need is a set of scores, a profile of the teacher across several competency indicators. Only a profile can reveal the teacher's strengths and weaknesses across a spectrum of competencies, and indicate just where efforts to improve can be concentrated with greatest effect.

Norms. In order to make a teacher's scores on different competency indicators in a profile comparable, you will need norms on all of the scoring keys based on a single large group of teachers, the larger the better. At first you will have to use the scores of the group you are working with to establish tentative norms, but as time goes by you should accumulate enough data on teachers in your school system to establish a relatively stable set of permanent systemwide norms. As you know, a set of norms enables you to transform a teacher's raw score on any competency indicator to a standard score which indicates where that teacher's performance would stand in the distribution of performances of all teachers in the norm group. Thus scores on all keys become comparable, and it is possible to find out whether a teacher has more (or less) of one competency than another.

COKER records are made on Opscan sheets like test answer sheets, so that they can be read and scored by a computer. At the same time the computer can be programed to print out, on request, various kinds of profiles of competency indicators.

Individual Profiles.   Figure 9.4 shows one teacher's profile across the 13 competency indicators supposed to relate to teacher effectiveness just as it was printed out by the computer. The profile is based on standard scores that have a mean of 50 and a standard deviation of 10. Note that this teacher's scores on competency indicators 12, 10, 7, and 3 are below average, which suggests that these would be the ones she could most profitably work on in order to become more effective. Another teacher's profile on the same 13 competency indicators is shown in Figure 9.5. This teacher like the first should be relatively effective, since she, too, is below average on only 4 of the 13 competency indicators; in this case, numbers 11, 8, 5, and 1.

Group Profiles.   Also useful is a profile of the mean scores of all of the teachers in a group. Such a group profile provides a much better indicator of the staff development needs of the teachers than the usual needs assessment based on teachers' perceptions of their own staff development needs, and enables you to target in-service training courses on the competencies with which the teachers need help the most, instead of those which they *think* they need most.

Once you have identified a particular competency as the one on which an in-service institute or workshop should focus, you can ask the computer to print out a profile of the group on the indicator of that competency; what you get will look like Figure 9.6, which shows how 43 teachers did on one Medley competency indicator. In this case, you will note that only 22 of the 43 teachers were below average on this competency indicator, which indicates that you should set up some other kind of training for the 19 who seem not to need help with this particular competency.

Measuring Changes in Teacher Performance.   The objectivity of measurements based on structured observation schedules makes them particularly suitable for assessing changes in teacher performance over time. If a group of teachers are observed and their records are scored before and after they take part in an in-service program you can compare their competency indicator profiles before and after, both individually and as a group. Such comparisons will give a picture of the effects of the program that is objective, precise, and detailed. And you can get such a picture of the effects on any individual teacher or subgroup as well as on the entire group.

If your staff development program is highly individualized, either with respect to the goals or to the kind of help given to each teacher, profiles like these can be particularly useful. In such cases, the goal each teacher adopts may be defined in terms of target scores on one or more of the competency indicators in the profile. Progress toward the goal can

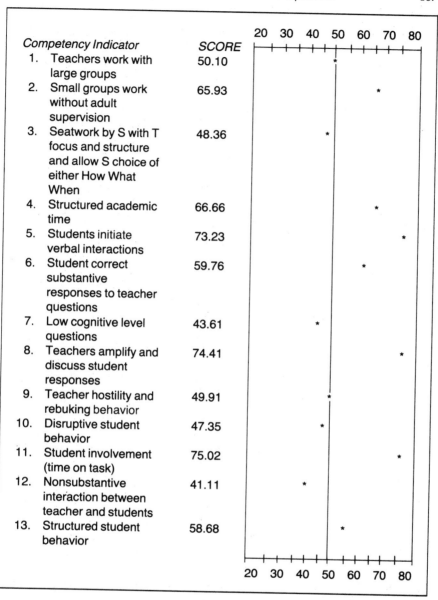

Competency Indicator	SCORE	20	30	40	50	60	70	80
1. Teachers work with large groups	50.10				*			
2. Small groups work without adult supervision	65.93						*	
3. Seatwork by S with T focus and structure and allow S choice of either How What When	48.36				*			
4. Structured academic time	66.66						*	
5. Students initiate verbal interactions	73.23							*
6. Student correct substantive responses to teacher questions	59.76					*		
7. Low cognitive level questions	43.61			*				
8. Teachers amplify and discuss student responses	74.41							*
9. Teacher hostility and rebuking behavior	49.91				*			
10. Disruptive student behavior	47.35			*				
11. Student involvement (time on task)	75.02							*
12. Nonsubstantive interaction between teacher and students	41.11			*				
13. Structured student behavior	58.68					*		

FIGURE 9.4 Medley competency indicator profile of teacher A.

then be assessed precisely, and in comparison with changes on other competency indicators in the teacher's profile, as well as with changes of other teachers on this same competency indicator.

Figure 9.7 reports pre- and post- scores for 10 teachers who were

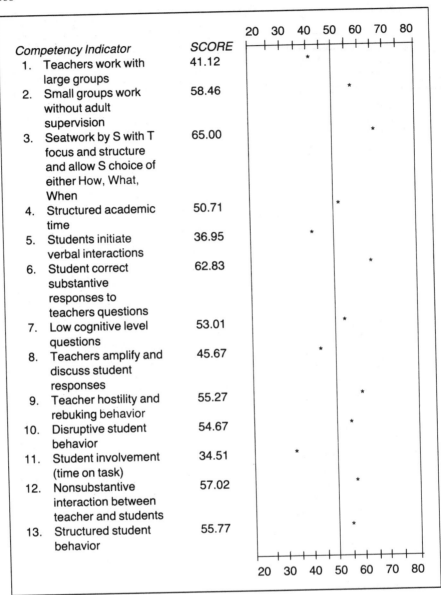

FIGURE 9.5   Medley competency indicator profile of teacher B.

observed before and after nine weeks of staff development designed to increase several behaviors, including the one listed. You will note, that teachers 2 had the most significant change, a decrease of two standard deviations.

Teacher No.	Score
1	64.83
2	75.02
3	41.05
4	60.81
5	42.76
6	47.39
7	39.92
8	52.69
9	36.43
10	54.30
11	50.47
12	67.20
13	69.34
14	38.69
15	64.97
16	53.27
17	47.45
18	34.51
19	50.50
20	44.62
21	47.44
22	47.34
23	50.91
24	37.98
25	54.12
26	57.60
27	35.81
28	45.14
29	42.50
30	48.02
31	52.65
32	49.96
33	66.90
34	47.31
35	42.17
36	42.15
37	40.35
38	44.22
39	55.17
40	35.11
41	55.47
42	65.37
43	49.88

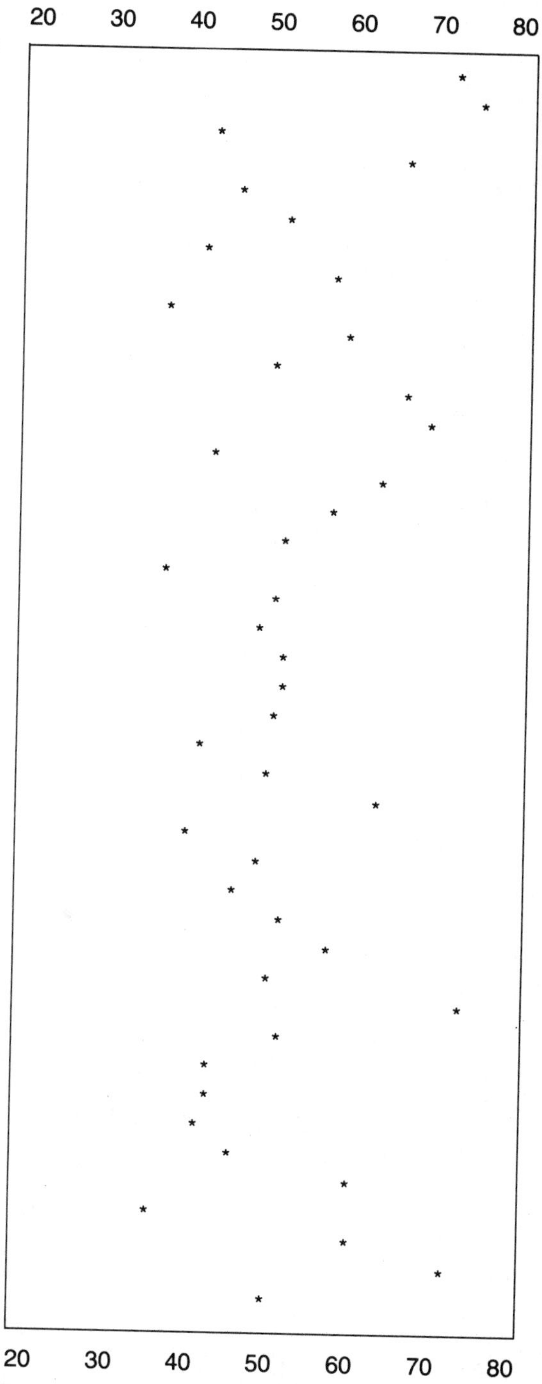

FIGURE 9.6 The profile of scores of a group of 43 teachers on Medley competency indicator 11: *student involvement (time on task)*.

Teacher Number	Score
1301 2301	39.58 (PR) 45.96 (PO)
1302 2302	71.89 (PR) 52.05 (PO)
1303 2303	53.96 (PR) 43.68 (PO)
1304 2304	53.15 (PR) 40.79 (PO)
1305 2305	60.30 (PR) 64.15 (PO)
1306 2306	46.05 (PR) 38.18 (PO)
1307 2307	47.92 (PR) 37.59 (PO)
1308 2308	60.45 (PR) 64.03 (PO)
1309 2309	36.75 (PR) 43.35 (PO)
1310 2310	43.16 (PR) 56.99 (PO)

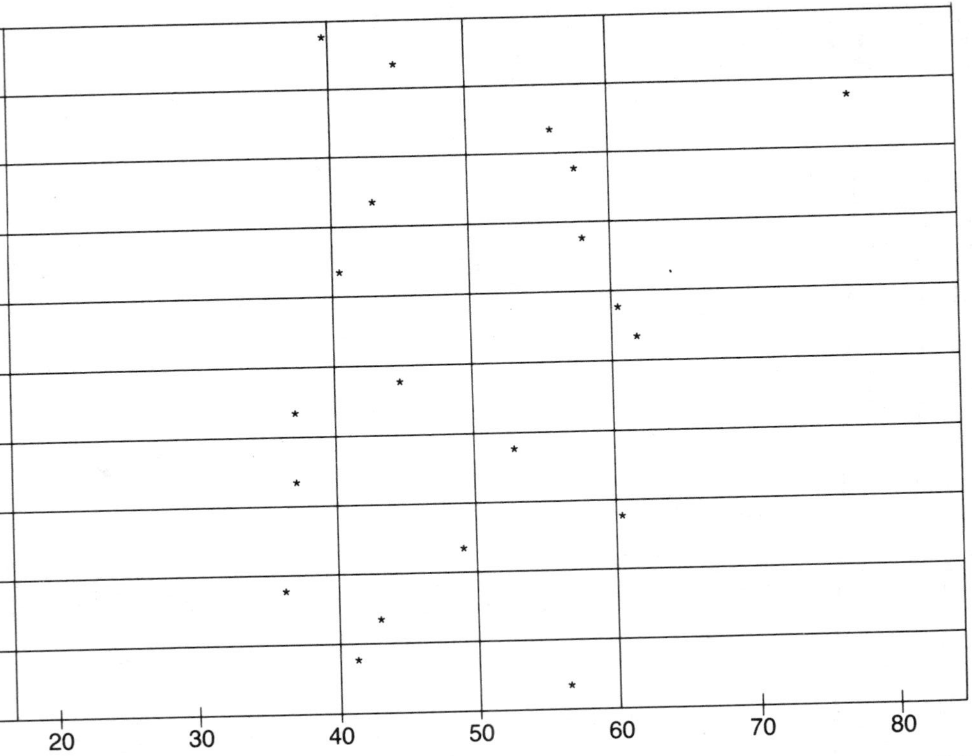

FIGURE 9.7 Profile of changes in scores of 10 teachers on a single competency indicator (PR represents pretest scores; PO represents posttest scores).

Monitoring Curriculum Change.   When the decision is made to intro-duce a new program or curriculum, before-and-after observations should be made in all the classes involved; and, if there is a control group in which no change is made, the same kinds of observations should be made in all the classes in the control group as well.

It will then be possible, by comparing group profiles, to ascertain whether and how the teacher behaviors in the classrooms changed with the introduction of the new curriculum. If there is a control group, it is possible to compare the changes in the experimental group with any changes that take place in the control group. In many cases, the nature of the new curriculum will be such that certain kinds of behaviors should be different in a class in which the new curriculum is being implemented correctly. In such instances it is possible to measure how well the curriculum is being implemented in each classroom in the study, or whether unintended side effects are occurring.

Researchers have found that this is likely to vary considerably from classroom to classroom; it is not unusual to find classrooms in which a new curriculum or method is, to all intents and purposes, not im-plemented at all. If effects on pupils' test scores are being examined in order to assess the effectiveness of the new curriculum, there is a possibility that the curriculum may be judged ineffective without having really been tried at all. Observational data can prevent such a fiasco by revealing the failure in implementation.

When there are wide variations in the degree of implementation in different classrooms, observational measurements can be used to adjust measures of pupil gains to remove the effects of these variations. In larger experiments, outcomes can be correlated with behaviors to see whether teachers who implement well produce greater pupil achievement gains than teachers who implement poorly. Spaulding (1982) has reported a series of well-designed studies which use both teacher and pupil observation measurements. These studies yield impressive results and illustrate this approach.

Comparing Programs.   Different programs may also be compared in similar fashion. Figure 9.8 shows mean profiles on the 22 Toledo competency indicators of four groups of teachers. Two of the groups consisted of student teachers from two different preservice programs, and the other two consisted of teachers employed full-time. The four profiles are superimposed on one another to facilitate comparisons. It is interesting to note that the profile of students from the University of Toledo, where these competencies are defined as program goals, as might be expected is much flatter than the others. It is also interesting to see that the Georgia State teachers' profile is more elevated, indicating generally higher level of competence than the student teachers at Toledo

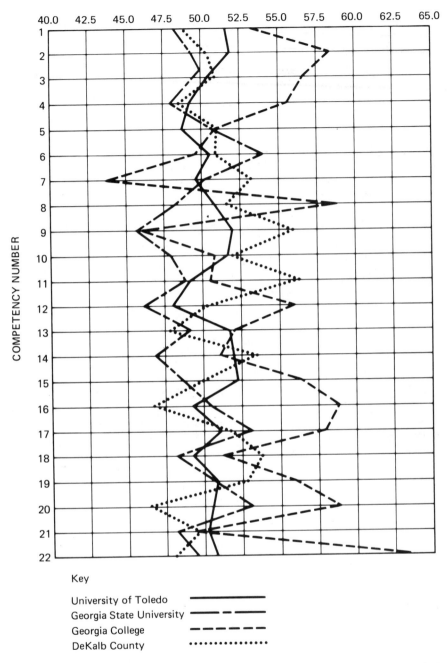

FIGURE 9.8 Profile of mean scores of four groups of teachers on 22 Toledo competency indicators.

possess. It would be interesting to know why certain competency indicators show greater differences than others.

Making Personnel Decisions. By personnel decisions we mean decisions related to staff utilization, such as decisions whether to hire or rehire a teacher, to recommend her for tenure or merit pay, and so forth. A full treatment of this difficult topic is, of course, outside the scope of this volume; we will only make some comments on how measurement-based teacher evaluations may be used to supply information relevant to such decisions.

Legal Issues. The view presented here parallels that of the development of science and of measurement devices. But we recognize that there is another view, and that the difference has not been resolved in the courts. One of the hallmarks of science is precision of reporting on the accuracy of its procedures and its findings. In teacher evaluation, the accuracy of our measuring instruments and the validity of our predictions are likely to be limited. One might conclude that by revealing this information about the limited accuracy of our measures, and their limited predictive power, we would arm a skillful defense attorney to argue a case in which a teacher has been denied certification, tenure, or promotion. The use of an explicit measurement system also opens the question of whether all the aspects of effective teaching have been identified and taken into account—and whether if this had been done the applicant might be differently evaluated. Nevertheless, it seems to us that the approach we are recommending is superior to any alternative based on subjective judgments. If a school district is reluctant to face the legal challenge of making decisions on the basis of objective scores and standards, there still is the compromise position of using objective measurement procedures as the basis for professional judgment.

Within legal limits, defensible use either of individual competency indicators or of profiles of competency indicators as a basis for personnel decisions is possible if the measures are valid and reliable, and if the criteria and standards to be used are public. This suggests the wisdom of doing everything possible to gain an advance consensus on both the criteria and the standards to be used. If that is not possible, differences should be negotiated until everyone concerned has had input and knows what the criteria and standards finally adopted are.

It will rarely be possible to define a decision criterion or standard based on a single competency indicator, although in many cases a single criterion or standard based on the total of the scores on several competency indicators may be satisfactory (especially if used in combination with other criteria not related directly to skill in interactive teaching). Of course, multiple criteria may be adopted. For example, if something like the Toledo competency indicators were used, criteria might be defined in each of three areas, all of which would need to be satisfied.

The problem of setting standards, minimum passing scores, is one to which no one, so far as we know, has a satisfactory solution. Our recommendation is that all standards be based on norms; that is, that a policy of requiring a score better than those of a specified proportion of teachers in the norm group be adopted. Just what this proportion should be is something the authors are not qualified to say.

Concluding Remarks. The examples we have given above represent only a few of the ways in which the rich and detailed information measurement-based teacher evaluation yields about what goes on in classrooms can be used. Although we have not emphasized the point, you must realize that the ultimate effect of any of these procedures on your school program depends on the validities of the competency indicators used. Content validity is not enough; the important question is whether what you and your staff agree to call competency indicators really deserve the name. This is the question we shall take up in the next section of this chapter.

VALIDATING COMPETENCY INDICATORS

A valid or true competency indicator is a dimension of behavior that is positively related to teacher effectiveness (i.e., to how much students learn from the teacher in question). Unless students learn more, on the average, from teachers who score high on a competency indicator than from teachers who score low on the same competency indicator, what that key measures is not a true competency, and scores on the keys are not competency indicators.

Estimating Outcomes of Teaching

In order to validate a measure of teacher performance believed to be an indicator of teacher competence we need an accurate, unbiased estimate of the results the teacher gets, that is, of the amount of student learning that can be attributed to her performance in the classroom.

Regressed Gain

The procedure for estimating the outcomes of teaching which has conventionally been followed is to estimate *regressed gain* or *residual gain* for each class—that is, to obtain an estimate of mean gains in the class in which the effects of mean initial ability (pretest, IQ or socioeconomic status) in the class is controlled statistically. These gain scores are then correlated across classrooms with the teacher competence measure to be validated. It has been recognized recently that this procedure is free of bias only when pupils are randomly assigned to classrooms (Campbell and Erlebacher, 1971), a situation which rarely if ever is found in schools.

An Alternative Approach

There is a relatively little-known alternative procedure which has been shown to be free of this kind of bias (Baldwin, 1981), which is described in Appendix D. This procedure yields a score Y' for each teacher which estimates how much a student with any given pretest score (or IQ, socioeconomic status, etc.) would be expected to learn in that teacher's class.

The validity of a competency indicator is estimated by calculating the partial correlation between the competency measure and Y' holding constant other factors, such as the average ability of the class, which may also affect the amount a student learns in that class.

A Caution and a Plan

What should you do when a competency indicator that you feel measures an extremely important competency fails to correlate with estimated gains of students? Should you conclude that the competency it is supposed to measure is not a true competency?

Not necessarily. A better plan would be to examine the scoring key carefully, and perhaps to refine it along the lines suggested in Chapter 8, and try out the new version. If you have a substantial amount of data, you might do an item analysis with student gains as the criterion, and revise or replace items that do not discriminate.

It is only through this sort of tinkering that our knowledge of the nature of teacher competence, and therefore our ability to measure it and help teachers increase their competence, can grow. If you have no time to do this yourself because you are too busy with more urgent tasks (surely none could be more important!), get help from some university—most professors would be willing to help you for the sake of the data alone, because such data are hard for professors to come by.

SUMMARY

Readers who have persisted to this point will scarcely need to be told that the implementation of a measurement-based teacher evaluation program is not a simple undertaking; not nearly so simple as adopting some teacher rating scale with important-sounding dimensions on it, passing it out to your administrators, and going on to some less troublesome task. But such simple solutions to complex problems almost never work; sooner or later the same problem will come up again. There is ample evidence that the current "solution" to the problem of evaluating teachers is not working.

The solution we have described in this volume may be difficult and complex, but it is a solution; if you keep after it the problem will at least diminish, if it does not go away altogether. The solution is difficult and complex only in the developmental stages; once a measurement-based system is in place it should be fully as easy to operate as what we do now, and probably cheaper than any reasonably adequate system based on ratings would be, if (indeed) any reasonable adequate system based on ratings were possible.

And, as we have seen in this chapter, a measurement-based system has two huge strengths that are unique. One is the wealth of useful information it provides; and the other is the capacity for self-correction intrinsic to it.

Sooner or later, we as educators or teacher educators will have to face up to the teacher evaluation problem; when we do, the direction indicated, however imperfectly, in this volume is the direction we will have to go. And the sooner we start, the better.

BIBLIOGRAPHY

Baldwin, G. L., Jr. "A Comparison of the Technique of Within-Class Regression to Analyses of Covariance in the Analysis of Non-Equivalent Groups." Ph.D. diss., University of Virginia, 1981.

Campbell, D. T., and A. Erlebacher. "How Regression Artifacts in Quasi-Experimental Evaluations can Mistakenly Make Compensatory Education Look Harmful." In J. Helmuth, ed., *The Disadvantaged Child.* vol. 3. New York: Brunner/Mazel, 1971.

Coker, Homer, and Joan G. Coker. *Classroom Observations Keyed for Effectiveness Research—Observer Training Manual.* Atlanta, GA: Georgia State University/Carroll County Teacher Corps Project, 1971(a).

——— *Classroom Observations Keyed for Effectiveness Research—User's Manual.* Atlanta, GA: Georgia State University/Carroll County Teacher Corps Project, 1979(b).

Medley, Donald M. *Teacher Competence and Teacher Effectiveness: A Review of Process-Product Research.* Washington, DC: American Association of Colleges for Teacher Education, 1977.

Medley, Donald M., Homer Coker, Joan G. Coker, Jeffery L. Lorentz, Robert S. Soar, and Robert L. Spaulding. "Assessing Teacher Performance from

Observed Competency Indicators Defined by Classroom Teachers." *Journal of Educational Research*, 1981, 74, 197–216.

Taebel, Donald K., and Joan G. Coker. "Teaching Effectiveness in Elementary Classroom Music: Relationships among Competency Measures, Pupil Product Measures, and Certain Attribute Variables." *Journal of Research in Music Education*, Fall, 1980.

Appendixes

The Research Base

RESULTS AND CONCLUSIONS

As we have pointed out, the primary objective of this report was to provide direct access to the findings of research on teacher effectiveness to teacher educators who lack the time, inclination, or technical competence it would take to dig them out personally. Tables 3–43 were designed to accomplish this. Anyone who reads the next few pages of this report can learn from them how to read these tables at a glance. Thus, whatever relevant, important, and reliable findings the research contains are at one's disposal.

Notes on Interpreting the Tables

Table 1 illustrates the format in which the 613 relationships are displayed in Tables 3–43. (These tables are grouped together following the text; Table 2 is not included because it is not pertinent to this discussion.)

The table title at the head of the page is meant to identify a common element in the process measures listed at the left under the heading *Behavior Item*. These are identified where possible by the actual item or category name used in the study; or when the name was not descriptive, a brief descriptive phrase is employed.

At the right of the list of behaviors is a column indicating the grade level or

This appendix was excerpted (with minor change) from *Teacher Competence and Teacher Effectiveness* by Donald M. Medley. Copyright 1977 by the American Association of Colleges for Teacher Education. Reprinted by permission.

Table 1 - PUPIL INITIATIONS

BEHAVIOR ITEM	GRADE	LOW SES PUPILS						HIGH SES PUPILS						SOURCE SYMBOL
		READING GAINS complexity		ARITHMETIC GAINS complexity		AFFECTIVE GAINS		READING GAINS complexity		ARITHMETIC GAINS complexity		AFFECTIVE GAINS		
		low	high	low	high	school	self	low	high	low	high	school	self	
Pupil-initiated vs. teacher-initiated interchanges	I									L[1]				WGC OScAR
Pupil-initiated interaction vs. response to teacher	I-II	L[1]		L[1]										S73 RCS1
Pupil initiates substantive interchange	II			L[1]						L[1]				WGC OScAR
Pupils speak freely	II		L[1]					L[1]						WGC OScAR
Pupil task-related comments to adults	III			L										SK 388a
Pupil questions, requests, commands--non-academic	III			L	L									SK 477c, 346a
All non-responsive pupil utterances to adults	III			L	L									SK 343a
Pupil initiates substantive interchange	III-VIII		H[1]	H[1]	H[2]					H[1]	H[2]			WGC OScAR
Pupil volunteers information vs. pupil asks for information	III-VIII	H[1]						H[1]						WGC OScAR
Total pupil-initiated contacts	IV									H	H			GG
Pupil-initiated vs. teacher-initiated substantive interchange	IX-XII	H[1]						H[1]						WGC OScAR

levels of the classes in which the behaviors were observed. At the extreme right, under the heading *Source Symbol*, are codes identifying the studies from which the relationships reported for each behavior item came; when available, the number assigned to the item in the actual instrument is also included. This will enable the reader to refer to the original study and identify specific items.

The studies are listed by code in Appendix A, with details about sample, instrumentation, and the like. Each letter in the body—*L, M,* or *H*—identifies a strong relationship; and the location of the letter identifies the two variables related: to the left is the behavior or process variable; above is the teacher effectiveness or product measure. Thus the first *L* on the upper left tells us that a strong negative relationship was found between *Pupil-initiated vs. teacher-initiated interchanges* and gains on an arithmetic test made up of items of high complexity, in classes which contained pupils of low socioeconomic status. We also note that they were first-grade classes, that the relationship was reported in the Carroll County-West Georgia study (WGC), and that the process instrument used was OScAR.

The superscript (in this instance, a 1) is used to indicate that the relationship is shown twice in the same row of the table; in this case, it also appears under high complexity arithmetic gains in classes with pupils of high socioeconomic status. Reference to Appendix A will verify that in the Carroll County (WGC) study, classes observed had pupils of mixed low and high socioeconomic status.

In the second line, we note a negative relationship between *pupil-initiated interaction vs. response to teacher* and gains on low-complexity reading test items, and between the same item and gains on low-complexity arithmetic test items, for pupils of low socioeconomic status in grades 1 and 2, reported in Soar 1973 and based on the Reciprocal Category System, Factor 1. The superscript on the two *L*s indicates that the measure used contained items on both reading and arithmetic.

In reading the tables, the reader may interpret *L* as meaning that the frequency of the behavior in question is *low* in the classes of effective teachers; or, in the case of bipolar measures (like the first two items in Table 1 which contrast two extremes), that the effective teacher will be at the lower of the two poles. Thus, effective teachers in the lower grades, according to these two studies, tend to initiate more, and permit their pupils to initiate fewer, interactions than the ineffective teachers do.

The line across the table divides results found in grades 3 or lower from those found in the higher grades. Because some studies combined results in grade 3 with those in higher grades, there is some overlap.

Note that the items below the line, which are similar to those above the line, tend to show strong positive relationships—*H*s. In the upper grades, the frequency of pupil initiations seems to be *high* in classes of effective teachers—a reversal from the lower grades.

This particular table does not show any curvilinear relationships—does not contain any *M*s. An *M* should be interpreted as meaning that the frequency of the behavior in question is intermediate in the effective teacher's class, and may be either low or high in the ineffective teacher's class.

Table 3 - GROUP SIZE

BEHAVIOR ITEM	GRADE	LOW SES PUPILS						HIGH SES PUPILS						SOURCE SYMBOL
		READING GAINS		ARITHMETIC GAINS		AFFECTIVE GAINS		READING GAINS		ARITHMETIC GAINS		AFFECTIVE GAINS		
		complexity low	high	complexity low	high	school	self	complexity low	high	complexity low	high	school	self	
Adult with large group of pupils-general	III	H		H		H								SK89 et al.
Adult with large group of pupils-arithmetic	III	H		H		H	H							SK 123,135
Adult with large group of pupils-reading	III	H		H		H								SK 146,158
Teacher, aide, or any adult with small group of pupils	III	L	L											SK 106,88, 94
Small group with teacher (arithmetic)	III		L	L										SK 122
Small group with any adult (arithmetic)	III	L	L											SK 134
Adult (other than teacher) working with (small) group	II			L^1			L			L^1				BTES AP
Small group with teacher, aide, or any adult (reading)	III	L	L				L							SK 157,145, 149

Table 4 - SMALL GROUP WITHOUT ADULT

BEHAVIOR ITEM	GRADE	LOW SES PUPILS READING GAINS (complexity low)	(complexity high)	ARITHMETIC GAINS (complexity low)	(complexity high)	AFFECTIVE GAINS (school)	(self)	HIGH SES PUPILS READING GAINS (complexity low)	(complexity high)	ARITHMETIC GAINS (complexity low)	(complexity high)	AFFECTIVE GAINS (school)	(self)	SOURCE SYMBOL
Pupils work without teacher--seatwork, parallel or instructional group	I	L^1	L^2	L^1	L^2									S73 FLA6
Pupils work without teacher--seatwork, parallel or instructional group	II	L^1	L^2	L^1	L^2	L								S73 FLA6
Hours of instructional learning without teacher vs. hours of structured learning with teacher	K,II	L^1	L^2	L^1	L^2									S73 CDR3
Small group working independently (arithmetic)	III	L		L		H	L							SK 138
Two pupils working independently (arithmetic)	III	L		L										SK 137
Two pupils working independently (reading)	III			L										SK 160

Table 5 - SEATWORK

| BEHAVIOR ITEM | GRADE | LOW SES PUPILS | | | | | | HIGH SES PUPILS | | | | | | SOURCE SYMBOL |
| | | READING GAINS | | ARITHMETIC GAINS | | AFFECTIVE GAINS | | READING GAINS | | ARITHMETIC GAINS | | AFFECTIVE GAINS | | |
		complexity low	high	complexity low	high	school	self	complexity low	high	complexity low	high	school	self	
Activity: seatwork	II	L^1						L^1						BTES R15
Pupil self-directed and task oriented	II	L^1		L^2				L^1		L^2				WGC FLACCS
All pupils work on same task at same time, are responsible for same assignments, no individualized assignments	II	L^1		L^1			L							S73 TP4
All pupils working independently (arithmetic)	III			L		H	L							SK 142
Teacher assigns large amount of seatwork	II-III	H		H^1						H^1				GE 18
Teacher individualizes assignments	II													WGC TP17

Table 6 - ACADEMIC TIME

BEHAVIOR ITEM	GRADE	LOW SES PUPILS READING GAINS complexity low	high	ARITHMETIC GAINS complexity low	high	AFFECTIVE GAINS school	self	HIGH SES PUPILS READING GAINS complexity low	high	ARITHMETIC GAINS complexity low	high	AFFECTIVE GAINS school	self	SOURCE SYMBOL
Structured vs. unstructured time	I-II	H^1	H^2	H^1	H^2									S73 CDR6
Total academic verbal interactions	I	H		H	H									SK 435a
Structured learning with teacher	II	L^1	H^2	L^1	H^2									S73 CDR3
Total academic verbal interactions	III			H	H									SK 566c
Percent of observations in which an academic activity is occurring	III	H		H	H									SK 242
Total class duration	III			H	H									SK 17
Unoccupied child	III			L	L									SK 77

Table 7 - TIME SPENT ON READING

BEHAVIOR ITEM	GRADE	LOW SES PUPILS						HIGH SES PUPILS						SOURCE SYMBOL
		READING GAINS complexity		ARITHMETIC GAINS complexity		AFFECTIVE GAINS		READING GAINS complexity		ARITHMETIC GAINS complexity		AFFECTIVE GAINS		
		low	high	low	high	school	self	low	high	low	high	school	self	
Reading activities (self report)	I	H												CRAFT log
Reading, alphabet, language development activities	I	H	H											SK 67
Number of pupils involved in reading	I	H	H											SK 163
Reading, alphabet, language development activities	III			H										SK 67
Number of pupils involved in reading	III			H	H									SK 163
Time teacher spends preparing and teaching reading (self report)	II	L^1	L^2					L^1	L^2					BTES WD1
Total reading time (self report) (Phonovisual method)	II		L											CRAFT log
Time teaching decoding skills in reading (self report)	V	L^1						L^1						BTES WD2

Table 8 – TIME SPENT IN READING-RELATED ACTIVITIES

BEHAVIOR ITEM	GRADE	LOW SES PUPILS — READING GAINS complexity low	high	LOW SES PUPILS — ARITHMETIC GAINS complexity low	high	LOW SES PUPILS — AFFECTIVE GAINS school	self	HIGH SES PUPILS — READING GAINS complexity low	high	HIGH SES PUPILS — ARITHMETIC GAINS complexity low	high	HIGH SES PUPILS — AFFECTIVE GAINS school	self	SOURCE SYMBOL
Supportive rate (self report)	I		H											CRAFT log
Supportive activities (self report) (Language experience method)	II	L												CRAFT log
Listening to stories (self report) (Phonovisual method)	I		H											CRAFT log
Listening to stories (self report) (Language experience method)	II	L	L											CRAFT log
Listening to poetry (self report) (Basal reader method)	II		H											CRAFT log
Percent of time in spelling	II-III							M	M	M				BE 5(T4)
Percent of time in language arts	II-III			L						L				RE 2(T4)

Table 9 - TIME SPENT ON ARITHMETIC

BEHAVIOR ITEM	GRADE	LOW SES PUPILS						HIGH SES PUPILS						SOURCE SYMBOL
		READING GAINS complexity		ARITHMETIC GAINS complexity		AFFECTIVE GAINS		READING GAINS complexity		ARITHMETIC GAINS complexity		AFFECTIVE GAINS		
		low	high	low	high	school	self	low	high	low	high	school	self	
Numbers, mathematics, arithmetic activities	III			H	H									SK 66
Number of pupils involved in arithmetic	III			H	H									SK 140
Frequency of teaching operation skills in arithmetic (self report)	II			H^1	H^2					H^1	H^2			ETES VD

Table 10 - TIME SPENT IN OTHER SUBJECTS

BEHAVIOR ITEM	GRADE	LOW SES PUPILS READING GAINS complexity low	high	ARITHMETIC GAINS complexity low	high	AFFECTIVE GAINS school	self	HIGH SES PUPILS READING GAINS complexity low	high	ARITHMETIC GAINS complexity low	high	AFFECTIVE GAINS school	self	SOURCE SYMBOL
Art work with reading (self report)	II	L												CRAFT log
Total science time (self report)	II	H	H											CRAFT log
Total social studies time (self report)	II		H											CRAFT log
Percent of time in social studies	II-III			M						M				BE 7 (T4)
Percent of time in art	II-III						L		H					BE 4 (T4)
Group time	III	L		L										SK 62
Story, music, dancing activities	III			L										SK 63

Table 11 – READING MATERIALS

BEHAVIOR ITEM	GRADE	LOW SES PUPILS READING GAINS complexity low	high	ARITHMETIC GAINS complexity low	high	AFFECTIVE GAINS school	self	HIGH SES PUPILS READING GAINS complexity low	high	ARITHMETIC GAINS complexity low	high	AFFECTIVE GAINS school	self	SOURCE SYMBOL
Use of basal reader other than state adopted (self report)	II		L^1						L^1					BTES WD
Use of books, etc. (secondary)	II	H^1	H^2					H^1	H^2					BTES R11
Wide range of informative materials available	II		L^1				H^2		L^1				H^2	WGC TP4
Use of games (self report)	II		L^1						L^1					BTES WD
Wide range of informative materials available	III-VIII	H^1					H^2	H^1					H^2	WGC TP4
Use of workbook other than basic (self report)	V							L^1						BTES WD
Use of board, etc. (secondary)	V							L^1						BTES R12

Table 12 – ARITHMETIC TEACHING MATERIALS

BEHAVIOR ITEM	GRADE	LOW SES PUPILS						HIGH SES PUPILS						SOURCE SYMBOL
		READING GAINS		ARITHMETIC GAINS		AFFECTIVE GAINS		READING GAINS		ARITHMETIC GAINS		AFFECTIVE GAINS		
		complexity low	high	complexity low	high	school	self	complexity low	high	complexity low	high	school	self	
Use of programmed materials (self report)	II			H^1	H^2					H^1	H^2			BTES WD
...teacher-made materials (self report)	II			H^1	H^2					H^1	H^2			BTES WD
...individualized materials (self report)	II				H^1						H^1			BTES WD
Games	II			L^1						L^1				BTES R19
Games, toys, play equipment present	III			L										SK 25
Audio-visual equipment present	III			L										SK 37
Audio-visual equipment used	III			L										SK 38

Table 13 – STEADY-STATE TEACHER TALK

BEHAVIOR ITEM	GRADE	LOW SES PUPILS — READING GAINS (complexity low)	LOW SES — READING GAINS (high)	LOW SES — ARITHMETIC GAINS (low)	LOW SES — ARITHMETIC GAINS (high)	LOW SES — AFFECTIVE GAINS (school)	LOW SES — AFFECTIVE GAINS (self)	HIGH SES PUPILS — READING GAINS (complexity low)	HIGH SES — READING GAINS (high)	HIGH SES — ARITHMETIC GAINS (low)	HIGH SES — ARITHMETIC GAINS (high)	HIGH SES — AFFECTIVE GAINS (school)	HIGH SES — AFFECTIVE GAINS (self)	SOURCE SYMBOL
Steady-state teacher talk vs. pupil talk	I	L^1		L^1										S73 RCS5
Teacher tells story, pupils attentive, interested	II	L^1	L^2					L^1	L^2					WGC CS1
Steady-state teacher talk vs. pupil talk	II			H^1				H^1						S73 RCS5
Teacher lectures, pupils bored	II	H^1	H^2					H^1	H^2					WGC CS2
Extended teacher talk and inquiry vs. drill	III-VI							H		H		H		S66 F3
Business-like lecture method, insistence on attention to tasks and conformity	IV,VI							H	H					Sp F6

Table 14 - PUPIL INITIATIONS

BEHAVIOR ITEM	GRADE	LOW SES READING low	LOW READING high	LOW ARITH low	LOW ARITH high	LOW AFFECT school	LOW AFFECT self	HIGH SES READING low	HIGH READING high	HIGH ARITH low	HIGH ARITH high	HIGH AFFECT school	HIGH AFFECT self	SOURCE SYMBOL
Pupil-initiated vs. teacher-initiated interchanges	I													WGC OScAR
Pupil-initiated interaction vs. response to teacher	I-II	L^1		L^1						L^1				S73 RCS1
Pupil initiates substantive interchange	II			L^1						L^1				WGC OScAR
Pupils speak freely	II	L^1		L^1				L^1						WGC OScAR
Pupil task-related comments to adults	III			L				L^1						SK 388a
Pupil questions, requests, commands--non-academic	III			L	L									SK 477c, 346a
All non-responsive pupil utterances to adults	III			L	L									SK 343a
Pupil initiates substantive interchange	III-VIII	H^1		H^1	H^2			H^1						WGC OScAR
Pupil volunteers information vs. pupil asks for information	III-VIII									H^1	H^2			WGC OScAR
Total pupil-initiated contacts	IV									H	H			GG
Pupil-initiated vs. teacher-initiated substantive interchange	IX-XII	H^1						H^1						WGC OScAR

Table 15 - TEACHER ENCOURAGES PUPIL PARTICIPATION

BEHAVIOR ITEM	GRADE	LOW SES PUPILS			HIGH SES PUPILS			SOURCE SYMBOL
		READING GAINS (complexity low high)	ARITHMETIC GAINS (complexity low high)	AFFECTIVE GAINS (school self)	READING GAINS (complexity low high)	ARITHMETIC GAINS (complexity low high)	AFFECTIVE GAINS (school self)	
Teacher listens to pupils and provides feedback	II	L^1			L^1			WGC FL27
Teacher pauses, asks for questions, and answers them before proceeding	II	L^1 L^2			L^1 L^2			WGC FLA
Short feedback on pupil question	II-III		H		L	H		BE L83
Teacher gives long feedback on pupil question	II-III	L	L		L			BE L84
Teacher praises pupil opinion question	II-III·	H						BE Q126

Table 16 - NUMBER OF TEACHER QUESTIONS

BEHAVIOR ITEM	GRADE	LOW SES PUPILS						HIGH SES PUPILS						SOURCE SYMBOL
		READING GAINS		ARITHMETIC GAINS		AFFECTIVE GAINS		READING GAINS		ARITHMETIC GAINS		AFFECTIVE GAINS		
		complexity low	high	complexity low	high	school	self	complexity low	high	complexity low	high	school	self	
Pupil responses, academic	I	H		H	H									SK 360a, 491c
Ratio of total opportunities pupil has to respond to total time (arithmetic)	II-III	L								H				BE T169
Group response to question, command, etc.	III	H		H	H				H					SK 363a
Pupil responses, academic	III			H	H									SK 360a, 491c
Pupil responses, total	III			H										SK 358a
Direct academic questions, requests, commands	III			H	H									SK 353a, 451a, 582c

Table 17 - PUPIL RESPONSE TO TEACHER QUESTIONS

BEHAVIOR ITEM	GRADE	LOW SES PUPILS READING GAINS (complexity low / high)	LOW SES PUPILS ARITHMETIC GAINS (complexity low / high)	LOW SES PUPILS AFFECTIVE GAINS (school / self)	HIGH SES PUPILS READING GAINS (complexity low / high)	HIGH SES PUPILS ARITHMETIC GAINS (complexity low / high)	HIGH SES PUPILS AFFECTIVE GAINS (school / self)	SOURCE SYMBOL
Percent correct	II-III	H	H			H		BE C7
Percent incorrect	II-III	L L	L L		H H	L		BE C9
Percent no response	II-III		L					BE C11
Percent don't know	II-III	H	H		M	M		BE C10
Number wrong	IV					L L		GG
No response	IV					L L		GG
Percent correct	IV					H H		GG

Table 18 - LOW COGNITIVE LEVEL QUESTIONS

BEHAVIOR ITEM	GRADE	LOW SES PUPILS						HIGH SES PUPILS						SOURCE SYMBOL
		READING GAINS		ARITHMETIC GAINS		AFFECTIVE GAINS		READING GAINS		ARITHMETIC GAINS		AFFECTIVE GAINS		
		complexity low	high	complexity low	high	school	self	complexity low	high	complexity low	high	school	self	
Convergent teaching--teacher central, low-level questions, quick response, feedback	I-II	H^1	H^2	H^1	H^2									S73 TP1
Narrow questions, drill, pupil response	I	H^1		H^1										S73 RCS3
Questions calling for translation, interpretation	K-I	H^1		H^1										S72 TCB3
Questions calling for interpretation	K-I	H^1		H^1										S72 TCB1
Narrow questions, immediate feedback	II	H^1	H^2				L^3	H^1	H^2				L^3	WGC TP23
Direct academic questions, requests, commands	III	H	H	H	H									SK 451a, 582c,353a
Percent of substantive questions that offer limited choice of answers (yes-no, etc.)	II-III			L						H				BE B6
Recitation (low-level questions, quick feedback, narrow focus)	V	M^1					M^2	M^1					M^2	S73a F11

Table 19 - HIGH COGNITIVE LEVEL QUESTIONS

BEHAVIOR ITEM	GRADE	LOW SES PUPILS						HIGH SES PUPILS						SOURCE SYMBOL
		READING GAINS complexity		ARITHMETIC GAINS complexity		AFFECTIVE GAINS		READING GAINS complexity		ARITHMETIC GAINS complexity		AFFECTIVE GAINS		
		low	high	low	high	school	self	low	high	low	high	school	self	
Broad answers vs. narrow ones	K-I	L¹		L¹										S72 TCB2
Open questions and pupil self-evaluation and free inquiry vs. closed, text-oriented questions, teacher evaluation	I-II	L¹		L¹										S73 TP7
Concept attainment by discovery method	II	L¹						L¹						WGC CS8
Teacher avoids causing pupil doubt or uncertainty	III-VIII	H¹				H²		H¹				H²		WGC TP6

Table 20 - TEACHER REACTION TO PUPIL RESPONSE--GENERAL

BEHAVIOR ITEM	GRADE	LOW SES PUPILS READING GAINS complexity low	high	ARITHMETIC GAINS complexity low	high	AFFECTIVE GAINS school	self	HIGH SES PUPILS READING GAINS complexity low	high	ARITHMETIC GAINS complexity low	high	AFFECTIVE GAINS school	self	SOURCE SYMBOL
Total feedback (academic)	I	H	H	H	H									SK 412a, 543c
Positive corrective feedback (academic)	I			H	H									SK 406a
Asks new question	II-III			H	H			L						BE J69
Repeats question	II-III	L	L					H	H	L				BE S163
Acknowledgement, task-related, non-academic	III			L										SK 397a
No feedback (when answer is correct)	II-III		H	L				H		L				BE D14
Rephrases question or gives clue	II-III	H	H	M				M		H				BE S164
Criticism	III-IV	L[1]	L[2]					L[1]	L[2]					S66 F1
Non-evaluative	V									L	L			BTES AP

Table 21 - TEACHER REACTION TO PUPIL RESPONSE--AMPLIFICATION, EXTENSION

BEHAVIOR ITEM	GRADE	LOW SES PUPILS						HIGH SES PUPILS						SOURCE SYMBOL
		READING GAINS complexity low	high	ARITHMETIC GAINS complexity low	high	AFFECTIVE GAINS school	self	READING GAINS complexity low	high	ARITHMETIC GAINS complexity low	high	AFFECTIVE GAINS school	self	
Teacher uses pupil ideas, probes	K-I													Perham
Teacher responds to pupil & amplifies	II	L[1]		L[1]						L[1]				S73 RCS2
Teacher discusses pupil answer (total)	II-III	L		L[1]				H						BE J68
Teacher discusses correct answer	II-III	L						H	H					BE D15
Teacher discusses wrong answer	II-III	M		L										BE F31
Teacher helps pupil correct misperception	II			H[1]						H[1]				WGC TP8
Teacher helps pupil correct misperception	III-VIII							L[1]						WGC TP8

Table 22 – TEACHER REACTION TO WRONG ANSWER

BEHAVIOR ITEM	GRADE	LOW SES PUPILS						HIGH SES PUPILS						SOURCE SYMBOL
		READING GAINS complexity low high		ARITHMETIC GAINS complexity low high		AFFECTIVE GAINS school self		READING GAINS complexity low high		ARITHMETIC GAINS complexity low high		AFFECTIVE GAINS school self		
Repeats, rephrases, or asks new question	II-III	M	M	M	M				M	H	H			BE F35, 36,38
No feedback	II-III	L												BE F30
Gives the answer	II-III	L	L	L	M				H					BE F32
Criticizes	II-III	L	L	L	L			H	H	L	H			BE F29, J66B
Negates (neutral rejection)	IV									L	L			GG

Table 23 - TEACHER REACTION WHEN PUPIL RESPONSE IS PART CORRECT

BEHAVIOR ITEM	GRADE	LOW SES PUPILS						HIGH SES PUPILS						SOURCE SYMBOL
		READING GAINS complexity low	high	ARITHMETIC GAINS complexity low	high	AFFECTIVE GAINS school	self	READING GAINS complexity low	high	ARITHMETIC GAINS complexity low	high	AFFECTIVE GAINS school	self	
Gives the answer	II-III	H	H	H				H	H		L			BE E21
Calls on someone else	II-III	M						H	H	M				BE E22
Asks a new question	II-III	H		H					L		L			BE E27
Rephrases or gives clue (morning)	II-III	H							H					BE E26
Repeat, rephrase, or ask new question	II-III	L	H					L	L					BE E24

Table 24 - TEACHER REACTION WHEN PUPIL FAILS TO ANSWER QUESTION OR SAYS "DON'T KNOW"

BEHAVIOR ITEM	GRADE	LOW SES PUPILS						HIGH SES PUPILS						SOURCE SYMBOL
		READING GAINS		ARITHMETIC GAINS		AFFECTIVE GAINS		READING GAINS		ARITHMETIC GAINS		AFFECTIVE GAINS		
		low complexity	high complexity	low complexity	high complexity	school	self	low complexity	high complexity	low complexity	high complexity	school	self	
Repeats, rephrases, or asks new question	II-III	H	M	H	H			L	H	L	L			BE 163, G44
Rephrases (or gives clue)	II-III	H		L					L	H				BE 164
Repeats question	II-III	H		M				L		L				BE S163
Another pupil calls out the answer	II-III	H		M	H			L						BE G43, J74
Calls on another pupil (no answer)	II-III	M		M	M			H	H	H	H			BE J73
Calls on another pupil (don't know)	II-III	L	L					H		H	H			BE G42
Gives the answer	II-III							H	H	H	H			BE G41
Criticizes	II-III							H	H					BE G39

Table 25 – TEACHER WORKS WITH INDIVIDUAL PUPIL

BEHAVIOR ITEM	GRADE	LOW SES PUPILS — READING GAINS (complexity low / high)	ARITHMETIC GAINS (complexity low / high)	AFFECTIVE GAINS (school / self)	HIGH SES PUPILS — READING GAINS (complexity low / high)	ARITHMETIC GAINS (complexity low / high)	AFFECTIVE GAINS (school / self)	SOURCE SYMBOL
Teacher checking pupil work	II	H^1		H^2	H^1		H^2	BTES AP
Teacher-initiated dyadic contacts per unit of teaching time (reading groups)	II-III		H					BE U170
Proportion of teacher-initiated contacts that relate to class work	II-III	H M	M		L M	M		BE P146
Percent of time pupil works alone with teacher (arithmetic)	II		H^1			H^1		BTES AP
Proportion of arithmetic contacts that are teacher-initiated, private	II-III	H			L L	L		BE T167
Proportion of pupil-initiated work contacts accepted	II-III	H H	H L		L L	H L		BE N105
Ratio of teacher-initiated contacts to pupil-initiated contacts	IV					L L		GG
Pupil-initiated work contact with teacher feedback	IV					H H		GG

Table 26 - CLOSE ATTENTION TO PUPILS

BEHAVIOR ITEM	GRADE	LOW SES PUPILS READING GAINS complexity low	high	ARITHMETIC GAINS complexity low	high	AFFECTIVE GAINS school	self	HIGH SES PUPILS READING GAINS complexity low	high	ARITHMETIC GAINS complexity low	high	AFFECTIVE GAINS school	self	SOURCE SYMBOL
Proportion of teacher-initiated work contacts that involve "mere" observation	II-III	L							H	L	L			BE P148
Long feedback on pupil-initiated work contacts	II-III	H						L						BE 168
Proportion of teacher-initiated work contacts that involve long feedback	II-III	H		L	M			L		L	M			BE P150
Teacher attends pupil closely in task setting	I	H¹ L²		H¹	L²									S73 FLA8
Teacher attends pupil closely	III-VIII	L¹						L¹						WGC FLA

Table 27 - TEACHER MOBILITY

BEHAVIOR ITEM	GRADE	LOW SES PUPILS						HIGH SES PUPILS						SOURCE SYMBOL
		READING GAINS		ARITHMETIC GAINS		AFFECTIVE GAINS		READING GAINS		ARITHMETIC GAINS		AFFECTIVE GAINS		
		low complexity	high	low complexity	high	school	self	low complexity	high	low complexity	high	school	self	
Adult movement	III	H	H	H	H									SK 444a
Teacher stays at desk (self report)	II-III							L	L					BE Q3
Teacher at desk--working or available	II			H^1						H^1				BTES AP
Teacher aloof, detached from pupil activities	II	H^1	H^2			H^3		H^1	H^2			H^3		WGC TP16
Positive pupil affect and free teacher movement	V		L^1					L^1						S73a F5

Table 28 - MISCELLANEOUS TEACHING TECHNIQUES

BEHAVIOR ITEM	GRADE	LOW SES PUPILS						HIGH SES PUPILS						SOURCE SYMBOL
		READING GAINS complexity low	high	ARITHMETIC GAINS complexity low	high	AFFECTIVE GAINS school	self	READING GAINS complexity low	high	ARITHMETIC GAINS complexity low	high	AFFECTIVE GAINS school	self	
Giving and receiving information	K-I	H[1]		H[1]										S72 TCB
Giving and receiving information	II	L[1]	L[2]	L[1]	L[2]									S73 TCB
Naming (pictures, objects, etc.)	II	L[1]		L[1]										S73 TCB
Teacher uses non-verbal communication skills	II	H[1]					L[2]	H[1]					L[2]	WGC FLA
Visual demonstration	II	H[1]												BTES R20
Games	II				L[1]						L[1]			BTES R19
Teacher always gives instructions for follow-up seatwork (self report)	II-III	L							H					BE 85
Clear explanations (teacher explanation not followed by pupil question)	III-VIII			H[1]	H[2]	H[3]				H[1]	H[2]	H[3]		WGC OScAR
Teacher uses non-verbal communication skills	III-VIII	L[1]						L[1]						WGC FLA

Table 29 - MISCELLANEOUS TEACHING TECHNIQUES

BEHAVIOR ITEM	GRADE	LOW SES PUPILS						HIGH SES PUPILS						SOURCE SYMBOL
		READING GAINS complexity low	high	ARITHMETIC GAINS complexity low	high	AFFECTIVE GAINS school	self	READING GAINS complexity low	high	ARITHMETIC GAINS complexity low	high	AFFECTIVE GAINS school	self	
Variety of instructional contexts (i.e., groupings)	II	L[1]	L[2]	L[3]	L[4]			L[1]	L[2]	L[3]	L[4]			BTES WD4
Class grouped by skill needs	II				L[1]						L[1]			BTES WD
Class grouped by reading level	II		H[1]						H[1]					BTES WD
Teacher selects respondent before asking question	II-III	L						H						BE A1
Teacher calls on volunteer	II-III	M		L				H	M	H	M			BE A3
Teacher uses non-patterned turns	II-III	H						L						BE 27
Structuring comments at beginning and end of lesson	K-I			H[1]						H[1]				Perham
Structured learning with teacher	II	L		L	H									S73 CDR3

Table 30 – METHODOLOGICAL APPROACH TO THE TEACHING OF READING

BEHAVIOR ITEM	GRADE	LOW SES PUPILS						HIGH SES PUPILS						SOURCE SYMBOL
		READING GAINS complexity low high		ARITHMETIC GAINS complexity low high		AFFECTIVE GAINS school self		READING GAINS complexity low high		ARITHMETIC GAINS complexity low high		AFFECTIVE GAINS school self		
Using basal readers (self report) (basal reader method)	I	H												CRAFT log
Behavior resembles that of teacher using language experience approach (language experience method)	I	H												CRAFT OScAR
Behavior resembles that of teacher using language experience approach with audio-visual enrichment (language experience method with audio-visual enrichment)	I	H												CRAFT OScAR
Behavior resembles that of teacher using skills-centered approach (language experience method with audio-visual enrichment)	I	H												CRAFT OScAR
Behavior implementing language experience approach (phono-visual method)	II	L												CRAFT OScAR

(Continued)

Table 30 - Continued

BEHAVIOR ITEM	GRADE	LOW SES PUPILS						HIGH SES PUPILS						SOURCE SYMBOL
		READING GAINS complexity		ARITHMETIC GAINS complexity		AFFECTIVE GAINS		READING GAINS complexity		ARITHMETIC GAINS complexity		AFFECTIVE GAINS		
		low	high	low	high	school	self	low	high	low	high	school	self	
Behavior resembles that of teacher using language experience approach (basal reader method)	II		H											CRAFT OScAR
Behavior resembles that of teacher using language experience approach with audio-visual enrichment (language experience method with audio-visual enrichment)	II	L												CRAFT OScAR
Behavior resembles that of teacher using skill-centered approach (basal reader method)	II	L												CRAFT OScAR
Minutes/day in phonics activities (self report)	II	L												CRAFT log
Using experience chart	II	L												CRAFT log

Table 31 - TIME SPENT ON MANAGEMENT

BEHAVIOR ITEM	GRADE	LOW SES PUPILS — READING GAINS (complexity low / high)		ARITHMETIC GAINS (complexity low / high)		AFFECTIVE GAINS (school / self)		HIGH SES PUPILS — READING GAINS (complexity low / high)		ARITHMETIC GAINS (complexity low / high)		AFFECTIVE GAINS (school / self)		SOURCE SYMBOL
Managing behaviors	I	L^1				L^2		L^1				L^2		WGC OScAR
Controlling behavior	I	L												CRAFT OScAR
Time spent in transitions	II-III							M	M	M				BE8 (T4)
Number of times when pupils line up	II-III	L	L					L						BE Q87
Teacher provides feedback to pupil on his/her behavior	III-VIII	L^1	L^2	L^3	L^4			L^1	L^2	L^3	L^4			WGC FLA

Table 32 – MANAGEMENT SKILL I-III

BEHAVIOR ITEM	GRADE	LOW SES PUPILS						HIGH SES PUPILS						SOURCE SYMBOL
		READING GAINS complexity		ARITHMETIC GAINS complexity		AFFECTIVE GAINS		READING GAINS complexity		ARITHMETIC GAINS complexity		AFFECTIVE GAINS		
		low	high	low	high	school	self	low	high	low	high	school	self	
Control without criticism	I		H^1						H^1					WGC OScAR
Teacher maintains self-control	I		H^1			H^2	H^3		H^1			H^2	H^3	WGC FLA
Teacher uses variety of control techniques, non-verbal	II	H^1	H^2				L^3	H^1	H^2				L^3	WGC FLA
Proportion of management errors that are overreactions	II-III		H						L	H	H			BE R161
Teacher supports appropriate, ignores inappropriate, coping behavior	II		L^1	L^2					L^1	L^2				WGC CS10
Proportion of management errors that are errors in timing	II-III	L	L						L					BE R160

Table 33 – MANAGEMENT SKILL III-VIII

BEHAVIOR ITEM	GRADE	LOW SES PUPILS						HIGH SES PUPILS						SOURCE SYMBOL
		READING GAINS complexity		ARITHMETIC GAINS complexity		AFFECTIVE GAINS		READING GAINS complexity		ARITHMETIC GAINS complexity		AFFECTIVE GAINS		
		low	high	low	high	school	self	low	high	low	high	school	self	
Control without criticism	III-VIII		H^1	H^3	H^4	H^2	H^3		H^1	H^3	H^4	H^2	H^3	WGC OScAR
Teacher maintains self-control	III-VIII	H^1	H^2				H^5	H^1	H^2				H^5	WGC FLA
Teacher supports appropriate, ignores inappropriate, coping behavior	III-VIII		H^1						H^1					WGC CS10
Teacher uses variety of control techniques, verbal and non-verbal	III-VIII	L^1		L^2	L^3			L^1		L^2	L^3			WGC FLA
Supportive classroom management	III-VIII	L^1		L^2	L^3			L^1		L^2	L^3			WGC FLA

Table 34 – REBUKING BEHAVIOR

BEHAVIOR ITEM	GRADE	LOW SES PUPILS						HIGH SES PUPILS						SOURCE SYMBOL
		READING GAINS (complexity)		ARITHMETIC GAINS (complexity)		AFFECTIVE GAINS		READING GAINS (complexity)		ARITHMETIC GAINS (complexity)		AFFECTIVE GAINS		
		low	high	low	high	school	self	low	high	low	high	school	self	
Teacher hostility	I	L^1						L^1						WGC OScAR
Teacher rebukes, desists with inappropriate pupil behavior	I	L^1				L^2		L^1				L^2		WGC CS5
Negative motivation (language experience method with audio-visual enrichment)	I	L												CRAFT OScAR
Negative motivation (phono-visual method)	II	L												CRAFT OScAR
Negative motivation (except language experience method with audio-visual enrichment)	II	L												CRAFT OScAR
Teacher hostility	III–VIII	L^1		H^1	H^2	L^2	L^3	L^1				L^2	L^3	WGC OScAR
Teacher rebukes, desists with inappropriate pupil behavior	III–VIII						L^3			H^1	H^2		L^3	WGC CS5
Teacher criticisms, rebukes, desists	III–VIII	L^1				L^2	L^3	L^1				L^2	L^3	WGC OScAR
Dominative teaching style with control through shame, ridicule, and threat	IV,VI	L						L					L	Sp F2
Teacher warns pupil	IV									L	L			GG

Table 35 - DISRUPTIVE PUPIL BEHAVIOR

BEHAVIOR ITEM	GRADE	LOW SES PUPILS						HIGH SES PUPILS						SOURCE SYMBOL
		READING GAINS complexity low	high	ARITHMETIC GAINS complexity low	high	AFFECTIVE GAINS school	self	READING GAINS complexity low	high	ARITHMETIC GAINS complexity low	high	AFFECTIVE GAINS school	self	
Teacher talks over pupil noise	I	H												Bemis T1
Hyperactive pupil behavior	I	H												Bemis P2
Disruptive pupil behavior	I	L												Bemis P1
Pupil negative affect	I-II	L^1		L^1										S73 FLA7
Negative pupil behavior	II			L^1	L^2					L^1	L^2			BTES AP
Inappropriate pupil talk	II		L^1						L^1					BTES AP
Reduced deviant behavior	II			L^1		H^2				L^1		H^2		WGC FLA
Freq. discipline problems attributed to lack of interest (self report)	II-III			L						L				BE Q2
Reduced deviant behavior	III-VIII	H^1	H^2			H^3	H^4	H^1	H^2			H^3	H^4	WGC FLA
Inappropriate pupil talk	V			L^1						L^1				BTES AP

Table 36 - PUPIL INVOLVEMENT

BEHAVIOR ITEM	GRADE	LOW SES PUPILS						HIGH SES PUPILS						SOURCE SYMBOL
		READING GAINS (complexity)		ARITHMETIC GAINS (complexity)		AFFECTIVE GAINS		READING GAINS (complexity)		ARITHMETIC GAINS (complexity)		AFFECTIVE GAINS		
		low	high	low	high	school	self	low	high	low	high	school	self	
Pupil not responding to adult	III	H		H	H									SK 544c
Absence of withdrawn behavior	II			L^1						L^1				WGC FLA
Pupil calls out answer to teacher question	II-III		L						H					BE A4
Pupil on task, actively involved	III-VIII	H^1						H^1						WGC FLA
Pupils on task, involved	III-VIII	H^1		H^2				H^1		H^2				WGC TP3, 10
Absence of withdrawn behavior	III-VIII	H^1				H^2		H^1				H^2		WGC FLA
Pupil joins in class or group activity	V	L^1				L^2		L^1				L^2		BTES AP
Pupil attentive to subject of lesson	V			H^1						H^1				BTES AP

Table 37 – PUPILS SPEAK FREELY

BEHAVIOR ITEM	GRADE	LOW SES PUPILS						HIGH SES PUPILS						SOURCE SYMBOL
		READING GAINS		ARITHMETIC GAINS		AFFECTIVE GAINS		READING GAINS		ARITHMETIC GAINS		AFFECTIVE GAINS		
		complexity low	high	complexity low	high	school	self	complexity low	high	complexity low	high	school	self	
Pupils permitted to speak freely	II			L¹						L¹				WGC FLA
Pupils speak freely	II	L¹	L²					L¹	L²					WGC OScAR
Teacher encourages pupils to speak freely	II				H¹						H¹			WGC TP7, 15
Social interaction among pupils	III			H										SK 234
Verbal interaction among pupils	III			L	L									SK 476c
Teacher listens while pupils interact	III–VIII						L¹						L¹	WGC OScAR
Teacher encourages pupils to speak freely	III–VIII	L¹				H²	L³	L¹				H²	L³	WGC TP7, 15
Pupils speak freely	IX,XII	H¹						H¹						WGC OScAR

Table 38 - POSITIVE AFFECT

BEHAVIOR ITEM	GRADE	LOW SES PUPILS						HIGH SES PUPILS						SOURCE SYMBOL
		READING GAINS complexity low	READING GAINS complexity high	ARITHMETIC GAINS complexity low	ARITHMETIC GAINS complexity high	AFFECTIVE GAINS school	AFFECTIVE GAINS self	READING GAINS complexity low	READING GAINS complexity high	ARITHMETIC GAINS complexity low	ARITHMETIC GAINS complexity high	AFFECTIVE GAINS school	AFFECTIVE GAINS self	
Teacher positive affect (enthusiastic, friendly, etc.)	I	H^1	H^2	H^1	H^2									S73 FLA9
Pupils happy, positive attitude and climate	II	H^1	H^2	H^1	H^2									S73 CDR2
Percent of management requests followed by thanks	II-III									L				BE P154
Pupil pride, cooperation vs. apathy, fear, etc.	II				L^1					L^1				WGC OScAR
Pupils enjoy class	II							L^1		L^1				WGC FLACCS
Teacher develops "we" feeling	II	L^1												WGC FLACCS
Teacher develops "we" feeling	III-VIII	H^1				H^2		H^1				H^2		WGC FLACCS
Pupils enjoy class	IX-XII	L^1				H^2	H^3	L^1				H^2	H^3	WGC FLACCS

Table 39 - REINFORCEMENT

BEHAVIOR ITEM	GRADE	LOW SES PUPILS READING GAINS complexity low	high	ARITHMETIC GAINS complexity low	high	AFFECTIVE GAINS school	self	HIGH SES PUPILS READING GAINS complexity low	high	ARITHMETIC GAINS complexity low	high	AFFECTIVE GAINS school	self	SOURCE SYMBOL
With token--task-related, non-academic achiever	I	H	H											SK 401a
With token--all	I					H	H							SK 469a
"Smiles", gold stars, etc. (self report)	II-III	L	L					L	L					BE Q46
Special privileges (self report)	II-III	L	L					H	H					BE Q47

Table 40 - PRAISE

BEHAVIOR ITEM	GRADE	LOW SES PUPILS						HIGH SES PUPILS						SOURCE SYMBOL
		READING GAINS		ARITHMETIC GAINS		AFFECTIVE GAINS		READING GAINS		ARITHMETIC GAINS		AFFECTIVE GAINS		
		complexity low	high	complexity low	high	school	self	complexity low	high	complexity low	high	school	self	
All adult praise	I													SK 398a
Positive motivation (with language experience method)	I	H		H	H									CRAFT OScAR
Positive motivation (with language experience method)	II		H											CRAFT OScAR
Positive motivation (with skills-centered method)	II	L												CRAFT OScAR
Public praise as motivation for others (self report)	II-III	H	H					H	H					BE Q39
Praise in pupil-initiated work contacts	II-III	H							L					BE P133
Ratio of praise to praise-plus-criticism (in reading groups)	II-III	H	H					L	L					BE Q155
Ratio of praise to praise-plus-criticism (general)	II-III	L	L	M				M	M	M				BE Q155
Praise after pupil response	IV									L	L			GG

Table 41 - DEPENDENT PUPIL BEHAVIOR

BEHAVIOR ITEM	GRADE	LOW SES PUPILS						HIGH SES PUPILS						SOURCE SYMBOL
		READING GAINS complexity low high		ARITHMETIC GAINS complexity low high		AFFECTIVE GAINS school self		READING GAINS complexity low high		ARITHMETIC GAINS complexity low high		AFFECTIVE GAINS school self		
Pupil asks for help, teacher gives it	I	L												Bemis T5
Pupils seek and get support from teacher	I			L^1										WGC CS6
Pupils seek and get support from teacher	II	H^1		L^2				H^1		L^2				WGC CS6
Pupils seek and get support from teacher	III-VIII	H^1				L^2		H^1				L^2		WGC CS6

Table 42 — NON-SUBSTANTIVE QUESTIONS

BEHAVIOR ITEM	GRADE	LOW SES PUPILS						HIGH SES PUPILS						SOURCE SYMBOL
		READING GAINS complexity		ARITHMETIC GAINS complexity		AFFECTIVE GAINS		READING GAINS complexity		ARITHMETIC GAINS complexity		AFFECTIVE GAINS		
		low	high	low	high	school	self	low	high	low	high	school	self	
Non-academic direct questions, requests, commands to individual pupils	III	L^1	L^2	L	L									SK 352a
Teacher non-substantive talk, pupils interested	II							L^1	L^2					WGC CS4
Pupil responses, non-academic	III			L	L									SK 359a

Table 43 - PERMISSIVE TEACHER BEHAVIOR

BEHAVIOR ITEM	GRADE	LOW SES PUPILS — READING GAINS (low)	READING GAINS (high)	ARITHMETIC GAINS (low)	ARITHMETIC GAINS (high)	AFFECTIVE GAINS (school)	AFFECTIVE GAINS (self)	HIGH SES PUPILS — READING GAINS (low)	READING GAINS (high)	ARITHMETIC GAINS (low)	ARITHMETIC GAINS (high)	AFFECTIVE GAINS (school)	AFFECTIVE GAINS (self)	SOURCE SYMBOL
Pupil choice of activities vs. teacher-structured activities	I-II	L^1		L^1										S73 TP5
Permissive teacher behavior	II	L^1	L^2		L^3			L^1	L^2		L^3			WGC OScAR
Proportion of pupil requests not granted	II-III	H							M	M				BE P142
Pupils speak aloud without asking permission	II	L^1	L^2					L^1	L^2					WGC FLA
Proportion of pupil-initiated work contacts delayed	II-III	H						H						BE P136
Permissive teacher behavior	III-VIII			L^1	L^2			H	H	L^1	L^2			WGC OScAR
Teacher control, structure vs. permissiveness, spontaneity	IV							H	H	H				SoK

BIBLIOGRAPHY

Medley, Donald M. *Teacher Competence and Teacher Effectiveness, A Review of Process-Product Research*, Washington, DC: American Association of Colleges for Teacher Education, 1977, Tables 1, 3–43.

A General-Purpose Design for Estimating the Reliability of Observational Data

In the pages to follow we will present a design that can be used to yield a number of estimates of the reliability of almost any set of scores based on observations of classroom behavior.

Three sources of unreliability may be identified in such scores, all of which should be taken into account. One is the degree of *inconsistency* in performance on different items on the key on which a score is based (when $K > 1$); the second is the *instability* of teacher behavior from one visit to another; the third is *observer disagreement* in coding behavior.

Internal consistency. Scores on two or more behavior items may be summed or averaged to obtain a single competency score for two reasons. One is to increase the reliability of the scores; the other, to refine the operational definition of the competency. Any single teacher behavior, such as asking one pupil to comment on another's answer (chosen, let us say, as an indication of *skill in questioning*), may occur for any of a large number of reasons, and might therefore reflect any of several different competencies. Calling on a nonvolunteer might also reflect *skill in questioning*; it might indicate *insensitivity to pupil needs*; it might be a control tactic; it might occur for some entirely different reason. The frequency of occurrence of either of these two behaviors may or may not reflect skill in questioning. The probability that either one in isolation does so is small, and hence either item's validity as a measure of the competency is likely to be low. Even if skill in questioning were highly correlated with teacher effectiveness, the correlation of a score based on either item with effectiveness would probably be low.

A score based on both items is likely to show a higher correlation, because when two items, each of which may reflect either the competency in question or some other factor, are combined, only the teacher who possesses that competency is likely to score high on both items. The chance that a teacher lacking a competency will get a high score on a key designed to measure that competency gets smaller as the number of items on the key increases. An a priori composite key made up of several items is almost certain to be a more reliable measure of the competency than any one-item key—and a more valid one as well. As more and more items that share a common factor are summed, the relative contributions to score variance of all factors other than the one common to all the items decrease rather rapidly.

The extent to which any set of items actually load on a common factor indicates whether or not the hypothesized competency really exists (in the sense that some teachers have more of it than others). A measure of this saturation on a common factor, as well as a test of the hypothesis that the factor exists, is provided by the coefficient of internal consistency of the total scores, referred to by Cronbach (1951) as coefficient *alpha*.

Coefficient alpha may be defined formally as an estimate of the correlation between the score of a teacher on one set of K items and the score that would be assigned to the same teacher on a different set of K items equivalent to the first. Coefficient alpha is in fact based on the average intercorrelation between pairs of items within the set, adjusted in Spearman-Brown fashion to allow for the fact that the score is based on the total of K items instead of on a single item. What is of concern here is if a parallel K-item scale could be constructed, how much an individual's score on that parallel scale would differ from his score on the existing scale.

Instability. There has been some controversy in the literature (cf. McGaw, Wardrop, and Bunda, 1972) about whether day-to-day variations in classroom behavior are properly regarded as errors of measurement. The argument against so regarding them is that a competent teacher intentionally varies her behavior from time to time as the immediate objectives of instruction change; and that since such variations are functional it is illogical to treat them as random errors. McGaw and his collaborators present a somewhat naive view of a problem which can be resolved only in terms of how the true score being measured is defined (cf. Medley and Mitzel, 1963, 309–310).

Suppose that the true score is defined as what the teacher did between 10 and 11 o'clock on a certain day. Behavior on other days is clearly irrelevant and should not be observed.

Suppose that the true score is defined as how a teacher behaves whenever she performs a certain task, such as reviewing an arithmetic lesson with a certain kind of class. Behavior when the teacher is performing any other task is clearly irrelevant and should not be observed. Variations in behavior from one such session to another clearly reflect instability of the behavior and should be regarded as errors of measurement.

Since it is the average amount of the behavior that would be observed over a long period of time (usually an entire school year) while the teacher is performing the task in question that measurements derived from these observations are meant to estimate, variations in behavior from one observation to another are therefore quite properly regarded as errors of measurement.

Observer Errors. Different observers recording the same behaviors at the same time do not usually produce identical records. The extent to which their records differ depends primarily on the nature of the recording instrument—on the demands it places on the recorder, how much of the complex phenomena of the classroom he is expected to observe, how subtle the cues he is to respond to in coding behavior are, the load of inference required, etc. When the true score to be estimated is defined in terms of what happens while the observers are present, that is, when the frequencies of events during a single visit are to be estimated, then disagreement between records made by different observers recording the same events is a major source of error. But when it is the average frequency over a semester or a year that is to be estimated from a few brief visits, observer errors tend to be negligible in comparison with those due to instability of behavior from visit to visit. Observer errors are the third source of errors of measurement that are identified as of concern.

Preliminary Treatment of Data. The design proposed here assumes that data will be collected in each classroom in the study by at least two observers at different times. Observers should work alone; that is, no two observers should record behavior in the same class at the same time. At least two observers should be trained to use the instrument and should be scheduled to see each teacher at least twice and equally often, making a minimum of four observations in each classroom. Under such conditions reliability analyses can be performed in a balanced design.

In most field studies, the raw data will contain a number of shortcomings (missing data, etc.) which make them unsuitable for analysis according to the original design without some preliminary adjustments. Following is an account of steps taken to adjust the data to remedy each of three principal difficulties.

Difficulty 1: Unequal Number of Visits. The design calls for each observer using each instrument to visit each class equally often, but exigencies in scheduling make this difficult. As a result the number of visits made by any one observer to any one class may vary. This problem can be dealt with by defining a unit called a *record* which consists of the set of *mean* frequencies on all items (on one scoring key) over all visits to one classroom by one observer. The unit of analysis used is this (mean) frequency on one item on one record made by one recorder.

One disadvantage of this procedure is that observer errors and errors due to instability of behavior are completely confounded. Another is that the scores vary in reliability according to the number of visits on which each record is based. Any reliability coefficients reported must, then, be averages. This is regrettable, but not unusual; indeed, most if not all reliability coefficients are averages in this sense. The advantage gained is that this greatly simplifies the analysis and the interpretation of the results of the analysis.

Difficulty 2: Nonnormality of Item Scores. Item frequencies on observational schedules are not usually distributed normally, and (in many instances) variances are not homogeneous between items. These characteristics of the data do not invalidate point estimates of reliability, but they do make interpretation difficult by invalidating the significance tests and interval estimates normally used. Even if conscious use of these procedures is avoided, there remains an unconscious tendency to look at findings as though the assumptions were fulfilled. Distortions in correlation coefficients due to skewness, in particular, can be extremely misleading when the correlations are visually inspected.

These problems may be dealt with by transforming the set of raw frequencies on each item in the set of records made by each observer in each year to a set of area T-scores. The process involves first ascertaining the rank of each class on each item on each record, and then assigning to that class on that item on that record whatever T-score would have the same rank in a set of normally distributed scores with mean of 50 and standard deviation of 10. One consequence of this is that any score on any item is based only on normalized rank information. Equal scores on different items mean equal ranks on both items; and equal scores from different observers indicate equal ranks in the sets of scores of the two observers. The unit of the analysis is now seen to be a T-score indicating the rank of a single class on a single item on a single record.

In addition to normalizing the data and equating variances on different items, as they were designed to do, these transformations equate all item means on all records. When an analysis of variance is made of a set of scores on K items and R records, instead of fitting one grand mean, as one does in a conventional analysis of variance, we fit KR means; and instead of losing one degree of freedom for fitting the grand mean, we lose KR degrees by fitting KR means. Moreover, the analysis will contain no main effects for *items* or *records*, or for the interaction between them. The only main effect that exists in any analysis in this approach is *classrooms*. The transformation also minimizes the effects of observer bias by setting each observer mean on each item to 50. This is important because, since the number of times an observer visits a given classroom varies from one observer to another, such biases could otherwise appreciably distort differences between classrooms.

Finally, as a result of these transformations, all items are weighted equally in any composite score based on more than one item.

Difficulty 3: Missing Records.   Some classrooms may not be visited at all by some of the observers. In each such instance, an entire record will be missing, so that the total number of missing values per record will equal the number of items on the scoring key. If the number of missing records in an analysis is M and the number of items is K, this means that, in all, MK item scores would be missing from the data, with a corresponding loss in degrees of freedom for total variation.

This problem will be dealt with by arbitrarily assigning a value of 50 to replace each missing item score. The effect may be expected to be conservative— that is, to reduce any reliability estimates obtained. This is part of the price that must be paid for failing to collect data in a balanced design.

Estimating the Reliability of a Single Instrument Key.   Table B.1 shows the design for estimating the reliability of scores on a K-item competency key scored on R records made in each of C classrooms with a single instrument, assuming M missing records. The function of the analysis is to provide empirical estimates of the amounts of variation in scores from different classrooms on different items based on different records attributable to each of the four sources. The four sources are: (1) differences between teachers in the competency being measured

TABLE B.1
Design for Reliability Analysis

Source of Variation	Degrees of Freedom*	Observed	Mean Squares Expected
Between classes	$(C - 1)$	a	$KR\sigma^2_C + R\sigma^2_{CK} + K\sigma^2_{CR} + \sigma^2$
Inconsistency	$(C - 1)(K - 1)$	b	$R\sigma^2_{CK} + \sigma^2$
Instability	$(C - 1)(R - 1) - M$	c	$K\sigma^2_{CR} + \sigma^2$
Residual	$[(C - 1)(R - 1) - M](K - 1)$	d	σ^2
Total variation	$(C - 1)\,KR - KM$		
Fitting means	KR		
Missing values	KM		
Grand Total	$\overline{CKR}$		

* In all equations, C = classrooms, K = items, R = records per class, and M = missing records.

(σ^2_C), (2) differences in the true scores of the same teacher on different items scored on the same record (σ^2_{CK}), (3) differences in true scores of the same teacher on the same item when scored on different records (σ^2_{CR}), and (4) variation due to any other source (σ^2).

Let us now develop some general reliability formulas that will estimate the reliability of a score based on a key of any length (say J items) and on any number of records (say P of them). In such a case, the *coefficient of reliability* ρ_{JP} is defined in Table B.2; and the appropriate estimate of the reliability of the scores is r_{JP}, which estimates ρ_{JP}.

If the J items on a competency indicator key, and only those J items, are taken as de facto definitions of a teacher competency (or other characteristic), then the true score of interest is the mean of all possible scores a teacher might *get on those items only*, regardless of when or by which observer a record is made. The precision of scores for this purpose is estimated by β_{JP}. This coefficient will be referred to, for convenience' sake, as *beta, the coefficient of stability of the score*. Although, since errors due to instability are confounded with observer errors, beta measures not only stability but observer agreement as well, the latter errors will be assumed to be negligible in comparison with the former.

If the true score on a competency indicator key is defined in terms of the performance on a single visit and if the J items used are regarded as a sample of a population of items reflecting the competency, the precision of a score based on J items and P visits is estimated by α_{JP} which will be referred to as *alpha, the coefficient of internal consistency* of the score.

Whether the set of J items included in a particular competency indicator key may be taken as an appropriate measure of that competency indicator is, of course, open to question. As has been noted, putting the J items together in a composite is tantamount to hypothesizing that the J items represent a population of items all of which reflect a single competency. If the hypothesis is true, the mean intercorrelation among the items will be greater than chance, and coefficient alpha will be large, since it estimates the expected score on the set of P records across all possible sets of J items.

Table B.3 shows a sample analysis with the numerical values of reliability coefficients given for the keys as scored ($J = K$, $P = R$), as well as for scores based on one item and one record ($J = 1$, $P = 1$).

An Example

To illustrate how this procedure is applied, let us look at an example. Consider a study involving seven classrooms ($C = 7$), and two recorders ($R = 2$). Suppose that a key called *content press* is scored on three items ($K = 3$).

The design calls for each recorder to visit each classroom on two different occasions, on each of which he records the frequency of behaviors observed on the three items. As it happens recorder 1 visits one classroom three times, and another only once. Otherwise the data were collected according to plan. The raw frequencies recorded on each item on each observation are shown in Table B.4.

The first step in the analysis is to calculate the mean of the frequencies for each recorder on each item in each classroom across all visits. Since recorder 1

TABLE B.2
Definitions and Estimation Formulas for Coefficients of Reliability, Internal Consistency, and "Stability" of Total Scores over J Items and P Records.

Definitions	Estimates*
(1) *Reliability* (true score is expected score in population of items and records) $$\rho_{JP} = \frac{JP\sigma^2_C}{JP\sigma^2_C + P\sigma^2_{CK} + J\sigma^2_{CR} + \sigma^2}$$	(1) *Reliability coefficient* $$\rho_{JP} (=) r_{JP} = \frac{a - b - c + d}{e_{JP}}$$
(2) *Internal Consistency* (true score is expected score for one set of P records in the population of items) $$\alpha_{JP} = \frac{JP\sigma^2_C + J\sigma^2_{CR}}{JP\sigma^2_C + P\sigma^2_{CK} + J\sigma^2_{CR} + \sigma^2}$$	(2) *Coefficient Alpha* (internal consistency) $$\alpha_{JP} (=) A_{JP} = \frac{a - b + \left(\dfrac{R - P}{P}\right)(c - d)}{e_{JP}}$$
(3) *"Stability"* (true score is expected score on one set of J items in the population of records) $$\beta_{JP} = \frac{JP\sigma^2_C + P\sigma^2_{CK}}{JP\sigma^2_C + P\sigma^2_{CK} + J\sigma^2_{CR} + \sigma^2}$$	(3) *Coefficient Beta* ("Stability") $$\beta_{JP} (=) B_{JP} = \frac{a - c + \left(\dfrac{K - J}{J}\right)(b - d)}{e_{JP}}$$ where: $$e_{JP} = a + \frac{P(K - J)b + J(R - P)c + (K - J)(R - P)d}{JP}$$

* Whenever b<d, b is set equal to d and whenever c <d, c is set equal to d. This has the effect of assuming that components estimated to be less than zero are equal to zero.

TABLE B.3
Sample Reliability Analysis—"Teacher Demonstrates Proper Listening Skills"
(Scored on STARS, four items and four records per classroom)

Source of Variation	*Analysis of Variance* D.F.	Sum of Squares	Mean Square
Classrooms	58	8,538	147.2
Inconsistency	174	18,320	105.3
Instability	163	14,722	90.3
Residual	489	25,965	53.1
Total Variation	884	67,545	
Fitting means	16	2,359,986	
Missing records	44	—	
Total	944	2,427,531	

	Coefficients as Scored	*Per Item Per Record*
Internal Consistency (alpha)	$A_{KR} = .285$	$A_{11} = .127$
Stability/observer agreement (beta)	$B_{KR} = .386$	$B_{11} = .047$
Reliability	$r_{KR} = .032$	$r_{11} = .004$

TABLE B.4
Raw Frequencies

	Recorder 1			*Recorder 2*		
Class	*Item 1*	*Item 2*	*Item 3*	*Item 1*	*Item 2*	*Item 3*
A	12, 16	13, 17	6, 12	12, 16	22, 26	13, 15
B	10, 8	12, 12	15, 19	8, 12	13, 15	18, 26
C	6, 7, 5	12, 12.15	7, 8, 12	7, 9	10, 12	2, 12
D	4	6	17	2, 6	2, 10	20, 26
E	1, 3	3, 3	3, 7	1, 5	4, 6	4, 8
F	6, 2	3, 5	0, 0	2, 4	2, 6	0, 6
G	0, 0	0, 6	0, 2	0, 2	0, 0	1, 1

tallied 12 and 16 occurrences of item 1 in classroom A, the mean for that recorder, item, and class is 14. This is the score on that item for the record made in classroom A by recorder 1. Table B.5 shows the scores on all 42 records (2 recorders × 3 items × 7 classes). These are the units of analysis we shall use.

The second step is to rank the classrooms in each column—that is, on each item on each record. Note that when two classrooms have equal scores in a column, as do classrooms D and E on item 1, record 1, they both receive the average of the ranks they share—in this case, they share ranks 4 and 5, so both get 4.5.

The third step is to convert the ranks to percentile ranks. The easiest way to

TABLE B.5
Scores for All 42 Records

Class	Item (I) × Recorder (R) Means (and Ranks)					
	I1, R1	*I2, R1*	*I3, R1*	*I1, R2*	*I2, R2*	*I3, R3*
A	14 (1)	15 (1)	9 (3.5)	14 (1)	24 (1)	14 (3)
B	9 (2)	12 (3)	17 (1.5)	10 (2)	14 (2)	22 (2)
C	6 (3)	13 (2)	9 (3.5)	8 (3)	11 (3)	7 (4)
D	4 (4.5)	6 (4)	17 (1.5)	4 (4)	6 (14)	23 (1)
E	2 (6)	3 (6.5)	5 (5)	3 (5.5)	5 (5)	6 (5)
F	4 (4.5)	4 (5)	0 (7)	3 (5.5)	4 (6)	3 (6)
G	0 (7)	3 (6.5)	1 (6)	1 (7)	0 (7)	1 (7)

do this is to begin by dividing 100 by twice the number of classrooms—in this case, $100 \div 14 = 7.14$. This is the percentile rank of the classroom with the lowest rank—i.e., 7. Now all we need to do is add 7.14 to 7.14 to get the percentile rank for the class where rank is next (6.5), getting 14.28; then add 7.14 to 14.28 to get the next one, and so. (This is a simple matter with a pocket calculator.) As a check, you should subtract the lowest percentile rank from 50, and then subtract 50 from the highest. These two numbers should be the same; if they are, you can be sure you have made no arithmetic errors. In our example, we get 42.9 and 42.8, indicating a rounding error too small to worry about.

Table B.6 shows you the T-scores that correspond to various percentile ranks; from it we get the results shown in Table B.7 for our particular problem. This completes step 4.

The fifth step in the process is to substitute T-Scores for the raw scores and ranks in Table B.5. The first pair (classroom A, recorder 1, item 1) is 14(1). Since according to Table B.6, a T-score of 64.6 corresponds to a rank of 1, Table B.8 shows a value of 64.6 as the first value.

The sixth step is to perform an analysis of variance of these 42 T-scores in the design shown in Table B.1. Because the mean of each column in Table B.8 is 50 (or as close to 50 as makes no difference), the sums of scores for recorders and for items, and the interaction between them will each turn out to be almost exactly equal to zero, so it is not necessary even to calculate them. Table B.9 shows the analysis with all sums of squares rounded to the nearest whole number.

You should be able now to calculate the reliability, alpha, and beta coefficients of these scores (which are based on 3 items and 2 records, so that $P = R$ and $J = K$) by using the formulas in Table B.2. They are, respectively, .90, .90, and .98. You should also calculate the coefficients per item per record ($L = 1, J = 1$), which are .72, .72, and .91.

As an exercise, you might assume that recorder 1 failed to visit classroom D at all and that recorder 2 failed to visit classroom G at all. This means that in Table B.5 you would put a rank of 4 in row D of each column under recorder 1, and in row G of each column under recorder 2 before ranking the other scores in each column.

Table B.10 shows the new ranks.

TABLE B.6
Area T-scores in Terms of Percentile Ranks

T-Score	Percentile	Rank	T-Score	T-Score	Percentile	Rank	T-Score
50.0	50.00	50.00	50.0		93.32	6.68	35.0
50.5	51.99	48.01	49.5	65.5	93.94	6.06	34.5
51.0	53.98	46.02	49.0	66.0	94.52	5.48	34.0
51.5	55.96	44.04	48.5	66.5	95.05	4.95	33.5
52.0	57.93	42.07	48.0	67.0	95.94	4.46	33.0
52.5	59.87	40.13	47.5	67.5	95.99	4.01	32.5
53.0	61.79	38.21	47.0	68.0	96.41	3.59	32.0
53.5	63.68	36.32	46.5	68.5	96.78	3.22	31.5
54.0	65.54	34.46	46.0	69.0	97.13	2.87	31.0
54.5	67.36	32.64	45.5	69.5	97.44	2.56	30.5
55.0	69.15	30.85	45.0	70.0	97.72	2.28	30.0
55.5	70.88	29.12	44.5	70.5	97.98	2.02	29.5
56.0	72.57	27.43	44.0	71.0	98.21	1.79	29.0
56.5	74.22	25.78	43.5	71.5	98.42	1.58	28.5
57.0	75.80	24.20	43.0	72.0	98.61	1.39	28.0
57.5	77.34	22.66	42.5	72.5	98.78	1.22	27.5
58.0	78.81	21.19	42.0	73.0	98.93	1.07	27.0
58.5	80.23	19.77	41.5	73.5	99.06	0.94	26.5
59.0	81.59	18.41	41.0	74.0	99.18	0.82	26.0
59.5	82.89	17.11	40.5	74.5	99.29	0.71	25.5
60.0	84.13	15.87	40.0	75.0	99.38	0.62	25.0
60.5	85.31	14.69	39.5	75.5	99.46	0.54	24.5
61.0	86.43	13.57	39.0	76.0	99.53	0.47	24.0
61.5	87.49	12.51	38.5	76.5	99.60	0.40	23.5
62.0	88.49	11.51	38.0	77.0	99.65	0.35	23.0
62.5	89.44	10.56	37.5	77.5	99.70	0.30	22.5
63.0	90.32	9.68	37.0	78.0	99.74	0.26	22.0
63.5	91.15	8.85	36.5	78.5	99.78	0.22	21.5
64.0	91.92	8.08	36.0	79.0	99.81	0.19	21.0
64.5	92.65	7.35	35.5	79.5	99.84	0.16	20.5
			65.0	80.0	99.87	0.13	20.0

TABLE B.7
Area T = Scores Corresponding to Ranks

Rank	T = Score
1	64.6
1.5	60.7
2	59.9
2.5	55.7
3	53.7
3.5	51.8
4	50.0
4.5	48.2
5	46.3
5.5	44.3
6	42.1
6.5	39.3
7	35.5

TABLE B.8
T-Scores

Class	Recorder 1 I1	I2	I3	Recorder 2 I1	I2	I3
A	64.6	64.6	51.8	64.6	64.6	53.7
B	57.9	53.7	60.7	57.9	57.9	57.9
C	53.7	57.9	51.8	53.7	53.7	50.0
D	48.2	50.0	60.7	50.0	50.0	64.5
E	42.1	39.3	46.3	46.3	46.3	46.3
F	48.2	46.3	35.5	42.1	42.1	42.1
G	35.5	39.3	42.1	35.5	35.5	35.5

TABLE B.9
Analysis of Variance

Source of Variation	Sum of Squares	Degrees of Freedom	Mean Square
Classes	2,679	6	446.4 = a
Item Heterogeneity	522	12	43.5 = b
Instability	53	6	8.9 = c
Residual	92	12	7.7 = d
Total Variation	3,346	36	
Means	105,040	6	
Total	108,386	42	

TABLE B.10
Item × Recorder Means (and Ranks) (with Missing Values)

I1, R1	I2, R2	I3, R1	I1, R2	I2, R2	I3, R2
14 (1)	15 (1)	9 (2.5)	14 (1)	24 (1)	14 (3)
9 (2)	12 (3)	17 (1)	10 (2)	14 (2)	22 (2)
6 (3)	13 (2)	9 (2.5)	8 (3)	11 (3)	7 (5)
–– (4)	— (4)	— (4)	4 (5)	6 (5)	23 (1)
2 (6)	3 (6.5)	5 (5)	3 (6.5)	5 (6)	6 (6)
4 (5)	4 (5)	0 (7)	3 (6.5)	4 (7)	3 (7)
0 (7)	3 (6.5)	1 (6)	— (4)	— (4)	— (4)

BIBLIOGRAPHY

Cronbach. S. "Coefficient Alpha and the Internal Structure of Tests." *Psychometrika*, 1951, 16, 297–334.

McGaw, B., J. L. Wardrop, and M. A. Bunda. "Classroom Observation Schemes: Where Are the Errors?" *American Educational Research Journal*, 1972, 9, 13–27.

Medley, Donald M., and Harold E. Mitzel. "Measuring Classroom Behavior by Systematic Observation." In N. L. Gage, ed., *Handbook of Research on Teaching*. Chicago, Rand McNally, 1963.

Factor Analysis

Factor analysis is an analytic procedure which uses the information of item intercorrelations to put items together into scales (factors) in such a way that the intercorrelations among items within a factor will be at a maximum and the intercorrelations from factor to factor will be at a minimum. It will identify the dimensions running through all of the items which are strongest in terms of the amount of variation which they identify, and it will identify the subset of items that makes up each dimension. Still another way of describing what the analysis does is to say that it will identify factors in such a way that they capture the most variation possible in the smallest number of factors. Given these characteristics, it will be clear that if there is, in fact, only one dimension present, the analysis will indicate this. And if scoring keys have previously been created for several dimensions the analysis will verify them if they do the best job of identifying subscales.

Each teacher observed can then be given a score which represents his or her position on each of these factors, called a factor score. This is one way of creating a measure—the factor score is a score on a measure. While the measures are created objectively, giving meaning to the measure is a subjective process and can be a problem. All the analysis does is tell you that these bits of behavior (the items) tend to occur together. The behaviors form a pattern—a constellation, which as a pattern occurs more often in some classrooms, less often in other classrooms. The analysis identifies the items which make up the pattern, but the logical problem of identifying what the items have in common—why they form a pattern, what the pattern means—is one for you to solve after the analysis process. Sometimes the meaning of the pattern is obvious, but sometimes it is not at all clear.

Mechanically the analysis is a two-step process in which the factors or dimensions are first identified (factor extraction) and then at the second step, factors are rotated so as to concentrate as much variance as possible in the smallest number of items within each factor. This second step also clarifies interpretation in most cases. But one of the problems which does not have a very good solution is the question of how many factors to rotate. There are statistical guidelines for making this decision, but with observational data it has seemed to us that the set of rotated factors which is most interpretable is typically a somewhat smaller number than most of the guidelines would lead one to retain. But let us emphasize again that this decision is ultimately a subjective, arbitrary one. As additional factors are rotated, what were formerly large factors with many items in them will split up into two or more smaller factors, which will be narrower and more specific. They may or may not make more sense. At some point in the process, farther division is likely to make less sense rather than more, but the decision is a judgmental one.

The most useful starting point for us for identifying an approximate number has been an inspectional procedure, the *scree test*. This is a simple procedure in which the eigenvalue for each factor from the extraction process is plotted against its factor number. The plot is inspected for the factor number at which the curve begins to level off and that is taken as the number of factors to rotate. Since this is subjective and inexact we have begun a factor or two below the number indicated, have gone one or two above, have interpreted each of the rotated matrices, and finally have used the one whose interpretation seemed clearest. It has more often been fewer than the scree test suggests rather than more, but the procedure provides a good starting point.

After the most desirable number of factors has been decided on and the rotated matrix has been created, then there is the question of how to create the factor scores which give each teacher or classroom a position on each of the factors. Glass and Maguire (1966) argue that the only suitable procedure is one in which every observation item enters every factor score, but with the weight determined by the loading of the item on the factor. These are called complete factor scores. Their primary reason for advocating this procedure is that it tends to minimize the correlations between factors. On the other hand, Horn (1965) presents arguments for and against each of a variety of methods for calculating factor scores, and concludes that for most purposes a method of calculating *incomplete* factor scores is preferable. This process is one in which items which load relatively heavily on a factor (we have used a cut off of .50, but that is arbitrary) are used to make up the measure. The scores for each teacher for each of the items on the measure are summed algebraically and averaged. Morris (1980) has shown that factor scores derived in this way are slightly, although not significantly, more reliable than the complete factor scores advocated by Glass and Maguire, and also that their predictive power in cross-validation is higher. This is consistent with the argument we advanced earlier from Dawes that a combining procedure which uses equal weights is usually preferable to any other. This appears to be one instance in which the simpler method is the better one, which is not always true.

We have discussed advantages and strengths of factor analysis, and a quantitatively oriented reader may wonder, "Why not start with this process?"

But it can also create patterns which are conceptually complex and perhaps not helpful, when carried out with complex sets of items. Table C.1 is such an example. The items are all from FLACCS, the predecessor to the Climate and Control System mentioned in Chapter 5. Factor scores on this dimension were negatively correlated with pupil achievement gain, indicating that where the sorts of behaviors which the factor identified were frequent, pupils learned less. Since at that time we had expected positive affect to be positively related to achievement we were surprised and suspected that the negative relationship was a function of other items reflecting a high activity level by pupils on the one hand, and the lack of any evidence of task focus on the other. It seemed to us that the factor might represent a "fun and games" classroom with little attention to learning activities. In the attempt to clarify the meaning of those components of the factor we created two rational composites, subsets of items, one reflecting positive affect expression (labeled PA) and the other reflecting the freedom of movement in the classroom (FM), indicated by the column titled *subset*. When the separate scores were correlated with achievement, free movement clearly correlated negatively with achievement, and although positive affect correlated positively with two pupil outcomes and negatively with two, the negative correlations were larger than the positive ones. At a minimum, there was no support there for the expectation that positive affect would be positively correlated with achievement.

When we have started with diverse sets of items, factors which are conceptually complex have not been unusual in our experience, and do create interpretive problems. In a setting in which improvement of instruction is the purpose of the activity, it would then be unclear what recommendations should be made to teachers about changes in their classroom behavior. Nor would it be clear how the data should be used in evaluating teachers. This appears to be a major disadvantage in the use of factor analysis for creating measures, and is why we have recommended starting with rationally homogeneous sets of items.

TABLE C.1
Factor 5—Free Movement and Positive Affect with Little Focus

Instrument	Subset[1]	Loading	Description
FLACCS	PA	.66	P positive affect, verbal and nonverbal
FLACCS	FM	.60	T moves freely among P
FLACCS	FM	.56	P seeks reassurance, support
FLACCS	FM	.55	T attends P briefly
FLACCS	PA	.52	T positive affect, verbal and nonverbal
FLACCS	FM	.48	P reports rule to another
FLACCS	FM	.42	P aimless wandering
FLACCS	FM	.43	P gives reason
FLACCS	PA	.42	Gentle T nonverbal control

Eigenvalue = 4.57

Source: After Soar and Soar (1974).
1.   PA = Positive Affect; FM = Free Movement

BIBLIOGRAPHY

Glass, G. V. and T. O. Maguire. "Abuses of Factor Scores." *American Educational Research Journal*, 1966, 3, 297–304.

Horn, J. L. "An Empirical Comparison of Various Methods for Computing Factor Scores." *Educational and Psychological Measurement*, 1965, 25, 313–322.

Morris, J. D. "On the Predictive Accuracy of Full-Rank Variables vs. Various Types of Factor Scores." *Educational and Psychological Measurement*, 1980, 40, 389–396.

Estimating Student Gains from Within-Class Regression

The first step in this process is to define what we mean by the "average student." For the present let us define the average student in a school in terms of his performance on an appropriate test administered near the beginning of the school year or before it begins, a student whose raw score on that administration of the test, which we shall call his *pretest score*, equals the mean raw score for his grade (or subject) on an appropriate set of norms for the test. Usually, if available, local system-wide norms are preferable.

The first step in estimating how much the average student would learn from any particular teacher is to set up what is called a "regression equation" for that teacher's class. Each teacher's regression equation will then be used to predict a student's *posttest score*, that is, the score he would get on an appropriate achievement test at the end of the school year.

It is, of course, very important that the posttest score used be a valid measure of achievement of the goals the teacher is supposed to achieve with that class. The test battery used in the regular school testing program will usually be a satisfactory posttest if it is administered at or near the end of the school year. The pretest can be any test that correlates with the posttest, such as a general intelligence test or a test of aptitude in the subject being taught. What works best is a previous administration of the same test that is used as the posttest (or a parallel form of it).

In order to set up a teacher's regression equation we must have a pair of pretest and posttest scores for each of the students in that teacher's class for one school year. For convenience' sake we shall call the pretest score of any student X and his posttest score Y. Using the correlation between X and Y within that teacher's class we can set up the regression equation for that teacher. The equation would look like this:

$$Y' = a + bX$$

where a and b are the *regression coefficients* for that teacher; they will be different for different teachers. Y' stands for the *predicted* posttest score of any student whose pretest score is X. Y' will not usually be the same as Y, which is the score a student with that pretest score will actually get on the posttest.

Suppose that, for a third-grade teacher named Ms. Rose, the value of a is 10.2, and the value of b is 1.8. Then Ms. Rose's regression equation is:

$$Y' = 10.2 + 1.8X$$

If the average pretest score a third-grade student should get according to the school norms is 21 points, then from the simple calculation:

$$10.2 + 1.8 \times 21 = 48$$

we estimate that the average third-grade student in the school system would be expected to get a posttest score of 48 points in Ms. Rose's class.

Suppose that we have a second teacher, Ms. Blue, whose regression equation is:

$$Y' = 28.6 + 0.9X$$

It is easy to calculate that the average student would be expected to get a posttest score of 47.5 in Ms. Blue's class. This is very close to what he or she would get in Ms. Rose's class, so we conclude that such a student would do just about as well in either teacher's class.

Suppose that the pretest score of a student on the 15th percentile of the norms was 11. It is easy to calculate that such a student's posttest score would be much higher (38.5) in Ms. Blue's class than in Ms. Rose's (30). In the same way we estimate that a bright student ($X=31$) would do a bit better (posttest score = 60) in Ms. Blue's class than in Ms. Rose's (posttest score = 56.5).

So long as X is set equal to the mean pretest score for the grade or subject to which the classes belong, Y', the measure of outcomes, will not be subject to any regression effect; that is, it will be free of the biases that distort differences in adjusted mean gain scores or regressed gain scores with which Campbell and Erlebacher were concerned. If X is set equal to any value other than the mean, Y' will be subject to a regression effect and will regress toward the mean; but this effect will be the same in every class and will not distort comparisons between classes.

It should be noted that differences between classes in Y' (like those in any other measures of pupil gains) cannot be attributed solely to differences in teacher performance unless pupils have been randomly assigned to classes (within grade and subject). If pupils are not randomly assigned, some portion of these differences may be due to differences in the classes rather than to differences in teachers. When you correlate Y' with scores on the measure of performance you are trying to validate, you will need to calculate partial correlations, holding major contextual factors (such as the average ability of the class) constant.

E

Selected Observation Instruments

Each of the following instruments has been found to be reliable and valid in a variety of research projects; each is judged to be a low-inference instrument; each has been used in research studies which yielded significant findings; and each measures enough different aspects of classroom behavior to be potentially useful in studies of teacher and student performances. They are presented here as examples of the type of observation instruments which can be used in the measurement-based evaluation of teachers.

1. The *Classroom Observations Keyed for Effectiveness Research* (COKER) is an objectively administered, low-inference sign system for observing teacher/student behaviors in on-going classrooms. The items on COKER have been reduced and adapted from more than 1,344 category and sign items on five separate observation instruments. These are the most reliable and valid items from the 1,344. They can be scored on a variety of keys to yield measures of a teacher's classroom behavior (Coker and Coker, 1979a, 1979b).

2. The *Coping Analysis Schedule for Educational Settings* (CASES). This is a system for measuring pupil socialization in terms of 13 categories of "coping" behaviors exhibited by pupils (Spaulding, 1982).

3. The *Spaulding Teacher Activity Recording Schedule* (STARS). This is a set of verbal categories for describing cognitive instructional strategies of teachers, organized under the subtitles of affective behavior, motor and social structuring, concept attainment, concept checking, and value expression (Spaulding, 1982).

4. The *Observation Schedule and Record. Form 5, Verbal* (OScAR 5V). This is a verbal category system designed to describe the classroom learning environment according to the relative frequencies of 80 different kinds of events in classroom interaction (Medley, 1979).

245

5. The *Climate and Control System* (CCS). This is a sign system that examines the control tactics of teachers as well as their affective behaviors and those of their pupils. It includes items relating to the nature of classroom structure, teacher and pupil control strategies, and teacher and pupil affective behaviors, both positive and negative (Soar and Soar, 1982).

CLASSROOM OBSERVATIONS KEYED FOR EFFECTIVE RESEARCH

The Classroom Observations Keyed for Effectiveness Research (COKER) is an objectively administered, low-inference sign system for observing teacher/student behaviors in on-going classrooms. The items on COKER have been reduced and adapted from more than 1,344 category and sign items on five separate observation instruments. These are the most reliable and valid items from the 1,344. They can be scored on a variety of keys to yield measures of a teacher's classroom behavior.

Procedures

Classroom observations can be done in a variety of ways. The ideal way is to schedule visits in advance and arrive in time to inform the teacher of your presence before the class begins. Upon entering the classroom, move to a position which will enable you to clearly observe the transactions and/or interactions among the teacher and students, remaining as unobtrusive as possible.

Complete the information at the top of the data sheet. Take time to get oriented to the situation, the interactions, the lesson. Start your watch and begin coding the first 5-minute observation period in Section A. At the end of five minutes, stop the watch and code Section B from memory. At this point, one observation has been completed.

When you are reoriented, complete the information at the top of another data sheet and start the watch again for the second 5-minute recording period. If the teacher has to leave the room, stop recording (stop the watch) and continue when she returns.

The total observation time per visit is 10 minutes; however, total time in classroom for one visit will be approximately 20–25 minutes.

Instrumentation

Section A in Figure E.1 consists of a matrix of numbered cells designating specific teacher and student transactions and/or interactions. The matrix is designed to accommodate one 5-minute observation. When an interaction represented by a numbered cell occurs, the cell should be marked. For example, if a teacher is "Directing-learning related" (13) and a student is "passively complying" (01) code the appropriate cell (13/01). A cell is coded only once in a given 5-minute observation period even though the behavior may occur numerous times. When using a sign system, code as many items as seen during a given coding period.

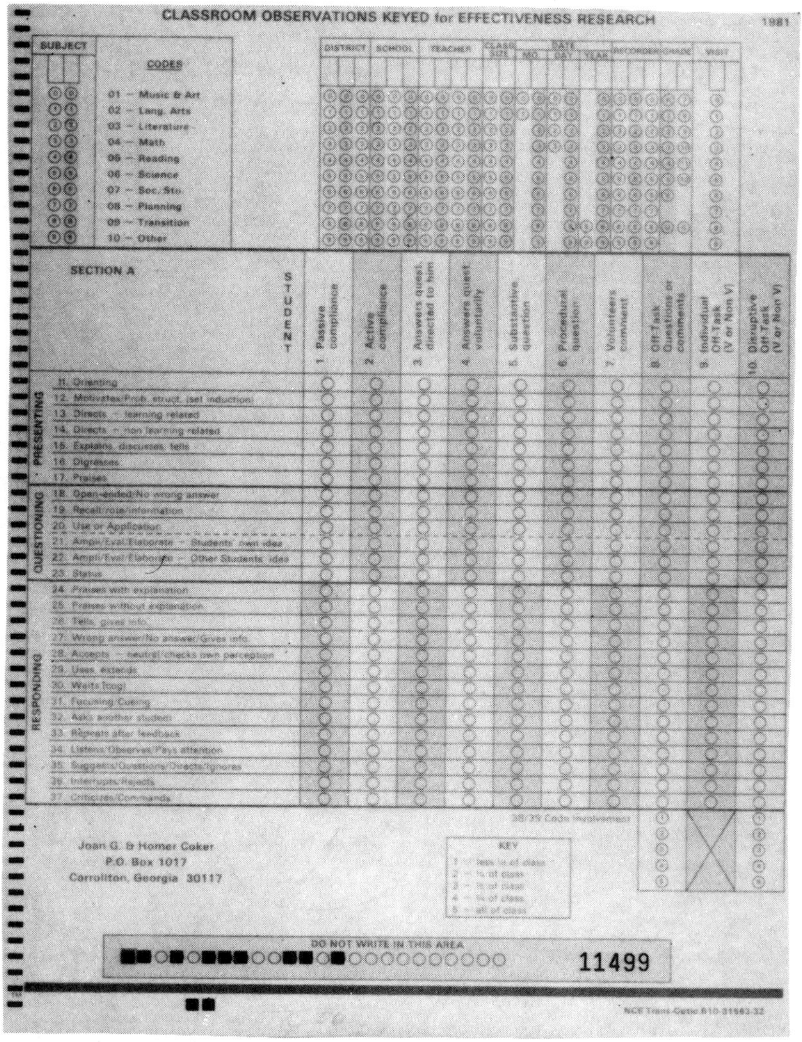

FIGURE E.1   First page of the COKER instrument.

Structure of the Instrument

The interaction matrix (Section A) in Figure E.1 is divided into two broad categories for student behaviors and three broad categories for teacher behaviors. The student behaviors include seven on-task student behaviors and three off-task behaviors. The major categories of teacher behaviors include 13 initiating behaviors, 7 of which are *presenting* and six of which are *questioning* behaviors. Also, there are 14 types of *responding* behaviors, two of which are negative responses.

The dotted line in the questioning section separates two kinds of teacher questions. Those above the line are initiated by the teacher whereas those below the line can be either initiating or responding behaviors (items 21, 22, and 23). Not every interaction can be recorded but the pervasive teaching pattern will be identified.

Section B in Figure E.2 is designed to record specific student and/or teacher cognitive and affective behaviors as well as teaching strategies which occurred during the previous 5 minutes. These behaviors may or may not be interactions. Code this section from memory.

Grouping in Figure E.2 (items 141 through 159) refers to the organizational plan or method used by the teacher, and whether the activities are prescribed by the teacher or not.

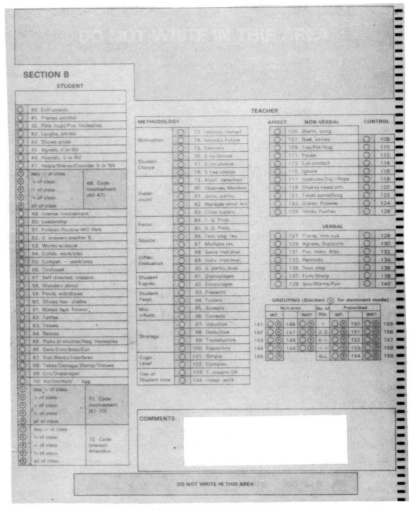

FIGURE E.2 Second page of the COKER instrument.

Recording and Scoring

The COKER uses NCS trans-optic forms to record observations which åre directly processed for computer scoring programs.

A large number of scoring keys are available and are presently being used in a number of studies. Users are encouraged to both review these keys and develop their own. A user's manual provides additional details.

THE COPING ANALYSIS SCHEDULE FOR EDUCATIONAL SETTINGS (CASES)

The Coping Analysis Schedule for Educational Settings (CASES) (Spaulding, 1982) and its use in classroom management were developed over a period of approximately 20 years as a result of more than 2,000 case studies of normal pupils from preschool through high school. Its categories are based on ego theory and reflect a number of dimensions of personality development. It was designed to measure the process of normal personality development and socialization occurring in structured settings. It consists of 13 basic categories of *coping* behaviors identified by descriptive statements. Subscripts are added to six categories to allow coding of child and adolescent behavior in terms of adult or cultural expectations (as determined by the setting). The augmented list numbers 19 categories. A brief form of CASES is given in Table E.1.

TABLE E.1
The Coping Analysis Schedule for Educational Settings—CASES
(Brief Form; Adapted from Spaulding, 1982)

Category	Abbreviated Description of Behavior
1	Aggressive, hurtful, destructive behavior
2	Negative attention-getting behavior
3a	Controlling others in a pro-social manner
3b	Controlling others in a self-serving manner
4	Resisting, delaying, defensive checking
5a	Appropriate self-directed, independent activity
5b	Inappropriate self-directed, independent activity
6a	Paying close attention in accordance with teacher expectations
6b	Paying close attention to events *unrelated to the task at hand*
7a	Integrative sharing and helping in accordance with expectations
7b	Integrative sharing and helping *in conflict* with expectations
8a	Integrative social transactions in accordance with expectations
8b	Integrative social transactions *in conflict* with expectations
9a	Integrative seeking and receiving help in line with expectations
9b	Integrative seeking and receiving *in conflict* with expectations
10	Following directions and teacher expectations submissively
11	Observing passively and checking on noise and movements
12	Responding to internal stimuli
13	Physical withdrawal, avoidance of involvement, and escape

Coping Categories

CASES categories are arranged with the more active coping categories grouped at one end and the more passive categories at the other, but the numerals do not represent an ordinal scale. Various psychological dimensions were used in the development of the schedule. Basic to its development were the concepts of integrative and dominative social behavior as delineated in the work of H. H. Anderson (1939, 1943). In addition to the generally active and passive styles of pupil response to environmental stimuli, CASES includes categories which reflect *overt aggression, passive aggression, independence, autonomy/dependence, avoidance,* and *withdrawal*. The term *coping* and many of the ideas implicit in CASES came from the work of Lois Murphy, especially from her book, *Personality in Young Children* (Murphy, 1956).

The Coping Analysis Schedule for Educational Settings permits the coding of all observable behavior in the classroom into one or another of the 19 categories. All but one of the categories (responding to internal stimuli *12*) are designed to characterize a person's economy with the external environment. How a given individual manages this economy is assumed, in this system of analysis, to be of crucial importance in the development of his or her social relations and, ultimately, his or her overall cultural adequacy.

Coping Styles Identified through Case Studies and Factor Analyses

The particular categories delineated in CASES were refined empirically through individual case studies conducted by students and research personnel at the Universities of Illinois, Hofstra, and Duke. Validity studies of the treatments devised for each of seven coping styles were made at San Jose State University from 1970 through 1982. In its present form, CASES provides a comprehensive technique of characterizing overt coping behavior in the classroom (or in any social setting). Combinations of category frequencies are used to produce coefficients representing eight coping styles first identified through factor analysis. The eight styles reflect the literature on personality development and are identified by letters and descriptive terms as follows:

Style A Dominative, active aggressive, annoying, bothering, controlling, manipulating

Style B Resistant, passive-aggressive, delaying, peer oriented, off-task

Style C Passive, withdrawn, avoidant, shy, dreamy

Style D Peer dependent, distractible, off-task

Style E Attentive, adult oriented, compliant

Style F Assertive, socially integrative, task oriented

Style G Appropriately self-directed, task oriented, self-motivated, independent, nonsocial

Style H Conforming, passive, submissive to directions

Uses of the Instrument

The instrument is useful as a means of measuring change in the overall process of socialization as well as providing day-to-day feedback to teachers on the effectiveness of specific techniques of classroom management and instruction. It has been used effectively with children as young as two. It has also been used to measure coping styles in adults in retirement homes, university classes, and hospital wards. In spite of the fact that the coding procedure requires interpretations of intent, it has been used successfully in case studies of autistic and mentally retarded pupils.

Data Collection

CASES data can be taken continuously or by means of time sampling techniques. Individual profiles or group norms by category or style can readily be obtained. An overall coefficient is available as a single measure of overall competency in coping with social and academic expectations in the classroom.

Training of Observers

Observers can be trained in approximately 25 to 30 hours. It is customary to obtain reliabilities of observation and recording in the high eighties to low nineties. The primary method of training is simultaneous observation of selected pupils by two or more observers. Data are gathered first by watching videotaped classroom sequences and secondly by observation of pupils in live settings. Data can be recorded by making tallies on a data sheet, by marking category numbers and letters, or by keying data online to a computer. Scoring is easily accomplished by hand, although computer programs can readily be written to score the data as they are keyed into the computer.

Norms and Standardized Scores

The CASES Style Coefficients are standardized on a norming sample of 1066 pupils in Santa Clara County, California. The standard is based on the concept of "standing out." A visibility threshold was set at a point one standard deviation above the mean of the norming sample. A coefficient of 1.00 was set as the threshold value, representing a point in the distribution where 84 percent of the scores were less than or equal to it. The style coefficients are used to identify the visible styles which characterize a given student and provide the information needed to decide upon an appropriate treatment to be applied in the classroom.

Validity

The validity of the categories and the treatments based on the style analyses has been established by a large number of case studies. Since the instrument is composed of low inference, descriptive categories, the validity of the categories rests primarily with the degree of agreement reached by experienced teachers, school psychologists, and classroom researchers in observations of well known pupils in specific case studies. Studies of convergent and discriminant validity have not yet been done. Predictive validity has been demonstrated in a limited number of studies (Coker, Medley, and Soar, 1980; Mahen, 1977; Spaulding and Papageorgiou, 1972).

Generalizability of CASES Scores

Generalizability studies (Spaulding and Spaulding, 1982) have indicated that a reliability of .71 can be expected after four visits to a classroom and that the coefficient increases to .75 with five visits (of about 15 to 20 minutes each). With 10 visits the generalizability coefficient can be expected to reach .86.

THE SPAULDING TEACHER ACTIVITY RECORDING SCHEDULE (STARS)

The Spaulding Teacher Activity Recording Schedule (STARS) is a classroom observation instrument designed to code the cognitive instructional methods, affective relationships, and behavior control strategies of teachers. The current form is a 1983 revision of earlier versions reviewed in *Evaluating Classroom Instruction* (Borich and Madden, 1977) and in *Mirrors for Behavior* (Simon and Boyer, 1967).

STARS consists of eight molar categories, under which are subsumed a number of subcategories. These categories are as follows:
- General
  - 01 Non-transactional with students

- Affective
  - 02 Disapproval (with aversive affect present)
  - 03 Withholding reinforcement by removal, "time-out"
  - 04 Withholding attention (ignoring behaviors of specific pupils)
  - 05 Approval (with positive affect expressed)

- Motor or Social Structuring and Restructuring
  - 06 Setting performance goals, limits, actions, and procedures
  - 07 Reminding and redirecting regarding limits, goals, procedures, rules
  - 08 Digressions, integrative off-task interaction with pupils

- Concept Formation, Attainment, or Development
  - 09 Concept formation or attainment by discovery methods (concrete concepts)
  - 10 *Complex* (formal) concept formation or attainment by discovery methods
  - 11 Concept formation or attainment by deductive methods (concrete concepts)

12 *Complex* (formal) concept formation or attainment by deductive methods
13 Concept formation or attainment by transductive methods
14 Concept formation or attainment by expository methods (concrete concepts)
15 *Complex* (formal) concept formation or attainment by expository methods
16 Concept formation or attainment by rote or repetitive processes

- Motivation, Information, and Focusing
  17 Motivational statements and/or giving or asking for incidental information
  18 Focusing attention, giving cues when pupils are in error, and refocusing

- Concept Checking, Testing, Strengthening
  19 Asking for recall of concrete facts or information
  20 Asking for recall of formal concepts, principles, rules, or generalizations
  21 Asking for use of concrete facts or information (asking applications)
  22 Asking for use of formal concepts, principles, rules, or generalizations

- Valuing
  23 Expressing values, needs, opinions, feelings, desires, likes, dislikes
  24 Eliciting pupil values, needs, opinions, feelings, desires, likes, dislikes

- Listening and/or Observing
  25 Listening to or observing pupil initiated behavior (with teacher awareness)

Reliability and Validity of STARS Style Scores

Studies of STARS data gathered using videotapes depicting junior high school teachers (Borich, Malitz, and Kugle, 1978; Weinrott, Jones, and Boler, 1981) demonstrated strong convergent and discriminant validity for 16 STARS categories grouped into five behavior constructs for comparison with categories from four popular classroom observation systems.

A study of the generalizability of STARS Style coefficients (Spaulding, 1982) found that odd-even correlations reached .80 after four observations were aggregated and correlated (using CASES and STARS in concert to obtain STARS Style coefficients) and .90 after eight observations were aggregated. In training observers, coefficients of agreement of .80 and above are normally achieved and maintained.

Norms

Norms have been obtained for STARS Style coefficients based on 640 samples of classroom teacher-pupil transactions in observations of 44 teachers.

Procedures for Use

STARS is generally used in conjunction with the Coping Analysis Schedule for Educational Settings (CASES) (Simon and Boyer, 1967). Samples of classroom transactions are made every 3 to 5 seconds using first CASES and then STARS (to reflect the transaction between a given pupil, or group of pupils, and the teacher). Normally, the recorded pairs (CASES and STARS category numerals) represent the observed behavior of a specific pupil (sampled in rotation from a preselected list of 6 or more pupils) and a simultaneous sample of observed teacher behavior using STARS. This "round robin" sampling of pupils is interrupted whenever the teacher transacts with a specific pupil. In such instances, the behavior of the specific pupil is sampled in tandem with the teacher.

Scoring

Scoring keys have been developed to produce style coefficients on 25 patterns of management and instruction commonly found in preschools, elementary class-rooms, and high schools. The first step in data reduction consists of computing the percentage of records (pairs) made by an observer that fell with-in each of the 25 teaching and management patterns (as represented by the keys). The percentage of pairs within each pattern is then reduced by the ratio of cells recorded in the pattern to the total number of cells in the pattern. This value is called the STARS "score" for the pattern in question. The score obtained for each pattern is then divided by the threshold value (or the "limen") established for each pattern. The limen is defined as "the minimum score that partitions the distribution so that 84 percent of the non-zero scores are less than or equal to it." This process results in a STARS Style "coefficient" which characterizes the "visibility" of the pattern in question. STARS Style coefficients of 1.00 represent the threshold of visibility. All scoring is accomplished using programs written for the Apple II microcomputer.

OBSERVATION SCHEDULE AND RECORD, FORM 5V

The categories used in OScAR 5V are shown in Figures 5.7 and 5.8 (see text, pp. 105–106). OScAR records may be scored on eight keys which were empirically derived by factor analysis, and represent approximations to ortho-gonal factors. (The approximations result from simplification of the factor weights.)

In addition to being roughly orthogonal in a factor-analysis sense, the keys are also orthogonal in the sense of orthogonal contrasts in the analysis of variance. This means that they are experimentally independent, or nonoverlapping in the same sense that separate behavior categories are nonoverlapping. This should eliminate any spurious intercorrelations between keys such as Q, A, S, and D that share certain categories in common. One result of this is that some keys are bipolar, that is, contrast two distinct behavior patterns seen as opposite. Keys Q, D, S, and A are of this type. Keys M, R, P, and L are independent because they do not share items with other keys.

In order to remove differences in total numbers of events recorded in different records, each category frequency may be divided by the total number of events on the record, and so reduced to a proportion independent of record length. To save work, this may be done after the scores are computed instead of before.

A brief description of each key follows.

M (Managing Behaviors). This is basically an index of the relative number of events that are concerned with procedural matters—with managing the class. Teacher statements which tell pupils to do (or not to do) something or which describe procedure are counted.

The factor analysis detected the fact that many teachers formulate commands in such a way that they appear on the surface to be requests. "Will you please turn to page 125?" "Would you mind closing the door?" Such utterances as these are coded as *considering* on OScAR 5V, even though pupils respond to them as *directing*. Hence, *initial considering* statements have a weight of +1 on *M*. However, *continuing considering* statements have a weight of −1. When two or more considering statements are made by the teacher in a row, the apparent consideration is much more likely to be preceived by pupils as genuine. A "really" considerate teacher tends to emit more continuing considering statements than initiating ones, and the net effect on his *M* score is negative.

R (Rebuking Behaviors). This reflects primarily how often a teacher criticizes pupil behavior. Since *initiating rebukes* are weighted three times as heavily as *continuing* ones, a high score does not reflect hostility as much as irritability, perhaps.

P (Permissive Behavior). A teacher gets a point on this key every time she offers a pupil a choice of courses of action, and loses one each time she refuses a pupil such a choice when the pupil requests it. The score, which is bipolar, contrasts permissive teachers (ones who let pupils make decisions) with autocratic ones (who do not).

L (Listening Behavior). A teacher earns a point on this scale each time she lets a pupil who has just volunteered a comment or question make a second comment without interrupting him. A high-scoring teacher is one who listens to a pupil and waits to be sure the pupil is finished talking before replying or interrupting.

A (Lecturing Behavior). This key contrasts the teacher who develops content by lecturing with the one who develops it by questioning pupils. It is the first of four keys which describe a teacher's questioning style.

Each time a teacher asks a question, she gets one negative point on the key. Each time she starts to give information herself, she gets a positive point. Each time she goes ahead to make another informing statement after she has already made one, she gets three positive points. A teacher who lectures—talks about content for long periods—gets a very high positive A-score; one who interacts a lot with pupils gets a high negative one.

S (Question Source).   This key contrasts classrooms where pupils initiate relatively more interchanges with classrooms where the teacher initiates relatively more of them. It is sensitive only to interchanges that are supported, acknowledged, or rejected. The highest positive score goes to a teacher whose pupils initiate many interchanges and who acknowledges the initiations without evaluating them, the lowest to the one who asks a lot of questions and acknowledges pupils' responses without evaluating them.

D (Question Difficulty).   This key is the most complex of the eight; it seems to contrast two kinds of teachers. A high positive score identifies a teacher who asks many questions, mostly convergent, which appear to be easy since the pupils almost always answer them correctly; but are rarely praised (as they should be if the questions are difficult). A high negative score identifies a teacher whose questions elicit answers of more varied quality—some are praised, some critized, some naturally rejected, etc., but very vew are merely approved.

Q (Question Quality).   This key also contrasts two kinds of teacher. One teacher (high positive) asks mainly elaborating questions (ones asking a pupil to enlarge on or react to a previous comment), and rarely evaluates a pupil response. (Presumably she asks a pupil to do so.) The other (high negative) asks mainly convergent questions, and either approves the pupil's response, criticizes it, or (more likely) acknowledges it and asks another question of another pupil. The first teacher, then, is probing, questioning to develop more subtle points; the second is conducting a rapid-fire drill.

Forms scorable on DIGITEK and IBM equipment are available, and an OPSCAN form is under development; should you decide to use OScAR, we will be glad to assist you in selecting and obtaining an appropriate form. For small-scale use, we record directly on the DATARAY form and keypunch from it. Computer programs for scoring and summarizing OScAR data are available.

CLIMATE AND CONTROL SYSTEM

This is the most recent in a series of instrument development efforts. An early instrument (Soar, 1966) was developed to add data to that collected by the Flanders System (Flanders, 1970). It was modified twice for data collection in Follow-Through and two locally conducted, federally sponsored projects (Soar and Soar, 1973, 1979). The most recent revision is shown in Figure 5.4. (See text p. 88.)

The matrix at the top of the page represents teacher-pupil interactions distinguished by whether pupil or teacher behavior initiated (or provoked) it. The teacher behaviors (the rows) scale is intended to represent increasing degrees of coerciveness on the teacher's part—both verbal and nonverbal.

The bottom of the page represents the kinds of groupings present, closeness of teacher attention to pupils, the reward system present, and the kinds of pupil behavior present, other than interactions. Finally, degree of pupil interest and involvement in task activity is coded.

Figure 5.5 (see text p.92) shows the second page. It codes affect expression—positive vs. negative, verbal vs. nonverbal, and teacher vs. pupil, with provision for coding how widespread pupil affect expression is, or how widely teacher affect is directed.

BIBLIOGRAPHY

Anderson, H. H. "The Measurement of Domination and of Socially Integrative Behavior in Teachers' Contacts with Children." *Child Development*, 1939, 10(2).

───── . *Dominative and Socially Integrative Behavior, Child Behavior, and Development.* New York: McGraw-Hill, 1943.

Borich, G. D., and S. K. Madden. *Evaluating Classroom Instruction: A Sourcebook of Instruments.* Reading, Mass.: Addison-Wesley, 1977. Borich, G. D., D. Malitz, and C. L. Kugle. "Convergent and Discriminant Validity of Five Classroom Observation Schedules: Testing a Model." *Journal of Educational Psychology,* 1978, 70, 119–128.

Brown, B. B. *The Experimental Mind in Education.* New York: Harper and Row, 1968.

Coker, Homer, and Joan G. Coker. *Classroom Observations Keyed for Effectiveness Research—Observer Training Manual.* Atlanta, Ga.: Georgia State University/ Carroll County Teacher Corps Project, 1979(a).

───── . *Classroom Observations Keyed for Effectiveness Research—User's Manual.* Atlanta, Ga.: Georgia State University/Carroll County Teacher Corps Project, 1979(b).

Coker, Homer, Donald M. Medley, and Robert S. Soar. "How Valid Are Expert Opinions about Effective Teaching?" *Phi Delta Kappan,* 1980, 62, 131–134, 149.

Flanders, N. A. *Analyzing Teaching Behavior.* Reading, Mass.: Addison-Wesley, 1970.

Mahen, R. G. "Relationships between Students' Classroom Behaviors and Selected Context, Process, and Product Variables." Unpublished doctoral thesis, University of Alberta, Edmonton, Canada, 1977.

Medley, Donald M. *The Development and Use of Observation Schedule and Record, Form 5V.* Charlottesville, Va.: School of Education, University of Virginia, 1979.

Murphy, L. B. *Personality in Young Children: Methods for the Study of Personality in Young Children* (Vol. 1). New York: Basic Books, 1956.

Simon, A., and E. G. Boyer. *Mirrors for Behavior: An Anthology of Observation Instruments* (Vol. 5) Philadelphia: Research for Better Schools, 1967.

Soar, Robert S. "An Integrative Approach to Classroom Learning." Philadelphia: Temple University, 1966, ERIC Document ED 033749.

Soar, Robert S., and Ruth M. Soar. "An Empirical Analysis of Selected Follow-Through Programs: An Example of a Process Approach to Evaluation." In I. J. Gordon (Ed.), *Early Childhood Education,* Chicago: National Society for the Study of Education, 1972.

————. "Emotional Climate and Management." In R. E. Peterson and H. J. Walbert (Eds.), *Research on Teaching.* Berkeley, Calif.: McCutchan, 1979.

————. "Climate and Control System." Gainesville, Fla.: College of Education, University of Florida, 1982.

Spaulding, R. L. "Generalizability of Teacher Behavior: Stability of Observational Data Within and Across Facets of Classroom Environments." *Journal of Educational Research,* 1982, *76,* 5–13.

Spaulding, Robert L., and M. R. Papageorgiou. "Effects of Early Intervention in the Lives of Disadvantaged Children." Final Report. San Jose, Calif.: San Jose State University, 1972, ERIC Document ED 066 246.

Spaulding, Robert L., and C. L. Spaulding. *Research-Based Classroom Management.* Los Gatos, Calif.: Authors, 1982.

Weinrott, M. R., R. R. Jones, and G. R. Boler. "Convergent and Discriminate Validity of Five Classroom Observation System: A Secondary Analysis. *Journal of Educational Psychology,* 1981, *73,* 671–680.

Index